CONTEMPORARY ISSUES IN LAW, MEDICINE AND ETHICS

Titles in the Series:

A Patient's Right to Know: Information Disclosure, the Doctor and the Law
Sheila A.M. McLean, University of Glasgow

New Reproductive Techniques: A Legal Perspective
Douglas J. Cusine, University of Aberdeen

Medico-Legal Aspects of Reproduction and Parenthood
J.K. Mason, University of Edinburgh

Law Reform and Human Reproduction
Edited by *Sheila A.M. McLean*, University of Glasgow

Legal and Ethical Issues in the Management of the Dementing Elderly
Mary Gilhooly, University of Glasgow

Legal Issues in Human Reproduction
Edited by *Sheila A.M. McLean*, University of Glasgow

Mental Illness: Prejudice, Discrimination and the Law
Tom Campbell, Australian National University, Canberra and
Chris Heginbotham, Riverside Mental Health Trust, London

Pregnancy at Work
Noreen Burrows, University of Glasgow

Changing People: The Law and Ethics of Behaviour Modification
Alexander McCall Smith, University of Edinburgh

Health Resources and the Law: Who Gets What and Why
Robert G. Lee, Hammond Suddards, Leeds and *Frances H. Miller*, University of Boston

Surrogacy and the Moral Economy
Derek Morgan, Cardiff Law School

Family Planning Practice and the Law
Kenneth McK. Norrie, University of Strathclyde

Mental Health Law in Context: Doctors' Orders?
Michael Cavadino, University of Sheffield

Artificial Reproduction and Reproductive Rights
Athena Liu, University of Hong Kong

Medicine, Law and Social Change
Leanna Darvall, La Trobe University

Abortion Regimes
Kerry A. Petersen, La Trobe University

Human In Vitro Fertilization: A Case Study in the Regulation of Medical Innovation
Jennifer Gunning, Agricultural and Food Research Council and
Veronica English, Human Fertilisation and Embryology Authority

Law Reform and Medical Injury Litigation
Edited by *Sheila A.M. McLean*, University of Glasgow

Medical Negligence Law
Andrew Philips, University of Strathclyde

Competence to Consent to Medical Treatment
John Devereux, Griffith University

Death, Dying and the Law
Edited by *Sheila A.M. McLean*, University of Glasgow

The Contractual Reallocation of Procreative Resources and Parental Rights: The Natural Endowment Critique
William Joseph Wagner, The Catholic University of America

Clinical Resource Allocation
Christopher Heginbotham, Riverside Mental Health Trust, London and
Peter Mumford, King's Fund College, London

Designer Babies
Robert Lee, Hammond Suddards, Leeds and *Derek Morgan*, Cardiff Law School

Legal Issues in Obstetrics
Vivienne Harpwood, Cardiff Law School

All titles are provisional

CONTEMPORARY ISSUES IN LAW, MEDICINE AND ETHICS

Edited by
SHEILA A.M. McLEAN

Dartmouth

Aldershot • Brookfield USA • Singapore • Sydney

Published by
Dartmouth Publishing Company Limited
Gower House
Croft Road
Aldershot
Hants GU11 3HR
England

Dartmouth Publishing Company Limited
Old Post Road
Brookfield
Vermont 05036
USA

British Library Cataloguing in Publication Data
Contemporary Issues in Law, Medicine and
Ethics. - (Medico-Legal Series)
  I. McLean, Sheila A.M. II. Series
  344.10441

Library of Congress Cataloging-in-Publication Data
Contemporary Issues in law, medicine and ethics/edited by Sheila
  A.M. McLean.
     p. cm. – (Medico-legal series)
    ISBN 1–85521–586–1
    1. Medical laws and legislation–Great Britain. 2. Medical
jurisprudence–Great Britain. 3. Medical ethics–Great Britain.
I. McLean, Sheila. II. Series.
KD3395.A75C66 1995
344.41'041–dc20
[344.10441]   95-31801
                                                                        CIP

Printed and bound in Great Britain by
Hartnolls Limited, Bodmin, Cornwall

ISBN 1 85521 586 1

Contents

Notes on Contributors

Patricia M.A. Beaumont is a barrister and a former tutor, Medical Law Unit, University of Glasgow. She is currently completing a PhD at the University of Glasgow and occasionally lectures on some aspects of Human Reproduction.

Iona Jane Brown is a graduate in Law from the University of Glasgow. She is currently completing a PhD at the University of Glasgow.

Chris Docker is Executive Secretary, Voluntary Euthanasia Society of Scotland. He is co-author of *Beyond Final Exit* (1995) and *Departing Drugs* (1993). He is the founder and director of the Living Will and Values History Project and the editor of *Collected Living Wills*.

R.S. Downie is Professor of Moral Philosophy at the University of Glasgow. He is author of many works on medical ethics, including *The Healing Arts: an Illustrated Oxford Anthology* (1994) and *Healthy Respect: Ethics in Health Care* (2nd ed., Oxford 1994).

Sarah Elliston is a Lecturer in Medical Law and a member of the Institute of Law and Ethics in Medicine at the University of Glasgow. She is a barrister and is also a member of a Research Ethics Committee.

Philippa Gannon is a Research Assistant at the Medical Law Unit at the University of Glasgow. She is conducting research on the legal and ethical implications of the Human Genome Project.

Graeme T. Laurie is a Lecturer in Law, Department of Private Law, University of Edinburgh. His research interests lie in the fields of medical law and intellectual property law.

Jane Mair is a Lecturer in the School of Law, University of Glasgow.

J.K. Mason is Professor (Emeritus) of Forensic Medicine in the University of Edinburgh. He is currently working and teaching medical jurisprudence in the Faculty of Law at that University.

Sheila A.M. McLean, the general editor of this series, is the International Bar Association Professor of Law and Ethics in Medicine and the Director of the Institute of Law and Ethics in Medicine at the University of Glasgow.

Derek Morgan is a Lecturer in Law at Cardiff Law School, University of Wales.

Kerry Petersen is a Senior Research Fellow, School of Law, University of Glasgow.

John Porter is Lecturer in Philosophy, Department of Philosophy, The University of Glasgow, and Regional Organizer of the Philosophy Group of the Royal College of Psychiatrists.

Preface

In 1976, I established an advanced class in what is now called Medical Law and Ethics at Glasgow University, followed in the next year by a full two-year honours programme. At that time, literature was sparse – indeed, it was extremely difficult even to work out what topics might be covered under this broad rubric. Even in the days before quality assurance, it was still the aim of all good academics (of which I fully intended to be one!) to be able to provide a reading list for one's students, and in my field this was in those days no easy task.

Accordingly, I put together a collection entitled *Legal Issues in Medicine*, which was accepted and published by Gower Press. In the intervening years, not only have people continued to buy this book, but the range, depth and complexity of the subject itself have grown exponentially. In the light of this Dartmouth Publishing suggested that I might consider producing a volume which roughly equates to 'Daughter of Legal Issues in Medicine'. This is it!

What is particularly fascinating for me, and probably for everyone who has been involved in this subject over the years, is not just the growth mentioned already, but the radical change in focus of this book from that of its predecessor. Although the importance of, for example, medical negligence is in no way diminished by the passage of time, it does not merit a chapter in this new book. Rather, no contemporary book would be complete without mention of, for example, the impact of the 'new genetics'. In addition, so much has now been written in the area of medical law and ethics that there is no longer the need to make the assumption that the reader has to be introduced to the topics considered at a relatively elementary level. Those who have followed the subject will be extremely well informed by the writings produced by my colleagues in the field.

The aim of this book, therefore, is also different from that of the earlier one. In this volume, the contributors have taken highly controversial issues and have sought to bring to them their own analytical and intellectual skills. In my view they have succeeded admirably, and I am grateful to them for their thoughtful and thought-provoking contributions.

It is a sobering thought that so much time has passed since I first launched myself in print on an unsuspecting public. It is a tribute to Dartmouth, and in particular to John Irwin, that I am still – in my own geriatric way – engaged with them in what I trust is the worthwhile attempt to contribute to a subject which never ceases to fascinate both intellectually and personally. I am, as always, grateful to all of the staff at Dartmouth whose tolerance, patience and professionalism are without question. Nearer to home, the time between beginning and finishing this manuscript has seen me through two secretaries, Maggie and Veronica. To both of them I offer my heartfelt thanks for managing (sometimes) to clear the diary long enough for me to get on with the book, and – most especially – for their friendship, support and excellent coffee!

The list of friends and colleagues who have also made their own particular contribution is too long to go into, but I am sure that I can speak for all of the contributors when I thank every one of them. As ever, this book is dedicated to my parents, without whose strength and care over the years, in the face of a workload which, in common with all academics, I find increasingly burdensome, I would have lacked the stamina even to start this book. I hope that the reader, when turning the final page, agrees that this would have been a shame, and that this collection will be a valuable and stimulating resource for all who are involved in this area.

The rapid growth of biotechnology in the last few decades has caused significant problems for law and ethics. In particular, this is true of issues surrounding intellectual property. It should be noted, therefore, that a decision is expected this year from the European Patent Office on the acceptability of patent protection for ONCO-mouse. Obviously, the author of chapter 12 will be unable to take account of this, but the issues that he raises remain pertinent.

SHEILA A.M. MCLEAN

1 Professional Ethics and Business Ethics

R.S. DOWNIE

Introduction

For centuries the doctor–patient relationship has been the essential idea in medical practice. Over the past decade, however, terms such as 'client', or 'customer', or 'consumer' have increasingly been used to refer to the patient. Emphasis in what is happening in the health service today is on efficient use of resources, value for money and the health service as a business, with the doctor as a 'purchaser' or 'provider' of medical services. This emphasis seems set to continue into the next century, as the cost of health care resources continues to rise while demand for them increases, and as patients become increasingly conscious of their rights as consumers of health care. Many doctors see the change as simply one of political rhetoric disguising but not really transforming the underlying reality of the traditional doctor–patient relationship. Others fear that political changes will in fact make for changes of substance in the traditional relationship and they deplore this as representing an attempt to replace the professional ethics of the doctor–patient relationship with the competing self-interests of the market-place. It may be, however, that such fears are based on an erroneous analysis of business and an over-idealistic view of the doctor–patient relationship. It may also be that the market which is emerging is not one in which the consumer (or patient) is the central figure but rather one in which the competition is between managers of purchasing health authorities and managers of provider units. Since these changes in medical practice seem inevitable as the decade progresses it is worthwhile to compare the professions, and especially medicine, with business. That comparison will occupy the first part of this chapter, and the second will be concerned with the nature of the market which is emerging.

1

The Professions and Business

The idea of professional ethics goes back to the Hippocratic oath and is entirely familiar and acceptable. Indeed, for reasons which will emerge, the idea of a profession entails that of ethics. By contrast, the idea of business ethics is very recent and not widely accepted. Indeed, the idea that business men and women have responsibilities other than those of maximising their own profits is widely thought to be absurd, and perhaps a majority of those who work in business, as well as doctors, would agree that it is an absurd idea. The contrast between the two points of view – the professional and the business – can be expressed via two quotations, from Chaucer and from Adam Smith. The ideal (if not the reality) of the professional is expressed by Chaucer (1389) in his account of the parson in the Prologue to *The Canterbury Tales*:

> A good man was ther of religioun,
> And was a poore persoun of a toun;
> But riche he was of holy thoght and werk.
> He was also a lerned man, a clerk,
> That Cristes gospel trewely wolde preche;
> His parisshens devoutly wolde he teche,
> Benigne he was, and wonder diligent,
> And in adversitee ful pacient;
> And swich he was y-preved ofte sythes.
> Ful looth were him to cursen for his tythes
> ....
> Wyd was his parisshe, and houses fer a-sonder,
> But he ne lafte nat, for reyn ne thonder,
> In siknes nor in meschief, to visyte
> The ferreste in his parisshe....[1]

(It should be noted that Chaucer's ideal professional is the parson and not the doctor, whose portrait is touched with irony!)

By contrast, the classic statement of the point of view of business or the market is to be found in Adam Smith (1776):

In almost every other race of animals, each individual, when it is grown up to maturity, is entirely independent, and in the natural state has occasion for the assistance of no other living creature. But man has almost constant occasion for the help of his brethern, and it is in vain for him to expect it from their benevolence only. He is more likely to prevail if he can interest their self-love in his favour, and show them that it is their own advantage to do for him what he requires of them ... It is not from the benevolence of the butcher, the brewer, or the baker that we expect our dinner, but from their regard to their own self-interest. We address ourselves, not to their humanity, but to their self-love, and never talk to them of our own necessities, but of their advantages.[2]

The implications of the two traditional views can be set out as follows:

The professions	*Business (the 'market')*
(a) Promote the interests of patients, clients and so on.	Promotes own interests, not those of customers.
(b) Fees incidental to professional activity.	Profits central to business activity.
(c) Professions concerned with real 'needs' of the public or important aspects of human life, such as 'health', 'justice' or 'education'.	Business concerned with wants or preferences (often trivial).
(d) Professions have duty to comment on broad matters of public policy.	No such public or social function.
(e) Professions have political and commercial independence which makes their comments relevant to public policy.	Business lacks independence and its comments on public policy express vested interests or right-wing politics.
(f) Professions have knowledge base which requires a broad education.	Business has a shallower, opportunistic knowledge base for which 'training' is a more appropriate term than 'education'.

These contrasts create a sense of moral superiority in the professions, whereas the business community responds aggressively with claims such as 'We live in the real world and not in an ivory tower' or 'We earn the wealth of the country on which the professions depend'.

The validity of these contrasts can be questioned: some are based on conceptual confusions and others are outdated by changes in the knowledge base of business and a changed economic structure in society. It should be noted that my concern is a philosophical one, directed at ideals, concepts and principles, rather than a sociological one, directed at *de facto* comparisons. For example, it will not be a relevant objection to anything I say that some businessmen are self-

seeking or corrupt, for so too are some professionals. The philosophical question concerns what practices must be so by the very nature of
businesses and professions.

Beneficence and Self-interest

The most important contrast is between the alleged beneficence of the
professions ('Benigne he was, and wonder diligent') and the 'self-love'
or 'self-interest' of business. Why is beneficence thought to be essential
to the professions, and self-interest to business? Is this the right sort of
contrast?

Beneficence is essential to the ethical ideal of the professions because
the professions provide a service for other persons. Now, many occu-
pations, such as those involved in transport or public health, provide
a service, but in the professions the service is provided specifically via
a *relationship* between the professional and his clients. What is here meant
by a 'relationship'? We can use the word 'relationship' in two ways; to
stand for the bond which links two or more people, or to stand for the
attitudes which people so linked have to each other.[3] As examples of
the first kind of relationship we might mention kinship, marriage,
business association or teacher–pupil. As examples of the second kind
we might mention fear, pride, respect, envy, contempt and so on. Thus,
someone seeing an adult with a child might ask, 'What is the relationship
between that pair?' and receive an answer in terms of the first kind of
relationship: 'teacher and pupil', 'father and son', and so on. Or he might
ask, 'What sort of relationship do Jones and his son have?' and receive
an answer in terms of the second kind of relationship: 'Jones has a great
affection for his son but his son has nothing but contempt for him.'

The two kinds of relationship are connected in various complex
ways. For example, if the situation is a business transaction, then the
attitude of the parties would not characteristically be one, say, of
affection or friendship. There is of course no logical impediment to such
an attitude developing out of the business transaction, and indeed it
is material for romantic comedy when the attitude in the relationship
is inappropriate for the bond, as in a film such as *Working Girl*. How
can we characterise a professional relationship?

Let us begin by anatomising the attitude aspect of the relationship.
To understand an attitude we must consider its object. The object of
the professional attitude is the patient and so on, conceived in terms
of vulnerability; typically there is inequality of power. This is obviously
the case in a doctor–patient or teacher–pupil relationship. It can be
argued that, because of the dominant position which the professional
occupies in the relationship with her/his client, and because as a professional s/he must supply a service, and often assess its success as
well, s/he must be governed more than others by principles of ethics;

in particular in this context s/he must be governed by a desire to be of assistance, often called 'beneficence'. That is why, as has already been said, the concept of a profession entails that of ethics.

The pathology of beneficence is paternalism, or the tendency to decide for individuals what they ought to decide for themselves. It is easy to understand how inequality of power coupled with beneficence can lead to paternalism. The antidote to paternalism, or an inappropriate or excessive expression of beneficence, is a sense of justice and honesty. I shall call this 'integrity' and stipulate that integrity must be combined with beneficence in the attitude component of the relationship between professional and patient or client. It is these moral qualities of the professional which are appropriate to the trust which the patient or client, because of his/her vulnerability, must have.

It is interesting in this context to compare the moral attitude of a doctor to a patient with that of an accountant to a client. In both cases the desire is to help, but it is a debatable matter in medical ethics how far a doctor is entitled to withhold some or all of the truth from a patient about his condition if, in the opinion of the doctor, telling the truth would or might upset the patient. Some, although by no means all, doctors regard it as obligatory to withhold the full truth if by so doing they will minister to the comfort or well-being of the patient. In other words, the attitude of beneficence prevails over that of justice and honesty in the doctor–patient relationship. But in the accountant–client relationship truth is of paramount importance. The accountant *cannot* help except through the truth. Justice to the client absolutely requires truth as the accountant sees it. That is why integrity is so important to the accountant.

The inequality of the professional relationship requires not only a special attitude, but also a special 'bond', which usually takes the form of an institutional role relationship. The need for a formal bond in addition to an appropriate attitude is evident if we consider the significant interventions which professionals can make in the lives of their clients, whether the interventions are medical, legal or educational. For example, a professional may on occasion be obliged to point out unpleasant truths, or he may discover facts which reflect adversely on the competence or even the integrity of clients. Again, in an educational context, there must be criticism of the work of pupil or student. The fact that it is an institutional bond or role which brings them together provides emotional insulation for both parties in such situations. Moreover, since it is important that the professional should know a range of personal details about their clients, there must be some assurance that no untoward use will be made of the information and that it will not be passed on as trivial gossip. An institution can impose confidentiality on the professional and provide security for the client.

The concept of a social role is helpful here as being a set of rights and duties to be analysed in terms of institutional concepts. An individual person is able to act not only in a private capacity but in that of a social role. In consenting to act in a role he or she thereby becomes morally responsible for actions which are done in its name. In accepting the role s/he identifies him or herself with the values of the profession and the rights and duties which go with the role. Moreover, by taking on the role, the individuals, we may say, are *authorised* by their professional associations to act in certain ways, depending on the function of the profession. Their authorisation is another element in their professional bond and their 'responsibilities to' and 'responsibilities for'.

The professions, then, provide a service through a special relationship. In view of the inequality and possibility of exploitation, the relationship involves a special attitude of beneficence tempered with integrity (justice and honesty) and a bond consisting of legal and ethical rights and duties authorised by the professional institution.

At this point it is tempting to take a wrong turning in the argument. Some writers draw a contrast between the market and the professions in this context. They claim that, while the professions aim at the interest of their clients, those involved in market transactions aim at their own self-interest. This point of view is an important one, for it largely accounts for the mistaken sense of moral superiority which many professionals adopt towards businessmen, industrialists, shopkeepers and others. It is based on several confusions, and it also obscures the important function which professions do fulfil. The source of the confusion may well be the well-known passage in the *Wealth of Nations*, already quoted.

Let us note to begin with that Smith is characterising the businessman in terms of an attitude – one of self-interest – yet it is not strictly accurate to describe the attitudinal component of an economic or business relation as one of self-interest or egoism. It is certainly true that each party in an economic exchange is attempting to maximise gain for him or herself, not for the other party. But by 'gain' we mean here a realisation of what the agents severally consider good, and this need not be egoistic at all, far less selfish. Thus a person's conception of what is good may include the realisation of the good of others. More helpful than the term 'self-interest' is the one introduced by the Revd. Philip Wicksteed, 'non-tuism':[4] 'What makes an economic transaction is that I am not considering you except as a link in the chain, or considering your desires except as the means by which I may gratify those of someone else – not necessarily myself. The economic relation does not exclude from my mind everyone but me; it potentially includes everyone but you.'[5]

Or again: 'The note of a business transaction between A and B is not that A's ego is consciously in his mind, but that, however many the *alteri* are, B is not one of them; and B, in like manner, whether he is thinking only of his own ego or of innumerable *alteri*, is not thinking of A.'[6] Thus Wicksteed concludes that 'The specific characteristic of an economic relation is not its "egoism" but its "non-tuism"'.[7]

A relation of this 'non-tuistic' sort is not simply regulative of conduct in the market – it is not just a guiding principle – but is a necessary constitutive condition of a market in the sense that where it does not obtain we do not have a market, but some other relationship between people. Whatever the defects of the market mechanism, therefore, it is superficial to attack it on the grounds that it is essentially based on an attitude of self-interest.

Moreover, there is a positive safeguard against the supposed corruption caused by the desire for profit to be found in the market; an economic relation by its very nature also involves a bond – a legal one. There are two reasons for saying this. The first is that an economic order assumes that there is an already existing system of rights, in that exchange is always at a 'price' and 'price' is an *agreed* exchange ratio. The second is that the establishment of an economic relation is *ipso facto* the establishment of a juridical relation in so far as it constitutes a 'contract' defining the rights and duties of the parties. In other words, a purely economic relation is an abstraction; all economic relations are integrated with juridical relations and the self-seeking of the parties is thereby limited, whatever their attitudes may be. Hobbes' man ruthlessly pursuing his self-interest is not in an economic order until the sovereign establishes a legal order. If I were attempting to seek a complete definition of an economic order I should of course need to refer to at least two other factors – the influence of scarcity, and of political conditions which allow a measure of freedom of choice – but for the purposes of this discussion the important point is that the 'non-tuism' of the economic relation is regulated by being from the outset a juridical relation.

The provisional conclusion, then, is that the trader, like the professional, may well be providing a service: he or she may be offering products of social utility such as watches, bread or any other product, and in so doing his or her attitude to his or her customers is not one of self-interest but 'non-tuism', and his or her conduct is restrained by legal bonds. By contrast, the professional's attitude is or ought to be one of 'tuism': in other words, he or she is concerned, through beneficence coupled with integrity, to promote the interests of his or her clients, although he or she too ought to be restrained by ethical and legal bonds.

Individuals and Organisations

Yet even this provisional conclusion must be expanded or it will be misleading. A contrast has been drawn between the institutionalised beneficence or 'tuism' of the professional and the 'non-tuism' of business. But to be fair the contrasts must be drawn at the same points in the chain of service. The professional is described as beneficent at the point where the service is delivered – during actual patient care. But this is compatible with saying that professional contracts for services rendered are being negotiated at another point in the chain in a non-tuistic manner. Equally, a business may establish its prices in a non-tuistic way: the astute business man or woman will consider what price the market will stand. But that is compatible with saying that at the point of delivery of service a salesman may offer his advice to a customer in a 'tuistic' manner by considering what it is that would best suit the requirements of the customer.

It is simply a muddle to contrast the benign service at which the doctor aims with the self-interested profit at which business aims. The doctor supplies medical services in a benign way but doctors are also fee-earners and it would be disingenuous to pretend that their professional associations do not attempt to maximise their fees. Equally, business men and women are also suppliers of the goods and services necessary for the well-being of social life, and it is unfair to suggest that at the point of delivery there is no attempt to provide a service fitting the needs of the consumer.

Sometimes medicine and other professions contrast the nobility of their causes – health, justice or education – with the triviality of the goods supplied by the market. But this is unfair too. There are trivial sides to the professions – the cosmetics of health care or the frivolities of litigation – whereas the market characteristically supplies the necessities without which we cannot exist.

Social Function

Another difference sometimes stressed between business and the professions concerns the alleged social function of the professions. It is clear that a profession will be concerned, as has been said, with the interests of *specific* clients, but it also has a broader social function. This broader social function involves the duty to speak out with authority on matters of social justice and social utility. Our concern above was with the duty of the professional to help and to be fair and honest to individuals, but now we are concerned with these duties in a wider social context. A good example of this is that provided by judges when, in giving judgement, they also comment on the need for changes in or additions to the law, or they comment on the practices of bureaucrats or the social services. Again, doctors have a duty to speak out on broad issues of health, as for example they might speak out against cigarette advertising or cast doubt on the effectiveness of care in the community. Accountants might be said to have a duty to speak out in the general interest of shareholders or against certain commercial practices which they regard as dishonest. In this kind of way the professions can be seen to have the important social function of regulators in the interest of general utility and justice. The existence of this function is recognised by the practice of including professionals on government enquiries or arbitration panels. To some extent professionals are invited for their expertise, but it is also because they are recognised as having this wider function as public commentators.

But business men and women can also have a wider social function outside the concerns of their specific industries. Bodies such as the Confederation of British Industry (CBI) are widely recognised as having the function of commenting on broad matters of social utility, and industry is increasingly involved in such matters as the sponsorship of the arts.

There was a historical period when it might have been claimed that only the professions have the political and commercial independence which enables their comments to be disinterested. But this is no longer true. All the professions are in varying ways dependent on governments and/or commercial support. For example, in medicine there is a suspicion that drug companies in many ways, some crude and some subtle, control at least some of the activities of the medical profession. In veterinary medicine the threat to independence comes from the farming industry which is more interested in furthering the interests of farmers than those of animals. To the extent that veterinarians go along with farming interests rather than the interests of animals, their professional independence is cast in doubt. As far as accountancy is concerned, the main pressure comes from commercialism in all its forms. On the other hand, whereas the primary duty of individual companies is no doubt to their shareholders, there are national bodies, such as the CBI, which speak their mind on broad policy issues and are no more subservient to the government than is the British Medical Association.

Education and Training

Finally, it is important that members of the professions should be educated, as distinct from merely trained, men and women. This is vital in view of the features which have been ascribed here to the professions. If a professional is to have integrity and independence, if he/she is to have the confidence to deal honestly and fearlessly with clients and be able to speak with authority on matters of broad public policy, he/she must be educated, as distinct from merely trained. What is the distinction? To give a full answer would involve providing a summary of many of the writings of Professor R.S. Peters,[8] and others, and of their critics. It may be adequate in this context to say first that, while the distinction is by no means hard and fast, the educated person has a wide cognitive perspective and can see the place of his/her skills within that wide perspective; second, that the educated person continues to develop his/her knowledge and skills; and third, that the knowledge and skills are developed within a framework of values.[9]

But the professions no longer have a monopoly of educated men and women. Large numbers of graduates enter industry and business, and indeed if we consider the complexities of the technology involved at all levels it is clear that business requires educated as well as trained men and women.

Thus, the conclusion of the first section of this chapter is that the traditional contrast between the professions and business is based on misunderstanding of the present position of each group. As we move into the next century it is plain that there is going to be much more overlap and that the professions have much to learn from business. It is therefore important to clear away uninformed, confused or emotionally based prejudice. It is also important to consider just what and how much the medical profession can learn from business, and that will be the concern of the second section of this chapter.

What Can the Professions Learn from Business?

The British government in a white paper entitled *Working for Patients*[10] is encouraging the medical profession to see their profession as a business. The hope is that there will be conspicuous improvements from the establishment of an internal market in health care services. What are these hoped for improvements, and are there signs that they are likely to be achieved as the decade progresses towards the year 2000? There are three connected aspects of medical care where we might expect to see improvements with the establishment of an internal market: patient choice, quality of service and expenditure.

If patients are to be encouraged to see themselves as consumers or as customers then one obvious benefit which should be expected is improved choice. A criticism of medical services of all kinds, which has grown in volume from the 1970s, is that they are essentially paternalistic. To be paternalistic, as has been seen, is to decide for others what they have a right to decide for themselves. Medical paternalism is thought to exist at two levels: at the point of delivery of the service (in the doctor–patient relationship) and in the selection of priorities in what is to be delivered (whether emphasis in the provision of services is to be, for example, on acute services or on the care of the elderly or the mentally handicapped). Will the much vaunted internal market improve patient choice in either of these respects?

There seems little sign that this is happening. In the first type of situation – the doctor–patient relationship – choice cannot be achieved by a market mechanism but only by the education of the doctor through medical ethics or the like.[11] The greater the patient's information the more meaningful the choice, and the nearer the doctor and the patient come to equality. But the perception of the desirability of this change can only come about through improved medical education, and indeed through the education of patients (for it is certainly the case that many patients prefer that the doctor should choose for them). It is not at all clear how such a change could come about through the introduction of a market mechanism.

When we move to the question of priorities in the provision of services, however, it is possible that market mechanisms can do more to improve choice. They can do so if patients, or at least bodies such as local health councils, are allowed to participate in decision making in the establishment of these priorities. For example, do we, the consumers, want a heart transplant unit or do we want improved services for the mentally handicapped? The answer is that we have no choice. Decisions are made for political reasons, or as the result of powerful medical lobbies; they are not made by consumers. Where, then, is patient choice thought to exist? Patients can choose what breakfast cereal they want in hospital! More seriously, they can choose their GP. But the latter choice can cut both ways. GPs with an eye to their budgets will not be anxious to accept high-cost patients such as the elderly. In short, in terms of possible increase in patient choice, the introduction of business terminology has achieved little.

In the second place, is the introduction of an internal market likely to improve the quality of medical services? Answers to this question will vary relative to the nature of those who are monitoring the services. In many of the large public services, such as British Telecom, the Post Office or British Gas, there are consumer councils which monitor service. Those bodies have many lay members. In smaller businesses quality control is provided by the discipline of the market – competition from rivals. What happens in medical services? How are standards of care monitored? The position of the British government is that 'the quality of medical work can only be reviewed by a doctor's peers'.[12] This does not sound like consumerism gone mad! It sounds more like the expression of a paternalistic monopoly. The users of medical services require to be empowered both in the matter of having a decisive say in the choice of the services they wish and in the matter of evaluating the quality of that service.

The third area which was expected to improve with the introduction of a market is expenditure. Will a business approach to medicine cut costs as the decade progresses towards the year 2000? In answering this question we must avoid an oversimplification. It is easy to have a simple version of the market relationship in which we are thinking of two parties only, the trader and the customer. But traders obtain their goods from wholesalers and manufacturers, and the market relationship holds there as well. In other words, retailer A will not pay more for his goods to manufacturer B if he can obtain cheaper and as good supplies from C. And larger market units may have many retail outlets which are obliged to give an account of their sales to the parent company, as pubs owned by a brewery will be obliged to give an account of their business to the parent company. There is a message here for medical practice. There is no reason why doctors should not be expected to buy or recommend cheaper drugs if they are as effective as more expensive equivalents in glossy packages.

This kind of change should certainly be encouraged, but it is not the kind of change which is of direct benefit to patients. The market here is one between different sets of managers – the managers of purchasing health authorities and the managers of provider units. The government may benefit here from cost cutting, a reasonable objective, but the benefits to the patient are marginal.

Possible disadvantages for the elderly in the new consumerism have already been referred to. But they are only one group who do not easily fit into the market situation. There are many disadvantaged groups, such as the mentally handicapped, who require active representatives to work on their behalf. It would, of course, be unfair to suggest that such groups are at more of a disadvantage now than they were previously. It is just that, since they are expensive, they require special attention or they will lose out in a market-based system of health care.

Some conclusions have emerged from this section. First, both the professions and business are evolving in this last decade of the century and, in particular, concepts from business, such as information, choice, quality control and cost cutting, can be used to improve medical services. However, there is a danger that these changes will not benefit patients in all cases. It is not, as some critics suggest, that the changes are cosmetic, or just political rhetoric; they are changes of substance. The danger is more that we shall have a manager-driven consumerism rather than a patient-driven consumerism, and it is far from clear that the result will be a 'user-friendly' service. If we are to have paternalism it may be preferable to have that of the old medical superintendent and GP rather than that of the general manager. A genuinely market-based medical service might free us from most sorts of paternalism, but the service must be modelled on the right areas of the market or we shall simply be substituting managerial bureaucracy for medical paternalism.

Limitations of the Market Model

In conclusion, it is suggested there are radical limitations to the extent to which market models are appealing as ideals for health care in the next century. In the first section of this chapter it was argued that there is nothing about business ethics properly understood which is inimical to the professions; indeed, the professions have much to learn from business. The second section went on to examine an actual attempt to transform the medical profession by creating an internal market in medical services. The analysis suggested that the attempt has not so far been very successful. But that failure is a contingent one. It may be that it is possible to improve medical services by choosing the right sort of market model. This final section turns from a critique of an actual attempt at changing medical paternalism to a proper philosophical concern with ideals, and to suggest there are limitations both in the older medical paternalism and in the newer market-based approach to health.

To the extent that there is emphasis on the *state* delivery of health care to individuals (such as in the paternalistic system of the National Health Service) there is an invitation to see health as a commodity to be supplied by the state. But the same is true if we think of health as a commodity bought in the market, by private health insurance or by whatever means. Yet health itself is not in any sense a commodity. Health and well-being are in the end a set of relationships among citizens. As Beauchamp put it:

> Collective goods are ultimately a set of relationships among the citizens of a community, relationships in which the community as a whole participates to obtain desired benefits. These collective goods include aggregate states of welfare or wellbeing, including declining rates of disease and premature deaths; efforts to limit the resources society devotes to personal health services; shared and common access to a good like medical care to foster the sense of community and membership in the group itself. And finally, there are those highly important collective goods, shared or common beliefs and values.[13]

It is clear that we can add a legal system to Beauchamp's list, and in particular one designed to stimulate social responsibility. Indeed, it is plausible to suggest that the increasing government intervention in drunk-driving issues has encouraged a greater social awareness about the dangers of alcohol more generally, and thus a greater sense of community and individual responsibility. In a similar way, legislation designed to assist disabled or handicapped persons can also increase a sense of community responsibility for those groups. In other words, in so far as health legislation and other governmental health policies are directed at increasing community awareness, as distinct from being directed at the good of specific individuals, they are not paternalistic.

My conclusion, then, is that market-based consumerism, with its assumptions of individualism, is in the end inadequate to secure health in its fullest sense.[14] Whereas the provision of *health care* may perhaps be improved if based on *appropriate* business or market models, *health itself* requires a set of relationships in which the community as a whole participates to obtain mutual benefits, which include a decline in ill-health and the enhancement of well-being through the shared values of citizenship. This is an ideal of society to which a re-educated medical profession can contribute greatly as the decade progresses, but it is an ideal which cannot be achieved solely by a consumer-oriented system of health care.

Notes

1   G. Chaucer [1389], *The Canterbury Tales*, Oxford, Oxford University Press, 1957.
2   A. Smith [1776], *The Wealth of Nations*, Oxford, Oxford University Press, 1976.
3   R.S. Downie and B. Charlton, *The Making of a Doctor*, Oxford, Oxford University Press, 1992.
4   P. Wicksteed, *The Commonsense of Political Economy*, London, Routledge, 1933.
5   *Commonsense*, at p.174.
6   Ibid., at p.179.
7   Ibid., at p.180.
8   R.S. Peters, *Ethics and Education*, London, Allen & Unwin, 1966.
9   K.C. Calman, and R.S. Downie, 'Education and training in medicine', *Medical Education*, **22**, (1988), 488.
10 *Working for Patients*, London, HMSO, 1989.
11 Downie and Charlton, *The Making of a Doctor*.
12 *Working Paper on Medical Audit*, London, HMSO, 1989.
13 D. Beauchamp, 'Life-style, public health and paternalism', in S. Doxiadis (ed.), *Ethical Dilemmas in Health Promotion*, Chichester, John Wiley, 1987, at p.72.
14 R.S. Downie, C. Fyfe and A. Tannahill, *Health Promotion: Models and Values*, 2nd edn, Oxford, Oxford University Press, 1996.

2 Health Rights, Ethics and Justice: The Opportunity Costs of Rhetoric

DEREK MORGAN

Nobody knows how much health care will be worth to him in terms of money and pain. In addition, nobody knows if the most advantageous form of health care is obtained from medical producers, from a travel agent, or by renouncing work on the night shift. ... The economics of health is a curious discipline, somewhat reminiscent of the theology of indulgences that flourished before Luther. ... You can count what the friars collect, you can look at the temples they build, you can take part in the liturgies they indulge in, but you can only guess what the traffic in remission from purgatory does to the soul after death. Models developed to account for the willingness of taxpayers to foot the rising medical bills constitute similar scholastic guesswork about the new world-spanning church of medicine.[1]

Without good health, people's ability to act upon at least some of the choices they make is curtailed. Providing the means by which citizens may preserve and restore their health may be thought to be a fundamental task of any modern state. If civil rights are to be of any value, then citizens must be able to exercise them and, in so far as ill health provides a major obstacle to this, it gives rise to fundamental questions about what the citizen may call upon the state to provide or to recognise. Indeed, it may be thought that, like rights to life and to liberty, the right to health care could be regarded as one of a group of basic rights which make active citizenship possible. As with all basic rights, the state would be required to take specific steps to recognise health rights.[2] This chapter, however, addresses two preliminary questions. First, what, if anything, is the responsibility of the state in securing the proper grounds of distribution of such health care as exists? Second, what role, if any, is there within this for arguments based on rights? The implications of these two arguments must be worked through in another place.

Allocation

The examples upon which I am going to draw and the arguments I am going to deploy are set against the background of the UK health care system; a system in transition, some would say turmoil.[3] It provides an example of the turbulence to which change gives rise and illustrates some of the problems necessarily involved in the distribution of what now seems universally to be acknowledged as a scarce good – health or, more precisely, health costs. The National Health Service and Community Care Act 1990 establishing the 'internal market' creates a system which significantly increases the likelihood of litigation concerning health care resources. The Act introduces buyers (district health authorities and GP fundholders) and sellers (hospitals) of health care. Decisions will more frequently be taken, not by central planning at ministerial level, but by business managers reacting to commercial pressures. Important conceptual questions, questions involving deep philosophical problems and giving rise to acute ethical dilemmas, will arise, such as whether one is addressing medical or social needs.[4] This has assumed enhanced importance in the United Kingdom following the 1990 Act because it has become important to know what is health care and what social care. The former is the responsibility of the health authority, the latter now lies exclusively in the province of the local authority.

Within this context, the proper grounds of allocation of the scarce good that health care has become assume particular significance. One possible approach is that health care should be given to those who in some way, judged against some sort of criterion, deserve it; that a just system of health care allocation should be backward-looking, asking what the individual has done in the past to safeguard, preserve or damage their own health such that the state should reward (or discipline) them in its response. In this sense, state policy would be delivered through its gatekeepers, the medical, nursing and other social welfare professions. An alternative model would be a needs-based model, a forward-looking model, in which treatments might still be denied, or prioritised, according to need.

Other possible grounds of distribution exist, but I want to take just two examples of the directly competing notions of what might be entailed in the state's responsibility and obligations for health care and compare the libertarian position offered by Bernard Williams with that of the leading conservative Robert Nozick. Williams argues:

> Leaving aside preventive medicine, the proper ground of distribution of medical care is ill health: this is a necessary truth. Now in very many societies, while ill health may work as a necessary condition of receiving treatment, it does not work as a sufficient condition, since such treatment costs money, and not all who are ill have the money; hence the possession

of sufficient money becomes in fact an additional necessary condition of actually receiving treatment.[5]

Nozick urges that 'it cannot be assumed that equality must be built into any theory of justice'.[6] He says of the passage quoted from Williams that he seems to be arguing that if, among the different descriptions applying to an activity, there is one that contains an 'internal goal' of the activity, then 'the only proper grounds for the performance of the activity, or its allocation if it is scarce, are connected with the effective achievement of the internal goal'. Thus, according to Nozick's reading of Williams, 'the only proper criterion for the distribution of medical care is medical need'. To this Nozick objects.

Does it follow, he asks, that the internal goal of an activity should take precedence over, for example, a person's particular purpose in performing the activity? If someone becomes a barber because he or she likes talking to a variety of different people, is it unjust of them to allocate services to those to whom they most like to talk? Or, if they work as a barber in order to pay tuition at school, may they not cut the hair of only those who tip well? Nozick ponders why the doctor's skills and activities should be allocated differently, via the internal goal of medical care. When the layers of Williams' argument are peeled away, he writes:

> what we arrive at is the claim that society (that is, each of us acting together in some organised fashion) should make provision for the important needs of all its members.... Despite appearances, Williams presents no argument for it. Like others, Williams looks only to questions of allocation. He ignores the question of where things or actions to be allocated and distributed come from. Consequently, he does not consider whether they come already tied to people who have entitlements over them (surely the case for service activities, which are people's actions), people who therefore may decide for themselves to whom they will give the thing and on what grounds.[7]

Nozick's argument has, of course, been criticised. Len Doyal and Ian Gough reject it as incorporating a Lockean view of ownership, an essentially individualistic view in which I and only I am entitled to decide what to do with the fruits of my labour. For them this is flawed in its descriptive nature of production. Production, they write, is 'a social process in which many mix their labour [and] any rights associated with ownership can no longer be focused exclusively on the individual'.[8] A further important recent criticism has come from within the conservative tradition to which Nozick appeals. John Gray has objected that the nightwatchman state of the kind advocated by Nozick (and increasingly abandoned in the proposed Clinton health care reforms in the United States) is incompatible with what he calls 'limited government', of which conservative government is the embodiment:

> A limited government has tasks that go well beyond keeping the peace. ... It has also a responsibility to tend fragile and precious traditions, to protect and shelter the vulnerable and defenceless, to enhance and enlarge opportunities for the disadvantaged, to promote the conservation and renewal of the natural and human environment and to assist in the renewal of civil society and the reproduction of the common culture without which pluralism and diversity become enmity and division.[9]

The implications of this argument for health care are important, far-reaching and challenging. Gray expounds these normative or evaluative criticisms in the concluding chapter of his book. Arguing, with critics such as Ivan Illich, that it must be accepted that there are limits to health care, Gray's first concern is with the over-medicalisation of life and death. Second, and this is related, he complains that modern medical care and treatment cannot be shown to have provided benefits proportionate to the claims made for it or indeed proportionate to the costs lavished on it. As Thomas McKeown has shown, improvements in health care have arisen much more from developments in sanitation, environment and personal lifestyle than they have from individual 'medical' breakthroughs.[10] Third, much of what has been incorporated within modern medical care lies, in truth, outside the medical domain 'and can be performed safely and intelligently by trained laypeople'.[11]

If Gray is correct in his analysis, it may be that insistence on rights is completely misplaced, unless those rights are rights to be left alone; rights to refuse invasive or unlooked for medical interventions, whether at birth or in death, rather than to insist upon the provision of certain types of high quality, but also high technology and unproven health care interventions.[12] That is an important caveat to the arguments which now ensue about what I have called conceptual limitations in respect of rights arguments in respect of health. An assessment of these arguments lies beyond the scope of the present chapter, but they illustrate the range of questions with which we are faced when considering the question of allocation.

Rights

The right to health has long been advocated as a basic human right but obviously not everyone can be assured of perfect health; much may depend upon genetic factors, natural and social environments, individual lifestyle and bad luck. It may, therefore, be more accurate and more limited to speak of a right to health care, rather than of health care rights. But the importance of the argument and its language is undeniable. As Michael Freeden puts it, 'the existence of scarce goods necessitates important decisions on distribution, whereas the insistence on the right to a good ensures that some of it will be available to any rights bearer'.[13]

The idea that patients have rights sits uncomfortably within the general shape of UK health care law. Issues such as informed consent are couched within ordinary malpractice principles, confidentiality is justified by reference to the public good and not by individual privacy rights and rights to health care under national legislation are for practical purposes unenforceable. But as Paul Craig has reminded us,

> One may reach the conclusion that a particular interest is incapable of being framed as a justiciable legal right, but still believe that it generates a constitutional obligation which the legislature is bound to advance. Such an obligation is of importance in itself, and may, moreover, have indirect implications for the interpretation of other legal doctrines.[14]

In other words, even if a legal right cannot be spelled out from a particular series of premises, it does not follow that some general (moral) obligation or expectation cannot properly be laid at the door of the state. To discuss fully that contention would require an extended dissertation on the relationship between moral and legal claims to rights and the role of the state, of which only a brief résumé can be given here. We might hold, however, that rights sum up our moral conclusions (that is, they are a useful way of speaking about the work that we have done elsewhere); they are a way of putting forward a moral case.[15] Of course, to assert that human beings have rights is not identical to asserting that they have human rights: 'The latter complex term has developed this century into a key phrase, denoting a pre-eminent notion of rights.'[16]

Human rights provide the criteria for making value judgements, reflecting normative judgements as to what it is permissible for free and responsible people, acting either individually or through their governments, to do. Human rights, then, can be used to evaluate the laws of states by deciding whether the standards inherent in such rights are reflected in positive law. They also provide justifications for conduct and arguments for changes to existing laws to give effect to them. Legal rights we may more usually understand to be those rights recognised in the law of individual states or at international law, where law refers to a body of binding rules, institutions and procedures regulating relationships and orderly change and protecting interests of men and women living together in a political society. Legal rights entitle the right holder to insist on their observance and various remedies, judicial and otherwise, are available.[17]

Law and legal rights are pervasive at all levels of social life; there are legal rights governing family relationships, education, working conditions, property (including wealth and resources) and state relationships with individuals. Many legal rights are the positive legal counterpart of human rights as moral rights and therefore reflect those values as well as protecting particular interests. Of particular interest here, however, is the relationship between law, rights and health care: the scope, boundaries and content of what we may call health care law. Of course, the question 'what is health care law?' admits of at least a descriptive and a conceptual answer; neither may be easy to articulate, and the boundary between the two may sometimes shade at the margins.

Patrick Devlin, writing only 30 years ago reflected: 'Is it not a pleasant tribute to the medical profession that by and large it has been able to manage its relations with its patients on the basis of such an understanding [that conduct be regulated by a general understanding of how decent people ought to behave] without the aid of lawyers and law makers'.[18] We might identify at least three levels of health care policy and practice which might be and are differently affected by law, or affected by different types of control exercised by the state. These may be in the form of or a manifestation of the state's legal authority, which may be called laws in a different or administrative sense, and some which may not be capable of being framed as a justiciable right but nonetheless impose obligations on the state. These three levels might be identified as the macro level – the form of the health care delivery system; the meso level – identifying the boundaries of that system – and the micro level, at which the specific patient–health carer relationship is defined.

At the macro level, there is little formal legal regulation but there is in addition a great deal of administrative regulation. The main legislative provisions are contained in the National Health Service Act 1977, the National Health Service and Community Care Act 1990 and the Medicines Act 1983. In this context, and recalling the discussion of allocation, it should be remembered that the role of primary care (90 per cent) vastly outstrips that of hospital care (10 per cent); and while the present cost structure is in inverse proportion to that, this itself is in the process of change.

The meso level, which identifies the legal boundaries of health care, suggests what may permissibly be done at law in the name of health care. Here, three examples of legislative intervention are the Human Organs Transplant Act 1989 (forbidding the commercial sale and purchase of human organs) the Surrogacy Arrangements Act 1985 (forbidding commercial involvement in the establishment and management of surrogacy arrangements) and the Human Fertilisation and Embryology Act 1990, but there are many others.

Finally, the micro level, which establishes the legal relationship between individual patients and doctors and other health care workers is replete with examples, drawn from various areas such as consent, confidentiality, negligence, non-resuscitation decisions, and many others. In these last two categories, the meso and the micro levels, in the sense suggested by Devlin, the relationship between doctors and their patients, although still largely bounded by law, is no longer one which is immune from legal regulation, control and direction. The important question which arises for present purposes is whether these functions have moral dimensions. Clearly, they *can* have moral dimensions, but the enforcement of morality is not itself necessarily numbered among them. However, I want to suggest there *are* areas of medical law where the goal comes closer to the enforcement of moral notions *as such* than perhaps in other cognate areas of the law, such as family law, or social welfare law. Examples of this, which are not incontestable, include those where the law is used to give shape to moral aspirations. Here we might consider abortion, sterilisation, assisted conception, embryo research, female circumcision, organ transplantation, the treatment of certain groups of patients, such as the severely handicapped newborn, those in persistent vegetative state or those living in coma, to take just selected examples. Notice, however, that very few of these examples are drawn from, or rely upon, what could be characterised as any positive programme of health care rights, or rights to health care, and it is to a consideration of that I want now to turn. Recall, however, the general point of departure: that there is little which could be said to represent such an agenda in UK law. The reasons for that is something upon which I shall offer some concluding reflections.

Rights to Health Care?

Before a detailed programme for implementation of health rights could be drawn up, there are a series of preliminary issues to be addressed. Conceptual difficulties exist in relation to the idea of health and the causes of ill-health. The former needs consideration to establish the content of health rights and the latter in order to address the strategies appropriate to realise them. A careful analysis of the types of rights and duties which are claimed by citizens is also needed. For example, individual entitlements which are claimed by citizens from the relevant agencies will be suitable for some areas, whereas in others collective or group rights of some sort will be more effective.[19]

In each country of Europe, including Central and Eastern Europe, similar questions arise with respect to law, medicine and bioethics. But there are differences of a philosophical, economic, social, political and even geographical nature which are not easily (even if desirably) bridged. The parallel between explosive political change within and across Europe and the rapid developments in bioethical sciences and their impacts on the fields of law, ethics and human rights have brought the focus upon differences in legislative response, differences in the extent to which questions such as those arising from the advent and adventure of reproductive technology, for example, constitute items on public, social and legal policy agendas. This will again depend on per-mutations and nuances in tradition, religion, culture, economics and wealth. Throughout the European Union and the member states of the Council of Europe moral and legal pluralism reflecting these variations is evident. Yet it is sometimes overlooked that that pluralism typically operates at the margins of what might be called the ethical stationery. The depth and breadth of agreement far outweigh and outpace moral disagreement, whether the supporting reasoning is of a broadly con-sequentialist or of a deontological kind.

Recognising this, the World Health Organisation Draft Declaration on the Rights of Patients (1 March 1990, revised August 1990) suggests that shared social, economic, cultural, ethical and political considera-tions have given rise to a movement throughout Europe towards a fuller elaboration and fulfilment of the rights of patients. Throughout Europe it is clear that there are shared principles which are being adopted in many countries and which seem to be independent of system charac-teristics. Health rights have a long established place in international rights documents. The United Kingdom, along with other contracting states, is committed to a number of international agreements to promote health rights, including the Universal Declaration of Human Rights, art. 25[20] and the International Covenant on Economic, Social and Cultural Rights, art. 12.[21] More recently, the Treaty of Maastricht, art. 129 provides:

> The Community shall contribute towards ensuring a high level of human health protection by encouraging co-operation between the member-states and, if necessary, lending support to their action. Community action shall be directed towards the prevention of diseases, in particular the major health scourges, including drug dependence, by promoting research into their causes and their transmissions, as well as health infor-mation and education.

But differences of an economic and political character serve only to underscore the problems of cultural comparisons when we move from the high levels of abstractions at which international documents pitch these aspirations to more concrete attempts to implement these 'rights'. Let me illustrate this by reviewing one attempt, in the United Kingdom, to give operational scope to these ideals.

The Patient's Charter (which shares some common themes and approaches with the Draft European Declaration on the Rights of Patients) is a government document which sets out non-legally enforceable expectations, which patients may properly have, of the health service. Although they may appear at first sight to be no more than loose formulations, they must be read in the light of what Craig has suggested regarding the moral weight of expectation: while a particular interest may not be framed as a justiciable legal right, it may nonetheless generate a constitutional obligation which the departments of state are expected if not yet bound to advance. The core of the Charter approach is spelt out in the following passage:

> The patient's charter sets out for the first time your rights to health care in the National Health Service and the National and Local Charter Standards which the Government intends to see achieved.
>
> In addition to seven well-established rights, the Government is introducing three new important rights ... [and] National Charter Standards in nine key areas. These are not legal rights but major and specific standards which the Government looks to the NHS to achieve, as circumstances and resources allow.[22]

These 'rights' cover such matters as receiving health care on the basis of clinical need, regardless of ability to pay; receiving emergency medical care at any time; referral to an acceptable consultant; expecting a clear explanation of any treatment, including risks and alternatives, before deciding to agree to the treatment; having access to your health records and knowing that those working in the health service are under a legal duty to keep their contents confidential; receiving detailed information on local health services, including standards and maximum waiting times; admission for treatment not later than two years from the day when your consultant places you on a waiting list; and full and prompt response to a complaint.

In addition to these Charter Rights are a series of what the Patient's Charter then goes on to identify as National and Local Charter Standards; those which are expressed not to be legal rights. These standards of service to which the NHS is to aim include more general notions such as respect for the privacy, dignity and religious and cultural beliefs of all patients; arrangements to ensure that everyone, including people with special needs, can use services; far more specific targets, such as arrival times for ambulances; immediate assessment for treatment in accident and emergency departments; and specific appointments to be seen in outpatients and consultations within 30 minutes of that appointment.

Some of these are highly specific, albeit not legally enforceable, targets for patient aspiration and service delivery. The caveat expressed in the Patient's Charter regarding resources shows how all these aspirations, even in a wealthy jurisdiction such as the United Kingdom, cannot be achieved costlessly, cannot be achieved without sacrificing possibilities and gains elsewhere and cannot be achieved without also addressing the conceptual and ethical questions of identification and allocation which have already been discussed above. Let me illustrate the problems which may beset any system which seeks to turn this rhetoric to reality through the mouthpiece of the law.

Rights to Health Care and the Opportunity Costs of Rhetoric

Two particular examples will serve to illustrate the concluding arguments which I want to pursue here. The National Health Service Act 1977 s.1(1) provides: 'It is the Secretary of State's duty to continue the promotion in England & Wales of a comprehensive health service designed to secure improvement (a) in the physical and mental health of the people of those countries, and (b) in the prevention, diagnosis and treatment of illness.' And section 3 provides:

> It is the Secretary of State's duty to provide throughout England & Wales, to such extent as he considers necessary to meet all reasonable require-
> ments –
> (a) hospital accommodation
> (b) other accommodation for the purpose of any service provided under this Act
> (c) medical, dental, nursing and ambulance services.

In *R. v. Secretary of State for Social Services ex parte Hincks*[23] several patients who had been waiting for up to three years for pain-relieving operations – longer than was medically advised – sued the health secretary. The delay arose in part from a shortage of orthopaedic beds in the Birmingham area, a wait caused in part by a decision not to build a new block on the hospital on grounds of cost. The Court of Appeal held that there was no right to bring the action. Lord Denning said that the minister could be considered to have failed in the discharge of the statutory duty only if his exercise of it was so thoroughly unreasonable as to be one which no reasonable secretary could have made. The Act did not create, according to the court, an absolute duty to provide services irrespective of economic decisions taken at a national level. According to Lord Denning, the provision had to be read subject to the qualification that the secretary of state's duty is to meet 'all reasonable requirements such as can be provided within the resources available'.[24]

Lord Justice Bridge gave a more convincing judgment when he rejected the plaintiffs' argument that, since the statute did not place any limits on the extent of the secretary's duty based on longer-term financial planning, none could be envisaged unless the statute expressly so provided. He held that if no limits in respect of longer-term financial planning were to be read into public statutory duties such as that apparently under consideration, then the Secretary would be faced with a bottomless (or at least ever-deepening) pit. The argument put forward on the plaintiffs' behalf was even more difficult to accept as a realistic claim when it was realised, he said, that the further the medical and technological advances go in the direction of even more comprehensive patient care, the greater would be the financial burden placed on the secretary if he were to avoid a dereliction of his duty under the NHS Act 1977.

A similar line of reasoning has been adopted in the three other cases which have sought a similar sort of challenge: *R. v. Secretary of State for Social Services ex parte Walker;*[25] *R. v. Central Birmingham Health Authority ex parte Collier*[26] and *Re J (a minor)(Medical Treatment).*[27] I cannot here consider each case, but *Re J* is of particular interest, because the patient tried to establish a right to a certain kind of treatment. A 16-month-old boy who had been injured in a fall suffered cerebral palsy and the court was asked by his natural parents to determine whether, if a life-threatening event arose, J should be given artificial ventilation and other life-saving measures whether the clinicians in charge of his care believed this was in his best interests or not. They indeed had argued that there was no medical evidence favouring ventilation. The issue was whether the court should ever require a medical practitioner to adopt a course of treatment which the doctor did not believe to be in the best interests of the patient. Lord Donaldson rejected any such argument and added, in response to a moral claim to treatment, a right imposing on someone else a duty to give treatment, that 'The sad fact of life is that health authorities may on occasion find that they have too few resources either human or material or both to treat all the patients whom they would like to treat in the way in which they would like to treat them. It is their duty to make choices'.[28] Lord Justice Balcombe said: 'I find it difficult to conceive of a situation where it would be a proper exercise of the jurisdiction to make an order positively requiring a doctor to adopt a particular course of treatment in relation to a child, unless the doctor himself or herself was asking the court to make such an order'.[29] He stressed 'the absolute undesirability of the court making an order which may have the effect of compelling a doctor or health authority to make available scarce resources (both human and material) to a particular child, without knowing whether or not there are other patients to whom those resources might more advantageously be devoted'.[30]

These limitations in the role of health care law are related to the economic limitations which lie at the root of the UK health service. Improvements will always be possible, and the demand for health care consumption will remain, in the economist's terms, elastic. This, of course, is one of the foundational problems which have bedevilled health service planning since the inception of the NHS.

Final Remarks: of Markets and Morals

The National Health Service sought the promotion of a comprehensive health service to secure improvement in the physical and mental health of the nation, and also to secure the prevention, diagnosis and treatment of illness through the provision of effective services. Such services were to be provided free. This was to be made possible by the state ownership and control of resources. These were to be allocated, at zero price, at the point of consumption, thereby ensuring freely available health care. It was assumed that the population would thereby grow healthier, and thus the costs would cease to rise and perhaps even begin to fall. As Lee points out,[31] the economic flaws in this argument are now obvious, and indeed should have been obvious at the time. Neoclassical writers such as Pigou as early as the 1920s had shown themselves well aware of the price elasticity of individual demand in relation to public services.[32] Notions of price elasticity dictate that an attempt to supply services at zero prices will be met by significant increases in demand above what would be demanded at prices set by marginal cost. Against this background, the attempt to establish a workable notion of rights to health care as a way of resolving or even responding to questions of just allocation of health benefits may seem to be a rhetorical nightmare. The territory of theory and the aspiration of practice which have been reviewed here illustrate briefly how attempts to make expectations realities through the language of rights are sometimes doomed to disappointment or failure: broken on the wheel of fortune, or its absence.

Notes

1   Ivan Illich, *Limits to Medicine*, London, Penguin, 1976, p.235.
2   This introduction draws on Jonathan Montgomery, 'Rights to Health and Health Care', in Anna Coote (ed.), *The Welfare of Citizens: Developing New Social Rights*, London, IPPR, 1992, pp.82 ff. Standard arguments about health rights are contained, *inter alia*, in Thomas J. Bole and William B. Bondeson (eds), *Rights to Health Care*, Dordrecht, Kluwer, 1991; and papers presented at the 'Symposium on the Rights of Patients', Lund and Orenas Castle, Sweden, 21–25 April 1993.
3   For an introduction to the background of the National Health Service, see Rudolf Klein, *The Politics of the National Health Service*, London, Longman, 1983, *passim*; for a brief survey of the recent changes set within that background, see Ian Holliday, *The NHS Transformed*, Manchester, Baseline Books, 1992, *passim*.
4   For an introduction to this vast literature see, for example, Caroline Currer and Margaret Stacey, *Concepts of Health and Disease: A Comparative Perspective*, Leamington Spa, Berg, 1986; and to some of the problems associated with one group of 'new' (reproductive) technologies, Marilyn Strathern, *Reproducing the Future: Anthropology, Kinship and the New Reproductive Technologies*, Manchester, Manchester University Press, 1992.

5   B. Williams, 'The Idea of Equality', in Peter Laslett and W.G. Runciman (eds), *Philosophy, Politics and Society*, 2nd series, Oxford, Clarendon Press, 1962, pp.110–31.

6   *Anarchy, State and Utopia*, Oxford, Basil Blackwell, 1974, p.233.

7   Ibid., at pp.234–5. I learned of this debate and began to understand its subtleties from lectures given by John Day, of the University of Leicester. His own interpretation of it, and his response, are now recorded in his essay, 'Justice and Utility in Health Care', in Lincoln Allison (ed.), *The Utilitarian Response: The Contemporary Viability of Utilitarian Political Philosophy*, London, Sage, 1993, p.30.

8   *A Theory of Human Need*, London, Macmillan, 1991, pp.137–8.

9   John Gray, *Beyond the New Right*, London, Routledge, 1993, p.50.

10 J. McKeown, *The Role of Medicine*, Oxford, Basil Blackwell, 1979, *passim*.

11 Gray, *Beyond the New Right*, at p.168.

12 Ibid., especially at pp.166–72.

13 Michael Freeden, *Rights*, Buckingham, Open University Press, 1991, p.92.

14 *Public Law and Democracy in the United Kingdom and the United States*, Oxford, Clarendon Press, 1990, p.7.

15 This sort of argument underlies the work of writers such as John Finnis, *Natural Law and Natural Rights*, Oxford, Clarendon Press, 1985. Others, such as Joseph Raz, in *The Morality of Freedom*, Oxford, Clarendon Press, 1986, and Ronald Dworkin, in *Taking Rights Seriously*, London, Duckworth, 1977, have sensitised us to the place of morality with respect to law, and have argued that morality (Raz) or principles (Dworkin) can be used as safety nets onto which judges may fall back and rely when gaps appear in the law. They do not explicitly address the questions of whose views, and what morality, but they fall within the mainstream of modern liberal thought on questions of the relationship between law and morality.

16 Freeden, *Rights*, p.6; see also Ian Kennedy, 'Agenda for Health Ethics and Law', (1991) **70** *Bulletin of Medical Ethics*, p.16.

17 For a more comprehensive review of these notions, from which this outline is derived, see Claire Palley, *The United Kingdom and Human Rights*, London, Stevens & Sons, 1991.

18 *Samples of Lawmaking*, Oxford, Oxford University Press, 1962, p.103.

19 For a further discussion of individual and groups rights, and important distinctions between and considerations within these categories, see Montgomery, 'Rights to Health and Health Care', pp.87–90.

20 'Everyone has the right to a standard of living adequate for the health and well being of himself and his family, including food, clothing, housing, and medical care and necessary social services.'

21 '... the right to enjoyment of the highest attainable standard of physical and mental health.'

22 *The Patient's Charter*, London, Department of Health, at p.6.

23 (1992) 1 BMLR, 93.

24 (1993) 1 BMLR, at 95.

25 (1993) 3 BMLR, 32.

26 6 January 1988, unreported.

27 [1992] 4 A11 ER, 614. To these should now be added the important case of *R*. v. *Cambridge Health Authority, ex parte B (a minor)* [1995] 23 BMLR 1.

28 Ibid., p.623.

29 Ibid., p.625.

30 Ibid.

31 For a summary of the history of the introduction of the NHS, from which this account is drawn, see R.G. Lee, 'Legal Control of Health Care Allocation', in Mark Ockelton (ed.), *Medicine, Ethics and Law*, Stuttgart, ARSP, 1987, pp.94–6.

32 See A. Pigou, *A Study in Public Finance*, London, Macmillan, 1928.

3 If You Know What's Good for You: Refusal of Consent to Medical Treatment by Children

SARAH ELLISTON

'The existence of the patient's right to make his own decision ... may be seen as a basic human right protected by the common law.'[1] In 1995, ten years after this statement was made, English law has shown itself reluctant to grant this basic human right to one class of patient – the competent child. Put simply, the law appears to recognise a decision made by a person under the age of 18 only if that decision is to follow the course of treatment recommended by the medical profession. The aim of this chapter is to describe the development of this approach to medical decision making by children and to argue that the current position is illogical, inconsistent and unjustified. To develop this discussion, it is first necessary to consider the relevant case and statute law governing medical decision making by children.

The Assessment of Competence

In the medical context, the law in England and Wales has set two standards by which it is determined, prima facie, whether a child is to be regarded as competent. The first is a presumptive test, by which a child is presumed competent provided that they have reached a certain age. The second is an evidential test, which requires the young person under that age to demonstrate to the satisfaction of a medical practitioner that they have achieved the requisite degree of competence to decide on the issue in question.

29

The Presumptive Standard

The position is largely governed by the Family Law Reform Act (FLRA) 1969, s.8 of which reads as follows:

> (1) The consent of a minor who has attained the age of sixteen years to any surgical, medical or dental treatment which, in the absence of consent, would constitute a trespass to his person, shall be as effective as it would be if he were of full age; and where a minor has by virtue of this section given an effective consent to any treatment it shall not be necessary to obtain any consent for it from his parent or guardian.
>
> (2) In this section 'surgical, medical or dental treatment' includes any procedure undertaken for the purposes of diagnosis, and this section applies to any procedure (including, in particular, the administration of an anaesthetic) which is ancillary to any treatment as it applies to that treatment.

Thus the statute appears to intend that the consent of a 16-year-old should be as valid in law as if they were an adult, that is that they are to be regarded as self-governing for this purpose. No stipulation is made as to the assessment of the competence of the 16-year-old, which ought therefore to be the same as for adults: that they are presumed to be competent unless the contrary is shown.

The Evidential Standard

The leading case is of course *Gillick v. West Norfolk and Wisbech Area Health Authority*.[2] This case, involving the provision of contraceptive advice and treatment to under 16-year-old girls, is too well known to require detailed exposition here.[3] For our purposes it is sufficient to note that those under 16 can consent to medical treatment on their own behalf if they are judged to be competent by a medical practitioner. In order to establish competence, differing tests were put forward in the leading judgements. According to Lord Fraser, children must demonstrate that they have 'sufficient discretion to be able to make a wise choice in their best interests'. By contrast, the judgement of Lord Scarman made no explicit reference to the 'best interests' test, instead basing the test of competence solely on the attainment of intelligence and understanding of the medical issues.

As will be seen, English law appears to have developed in accordance with Lord Fraser's judgement.[4] Under either test, however, the presumption as to competence is reversed and the child is presumed not to be competent unless they satisfy the medical practitioner. In effect the child must satisfy an evidential rather than a presumptive test as to competence.

The first question to ask is why an arbitrary age limit of 16 is to determine when a child is presumed to be capable of making decisions about medical treatment. A study of children appears to show that the competence of children in these matters may be significantly under-estimated.[5] As will be argued below, a possible answer to this question is that the age limit was set as a notional age intended more to provide an additional avenue of protection to the medical practitioner seeking to provide treatment to a child which might otherwise be vetoed by the child's parents than to empower children to make the ultimate decisions about their own treatment. Secondly, it might be supposed that a young person who is deemed to be competent under either of the standards should also be considered competent to refuse it. The falsity of this supposition is shown by recent English case law. None of the aforementioned tests for determining the legal capacity of children to consent to medical or similar treatment explicitly considers the question of refusal. In the absence of specific statutory guidance on this point, a distinction has been drawn between these situations. In order to achieve the desired outcome in medical terms for the child, the courts have in fact reassessed the criteria for competence and created additional requirements where a child refuses consent.

The Child who is Competent to Consent to Treatment but not to Refuse it

The first case to deal with this matter was the case of *Re E (a minor) (wardship: medical treatment).*[6] It concerned a boy who was within three months of his sixteenth birthday. He was suffering from leukaemia and had refused to consent to a blood transfusion. He and his parents, who fully supported his decision, were Jehovah's Witnesses and blood transfusions were contrary to their religious beliefs.

The main strand of the judgement by Ward J. was that, although the boy was intelligent enough to make most decisions regarding his own well-being, he did not understand what the effect of his refusal would be. Therefore he was not competent to make a decision. The test applied was a particularly stringent one to satisfy, since it required the boy to be able to turn his mind to the manner in which he might die and to the extent of his and his family's suffering. It is doubtful whether many adults in similar circumstances would be able to fulfil this as a test of competence, and certainly nothing like it has been suggested in cases concerning adult Jehovah's Witnesses. The use of this test is particularly ironic since it is clear from the judgement that the child in *Re E* had not even been asked to turn his mind to such matters.[7]

A second idea expressed in this case is that, even if a particular child has sufficient understanding and intelligence to weigh up the issue in question, it is assumed that children are unable to consider the long-term effects of their decisions.[8] This introduces another explicit requirement into the test of competence for children that it is either presumed adults have by virtue of being adults, or that it is not necessary for them to have. It also proceeds on the assumption that the decision they have taken *is* against their long-term interests; that is, that it has already been decided that the decision taken by the child is 'wrong'. Further, it fails to recognise the individuality of that child by focusing instead on the patient as a member of a class, that class being children.

If the boy had chosen to accept medical advice to have treatment, it seems probable that this case would never have reached a court since a medical practitioner would have been justified in proceeding on his consent, as it is unlikely in the extreme that the boy would have been judged to have failed to consider his own long-term interests by consenting to such treatment. According to the ratio in *Gillick*, the competent child may accept treatment, even if the parents object. This point will be returned to later. *Re E* involved tinkering with the traditional idea of competence: what ability a person must show in order to be deemed capable of undergoing a rational decision-making process. It might be argued that, in *Re E*, competence assumed critical importance because the boy was under the age of 16. The argument that the boy was very nearly 16 was rejected because he had not yet attained that age. Therefore competence was judged on the evidential standard which imposes a higher burden of proof on the child.

Indeed, this approach was approved in the case of *Re R (a minor) (wardship: medical treatment)*,[9] which reached the Court of Appeal, Civil Division. The leading judgement was delivered by Lord Donaldson of Lymington M.R. This case concerned a 15-year-old girl with fluctuating mental health. The adolescent psychiatric unit in which she had been placed wished to treat her with anti-psychotic drugs, which they considered she needed to receive even during periods of remission from her mental illness. However, in her lucid intervals she objected to taking these drugs. The local authority therefore commenced wardship proceedings and sought leave from the court for the unit to administer medication, including such drugs, with or without the girl's consent.

On the facts, it was held that the ward was not competent even in her lucid intervals.[10] This is a curious conclusion to reach, since it allows competence to be judged not on the present but on the past or the predicted mental condition of the person. In addition it was held that the drug treatment was in the girl's best interests and that the medical staff should be authorised to provide it. The appeal was dismissed on both these grounds.

This fundamental shift in approach to medical decision making by children was taken a stage further in the case of *Re W (a minor) (medical treatment)*,[11] a case again heard by the Court of Appeal, Civil Division with the leading judgement given by Lord Donaldson of Lymington

M.R. The case involved a girl under local authority care and suffering from anorexia nervosa. She was 16 years old when her physical condition deteriorated to the extent that the authority wished to transfer her from the specialist residential unit in which she was being cared for to a hospital and for treatment to be administered to her there. She objected, saying that she would cure herself when she felt ready to do so and the local authority sought directions from the court under the inherent jurisdiction, rather than under the wardship jurisdiction. At first instance it was held that, although she did have sufficient under-standing to make an informed decision, nevertheless the court had inherent jurisdiction to make the orders sought.

The decision to make the orders sought by the local authority was upheld on appeal. However, the Court of Appeal based their decision on the finding that the nature of the condition itself involved a desire not to be treated. In these circumstances the girl's refusal of consent could be overruled, despite the fact that she appeared quite capable of understanding the information given on the consequences of a failure to treat her, and although, being 16 years old, she ought to have been presumed to be competent. It appears therefore that the courts adopt a much stricter test in determining the competence of a child, a test that even a presumptively competent child is unlikely to satisfy.

It could be argued that it would be wrong to base general proposi-tions on the court's attitude to determining the competence of minors on the cases of *Re E*, *Re R* and *Re W* because of their particular cir-cumstances. After all, *Re E* and *Re R* concerned minors who were required to establish their competence as they were under 16. A further factor arising in *Re R* and also in the case of the presumptively competent girl in *Re W* was that the very condition for which treatment was proposed involved mental and emotional disturbance. This, it might be thought, would make it impossible for them to undergo a rational decision-making process.[12] However, this argument loses its force when it is remembered that the court's tests in *Re E* are such that most competent adults would find them almost impossible to meet. Similarly, the girl in *Re R* was lucid when she made her decision. It might be thought reasonable to attempt to prevent her lapsing back into a mentally disordered state. However, this sets a dangerous precedent whereby various forms of treatment may be administered to competent patients against their will in the belief that this will avert mental disorders which may in fact never materialise.

Re W poses rather more problems since, if a desire not to be treated is indeed part of a condition of illness, it is difficult to conclude that the decision to refuse treatment was a true expression of the patient's own will, since her decision was directed by the disorder. This appears to have been the approach of the medical profession and the courts in relation to adults suffering from this condition who have been treated under the

Mental Health Act 1983.[13] However, such a finding should be made only with a great deal of care, since it may be all too easy to subvert the concept of competence in order to hold that a patient's desire not to be treated is a symptom of mental disorder, rather than an expression of their autonomy. In addition, apart from these difficult cases where competence may genuinely be in doubt, the judgement went much further than this in stating that even a competent minor could never override the consent given by either the child's parents or a court. Although strictly *obiter*, since it was found as a fact that W was not competent, the tenor of the judgement and the approach of the courts where children refuse consent leads to the suspicion that it will be followed.

It is submitted that there is no justification for the courts' adopting a more stringent test in order to determine whether a child is competent or not. In addition, to draw a distinction between the ability to consent to treatment and the ability to refuse is quite illogical. As has been said, the right to say yes must carry with it the right to say no.[14] If one is able to weigh up the considerations in order to agree to treatment, surely one is equally capable of weighing up the same considerations even though arriving at a different conclusion? It has been suggested that a difference may lie between consenting and refusing to consent in that consent 'involves the acceptance of an experienced view, refusal rejects that experience – and does so from a position of limited understanding'.[15] While this may be true, the same is also likely to be true where adults are asked to make the same choice. Most patients are likely to know less about the treatment of disease than a qualified doctor. The critical point should surely be whether the patient, whatever their status, is in fact able to understand the risks, benefits and possible outcome of their decision. To assume that no-one under the age of 18 is able to do so, whereas those over 18 are assumed to have this ability, again ignores the individuality of the patient by focusing on the status of minority.

A further suggestion is that refusing consent 'may close down the options'.[16] Again, however, it might be argued that embarking on a particular course of treatment may also close down options, necessitating adherence to a particular regime of surgical or pharmacological interventions, with significant physical and emotional consequences for the patient. One cannot help but think of the case of the young child, Laura Davies, who in her tragically short life underwent a series of complex medical procedures. Here even the medical team involved later questioned whether such prolonged attempts to save her life had been justified. A distinction between consenting and refusing to consent to treatment is therefore hard to maintain, and implying that a different level of competence is required by children seeking to refuse consent to treatment is unjustified.

By introducing such additional criteria, the courts are shifting the determination of competence from being a test of a person's ability to undergo a rational decision-making process to one of the ability to make what is, in their view, a rational decision. In other words, the crucial factor is the predicted medical outcome of the minor's decision.

The Primacy of Autonomy

While the law has intervened to prevent even well-intentioned inter-ference with the decisions of competent adults, it has been notably reluctant to do so in the case of children. In English law at least, whether a competent child will have their wishes respected seems to have nothing to do with autonomy and everything to do with outcome. This point can be demonstrated by examining the different attitudes of the English courts to consent and refusal of consent to medical treatment.

Competent Children: Consent

It might be assumed that, when a competent child makes their own decision on medical treatment, no-one who might otherwise have been able to make a decision on behalf of a child need, or should be allowed to, interfere with that decision. This certainly appears to be the approach of the law to the role of parents when considering the question of the competent child's decision to accept recommended medical treatment.[17]

In England and Wales it is stated in the case of the presumptively competent child in the FLRA 1969 that their consent is sufficient and the consent of a parent shall not be necessary; that is, a parent's consent is not needed *in addition* to that of the competent child.[18] The same is true for the evidentially competent child. In England it has been held that the parental right to consent to medical treatment for their children is subject to erosion as the child gains intellectual, physical and emotional maturity. As Lord Scarman put it in *Gillick*: 'The underlying principle of the law was exposed by Blackstone and can be seen to have been acknowledged in the case law. It is that the parental right yields to the child's right to make his own decisions when he reaches a sufficient understanding and intelligence to be capable of making up his own mind on the matter requiring a decision.'[19]

Indeed, by virtue of the doctrine of confidentiality between doctor and patient, the parents may not even be aware that a competent child has sought treatment.[20] Furthermore, where a parent is aware that a child is being offered medical treatment and objects, the treatment may proceed despite their objections. Such a situation occurred in the case of *Re P (a minor)*,[21] where a 15-year-old girl was seeking an abortion, against the wishes of her father. It was held that she was competent to make her own decision and that her father's objection did not operate to override her consent. This case supports the idea that a medical practitioner may not only proceed without seeking the opinion of a parent where the consent of a competent young person is obtained, but that in these circumstances she may proceed where a parent explicitly withholds consent.

However, it should be noted that, although a parent cannot override a competent child's consent, a court retains its protective role and may veto the child's consent if it considers this to be in the child's best interests, following the line of reasoning by Lord Fraser in *Gillick*. The power of the court is therefore greater than the power of a parent in this respect. The court in *Re P (a minor)* chose not to exercise its discretion since the abortion was expressed by medical opinion to be in her best interests.

Competent Children: Refusal of Consent

Where the decision made by the competent child is to reject the advice given by medical practitioners, according to the English courts the decision of the child can be overruled not only by the court but also by that child's parent and this is so regardless of whether the child is able to demonstrate competence even under the already strict criteria. This proposition was developed in the case of *Re R*, above, where it was stated that, even if the girl had been deemed competent to make a decision refusing treatment, this decision could be overruled by parents or by the court exercising its wardship jurisdiction if it considered the treatment to be in her best interests.

The principle was stated again by Lord Donaldson in *Re W*, where the best interests test was held to be equally applicable to cases brought under the inherent jurisdiction of the court, rather than under its wardship jurisdiction:[22] 'No minor of whatever age has power by refusing consent to treatment to override a consent to treatment by someone who has parental responsibility for the minor and *a fortiori* a consent by the court.'[23] Thus, while only a court may override the consent of a competent child, both court and parents may override a refusal of consent, and this power lasts until the child's eighteenth birthday.

One may well ask then why the competence of the child is an issue at all. It can be argued that it is not and that the real issue in deciding whether or not medical treatment can be provided to children, in contrast to adults, is the predicted medical outcome. This approach fundamentally undermines the concept of autonomy. It is submitted that there is no justification for the difference of treatment of children in this respect and that it is based on a misinterpretation of the existing case and statute law. To explore this argument, it is necessary to compare the laws regulating consent to medical treatment by adults and minors.

The Purpose of Consent to Medical Treatment

At the heart of the issue of consent lies the tension between the principle of autonomy and the principle of beneficence. That there is such a tension is well recognised and it is beyond the scope of this chapter to provide more than an outline of this debate.[24] Requirements for consent are based on the principle of autonomy and are grounded in the idea that respect is due to the individual. Several reasons have been put forward for requiring the patient's consent before medical treatment is given. These include protection of bodily integrity, freedom of choice and therapeutic benefit.[25] There is considerable debate over the extent of health care professionals' duty in promoting these principles.[26]

The adult patient of sound mind is taken as the benchmark for determining whether a person is to be legally recognised as having capacity and competence to determine their own medical treatment. The statement by Cardozo J. is, of course, the classic formulation of this concept: 'Every human being of adult years and sound mind has a right to determine what shall be done with his own body, and a surgeon who performs an operation without his patient's consent, commits an assault.'[27] Adults are thus entitled to the benefit of the presumption that they are competent to make their own decisions. The law assumes that they will have both the intellectual ability and the maturity of judgement developed through experience to be able to undertake a rational decision-making process. Adult status of itself provides evidence of capacity to exercise choice as to treatment. The importance of exercising choice is recognised by the legal requirements for information disclosure which will enable the patient to consider the available options, risks and benefits of proposed treatment or a failure to treat.[28]

Whether a person is competent or not is ultimately a question for the court,[29] although in reality such decisions are made on a daily basis by practitioners. Although medical practitioners may receive no specific training on assessment of competence, the courts appear to accept that any registered medical practitioner is capable of making this assessment. The presumption of competence applies equally to adults suffering from a degree of mental impairment. However, this presumption can be rebutted if it is shown that they do not understand the particular procedure or its implications, or are unable to arrive at a choice by rational means. The question arose in the case of *Re C*.[30] C had been diagnosed as suffering from paranoid schizophrenia. He developed gangrene in a foot and the medical opinion was that he would die if the leg were not amputated below the knee. C, however, refused consent to such an operation and it was argued by the hospital treating him that his ability to make a definitive decision was impaired by his mental illness.

The judge adopted a three-stage analysis, since competence was in doubt, proposed by the doctor treating C. This analysis is in line with the recommendations set out by the Law Commission:[31] 'i. comprehending and retaining treatment information; ii. believing it; and iii. weighing it in the balance to arrive at choice.' This approach, building on previous case law, stresses the importance of patient choice and the exercise of autonomy. The capability of the patient to reach a decision must be considered in the precise context of the question being posed. In other words, is this person capable of making a decision on the proposed form of medical treatment consistent with their own values and beliefs? Although dicta in *Re C* and the earlier case of *Chatterton v. Gerson*[32] suggest that the patient need have only a broad understanding of what is involved in order to give a valid consent, it could be argued that the case of *Re T* is authority for requiring a greater degree of competence where the effects of the decision may be more serious. The judgement in *Re T* suggested that, where a patient refused consent, he must show an understanding 'commensurate with the gravity of the decision which he purports to make. The more serious the decision, the greater the capacity required'.[33]

Whether this in fact adds anything to the requirement that the adult does understand the nature, effect, risks and benefits of the proposed treatment is doubtful. It probably does no more than to put more of an onus on the health carers to be satisfied that they have provided a sufficient explanation to the patient on the seriousness of the expected consequences of a refusal of consent, and that the patient has understood this information. To hold otherwise would suggest that it is for the adult patient to prove he is competent, which is clearly wrong in both law and principle.

This proposition ought to apply equally strongly to the presumptively competent minor, where the statute itself provides for no additional criteria. Obviously, where the evidentially competent child is concerned, *Gillick* establishes that the burden of proof is reversed, but once the requisite level of competence is achieved, this ought to settle the matter in favour of respecting the child's decision. There seems to be no reason why a test that is applicable to an adult, where competence is in doubt, ought not to be equally applicable to a child, unless the view is taken that all persons below the age of 18 exhibit wholly different characteristics and reasoning abilities to those above that age. Such a view is patently absurd.

A relatively strong burden of proof would appear to lie on those who seek to challenge this presumption of competence, if all that is required is the patient understands in broad terms the procedures, risks, benefits and options. However, it is worth remembering at this point that even an adult may have to demonstrate some ability to undergo a rational decision-making process if doubts are raised on this matter. It is likely that there will be greater scrutiny of this ability where the decision is regarded by the medical profession as irrational. The temptation may well be to judge that a person is not in fact competent to make the decision in question, particularly where the decision is to refuse medical treatment. It should be borne in mind that, in the case of an assessment of competence to consent to medical treatment, the doctor making this assessment will often be the one proposing the treatment.

This problem is raised in an even more acute form where the patient has not achieved adult status. As discussed above, the English courts appear to have developed more stringent criteria for the establishment of competence and capacity in the case of those under the age of 18. Even if a minor is able to satisfy the additional requirements, their decision may still be overruled by either the court or the minor's parents. The establishment of competence of a minor therefore appears to be a meaningless exercise. The question then becomes: how have the courts reached their decisions regarding the choices of minors? According to the judiciary, their decisions are reached by applying the concept of the best interests of the child (or an application of the 'welfare' principle). This idea of best interests is a convenient shorthand expression, but what does it really mean and how will it apply to a particular case?

The Best Interests of the Child or Young Person

The first idea of what might be meant by the concept of best interests, as has been demonstrated, can be dismissed relatively swiftly. This is the notion that it is in a person's best interests, and incidentally in the best interests of society, to respect their autonomous decisions (except in circumstances where significant harm to others may result). As the above cases illustrate, the fact that a child has been deemed competent does not mean that their wishes are regarded as determinative. The opinions of the courts in *Re R* and *Re W* suggest that the child's wishes should carry more weight with increasing age and maturity,[34] but whether this amounts to anything more than paying lip-service to the principle of autonomy is to be doubted since in no reported English case on the refusal of consent by children have their wishes been respected. Their wishes are, at most, a factor for the court to take into account in determining what the welfare of the child requires.

If the autonomy of the individual is not the principle to be respected by the best interests test, then what is? The autonomy of the family might seem to be a candidate.[35] Since in the case of young children, parents have the right to decide upon medical treatment, they are felt to be in the best position to judge what is right for their child. However, this is true only up to a point. Parents do not have an absolute right to determine medical treatment. In the case of older children, as we have seen, the parental right to consent or withhold consent is a dwindling one that gives way to the right of the child to make up their own mind. But even where children are clearly too young to reach a decision for themselves, parents can neither veto treatment that is determined to be medically necessary nor insist that it be provided.[36]

The English courts have reserved to themselves greater powers over children than those of natural parents[37] and have consistently taken the view that it is not their function to act as the real parents would (otherwise the parents' views would always be determinative and recourse to the courts would be neither necessary nor possible) but as an 'objective parent'. This test seems to have its origin in the approach of Lord Upjohn in the case of *J* v. *C*,[38] dealing with custody of infants, where he said:

> The law and practice in relation to infants have developed and are developing and must and no doubt will continue to develop by reflecting and adopting the changing views as the years go by of reasonable men and women, the parents of children, on the proper treatment and methods of bringing up children, for after all that is the model which the judge must emulate, for he must act as the judicial reasonable parent.

This is therefore an objective test, and is also described as the standard of the ordinary mother and father, but it is only part of the test, since it is also subjective in that the test must be applied not to the ordinary child but to the particular child.[39]

Though this test has its value in protecting children from neglect or abuse by their parents, it is difficult to see why it is an appropriate one for determining whether the wishes of a competent young person should be respected. In any event, to say that the judiciary will act in the manner of the ordinary mother or father is only to raise another question: how would these mythical parents – the parents on the Clapham omnibus – act in the particular circumstances? The courts' power to determine questions involving children appears to be exercised in accordance with a certain set of presumptions, all of which are problematic.

The first is based on sanctity of life or quality of life arguments. Health risks for a competent adult as a result of their refusal of consent are not a relevant consideration for the courts. The sole question seems to be whether the patient has the basic requirements to make an autonomous decision. When a person has adult status and the presumption of competence has not been rebutted, their decision must be respected by the health care professionals and will be upheld by the courts regardless of the anticipated consequences of a failure to treat. The position is perhaps most clearly set out in *Re T (adult: refusal of medical treatment)*,[40] where Lord Donaldson M.R. stated in summary:

> Prima facie every adult has the right and capacity to decide whether or not he will accept medical treatment, even if a refusal may risk permanent injury to his health or even lead to premature death. Furthermore, it matters not whether the reasons for the refusal were rational, or irrational, unknown or even non-existent. This is so notwithstanding the very strong public interest in preserving the life and health of all citizens.

This conclusion also finds support in Commonwealth jurisdictions such as in Canada, per Robins J.A. in the case of *Malette v. Shulman*:[41] 'The right of self-determination...obviously encompasses the right to refuse medical treatment. A competent adult is generally entitled to reject a specific treatment or all treatment, or to select an alternative form of treatment, even if the decision may entail risks as serious as death and may appear mistaken in the eyes of the medical profession or of the community.' In this context, the best interests of the patient are seen in terms of ensuring respect for the autonomy of the patient. Their best interests are not measured in terms of health or even life itself, and refusal of consent is seen as a necessary aspect of this principle. A competent adult's decision to refuse treatment may not always be respected. *Re S*[42] provides a controversial example (see Chapter 5). Others may be found: for instance, public health measures. However, it should be noted that the individual's autonomy in such situations is said to be overridden to protect others, not the individual. In so far as *Re S* suggested that the pregnant woman's refusal of consent could be overridden in her own vital interests, this is clearly contrary to authority.

Where children are concerned, the majority of the cases that have reached the courts have arisen in circumstances where the life of the child has been considered by medical opinion, of which more later, to be seriously threatened. In such situations, the courts have unanimously regarded the fact that the treatment proposed was said to offer at least some chance of survival as being the crucial factor in overriding the refusal of consent by the competent child. For example, per Ward J. in *Re E*:[43] 'When, therefore, I have to balance the wishes of a father and son against the need for a chance to save a precious life, then I have to conclude that their decision is inimical to his [the boy in the case] well-being.' However, this ignores the fact that in other circumstances it has increasingly been recognised that life is not always better than death – *for that individual*. This is implicitly recognised in the case of competent adults,[44] and also in other cases where the individual lacks the capacity to decide for themselves, as with handicapped neonates, and the case of *Airedale NHS Trust* v. *Bland*.[45] In these cases the argument for not providing treatment is perhaps weaker than in the case of competent children, since the individuals in such cases are incapable of forming or expressing any view on the matter.

These cases illustrate the principle that sanctity of life *in itself* does not provide a ground for overriding a decision that may or will result in death. The issue is in fact more to do with quality of life and whether, to paraphrase the judge in *Re B*, the life of the child is demonstrably going to be so awful that in effect the child should be allowed to die.[46] In the case of the competent adult, as we have seen, the law has refused to intervene in such a patient's own assessment of what would be tolerable for them, allowing them to refuse to undergo a particular form of treatment that would result in physical disability or psychological distress, even if the result will be the patient's death.

A striking example of judicial unwillingness to pass judgements on the reasonableness of an adult's set of values was provided in the criminal case of *R* v. *Blaue*,[47] where the defendant to a charge of manslaughter raised the argument that the refusal of the victim to consent to a blood transfusion was a supervening cause of death because it was unreasonable. Lawton L.J. responded:

> At once the question arises – reasonable by whose standards? Those of Jehovah's Witnesses? Humanists? Roman Catholics? Protestants of Anglo-Saxon descent? The man on the Clapham Omnibus? But he might well be an admirer of Eleazer who suffered death rather than eat the flesh of swine [see 2 Maccabees 6:18–31] or of Sir Thomas Moore who, unlike nearly all his contemporaries, was unwilling to accept Henry VIII as Head of the Church of England. Those brought up in the Hebraic or the Christian traditions would probably be reluctant to accept that those martyrs had caused their own death.

However, this approach has not been endorsed in relation to competent children where courts will make decisions that in effect balance the predicted outcome of treatment against non-treatment. In so doing they make judgements on behalf of those children about the quality of life expected with treatment. This may in part stem from the view that the best interests of children are served by enabling them to 'come to an enjoyment of autonomy'.[48] This might seem to be reasonable, were it not for the fact that the time when such autonomy may be 'enjoyed', in respect of refusing treatment, is set at the wholly arbitrary age of 18. It should be remembered that the age of majority has varied over time and was until comparatively recently set at 21.

While setting an arbitrary age for such reasons as ability to vote is acceptable, since the administrative difficulties involved in question-

ing every citizen in order to establish their competence for enfran-
chisement would be practically insurmountable, the same is not true
where decisions about the management of health of an individual are
concerned. Here the individual's ability to make a decision can be
scrutinised and indeed this must be done where a person under the
age of 16 is seeking medical treatment without the knowledge or
consent of their parents. The situation we are faced with now is that
the most that a competent child can expect is that their consent to
medical intervention will be determinative. Therefore it may be seriously
doubted whether any real question of autonomous decision making
by them arises. Their consent is a mere acceptance or endorsement of
a procedure that may be authorised to be carried out anyway.

Judges, as seen above, will in almost all cases place life itself above
all other considerations in considering competent children. Although
it was open to C, a sufferer from schizophrenia, to say that he would
rather die with two feet than live with one, it is very much to be
doubted whether a court faced with a competent 16-year-old would
respect similar statements. It is likely that the court may have been
influenced in the case of C by a number of factors, including the
patient's age (C was 68). Considerations of the life expectancy of the
child with an amputation might well tempt a court to say that survival
with a disability is preferable, thereby perhaps forcing a child to live
for many years with a disability that an adult might find intolerable
for a much shorter period and be allowed to reject. In this connection,
the courts appear to place much greater weight on physical than on
emotional considerations.

This question of emotional trauma was discussed briefly in the case
of *Re E*, where the judge had been referred to the Canadian case of *Re
LDK*.[49] In *Re LDK* the court found that the emotional trauma of the blood
transfusion would have a negative effect on the treatment. Evidence
had been led that, if an attempt had been made to transfuse her with
blood, she would 'fight that transfusion with all the strength she could
muster. She would scream and struggle, pull the injecting device out
of her arm and attempt to destroy the blood in the bag over her head'.[50]
The thought of such scenes taking place in an institution dedicated to
ensuring the well-being of patients in all respects, not just in physical
health alone, is surely not an edifying one.

It further illustrates the point that, while the court would not intervene
if the sole cause of an adult's refusal of treatment was a religious one,
it would have no hesitation in doing so where a child is concerned. Ward
J. was able to hold in *Re E* that there was no evidence to suggest that
the boy would make such efforts to resist treatment here: 'On the
contrary, any emotional trauma in the immediate course of the treatment
or in the long term will not outweigh, in my judgment, the emotional
trauma of the pain and the fear of dying in the hideous way he could

die.'[51] This from a judge who admitted he had no real conception of the strength of the boy's belief: 'One has to admire – indeed one is almost baffled by – the courage of the conviction that he expresses.'[52]

Several questions then arise: how much physical disability must a child be forced to endure because others feel it is better for that child to remain alive and why might a child be considered to be better off surviving in circumstances that an adult might choose to avoid? Would a child who had the strength to physically resist treatment have their objection to treatment respected, whereas the possibly more mature child, seeking to resist using only argument, have their objections ignored? It also poses the problem of what right a child has to refuse treatment that is neither life-saving nor life-prolonging, but that medical opinion, with parental or court approval, believes the child would benefit from. Halo therapy, a painful and lengthy treatment designed to attempt to correct growth deficiencies, is but one example.

It may be that the opinions expressed in the judgements so far can be confined to treatment for seriously debilitating or life-threatening conditions, but they are certainly wide enough to include any treatment thought to be in the child's best interests. They do nothing to encourage intelligent and thoughtful participation by children in the management of their health and may set a precedent by which health care professionals are discouraged from providing information to children, safe in the knowledge that they can obtain consent from the parents anyway. It may also lead to a breakdown in the relationship of trust between doctor and competent minor patient, since, if the doctor is unable to obtain consent from them, but the law will sanction consent given by parents or a court, doctors may feel under a duty to breach patient confidentiality in order to obtain that consent.

In addition to the factors already mentioned, it appears that a child cannot seek an alternative form of treatment, that is more acceptable to them, if the treatment they reject is considered to be the most effective. The boy in *Re E* was already being treated with a combination of drugs to combat his condition. However, the drug that was considered to be most effective had side-effects that would almost certainly require him to have a blood transfusion. It was held that, even though the conservative treatment held *some* prospect of success, some might say a reasonable prospect, that was not sufficient and that he should be given the additional drug necessitating the objected to transfusion.[53] Such decisions again negate the autonomy of the child in that they do not allow for the pros and cons of different forms of treatment or alternative treatments to be considered by the individual. They also place a high value on the medical profession's assessment of what is, at best, a speculative question. This reliance on medical opinion will now be examined in greater detail.

The second crucial factor that appears to influence the courts' determination of the child's best interests is indeed the role played by the medical profession. Since autonomy is the principal consideration when dealing with a competent adult patient, the medical opinion of the health carers as to the merits of the decision is not a relevant factor save in the exceptional circumstances described above where the health or safety of others is said to be threatened. In such situations, the opinion of the health carers will assume crucial importance as it is largely on this evidence that the court will decide whose interests are to prevail.

In cases involving children, the opinion of the child's medical practitioners will almost invariably be the decisive factor and they will be given leave to carry out such medical procedures as they deem necessary. This can be demonstrated by the fact that in every reported case the medical practitioners have been given such leave to proceed despite the refusal of consent by the minor. This is the position regardless of whether the child is deemed competent or not or whether their decision is supported by their parents. It is also evident in the reasons given by the judiciary for their judgements. Particularly striking examples are to be found in the cases mentioned earlier presided over by Lord Donaldson M.R., namely *Re R* and *Re W*. In the first of these, he referred to the giving of a consent as being comparable with the holding of a key. He relied on his interpretation of a statement of Lord Scarman in the *Gillick* case[54] in holding that, until a child obtains *Gillick* competence, only the parents of the minor hold the key to unlock the door to treatment. Where a child is *Gillick* competent, the right of the parent to consent to treatment and to override the refusal of consent remains in addition to the newly acquired right of the minor – both are keyholders.

In other words, the attainment of *Gillick* competence does not extinguish a parent's rights to consent to treatment (and *a fortiori* the power of a court). All that a doctor needs is consent by *one* of the keyholders (and it apparently does not matter which one) in order to proceed lawfully with treatment. However, although it allowed medical treatment to proceed, it in no way compelled a doctor to do so. This approach endorses the view that the crucial factor is that someone is able to sanction the provision of medical treatment to the minor, if the doctor is willing to provide it, whether this is in accordance with the minor's wishes or not.[55] Donaldson M.R.'s conclusion was not explicitly approved by the other members of the Court of Appeal on this point and was roundly criticised by commentators.[56] Fears were expressed in particular over the possible practical consequences of his judgement, for example that a girl might be forced to have an abortion against her wishes because her parents consented to it.

In addition to being a questionable interpretation of the dicta of Lord Scarman in *Gillick*, drawing a distinction between giving consent and refusing it is quite unsustainable in logic. Lord Scarman held that the parental right to consent not only yields to the child's right when that child is deemed to be competent, but in fact terminates. Lord Donaldson's interpretation wholly undermines autonomous decision making, which ought to be the basis and the justification for the legal requirements of obtaining consent to medical treatment. An adult patient is asked to consent precisely because it is anticipated that they may, for whatever reason, refuse. Proceeding without permission is a violation of the respect due to the patient in terms of both their bodily integrity and their freedom of choice. Are competent minors really unworthy of similar respect?

Furthermore, Lord Donaldson's view seems to run counter to the spirit and express provisions of The Children Act 1989, which seems to vindicate the right of children to refuse medical or psychiatric examination or other assessment.[57] Where a child is subject to a supervision order, a court may include a term requiring a child to undergo psychiatric or medical examination or treatment. However, such a requirement may not be included unless the court is satisfied that, where a child has sufficient understanding to make an informed decision, he consents to its inclusion. The same is also true where the court is making an interim order in relation to the child. It might be thought that, where either a child is under a supervision order or one is being considered, a greater degree of control might be accorded to a person or body having parental responsibility, since such orders will be made only where the child appears to be at some degree of risk. However, the statute specifically provides that not even a court may require a competent child to submit to examination or treatment where the competent child objects. These provisions were inserted in the Children Act 1989 after a Commons amendment in response to fears that a competent minor's wishes might be disregarded. It was also felt that doctors would object, in any case, to complying with a court order to this effect.[58] The provisions were felt to be uncontroversial since they were taken to be in accordance with the existing law on the matter.

These views and the arguments by analogy to the position taken in the Children Act 1989 proved to have no influence on subsequent legal developments. Lord Donaldson was given the opportunity to reconsider the matter in *Re W*, but, despite retracting from the keyholder analogy, he in fact went even further towards defining the purpose of consent to treatment for minors as a method of achieving the desired medical outcome. He rejected the keyholder analogy because 'keys can lock as well as unlock', so that a competent child could choose to refuse treatment. Instead he likened provisions for the consent to treatment of minors to a 'legal "flak jacket"' whether consent is obtained from a competent minor or anyone, including the court, with parental responsibilities. The purpose of this was expressly stated to be 'to protect the doctor from the litigious'.[59] In so doing he drew a distinction between the clinical purpose of seeking consent and the legal purpose. He recognised the therapeutic benefit to the patient in understanding and agreeing to proposed treatment, and the benefit to medical staff in terms of ease of administration to the patient.

This judgement at last made explicit the reasoning implicit in all the reported cases in these situations – that the ultimate decision on whether to treat is in essence one that will be made by the medical practitioner. Lord Donaldson dismissed the fears raised over abortions being carried out on protesting 16- or 17- year-old girls in reliance on their parents consent as follows: 'Whilst this may be possible as a matter of law, I do not see any likelihood taking account of medical ethics [*sic*], unless the abortion was truly in the best interests of the child'.[60] Despite his optimism concerning medical ethics, Lord Donaldson himself foresaw the possibility that such a flagrant disrespect for a competent child's autonomy might occur, in concluding ominously, 'That is not to say that it could not happen', citing a sterilisation case as an example of medical ethics failing to provide an obstacle to medical treatment against the child's best interests.[61]

In such a situation, he appears to place reliance on the judiciary to protect the child, as he believes that they would prevent any such abuse by requiring the treatment to be in her best interests.[62] This is ironic, since resort to the judiciary in this scenario is only necessary because the courts have declared that her decision can be overruled by her parents. If a child's refusal of consent was regarded as determinative, there would be no need to bring in the judiciary to consider whether her decision was better calculated to be in her best interests than that of her parents.

In addition to subjecting minors in such circumstances to additional pressure and the trauma of a court hearing on what are deeply personal matters, as we have seen the judiciary may in fact prove less of a protection than Lord Donaldson would have us believe. The case of *Re D* is an apposite example. It only reached the court as a result of the intervention of one of the health care professionals who brought it to the attention of the court because of his concerns over the case. To rely upon such an intervention where the professional opinion of the health carers may be unanimous is a slender thread on which to hang a means of protection of a child, whether protection is based on the best interests approach as understood by Lord Donaldson or on the wider principle of the autonomy of the individual. In any event, it should be remembered that in all cases where children have refused consent to medical treatment, the courts have relied upon the opinion of the medical profession. It is therefore they, rather than the judiciary, that are likely to have the final say, even if the case is heard. There are various reasons why expert opinion will carry such weight, some of which are relevant in other areas of judicial consideration, others of which are peculiar to the treatment of children.

First, the judiciary have shown a traditional bias towards accepting the expert evidence given by medical witnesses. This bias is perhaps exemplified by the UK formulation of the test for negligence in medical malpractice. Second, it is most likely that the case will come before the courts on an application by the medical practitioners wishing to provide treatment for the child. The application is most often brought by a health authority or health board. Applications are also often made by local authorities where children are already, or are soon to be, in care. All these institutions have considerable resources, and are likely to have recourse to specialist teams of lawyers and medical experts familiar with this type of legal proceedings. By contrast, parents wishing to support their child's refusal of consent are likely to be receiving legal aid, and may be less able to obtain representation by specialist legal practitioners and expert witnesses.

This problem will be even more apparent where both the medical profession and the parents wish treatment to proceed and it is the child alone who objects. It may be extremely difficult for a child to obtain legal representation of any kind or to give instructions, since they will in all probability be unaware of the possibility of doing so and would be hampered by their physical condition and location (most often being confined in a hospital). While the child in *Re D* was suffering from a mental disability which prevented her from giving or refusing consent to sterilisation, and was therefore particularly reliant upon others to bring her case before a court, otherwise competent children will arguably be in no better position. This may account for the dearth of case law where a child has not been supported in their refusal of consent by at least one of their parents, even before Lord Donaldson's contention that parents could in any event overrule the refusal of consent by their child.

Third, the proceedings themselves usually relate to some potentially life-threatening situation and hence are apt to arise at short notice, which may adversely affect parents or children seeking to challenge the proposed medical treatment in marshalling medical evidence and in obtaining suitably qualified legal representation.[63] All these factors will make it relatively easy to persuade a judge that the medical treatment suggested is not only advisable but is essential for the child. In this way, the medical outcome approach, synonymous with the idea of medical paternalism, takes precedence over the principle of autonomy in the case of the refusal of consent to treatment by a competent child.

But the reason why this should be so is still unclear. Is it, perhaps, due to the fact that we are referring to an individual as a child, with all the emotive connotations of that word? One can imagine judicial reluctance to be the cause of newspaper headlines claiming that a court allowed a child to die. This might be felt to be a dereliction of duty – the duty to protect those who are perceived as being vulnerable, even from themselves. Perhaps the reason is more pragmatic, in that the judiciary *can* make these decisions for a child but cannot, though they might wish to do so, in the case of an adult. It should be remembered at this point that the power of the court to intervene in a person's decision for their own good ceases abruptly when that person reaches their eighteenth birthday.[64] All the same reasons why a court might wish to intervene in that person's decision may still exist, but the court is powerless to act unless it can find some reason for disputing the person's competence or free will, or can use the premise that social policy or the needs of others require treatment to be given.

But the fact that a court has given itself the power to overrule a competent child's refusal of consent does not mean that it *should* have done so. The English courts did not have to deny autonomy to competent children. Nothing in statute or common law forced them to take this position. By way of comparison, it is worth considering the position in Scotland, where at present the question of refusal of consent to medical treatment by competent children is still open. The situation here is comparable to that in England at the time that the decision in *Gillick* had been reached.

An Alternative UK Approach: Scotland

Although the question of a child refusing consent to treatment has yet to be litigated in the Scottish courts, there are powerful arguments that suggest a child who is competent under either the evidential or the pre-sumptive standard would have their decision respected. Such arguments hinge first on an interpretation of the existing legislation and second on the grounds of public policy. Medical decision making by children in Scotland is now regulated by statute after the passing of the Age of Legal Capacity (Scotland) Act (ALC(S)A) 1991.

Although the structure of the statute appears to mirror the English position, providing for a presumptive and evidential test of competence, there are in fact significant differences which suggest that the Scottish courts may not take the same line as their English counterparts. Although this view is speculative, as the issue remains untested, certain historical factors and features of the statute do give force to the argument that a Scottish child has greater control over medical decision making than an English one.

The Presumptive Test

The ALC(S)A 1991 abolished the previous system of pupilarity. A person of or over the age of 16 has legal capacity to enter into any legal transaction (s.1(1)(b)). A legal transaction is defined in s.9 as including 'the giving by a person of any consent having legal effect', and will therefore include the giving of consent to medical treatment. Again, as in England and Wales, no criteria are set for the assessment of the 16-year-old's competence: the mere fact of attaining that age creates the presumption of the ability to make medical decisions, as does the attainment of adult status.

The Evidential Test

Specific provision as regards medical treatment is made for those under the age of 16, where the Act provides as follows in s.2(4): 'A person under the age of 16 years shall have legal capacity to consent on his own behalf to any surgical, medical or dental procedure or treatment where, in the opinion of a qualified medical practitioner attending him, he is capable of understanding the nature and possible consequences of the procedure or treatment.'

Refusal of Consent to Medical Treatment

The ALC(S)A 1991 shares the same defect as the FLRA 1969 by failing to deal explicitly with this issue. However, the difficulty that has arisen in England has not arisen solely because the FLRA 1969 does not make express provision for refusal; rather it is because the interpretation of the legislation and case law allows others, namely parents and the courts, to veto the decision of the child. The real problem lies in not granting exclusive decision making power to the competent child. In Scotland, interpretation of the statute may yield a quite different result.

An important difference to the corresponding English statute is that the ALC(S)A 1991 makes no reference to the parental power of consent. Thomson has argued that the effect of this is to make it unnecessary to consult parents or seek their approval once a child reaches the age of 16, unless the child cannot understand information or make a choice. This is partly due to the effect of the ALC(S)A 1991 defining parental rights in terms of 'guardianship, custody and access'.[65] According to the Scottish Law Commission, in their report preceding the enactment of the ALC(S)A 1991, while the decision to take a child to a doctor was an exercise of the power of custody, consent to medical treatment on the child's behalf was an exercise of the right to act as the child's legal representative.

Since the purpose of allowing a parent to represent the child legally was to empower a child without the requisite competence to make legally binding decisions, once the child is deemed to have legal capacity, such parental rights cease to be necessary and are extinguished. The ALC(S)A 1991 states that children that are either presumptively or evidentially competent shall have legal capacity to consent to their own medical treatment. Unless Scottish courts are to reject the views of the Scottish Law Commission, that the power to consent must include a right to refuse, it would seem that Scottish parents cannot override competent children's decisions.

There may be a further factor in support of this approach. The ALC(S)A 1991 does not include a definition of what is meant by 'surgical, medical or dental procedure or treatment). Commentators have noted that this could be interpreted to allow a child to consent to medical procedures that need not be directly for the benefit of that child, such as consenting to donation of non-regenerative tissue.[66] If this is accepted, it might provide evidence that, since children have the capacity to consent to procedures that are not for their own benefit, they may decline treatment that it is felt would be beneficial. In other words, children may choose to make decisions that are not in their best interests. Against this position, it could be suggested that, although children may make a decision that does not further their own interests, they may not make one that will positively harm them. Furthermore, it may be argued that, where children donate organs to siblings, they gain a benefit in terms of their emotional or psychological well-being which would be harmed if they were unable to consent and thereby save the life of their sibling.

However, the above does go some way to suggest that the reliance on the best interests test may not be as absolute in Scotland as it appears to be in England and the purpose of the legislation is more to enhance the autonomy of the individual than to provide a means of protecting doctors from litigation or ensuring that medical treatment may be forced on unwilling patients. If parents lose their right to override a competent child's refusal of consent, the final question is whether a court has the power to do so. If in Scotland, as has been suggested, the basis on which children may make their own medical decisions is the attainment of legal capacity, then it would seem to follow that Scottish courts have neither the need nor the power to intervene. Either a person is competent and has legal capacity to make their own decisions, or they are not. Unless the protection of others requires a medical decision to be overruled, a court cannot interfere. To hold otherwise would mean that the decision of a competent adult, who by nature of being an adult automatically has legal capacity, could also be overruled. This is a position that has so far been rejected by the courts.

Conclusions

To return to my starting point, if, as Lord Scarman asserts, the patient's right to make their own decision is a basic human right, there ought to be very strong and compelling reasons why this right should be denied to an individual. Although there is an obvious need to protect the health and welfare of those who are incapable of forming their own decisions, this does not justify making decisions on behalf of those who are competent to decide for themselves.

There is no rational reason to assume that a person of 17, for example, is any less competent, by virtue of their age alone, to make a decision to refuse medical treatment than a person of 18. The present approach of the English courts diverts attention away from the individual and towards the membership of the class of children, with all the attendant misconceptions and assumptions that go with it, such as that children are incapable of considering their long-term interests simply because they are children. In addition, it fails to take into account considerations other than health-oriented ones and in this way frustrates the underlying rationale for the legal requirements of consent to treatment, that of ensuring the autonomy of the individual. Its purpose is not to ensure that treatment is provided to unwilling recipients, nor is it to protect health care professionals from litigation.

It is suggested that, instead of fixing an age below which competent patients may have their refusal of treatment overridden by others, the sole question should be that of competence and that the standard of competence should be the same as that for adults as set out in the judgement in *Re C*, not a redefinition of competence that assumes the patient is incompetent if they do not accept recommended medical treatment. The role of the law regarding consent to medical treatment should be to protect the decision making of competent persons, not the competent person themselves.

At present, the law in England permits those under 18 to have their medical decisions respected if, but only if, they know what is good for them and accept the treatment that is proposed. Such a situation is both illogical and unjust and may have wider implications for the way in which children are viewed in our society, in that it suggests that children are in some way less entitled to full respect as members of our society by virtue of their status. This is a view that should be resisted, not least in the context of the refusal of medical treatment by children.

Notes

1   Per Lord Scarman in *Sidaway* v. *Bethlem Royal Hospital Governors* [1985] AC 871, at 882.

2   [1986] AC 112; [1985] 3 A11 ER 402, HL.

3   For fuller discussions see, for example, M. Brazier, *Medicine, Patients and the Law*, 2nd ed., Harmondsworth, Penguin, 1992, ch.15; I. Kennedy, 'The Doctor, the Pill and the 15-Year-Old Girl', in *Treat me Right*, Oxford, Clarendon Press, 1994, ch.5;

D. Brahams, 'The Gillick Case: a Pragmatic Compromise', *New Law Journal*, 24 January 1986, 75–7.

4   For a discussion of this point, see K. Norrie, 'Medical Treatment of Children and Young Persons', in D. Morgan and G. Douglas (eds), *ARSP – Beiheft*, **57**, 'Constituting Families' (1994), at 109–17.

5   C. Eiser, 'Changes in Understanding of Illness as the Child Grows', *Archives of Disease in Childhood*, **60**, (1985), at 489. See also results of research and interviews in P. Alderson, *Children's Consent to Surgery*, Buckingham/Philadelphia, Open University Press, 1993.

6   [1993] 1 FLR 386. The case was in fact heard in September 1990.

7   See at 391C: 'I did not judge it right to probe with him whether or not he knew how frightening it would be, Dr. T did not consider it necessary to spell it out for him and I did not feel it was appropriate to do so.'

8   See, for example, in *Re E*, at 393E, where Ward J. said 'I have to take into account the fact that teenagers often express views of vehemence and conviction – all the vehemence and conviction of callow youth! Those of us who have passed beyond callow youth can all remember the convictions which we have loudly proclaimed which we now find somewhat embarrassing.' The fact that adults may also loudly proclaim convictions which they later regret does not seem to enter into the assessment of the competence of adults.

9   [1991] 4 A11 ER 177.

10 In discussing Gillick competence, Lord Donaldson M.R. said that 'there is no suggestion that the extent of this competence can fluctuate upon a day-to-day or week-to-week basis' (at 187 d). However, this is precisely what a test of competence should be aimed at: ensuring that the person is, at the time when they are asked to make a decision, capable of doing so and that this wish is sustained at the time of treatment. Where competence fluctuates on a more rapid basis it is perhaps more arguable that the person concerned does not have the ability to make their own medical decision.

11 [1992] 4 A11 ER 627.

12 This would be equally true where the patient in question was an adult; however, given the fact that the judiciary are already over-disposed to authorise treatment on unwilling minors, their position appears to be even more precarious.

13 See *R. v. Riverside Health Trust* 20 BMLR 1; *Re KB (adult) (mental patient: medical treatment)* 19 BMLR 144. For a brief survey of the law surrounding the forcible feeding of adults see I. Kennedy and A. Grubb, *Medical Law: Text with Materials*, 2nd ed., London, Butterworths, 1994, part ii, ch.4, at 334–41.

14 K. Norrie, 'The Age of Legal Capacity (Scotland) Act 1991', *Journal of the Law Society of Scotland*, **36**, November 1991, 111–13.

15 J.K. Mason and R.A. McCall Smith, *Law and Medical Ethics*, 4th ed., London: Butterworths, 1994, ch.10, at 229.

16 Ibid.

17 This appears to be the reasoning in the majority opinions in *Gillick* and also the judgement in *Re W*.

18 Section 8(1).

19 At 186.

20 See *Gillick* and the translation of this into guidance to the medical profession by the General Medical Council in *Professional Conduct and Discipline: Fitness to Practice*, December 1993, paras. 80–84, at 26 and 27.

21 [1986] 1 FLR 272; (1982) 80 LGR 301.

22 For a comparison of the wardship and inherent jurisdiction of the courts, see J. Gilham, 'The Dilemma of Parental Choice', *New Law Journal* (August 20, 1993, 1219–20. For a discussion of the development of the *parens patriae* jurisdiction, see

J. Seymour, 'Parens Patriae and Wardship Powers: Their Nature and Origin', *Oxford Journal of Legal Studies*, **14** (1994), 159–88.

23   At 639 j.
24   See, for example, M. Komrad, 'A Defence of Medical Paternalism: Maximising Patients' Autonomy', *Journal of Medical Ethics*, **9** (1983), 38–44; H. Teff, 'Consent to Medical Procedures: Paternalism, Self-Determination or Therapeutic Alliance?', *Law Quarterly Review*, **106** (1985), 432–43; E. Pellegrino and D. Thomasma, 'The Conflict Between Autonomy and Beneficence in Medical Ethics: Proposal for a Resolution', *Journal of Contemporary Health Law and Policy*, 3 (1987), 23–46.
25   See, for example, the discussions by G. Robertson, 'Informed consent to Medical Treatment', *Law Quarterly Review*, **97** (1981), 102–26; T.K. Feng, 'Failure of Medical Advice: Trespass or Negligence?', *Legal Studies*, 7 (1987), 149–68; I. Kennedy, *Treat me Right*, Oxford, Clarendon Press (reprinted 1994), ch.9; S.A.M. McLean, '*A Patient's Right to Know: Information Disclosure, the Doctor and the Law*', Aldershot, Dartmouth, 1989.
26   See the references in note 24.
27   *Schloendorff* v. *Society of New York Hospital* (1914) 211 NY 125, 126.
28   *Sidaway* v. *Bethlem Royal Hospital Governors* [1985] AC 871.
29   *Richmond* v. *Richmond* (1914) 111 LT 273.
30   *Re C (adult: refusal of treatment)* [1994] 1 WLR 290.
31   Law Commission consultation paper 129, 'Mentally Handicapped Adults and Decision-Making', para 2.20.
32   [1981] QB 432.
33   *Re T (adult: refusal of medical treatment)* [1992] 4 A11 ER 649 at p. 661 j.
34   For example, Lord Donaldson M.R. stated that a child's refusal was 'a very important consideration in making clinical judgments and for parents and the courts in deciding whether themselves to give consent. Its importance increases with the age and maturity of the minor' (*Re W* at 639 j – 640 a).
35   See, for example, J. Thomson, (1991) 'It is the hallmark of a democratic society that, while parents have the primary responsibility for the care of their children, they are free to bring up their children in the manner which they deem best for their children's welfare' (*Family Law in Scotland*, Edinburgh, Butterworths, 1991, p.177).
36   *Re J (a minor)(wardship: medical treatment)* [1992] 4 A11 ER 614; (1992) 9 BMLR 10.
37   This power may be exercised in England and Wales either under the wardship jurisdiction or as part of the *parens patriae* jurisdiction (see *Re W*, per Lord Donaldson: 'the High Court's inherent jurisdiction over children – the parens patriae jurisdiction – is equally exercisable whether the child is or is not a ward of court'). For a detailed analysis of the origins of these powers, see J. Seymour, 'Parens Patriae and Wardship Powers: Their Nature and Origin', *Oxford Journal of Legal Studies*, **14** (1994), 159–88. The Scottish courts have a similar extensive jurisdiction under the Nobile Officium (see J. Thomson, *Family Law in Scotland*, p.195).
38   [1970] AC 668, 672.
39   *Re E*, 392H–393A.
40   [1992] 4 A11 ER 649; (1992) 9 BMLR 46 (CA).
41   (1990) 67 DLR (4th) 321, 328.
42   *Re S (adult: refusal of medical treatment)* [1992] 4 A11 ER 671; (1992) 9 BMLR 69.
43   At 393 G.
44   *Re T*, case cited in note 33.
45   [1993] 1 A11 ER 821; (1993) 12 BMLR 64.
46   *Re B (a minor)(wardship: medical treatment)* (1981) [1990] 3 A11 ER 927 at 929; [1981] 1 WLR 1421 at 1424 (CA), per Templeman L.J.
47   [1975] 3 A11 ER 446 at 450 b–c.
48   This point was made by I. Kennedy, *Treat Me Right*, ch.5.

49   The Canadian case is untraceable but is cited, without a reference, in *Re E (a minor) (wardship: medical treatment)* [1993] 1 FLR 386.

50   *Re E*, case cited at 393H.

51   At 394B.

52   At 394F.

53   On commencing conservative treatment, it was estimated that the boy would have a 60 per cent chance of remission as opposed to 80 per cent with conventional treatment. By the time the case was heard the ratio was 40–50 per cent as against 70 per cent. See *Re E*, at 388D–389A.

54   '...the parental right to determine whether or not their minor child below the age of 16 will have medical treatment terminates if and when the child reaches a sufficient understanding and intelligence to enable him or her to understand fully what is proposed' ([1985] 3 A11 ER 402 at 423; [1986] AC 112 at 188–9).

55   This contrasts markedly with the situation where a child seeks medical treatment against the wishes of her parents, as in *Gillick* itself. Here it is the child's view that is said to be determinative, *not* the parents'.

56   See, for example, I. Kennedy, 'Consent to Treatment: the Capable Person', in C. Dyer (ed.), *Doctors, Patients and the Law*, 1992, Oxford: Blackwell Scientific Publications, ch.3; A. Bainham, 'The Judge and the Competent Minor', *Law Quarterly Review*, 108 (1992), 194–200; R. Thornton, 'Multiple Keyholders – Wardship and Consent to Medical Treatment', *The Cambridge Law Journal* (1992), 34–7.

57   Schedule 3, Part I, paras. 4–7.

58   See Baroness David, House of Lords, Official Report, 19 January 1989, col. 405.

59   At 635c–d.

60   At p.635j.

61   *Re D (a minor)(wardship: sterilisation)* [1976] 1 A11 ER 326.

62   At p.636a.

63   Of course, no imputation is cast on the quality of the legal representation obtained by the children and parents in the cases referred to.

64   See the judgement in *Re W*.

65   See s.8 Law Reform (Parent and Child) Act 1986, as amended by the ALC(S)A 1991.

66   J.K. Mason and R.A. McCall Smith, *Law and Medical Ethics*, 4th edn, London, Butterworths, 1994, p.373.

4 Private Decisions and Public Scrutiny: Sterilisation and Minors in Australia and England*

KERRY PETERSEN

It is in supervising those social and moral areas of work where technical peer review is overly narrow that evaluation and control by those outside the professions become essential. (Eliot Freidson, *Professionalism Reborn*[1])

Introduction

The medical profession is one of the most powerful institutions in the common law countries. It has autonomy over its work and the right to self-regulation. The mantle of professional autonomy protects the clinical decision from external scrutiny because the state has given medical practitioners authority over the technical aspects of medical work. Moreover, by adopting a posture of ethical neutrality, medical practitioners have exercised authority over social and moral questions tangential to the technical part of the medical decision. This has enabled the medical profession to include the non-technical, or social and moral, aspects of medical work within its protected professional boundary. For example, when the law recognised mental health as a lawful ground for abortion in *R. v. Bourne*[2] it introduced a non-physical

* I would like to express my gratitude to the following friends and colleagues who have commented on early drafts of this paper: Professor Sheila McLean, Lee Ann Basser Marks and Professor Ken Mason. Thanks also to Laurence Davies for editorial assistance.

ground for lawful therapeutic abortion and ultimately the concept of mental health became a generic euphemism for a range of social indications. It was also the case that mentally incompetent people were sterilised for eugenic reasons with little open discussion about this important aspect of the issue until these private medical decisions were subjected to the public gaze of judicial proceedings.[3]

In its self-regulatory role, medicine as a professional body has established ethical principles and standards of conduct through internal organisational structures and professional associations.

Traditionally, the medical profession has addressed and debated medical ethics but paid less attention to questions of human rights. The profession has accorded a higher priority to concerns about professionalism and ethics.

The ethical principles of beneficence and respect for autonomy have played a significant role in ethical developments. Beneficence – the foundation principle of medical ethics – can be traced back to the Hippocratic Oath. It has been handed down from generation to generation of doctors and is shaped and moulded by internal professional influences such as debates and statements on medical ethics issued by professional associations. Beneficence requires a medical practitioner to protect and promote the interests of the patient. Beneficence has also been used to justify medical paternalism. Unlike beneficence, autonomy is a 'creature of our own century'[4] which has 'developed outside medicine, in the law and in political philosophy'.[5] By way of criticism Giesen notes: 'Medical ethics, from the Hippocratic Oath on, has taken a thoroughly paternalistic position, emphasising the patient's somatic well-being above his dignitarian interest in determining whether and to what extent he shall undergo any recommended medical procedure.'[6]

Patient autonomy was recognised as a human right as long ago as 1914, in the landmark US case, *Schloendorff v. Society of New York Hospital*.[7] This case acknowledged a patient's right to self-determination and signalled a shift away from medical paternalism. Since *Schloendorff* the law governing consent to medical treatment and patient autonomy has undergone profound changes in the common law countries.[8] Although patient autonomy has been the eleventh commandment of medical practice, some modification of this view is developing.[9] Equally important is the issue of non-voluntary treatment in cases where the patient is unable to consent to treatment or to refuse treatment because of mental incompetence. The medical profession has been subject to public and legal scrutiny as the result of growing concerns about non-voluntary medical treatment and the human rights of mentally incompetent people. In turn, this has promoted a heightened awareness of medical paternalism and non-technical aspects of clinical decision making, and has led to further encroachment on professional autonomy.

There has never been legislation in Australia or England (unlike the situation in some American states[10]) providing for the compulsory sterilisation of incompetent people. Whilst it is impossible to estimate the number of non-voluntary sterilisations performed in Australia and England prior to intervention by courts, there are enough random figures from different sources to suggest that these procedures were fairly common.[11] Doctors, parents, families and institutional authorities made these decisions privately. There was little public interest in moral or ethical questions. Views about the medical treatment of mentally incompetent women were generally entwined in notions of medical autonomy, beneficence and medical paternalism. As a result, no-one considered in great depth important matters such as consent, non-voluntary treatment or decision-making criteria.[12] The issue of sterilising mentally incompetent women under 18 years of age became public when proceedings were initiated in the English courts in the mid-1970s and the Family Court of Australia more than a decade later. In discussing the key sterilisation cases in Australia and England, it will be shown how the unveiling of medical decision making has brought about a fundamental change in our perceptions of the role of the medical practitioner in cases concerning the sterilisation of mentally incompetent women under 18 years of age. This confrontation with professional autonomy and parental authority has forced a reassessment of the ethics governing sterilisation when a young woman does not have sufficient autonomy to make an informed choice about whether or not to be sterilised. The shift in social control permits judges to be informed by a range of experts – not just medical practitioners. This chapter compares developments in Australia and England and illustrates some distinctive differences in the way the judiciary has utilised medical and non-medical evidence. The chapter begins with an examination of some early sterilisation cases dealing with medical decision making, and then moves on to a discussion of medical and non-medical evidence.

Clinical Decisions

Court involvement in Australia and England concerning the sterilisation of young mentally incompetent women commenced with applications to restrain the implementation of clinical recommendations and decisions made by medical practitioners with the consent of the parents. It is important to be aware that individuals who had no personal involvement with the families initiated these proceedings.

England

An indication of the changes ahead was signalled in the 1970s. In the first English case, *Re D (a minor)(wardship: sterilisation)*[13] Heilbron J. found a sterilisation operation was neither medically indicated nor necessary and refused authorisation on the ground that it would be a violation of a basic human right to perform a non-therapeutic sterilisation on an 11-year-old girl, who suffered from Sotos Syndrome, without her consent. Wardship proceedings[14] had been instituted as a result of a disagreement between Dr Gordon and other professionals who cared for the child in a special school. The plaintiff, an educational psychologist, initiated the application to prevent the proposed hysterectomy from being carried out. It was accepted as common ground that D had the intellectual capacity to marry and that sterilisation could have serious consequences for a potential marital relationship. It was also accepted as common ground that D was not sexually active and the opportunity for sex was virtually non-existent. Both Dr Gordon and D's mother were opposed to abortion if D became pregnant.

The court heard medical evidence from Dr Gordon and a number of medical practitioners who had been called upon by the plaintiff and the official solicitor. Dr Gordon was the only medical witness who favoured the sterilisation and he recommended the procedure to prevent D from ever having a child. His recommendation was based on a mixture of medical and social grounds. He believed the operation was medically indicated because D could have a disabled baby. He also believed that her epilepsy could cause her to harm a baby. The other doctors agreed that there was an increased risk of such an eventuality but because no-one with Sotos Syndrome has ever been known to have a baby it was impossible to make a precise prediction. Dr Gordon was opposed to contraception for D but Heilbron J. accepted other medical evidence that suitable contraception could be used when and if necessary. The three medical witnesses called by the plaintiff and the official solicitor all opposed the operation on the grounds that there were no appropriate medical indications. In addition, Dr Snodgrass and Professor Huntington expressed grave concern about performing a non-consensual sterilisation for non-medical reasons on such a young girl.

Apart from the risk of pregnancy, the social reasons which formed part of Dr Gordon's clinical judgement included concerns about D ever having the capacity to live outside a sheltered environment; her inability to cope with a family if she were to marry; and the possibility of future institutionalisation. Both D's headmaster and the plaintiff challenged Dr Gordon's social and behavioural reasons for recommending the operation. They believed she was responding well to the special school and her behaviour was continuing to improve.

Heilbron J. took the view that social reasons were beyond the scope of the clinical judgement. She was obviously influenced by the facts that the operation was irreversible and that D was only 11 years old. Moreover, evidence that there had been a marked improvement in her overall capacities since attending the special school impressed the court. Heilbron J. said: 'In my judgment Dr Gordon's views as to D's present and future social and behavioural problems were somewhat exaggerated and mistaken. I think in this area his views were clouded by his resentment at what he considered unjustified interference.'[15]

On the question of D's competence, Heilbron J. accepted that D would most likely understand the implications of a sterilisation operation by the time she reached 18. She found that a decision to sterilise was not entirely within the discretion of one doctor's clinical judgement, unless performed for medical reasons. Accepting medical evidence which opposed the operation, she said: 'I cannot believe, and the evidence does not warrant the view, that a decision to carry out an operation of this nature performed for non-therapeutic purposes on a minor, can be held within the doctor's sole clinical judgment.'[16] By contrast, Dr Gordon maintained that 'provided the parent or parents consented, the decision was one made pursuant to the exercise of his clinical judgment, and that no interference could be tolerated in his clinical freedom'.[17]

Australia

The major question for the Family Court of Australia in the early cases was whether parents, as guardians, had the authority to authorise sterilisation operations without court involvement. Four first instance decisions of the Family Court of Australia divided evenly on the issue. *Re a Teenager*[18] and *Re S*[19] held that parents, as guardians, did not need court authorisation. Conversely, *Re Jane*[20] and *Re Elizabeth*[21] held that court authorisation was required. The conflict was resolved in *Secretary, Department of Health and Community Services* v. *JWB and SMB*[22] (hereafter referred to as *Re JWB*) where the High Court ruled that parents as joint guardians could not lawfully authorise a sterilisation operation upon a child in the Northern Territory without the order of the court and that the Family Court of Australia exercising its *parens patriae* jurisdiction could provide authorisation pursuant to the powers set out in the Family Law Act 1975 (Aust.).[23] The majority of the Australian High Court in *Re JWB*[24] stated: 'The function of a court when asked to authorise sterilisation is to decide whether, in the circumstances of the case, that is in the best interests of the child. We have already said that it is not possible to formulate a rule which will identify cases where sterilisation is in his or her best interests.'[25] The High Court emphasised that the best interest test in these cases was subject to sterilisation being a step of last resort. Accordingly, the majority further stated: 'In the context of medical management, "step of last resort" is a convenient way of saying that alternative and less invasive procedures have all failed or that it is certain that no other procedure or treatment will work.'[26]

In the first two Australian sterilisation cases, *Re A Teenager*[27] and *Re Jane*[28] the facts were very similar, and the court decided in each case to let the operation go ahead. Nevertheless, these cases illustrate two very different judicial approaches to professional autonomy, parental authority and human rights and for these reasons they are worth considering in some detail. In *Re a Teenager*,[29] an application was made to His Honour Justice Cook by a 14-year-old girl through her 'next friend' to restrain her parents from permitting a hysterectomy operation to be performed on her. She lived at home with her family and was assessed as having the mental ability of a 2–3-year-old child. Because the brain damage had been caused by birth trauma there was no concern about the transmission of disability. Although severely disabled intellectually, her general physical health and development were 'normal'. Unlike the child in *Re D*, her mental ability was unlikely to improve in any significant way. Her parents and her general practitioner made the decision after a number of other medical specialists had been consulted. The operation was to be performed by the general practitioner who had been caring for the family for about ten years and who was familiar with the girl's health and well-being. Shortly before the operation, the father discussed the procedure with a staff member at the government centre for the care of disabled people. He believed the discussion was confidential. However, the staff member was vehemently opposed to the operation and presumably the staff member was responsible for initiating legal proceedings.

It was understood in *Re a Teenager* that she would never marry or enter into a relationship which would involve parenting and could not understand the process of conception and birth. It was assumed that if a sterilisation was not authorised and she became pregnant an abortion would be indicated. Non-medical witnesses claimed that the operation was premature and that other options had not been properly explored. Evidence was given about a number of menstrual management and desensitisation programmes, although at the time of the hearing the child had not commenced menstruating. Her mother believed that it would be too stressful for her daughter to learn menstrual management skills and that her limited capacities would be better used learning basic hygiene, toileting and social skills. The elimination of menstruation was the primary motivation for the operation. Presumably, this is why Cook J. said this was not a sterilisation case – even though the removal of the uterus would have the effect of sterilisation.

Cook J. held that it was within the scope of parental power to authorise the sterilisation. His Honour's decision was based on his view that a caring family in these circumstances was in a better position to determine the special needs of a child than a court. Although evidence was given from teaching and health care professionals, Cook J. viewed evidence from the family's general practitioner as being more significant because of his long-term involvement with the child as a patient and with the family. The general practitioner's recommendation was based on the following medical indications: first, a phobic reaction to blood; second, the difficulties associated with attempts to give the child medication and injections; third, a full consideration of the effects of the hysterectomy on the girl's body compared to the unknown long-term effects of hormonal pills and injections. Evidence given by other medical witnesses both supported and refuted the general practitioner's recommendation.

There is a remarkable contrast between the attitudes of Cook J. in this case and Heilbron J. in *Re D* to the scope of the clinical judgement. Cook J. did not exclude non-technical factors from the scope of the clinical judgement. He placed considerable weight on the general practitioner's evidence and took into account the general practitioner's assessment of 'interrelationships and psychic dynamics within the family',[30] together with 'the effect the caring for the child was having upon her mother, her father and her brother'.[31] In addition Cook J. placed a great deal of faith in the capacity of medical practitioners to make ethical decisions. He said: 'It is not conceivable to this Court that medical advisers would prostitute their Hippocratic Oath to perform unnecessary or ill-advised and untimely operations, particularly of a major kind.'[32]

In *Re Jane*,[33] decided shortly after *Re a Teenager*, the facts were essentially the same, although the cause of the disability is not mentioned in the judgement. The purpose of this operation was to prevent menstruation and the risk of pregnancy, even though Jane had not commenced menstruating. In this case the restraining order had been sought by the acting public prosecutor. Evidence was given by teachers, psychologists and social workers. Once again it was argued on behalf of the child that the operation was premature and that alternatives had not been adequately considered. However, the medical evidence was overwhelmingly in favour of a hysterectomy.

Unlike Cook J., Nicholson C.J. was opposed to leaving these important decisions in the hands of medical advisers and parents. He observed 'Not all parents are wise and caring and not all medical practitioners are ethical and reasonable.'[34] Nor did he regard beneficence as providing adequate guidance for medical practitioners or protection for mentally incompetent people. He said:

I note that in *re Teenager* (1989) FLC 92-006 Cook J. would be prepared to trust the ethics of the medical profession not to engage in improper unethical conduct. With respect to His Honour and to the vast majority of that profession, I am unable to accept this proposition. Like all professions, the medical profession has members who are not prepared to live up to its professional standards of ethics and experience teaches that the identity of such practitioners becomes known to those who require their assistance and their services are availed. Further, it is also possible that members of that profession may form sincere but misguided views about the appropriate steps to be taken.[35]

It was held that the consent of the court was required because it was a medical procedure which involved interference with a basic human right and had a non-therapeutic purpose as a major aim. Accordingly the court had to apply the best interest test. Section 60D of the Family Law Act 1975 provides: 'In proceedings ... in relation to a child, the court shall regard the welfare of the child as the paramount consideration.' The court sanctioned a hysterectomy operation on the ground that it would improve Jane's quality of life. It is worth noting that the Chief Justice recognised the difficulty of distinguishing between a thera-peutic and non-therapeutic medical procedure – assuming that therapeutic procedures connote the treatment of a malfunction or disease, and acknowledging that a procedure can be performed for a mixture of reasons. He said, 'I think that this difficulty can be overcome, however, by asking whether the principal or major aim of the procedure has a non-therapeutic purpose. If it does have as a principal or major aim a non-therapeutic purpose, then the court's consent should be obtained.'[36]

Medical Evidence

This section will consider the role of medical opinion in some of the sterilisation cases. However, before looking at the role of medical opinion in these cases it is worth briefly commenting on the best interest test. This test, which allows for broad judicial discretion, inevitably reflects the values and attitudes of individual judges. In *Re Jane* and *Re Marion (No.2)*,[37] the Chief Justice of the Family Court of Australia attempted to impose more structure and coherence on judicial decisions by establishing guidelines to assist in the application of the best interests test. They are significant because they require more precise information from practitioners than evidence about the circular state-of-the art term 'current medical practice'.[38] Broadly, the relevant factors include the particular condition which requires treatment; the nature of the treatment and the reasons for it; alternative courses of treatment; the risks of the proposed treatment; and the consequences of each possible course of action. According to these guidelines a court is also required to take into account the psychological and social impli-cations for the child and ensure that the views of the parents, guardians or custodians are considered. This last requirement checks the diminution of parental authority.[39] Nevertheless, the courts have emphasised that what is critical is the child's interests rather than the parents', although the latter are usually relevant in the determination of the child's interest. The English cases have not established similar guidelines to assist in decisions about sterilising minors.[40]

England

In *Re B*,[41] the House of Lords heard an appeal concerning a sterilisation by tubal ligation of a disabled epileptic 17-year-old girl who had the mental age of a child of 5 or 6 years of age. The girl, Jeanette, had been received into care at 4 years of age. It was envisaged that, when she was 19 years old, she would go to an adult centre where there would be comparatively little supervision and a danger of becoming pregnant. The House of Lords was responding to an application by a local authority to have Jeanette sterilised, rather than intervening in a clinical decision or attempting to trespass upon professional boundaries, as in *Re D*. The facts in B's case were remarkably similar to those of the Australian Family Court decisions in *Re a Teenager* and *Re Jane*. Jeanette was nearly 18 and soon due to pass out of the wardship jurisdiction. At the time *Re B* was being decided, there was some doubts as to whether the court had jurisdiction to authorise the sterilisation of adults. There was, therefore, a sense of urgency about the case and Lord Hailsham noted: 'We should be no wiser in 12 months' time than we are now and it would be doubtful then what legal courses would be open in the circumstances.'[42] The question of jurisdiction and mentally incompetent adults was decided later in *F* v. *West Berkshire Health Authority and Another*.[43] In this case, the House of Lords held that court sanction was desirable but not required, and the *Bolam*[44] test should determine the legality of the procedure.

Jeanette would never be competent to consent to any medical procedure or to marriage. It was accepted as common ground that a therapeutic abortion would have to be performed if Jeanette became pregnant and the main issue concerned the best means of preventing her from becoming pregnant. The three medical experts agreed that Jeanette should not become pregnant and the only disagreement concerned the means of achieving this objective. One consultant favoured the pill over irreversible sterilisation. However, his assessment of a satisfactory contraceptive regime along these lines was less than optimistic. The other two recommended occlusion of the Fallopian tubes. The only non-medical evidence referred to was given by a social worker who described how difficult it was to administer pills to Jeanette – particularly when she was in an aggressive mood.

Upholding the decisions of the Family Division and the Court of Appeal, the House of Lords held that it was in Jeanette's best interests to be sterilised and further that a sterilisation can only be authorised in these circumstances if the ward lacks the capacity to make decisions about pregnancy and childbirth.[45] Lord Hailsham said: 'There is no doubt that, in the exercise of its wardship jurisdiction, the first and paramount consideration is the well-being, welfare or interests (each expression occasionally used, but each, for this purpose, synonymous) of the human being concerned that is the ward herself or himself. In this case I believe it to be the only issue involved.'[46] The House of Lords emphasised that questions of eugenics, social interests, public policy and the convenience of the care givers were invalid considerations. Moreover, the decision was reached on the assumption that a tubal ligation was not reversible. Lord Oliver of Aylmerton said: 'My Lords, the arguments advanced against the adoption of a sterilisation are based almost entirely (and, indeed, understandably so) on its irreversible nature. It was observed by Dillon L.J. in the Court of Appeal that the jurisdiction in wardship proceedings to authorise such an operation is one which should be exercised only in the last resort and with that I respectfully agree.'[47]

The medical evidence played a significant role in the process of reasoning adopted by the court in this case. For example, on the basis of medical evidence, it was accepted by Bush J. in the Family Division that it would be a disaster for B to get pregnant. This assumption was never challenged and largely determined the boundaries of the case. The degree of disability suggests that it would indeed have been traumatic and frightening for Jeanette to have become pregnant and that it could have been difficult to diagnose pregnancy in the early stages because of her obesity and menstrual irregularity. However, the interpretation of 'last resort' appears to have been influenced by the urgent circumstances in this case. Would sterilisation have been the last resort if *Re B* had been decided after F's case? By contrast, Heilbron J. in *Re D* thought it was a pity that D's mother and doctor had not sufficiently considered the alternative of abortion. Admittedly, in this case the child was only 11 years of age and the possibility of pregnancy was more remote.

It was assumed in *Re B* that it was in Jeanette's best interests to have the physical freedom that would be available at the adult training centre without evidence on this question being given by experts in the area. Surely, pregnancy was not the only danger posed by some degree of physical freedom? Other physical and life-threatening dangers, such as sexually transmitted diseases, rape or abuse, were also potential problems. In the Australian case, for example, *Re L&M*,[48] Warnick J. stressed that the risk of abuse was not removed by sterilisation and that the problem of abuse should be addressed specifically. Moreover, while it would be discriminatory to deny Jeanette the opportunity to enjoy protected sex, questions about her intellectual capacity to give consent to sex were not addressed. Why was evidence on this question not received from a non-medical expert such as a psychologist?

Re B is a very good example of professional 'back-patting'. As has been noted, the medical evidence was never challenged and the assumptions which arose from the medical evidence locked the courts, at all levels of adjudication, into an inevitable path of reasoning. It is a matter of some concern that the House of Lords applied the best interests test on the basis of such limited sources of information. In terms of precedent value, the case provides minimal judicial guidance on how to make decisions about non-voluntary sterilisations – other than to base the decision primarily upon medical evidence even when non-medical interests are relevant.

Since *Re B* two further wardship applications concerning sterilisation have been reported in England. Hinting at the dangers of the slippery slope, Mason and McCall Smith point out that both these cases can be seen as sterilisations which were authorised on social grounds for the benefit of the wards, that is, to protect their lifestyles.[49] In *Re M (a minor)(wardship: sterilisation)*,[50] an order was made authorising a tubal ligation on a 17-year-old girl with Fragile X Syndrome. She was referred to as J. The girl lived at home with her parents and was becoming sexually active. It was common ground that if she were to have the freedom to move around in the community and attend college she was at risk of becoming pregnant. Possible pregnancy was the main issue, complicated by a 50 per cent chance of her transmitting her disability to a baby. Although it was possible that J could have maternal feelings she would never be able to look after a baby and thus it would be taken from her.

Medical witnesses advised the court that all other forms of prevention were inappropriate and the complications of possible recurrent abortions supported the case for sterilisation. Professor Tindall also advised the court that there was a 50–70 per cent chance that the operation could be reversed. He preferred to describe the procedure as a form of contraception in order to avoid the emotive connotations associated with sterilisation. Bush J. authorised the sterilisation on the ground that a sterilisation would promote the ward's best interest by ensuring that she did not become pregnant. He also stressed that eugenic grounds did not form part of his decision to authorise the operation and that a legal abortion would be an option if these came into question. Brazier makes the relevant observation that this is really a backdoor way of dealing with the eugenic question.[51]

The ward in *Re P (a minor)(wardship: sterilisation)*,[52] who was referred to as T, was more disabled than D but less disabled than Jeanette. She was 17 years old, with a mental age of six and reasonable social skills.

Her disability was connected with birth trauma, therefore inherited disability was not an issue. T attended a college and was deemed capable of using public transport. Moreover, a future move to a residential home was most likely. At the time of the hearing she was living at home with her divorced mother. T needed special care and supervision but could attend to her own bodily needs. She was an attractive teenager with normal sexual drives; however, contraception had been abandoned because of side-effects. It was recognised by the court that this was a marginal case.

Evidence from Professor Winston, a consultant obstetrician and gynaecologist, of a 95 per cent chance of reversing the tubal ligation was an influential factor in this case. In view of the advances in reversal surgery, Eastham J. queried the weight that should now be given to sterilisation as a step of last resort. Two psychiatrists agreed that there would be no change in T's intellectual capacity but with appropriate care her social skills could improve. However, they disagreed on the question whether she would ever be able to give a fully informed consent to a tubal ligation. Further, Dr Heller indicated in his evidence that he believed the issue of reversibility was academic because it was his firm opinion that T should never have a child. Eastham J. gave more weight to the less optimistic prognosis of T's general capacities given by Dr Heller, without any explanation of why he chose one doctor's evidence over the other.

Medical opinions from two eminent gynaecologists and surgeons also differed. Professor Robert Winston was prepared to carry out the operation if the court granted authorisation, whereas Mr Barron considered the operation was premature and that it would be better to wait until T was older. Even though this was clearly a borderline case, Eastham J. approved the sterilisation on the ground that pregnancy should be avoided at all costs. He believed it would have been disastrous for T to become pregnant because the baby would have to be removed from her for its own well-being, and so there would be a violation of maternal feelings.

As has been noted, the major concern in these cases was to avoid the risk of pregnancy, because the young woman in question would not have been able to rear a child. Other broader concerns such as whether the sterilisation was premature do not appear to have been seriously examined by the court. Evidence about the reversibility of sterilisation procedures was an important feature of the decisions. In neither case, however, was there any real suggestion that the handicap would ever be resolved or that the young women could possibly become capable of parenting a child. The question of reversibility should surely be relevant only if there was a realistic possibility of improvement in these capacities.

In addition, a number of important legal and ethical questions were avoided. First of all, it is not clear that either of these women would ever be able to give an informed consent to an operation reversing the tubal ligations. Moreover, they would be beyond the wardship juris-diction of the court shortly after the cases were decided. As has been noted, since the House of Lords decision in *F's case*, doctors are not required to obtain court authorisation before performing surgery or treatment on mentally incompetent adult patients. However, it is expected that doctors will as a matter of practice choose to make appli-cations when radical or irreversible treatment is contemplated. What criteria will be used if a reversal operation is under consideration? How much scope will there be for medical paternalism if the doctors and either the woman or her care givers disagree about reversing the operation? Moreover, as Brazier observes, how realistic is it to expect that a disabled woman would be offered reversal surgery?[53] Finally, it is also worth observing that if women in these circumstances are not protected from pregnancies it is most likely that their babies will be adopted. The shortage of babies available for adoption in Australia and England could lead to pressure being placed on these women to be used as 'foetal incubators', and this would pose serious ethical questions for a medical practitioner.

Australia

Before considering *Re L&M*,[54] one of the most recent sterilisation cases decided in Australia, it is worth referring briefly to *Re Marion (No.2)*.[55] In terms of legal history, this case is a celebrated one because it went to the High Court on appeal and clarified the Australian law on consent in these cases. After the High Court handed down the decision in *Re JWB*,[56] Nicholson C.J. was required to decide the facts in *Re Marion (No.2)*[57] in accordance with the law as declared by the High Court. *Re Marion* concerned a highly dependent 14-year-old girl suffering from severe intellectual and physical disabilities. Like many of the other young women in these cases she did not understand reproduction, nor could she cope with pregnancy or child rearing. However, this case differed from the other cases discussed in this chapter because the hysterectomy and ovariectomy were ordered for medical reasons: to minimise her seizures and reduce the possibility of further brain damage.

Nicholson J. held that the procedure was in the best interests of the child after considering strong medical evidence and overwhelming non-medical evidence in favour of the operation.[58] He said, 'this case probably falls into the category where the court's consent is unneces-sary since, on the facts as I have found them, the procedure was required for medical and therapeutic reasons'.[59] *Re Marion*, therefore, raises a difficult 'chicken and egg' dilemma. How does a medical practitioner know if her or his diagnosis will be accepted as lawful until the diagnosis has been validated by a court? Doctors may well be reluctant to go ahead with any non-therapeutic sterilisation in the absence of court authorisation – which of course can place a great emotional and financial strain on all those involved.

Re L&M,[60] the final case to be discussed in this chapter, concerns a similar set of facts to *Re B*.[61] The parents of Sarah, a severely physically and intellectually disabled 17-year-old girl, sought authorisation from the Family Court of Australia to consent to the performance of a hysterectomy and an ovariectomy upon their daughter. The disability had been caused by birth trauma, so there was no question of eugenics in this case. Sarah was dependent on her care givers for all her basic needs and was doubly incontinent. She wore nappies at all times. She was also epileptic and her condition was not expected to improve. Sarah had commenced menstruating and fertility was assumed. She had been in permanent care from a young age and was visited by her parents about four times a year. At the time of the hearing, she lived in a disabled persons' ward in a country hospital. However, future plans included the possibility of shared accommodation for disabled people, where other residents and care providers could be male.

Sarah, like Jeanette, lacked the capacity to give informed consent to a medical procedure and her inability to understand reproduction, contraception and birth was a permanent state of affairs. It was highly unlikely that she would ever form an enduring personal relationship and she could not possibly care for a child. The parents and Dr Py, the medical practitioner who would have performed the sterilisation, were opposed to abortion.

The trial judge in the case conducted a very broad inquiry into a number of factors relevant to the determination of Sarah's best interests. Evidence was received from a range of health care practitioners as well as the parents and the teacher at the special school attended by Sarah. Warnick J. addressed the application of conventional evidentiary rules when a court was exercising the *parens patriae* jurisdiction. He ruled that compliance with the conventional rules was not always necessary and could be waived if they imposed an intolerable burden on those involved in the case. On this basis he admitted a report by Ms C, an occupational therapist, who had undertaken post-graduate research investigating menstrual and fertility decision making on behalf of intellectually disabled women. The report referred to a number of studies dealing with medical matters concerning which Ms C could not be said to have expertise. Warnick J. said:

> I admitted most of the evidence from the occupational therapist, however, without qualification, because it seemed to me that the issues raised in applications of this nature, being medical, social, philosophical, moral and

even economic, were so varied and far-reaching, that to require direct evidence on each issue or consideration, from a person with formal expertise, would add intolerably to the cost and length of hearings such as this.[62]

By way of qualification, he admitted the part of the report dealing with the consequences of hysterectomy as evidence only of the information upon which the author relied.

Evidence from medical practitioners indicating whether or not they would decide to carry out the procedure was also admitted. Warnick J. noted the significance of this information to his inquiry and ruled that it did not infringe the rule against 'swearing the issue' because it answers the same questions as that which the court has to decide. Furthermore, as will be shown later, Warnick J. attached considerable importance to evidence received from non-medical witnesses and did not hesitate to disagree or take issue with medical opinion.

Evidence was given about a large number of issues concerning Sarah's welfare, including hygiene, the proposed move to residential accommodation, the risk of sexual abuse, pregnancy, epilepsy, menstrual discomfort and surgical risks. Fears that she could be sexually abused by a male care giver or fellow resident were also expressed in evidence. Ms T, a qualified occupational therapist who specialised in arranging accommodation for disabled people, and one of Sarah's teachers, both testified that menstrual management was an additional, but minor, burden in Sarah's case. Ms T, who had known Sarah for more than ten years, also advised that Sarah's problems with menstruation would not prevent her from being moved to residential accommodation if the opportunity arose, and that there were sufficient safeguards built into the selection and monitoring of care givers to provide adequate protection against sexual abuse.

Three of the four medical witnesses favoured sterilisation. Broadly, the major reasons advanced for sterilisation concerned the possibility of menorrhagia, menstrual management in residential accommodation, the medical risks associated with pregnancy and the risk of pregnancy. The only doctor who opposed the operation was Dr Pg. In his view, there were insufficient medical reasons to justify the procedure. After hearing evidence from the three doctors who favoured sterilisation, Warnick J. found there was not sufficient medical evidence to justify authorising the sterilisation and observed that some of the medical evidence was emotive. He also observed that Dr Pg seemed to have 'a more accurate perception of the issue and facts involved than some other practitioners'.[63] Further, he found that Sarah did not have to be sterilised to move into residential accommodation. Preferring evidence from non-medical witnesses on the issue, he said: 'It is not the evidence that

Sarah's incapacities during menstruation would produce great problems outside a hospital environment.'[64]

Weighing up the benefits and the detriments, Warnick J. found that the surgical risks and the possible long-term harmful effects of the procedure outweighed the benefits. Warnick J. held that sterilisation was not in Sarah's interest, and he refused the application on the ground that, although the operation would remove the risk of pregnancy, (the primary motivation for the operation), it would not achieve any other real benefit for Sarah or improve her life in any meaningful way. Noting that the probability of Sarah's becoming pregnant was relatively remote and would most likely result from abuse, he said, 'Thus pregnancy itself is a number of steps removed from probability.'[65] In his view the risk of abuse was not removed by sterilisation and did not justify the violation of her personal integrity. On the broad policy issue he took a strong stand, observing: 'To make a decision in this case, in favour of sterilisation, would be virtually equivalent to establishing a policy that all females, with profound disabilities resembling those afflicting Sarah, should be sterilised.'[66]

The decision in *Re L&M* shows that the Australian courts, unlike their English counterparts, still place considerable weight on sterilisations being a step of last resort. The guidelines established in *Re Marion (No.2)* require courts to conduct a broad and extensive inquiry into the circumstances of each case. As part of this process all possibilities and alternatives must be thoroughly examined and evaluated – the possibility of reversibility would be only one factor amongst many for the court to consider.

Conclusions

The development of a therapeutic and non-therapeutic dichotomy in the sterilisation cases echoes the history of Australian and English abortion laws where professional autonomy has had a direct influence on the evolution of lawful abortion.[67] In a broad sense, therapeutic sterilisations are performed for medical reasons and non-therapeutic sterilisations are performed chiefly to avoid pregnancy. As Nicholson C.J. pointed out in *Re Jane*, it is sometimes difficult to disentangle therapeutic from non-therapeutic aims.[68] It may also be argued that the drawing of the distinction is an exercise of clinical autonomy, and in Australia it is not clear how this is to be determined.

The sterilisation of mentally incompetent young women for non-therapeutic reasons is not a new practice. Traditionally, the thorny question of consent was buried in the privacy of clinical autonomy and parental autonomy. Faith was placed in the ethical principle of beneficence and parents were deemed to have the right to make medical decisions about their offspring. The shift away from medical paternalism towards patient autonomy has highlighted the question of consent and has focused attention on the human rights involved. The mood has changed, and the major issue is now the welfare of the young woman. Do the benefits of sterilisation outweigh the detriments? As part of this inquiry, courts in Australia must consider the views of parents as well as a range of care takers who may be able to assist the court as a result of their relationship with the young woman. In both Australia and England the courts are required to apply the best interests test, although in Australia it has been described by the High Court as being confined by the notion of the step of last resort;[70] there is no provision for a substituted judgement principle.[71] The major advantage of the best interests test is its flexibility. It enables the individual circumstances of each case to be considered. Although time-consuming, this is important because, as the cases in this chapter demonstrate, the degree of disability and individual circumstances vary a great deal. In some cases, for example, it may be very repressive to impose physical restraints on a young woman because of the fear of pregnancy. On the other hand, the best interests test is based on the assumption that there is a set of common values upon which judges can draw to make the right decision, even though there is no such thing as an objective evaluation.[72] Each judge is influenced by her or his standards, prejudices and moral framework. In addition, the inherent vagueness of the test encourages judges to defer to medical opinion and to rely on medical evidence about common medical practice.

In England, the decision by the House of Lords in *F's case* to apply the *Bolam* test to adult sterilisation cases has filtered down to the lower courts. As Brazier points out:

> Sterilization will be lawful if the decision to sterilize that particular woman is in conformity with a responsible body of medical opinion. *Re P* illustrates that, in practice, hypothetical reversibility of sterilization has convinced some responsible gynaecologists that it is now appropriate for a much broader category of women. Sterilization need no longer be the last resort, merely perhaps the most 'convenient' means of contraception.[73]

She makes the further point that other doctors may offer a different view about the influence that the reversibility should have on the decision, with the result that the case may be 'determined by geography'.[74]

The Australian courts have tackled the vagueness aspect of the best interests test with the establishment of special guidelines in *Re Marion (No.2)*. These guidelines require courts to consider specific medical, as well as social and psychological, information. Nevertheless, the weight to be placed on any evidence depends on judicial attitudes. The reports of the Australian cases before and after *Re Marion (No.2)* show a willingness to give credence to non-medical testimony. With the exception of Cook J. in *Re a Teenager*, it may also be said that Australian judges are less deferential to medical opinion than their English counterparts. In *Re L&M*, Warnick J. not only disagreed with some aspects of medical evidence but favoured evidence from non-medical witnesses. Non-medical evidence played a less influential role in the English cases discussed in this chapter.

Making the sterilisation of young mentally incompetent women public in the Australian and English jurisdictions has created a considerable dent in professional autonomy. This unravelling of clinical decision making has exposed the extent to which social and moral considerations have become part of medical work and have therefore been subject to minimal external control. The transfer of sterilisation decision making from the private to the public arena has provided for more external scrutiny, by giving courts jurisdiction over a matter which was previously regarded as belonging to the private realm of the medical practitioner and the family. Most importantly, this process has placed the issue of sterilising minors on the public agenda and has drawn attention to the ethical and human rights issues.

Notes

1   E. Freidson, *Professionalism Reborn*, Cambridge Polity Press, 1994, p.166.
2   [1939] 1 KB 687. See K.A. Petersen, *Abortion Regimes*, Aldershot, Dartmouth, 1993, p.63–5.
3   For discussion on the historical context, see M.D.A. Freeman, 'Sterilising the Mentally Handicapped', in M.D.A. Freeman, *Medicine, Ethics and The Law*, London: Stevens and Sons, 1988, p.56–60.
4   L.B. McCullough and F.A. Chervenak, *Ethics in Obstetrics and Gynecology*, New York, Oxford University Press, 1994, p.48.
5   Ibid. p.49.
6   D. Giesen, 'From Paternalism to Self Determination to Shared Decision Making in the Field of Medical Law and Ethics', in L. Westerhall and C. Phillips (eds), *Patient's Rights*, Stockholm, Nerenius & Santerus, 1994, p.20. See also T.L. Beauchamp and J.F. Childress, *Principles of Medical Ethics*, 4th edn, New York, Oxford University Press, 1994.
7   211 N.Y. 125, 105 N.E.92 (1914).
8   See S.A.M. McLean, *A Patient's Right to Know: Information, Disclosure, the Doctor and the Law*, Aldershot, Dartmouth, 1984.
9   C. Wells, 'Patient Consent and Criminal Law', *Journal of Social Welfare and Family Law*, (1994), p.65.
10 J.K. Mason and R.A. McCall Smith, *Law and Medical Ethics*, Edinburgh, Butterworths, 1994, p.83–4. In 1994, Judge Souter of the United States Supreme Court refused to bar the sterilisation of a severely disabled adult woman. Although the decision will probably be the subject of appeal, it will be too late to stop the sterilisation. The Supreme Court has not ruled on sterilisation for disabled people since 1927, when in *Buck* v. *Bell*, 274 US 200 (1927) it upheld a Virginia law allowing the sterilisation of disabled people living in institutions.

11 Freeman, *Medicine*, p.59–60; *Re Jane* (1989) FLC 92-007 77,259. See also J. Godhar, 'The Sterilisation of Women with an Intellectual Disability' *University of Tasmania Law Review*, **10**, (1991) 157; M.Jones and L.A. Basser Marks, 'The Dynamic Developmental Model of the Rights of the Child: A Feminist Approach to Rights and Sterilisation', *International Journal of Children's Rights*, **2**, (1994), 1.

12 For information on the law concerning parental consent and the medical treatment of minors, see Mason and McCall Smith, *Law and Medical Ethics*, chap.10.

13 [1976] 1 A11 ER 326.

14 In England the wardship jurisdiction is derived from the prerogative powers of the Crown as *parens patriae*.

15 [1976] 1 A11 ER 326, 331.

16 [1976] 1 A11 ER 326, 335.

17 [1976] 1 A11 ER 326, 334.

18 (1989) FLC 92-006.

19 (1990) FLC 97-124.

20 (1989) FLC 92-007.

21 (1989) FLC 92-023.

22 (1992) FLC 92-293.

23 Family Law Act 1975, s.63(1); 63E(1); 64(1).

24 (1992) FLC 92-293.

25 (1992) FLC 92-293, 79,185.

26 (1992) FLC 92-293, 79,185; see also *Re B* [1987] 2 A11 ER 206 per Lord Oliver of Aylmerton at 215.

27 (1989) FLC 92-006.

28 (1989) FLC 92-006.

29 (1989) FLC 92-006.

30 (1989) FLC 92-006, 77,203.

31 (1989) FLC 92-006, 77,203.

32 (1989) FLC 92-006, 77,226.

33 (1989) FLC 92-007, 77,257; Jones and Basser Marks, 'The Dynamic Developmental Model', 25–6.

34 (1989) FLC 92-007, 77,258.

35 (1989) FLC 92-007, 77,257.

36 (1989) FLC 92-007, 77,261.

37 (1994) FLC 92-448. In the recent 1995 Appeal decision, *P* and *P* (Appeal No. EA 85 of 1994), the Full Court of the Family Court of Australia overruled a decision of Moore J. dismissing an application to have a disabled child sterilised. The Full Court agreed broadly with the need for judicial guidelines in sterilisation cases but took the view that great care must be taken before establishing prescriptive guidelines. The Full Court reiterated and applied the guidelines adopted by Nicholson C.J. in *Re Jane* (1989) FLC 92-007 and *Re Marion (No.2)* (1994) FLC 92-448 and also maintained that the principle of judicial discretion must be retained in these cases.

38 See D. Giesen, 'Medical Malpractice and the Judicial Function', *Medical Law International*, **1**, 1993, 3.

39 *Gillick* v. *West Norfolk and Wisbech Area Authority* [1985] 3 A11 ER 402 AC 112; for discussion on this issue see Mason and McCall Smith *Law and Medical Ethics*, pp.224–5. See also Jones and Basser Marks, 'The Dynamic Developmental Model', 25–6; L.A. Basser Marks, 'Family Privacy versus Individual Autonomy: The Role of the State in Children's Medical Treatment Decisions', paper presented at the 4th AIFS Australian Family Research Conference, NSW, 1993.

40 But see *In Re GF* [1993] 4 MED.L.R 77 where Sir Stephen Brown states that an operation could be performed which has the incidental effect of sterilising a mentally incompetent adult without court authorisation if two doctors agree that

the procedure was necessary for therapeutic purposes and was in the patient's best interests; and that no practicable less intrusive procedure was available. This is really a beneficence model of decision making which, like abortion decisions, requires two medical practitioners. It could be described as a form of statutory peer review.

41 [1987] 2 A11 ER 206.
42 [1987] 2 A11 ER 206, 212–13.
43 [1989] 2 A11 ER 545. The House of Lords confirmed in *F's* case that the *parens patriae* jurisdiction no longer exists in England and the court has no power to give or withhold consent to a sterilisation operation on an adult woman disabled by mental incapacity. Their Lordships considered that, as a matter of good medical practice, doctors should seek a Declaration in these circumstances. Moreover, when assessing the best interests of the patient the Court should apply the test of what would be accepted as appropriate treatment at the time by a reasonable body of medical opinion skilled in that particular form of treatment, as established in *Bolam* v. *Friern Hospital Management Committee* [1957] 2 A11 ER 118.
44 See note 43.
45 Lord Hailsham L.C. disagreed with the view of La Forest J. in the Canadian case *Re Eve* (1986) 31 DLR (4th)1, that sterilisation should never be authorised for non-therapeutic purposes on the grounds that such an approach was in contradiction to the welfare principle.
46 [1987] 2 A11 ER 206, 212.
47 [1987] 2 A11 ER 206, 218.
48 [1993] 17 Fam LR 357.
49 Mason and McCall Smith, *Law and Medical Ethics*, p.85.
50 [1988] 2 FLR 997.
51 M. Brazier, *Medicine, Patients and The Law*, 2nd edn, London, Penguin, 1992, p.390.
52 [1989] 1 FLR 182.
53 Brazier, *Medicine, Patients and the Law*, pp.390–91.
54 [1993] 17 Fam LR 357.
55 (1994) FLC 92-448.
56 (1992) FLC 92-293.
57 (1994) FLC 92-448.
58 See also *Re X* [1991] 2 NZLR 365, where the court found that it was in the best interests of a severely intellectually disabled girl to have an operation to prevent menstruation. Hillyer J. also upheld medical and parental autonomy and provided that court authorisation was not necessary if the guidelines set out in that case were followed.
59 [1993] 17 Fam LR 337, 355.
60 [1993] 17 Fam LR 357.
61 [1987] 2 A11 ER 206.
62 [1993] 17 Fam LR 357, 362.
63 [1993] 17 Fam LR 357, 369.
64 [1993] 17 Fam LR 357, 376.
65 [1993] 17 Fam LR 357, 374.
66 [1993] 17 Fam LR 357, 374.
67 K.A. Petersen, *Abortion Regimes*, passim.
68 *Re Jane* (1989) FLC 92-007, 77,260; see *Re JWB* (1992) FLC 92-293, Brennan J. at 79,190.
69 In the guidelines established in *Re Marion (No.2)*, the court must take into account 'the relevant factors which go to determining whether the procedure is in the best interest of the child as follows:
The views (if any) expressed by:
a)   the guardian/s of the child
b)   the person who is entitled to the custody of the child

c)   a person who is responsible for the daily care and control of the child

d)   the child

about the proposed procedure or treatment and to any alternative procedure or treatment.'

70   (1992) FLC 92-293, 79, 185.

71   R. Gillon, 'On Sterilising Severely Mentally Handicapped People', *Journal of Medical Ethics,* **13**, (1987), 59–61.

72   P. Parkinson, 'Children's Rights and Doctor's Immunities: The Implications of the High Court's Decision in *Re Marion'*, *Australian Journal of Family Law,* **10**, (1992), 121–2.

73   Brazier, *Medicine, Patients and the Law*, pp.391–2.

74   Ibid., p.392.

5 Maternal/Foetal Conflict: Defined or Defused?

JANE MAIR

In recent years a disturbing image has emerged of pregnancy and childbirth: that of the maternal/foetal conflict. It is a violent image which disrupts the coexistence of mother and foetus. It is an emotive phrase which suggests unmotherly feelings and a grotesque perception of the struggling foetus. What is this maternal/foetal conflict? The label has been applied to a number of situations where there appears to be a conflict of interests between a pregnant woman and the foetus which she is carrying. The conflict arises in situations where there is a clash between the conduct of the woman and the well-being of the foetus as presented by medical opinion. The conflict is evident in two scenarios: first, where the woman behaves during pregnancy in a way which is considered as potentially harmful to the development of the foetus and, second, where surgery is deemed to be necessary for the birth of the child but the mother refuses to consent. Thus maternal/foetal conflict incorporates the dual issues of prenatal injury and enforced Caesarians.

The conflict is presented initially in a medical context. It is likely to be the doctor who identifies the existence of a conflict of interests. An increasing trend has developed whereby the courts are then involved, apparently to adjudicate between the parties but also to protect the doctors against claims of negligence or medical malpractice. The involvement of the courts has led to discussion of the possible existence of foetal rights which can either be exercised to defeat the mother's rights or be used as a basis for raising a legal action against the mother for compensation. In practice these dilemmas are of importance to the medical profession in the development of treatment for pregnant women. They are becoming of importance to the law, which is being asked to provide guidance to doctors and to authorise increasing control of pregnancy. The approach of both medicine and law has considerable implications for women's lives, their relationships and their legal status.

Much has been written about maternal/foetal conflict, which contrasts with the relative scarcity of legal judgements and the notable lack of reasoned judicial opinion within these judgements. In this chapter it is intended to review the current legal approach to maternal/foetal conflict, to consider the potential for legal development within the framework of this conflict and finally to question the use of a conflict model.

Issues of maternal/foetal conflict have only recently – and very rarely – been considered by courts within the United Kingdom,[1] although they have more frequently appeared before the US courts. In the United Kingdom, there have been few reported cases arising from circumstances which indicate the potential for conflict. Two which directly highlight this conflict are *D* v. *Berkshire County Council*,[2] which relates to the issue of conflict during pregnancy between the woman's behaviour and the development of the foetus, and *Re S (adult: refusal of medical treatment)*,[3] which deals with enforced Caesarian sections. In neither case do we find any detailed discussion of the legal, social and philosophical issues which are involved but they do provide factual examples of the types of situation in which a conflict between the woman and the foetus might be argued to exist. In addition to these decisions, consideration can be given to a number of US cases in which there has been further discussion of these issues.

Where is the Legal Conflict?

What is the current legal approach to maternal/foetal conflict? An indication of this can be obtained by looking at recent UK cases against a background of further developments in the United States. Although there are issues which are common to all of the cases, disputes tend to arise in two discrete ways: those which emerge from conflict during pregnancy – conflict between the autonomy of the woman to behave in a certain way and the healthy development of the foetus, and those which emerge from conflict at the point of birth – cases concerning enforced Caesarian sections or other intrusive surgery. The fundamental legal question in all of the cases would seem to be whether a foetus is recognised as having any legal status. Is a foetus a legal person which is capable of having (or enforcing) legal rights? If the answer to this question is yes, what are the rights of the foetus and how can these be reconciled with the rights of the woman? These questions are not always directly addressed by the courts, although the recognition of foetal rights would appear to underpin a number of the decisions.

Female Autonomy v. Foetal Development

The question of whether a foetus has a legally recognised existence was addressed by the courts in *D* v. *Berkshire County Council*,[4] a case which highlighted the potential for conflict between the autonomy of a pregnant woman and the development of the foetus. This case concerned a care order made under s.1(2)(*a*) of the Children and Young Persons Act 1969[5] in respect of a child born on 12 March 1985. The mother was a registered drug addict who had taken drugs throughout her pregnancy, as a result of which the child, at birth, was suffering from drug withdrawal symptoms. Care was granted to the local authority on the ground that 'the child's proper development is being avoidably prevented or neglected or his health is being avoidably impaired or neglected or he is being ill-treated'.[6] The child was at no time in the care of the mother and, therefore, the controversial issue was whether the court was entitled to take account of the mother's conduct during pregnancy in relation to the neglect/impairment of the child's development/health. A care order was made by a juvenile court on 1 August. On appeal to the Divisional Court of the Family Division, the order was discharged but was subsequently reinstated by the Court of Appeal and upheld by the House of Lords. Throughout the various stages of this case, the courts concentrated on the interpretation of s.1(2)(*a*) of the 1969 Act. Their concern was with a point of statutory interpretation rather than with any consideration of the wider social and philosophical implications of their decision. The court 'took the view that a child's development is a continuing process which encompasses the past and the present and [they] considered that events in the past life of this child, even during the time when it was a foetus in the womb, were relevant'.[7]

In the circumstances of this particular case, it is perhaps difficult to perceive a conflict. With regard to the care of the child, there was no disagreement as to the need of the child for care and control. The dispute related to what was, to some extent, a technical matter: whether care should be sought under the 1969 Act or by means of wardship proceedings. The decision is significant, however, in that it recognises the legal existence of the foetus. It takes account of the woman's behaviour, as it affected the foetus, as a factor in deciding on the care of the child. There was no question of the courts recognising the foetus as a legal person capable of having or enforcing legal rights. There was agreement as to the need for a live birth before the Act could be applied, but there was recognition of the importance of prenatal conduct by the mother as affecting the subsequent care of the child.

Legal recognition of the importance of foetal development might give rise to concern that the law would be developed to permit prenatal intervention where the woman's conduct is identified as endangering the foetus and the subsequent health of the child. This potential line of development has subsequently been blocked by the English courts. In *Re F (in utero)*[8] a local authority sought to make a foetus a ward of court in order to protect it from the mother on account of her lifestyle. The Court of Appeal refused to grant the application until the child was born on the basis that to do so would necessarily involve restraining the woman. The court stated that the foetus had no separate legal personality and that, even if it did, the freedom of the mother must take priority. Thus, having taken a step towards foetal rights in *D* v. *Berkshire County Council*, it was clear that the court was unwilling to take the extreme step of upholding those 'rights' against the woman's right to physical liberty.

Attempts to seek custody of a foetus have been considered in the United States. A Superior County Court in Georgia in *Jefferson* v. *Griffin Spalding County Hospital Authority*[9] awarded temporary custody of a foetus to the county department of family and children services. A woman in the 39th week of pregnancy was advised by the hospital that she had a complete placenta previa and that there was a 99 per cent chance that the child could not survive vaginal delivery. She refused her consent to a Caesarian section on the basis of her religious beliefs, beliefs which were shared by her husband. The hospital sought and obtained authority to carry out a Caesarian if and when the woman presented herself at the hospital. The following day, a petition was brought forward for an award of temporary custody. The court granted temporary custody of the foetus to the county department, giving it 'full authority to make all decisions, including giving consent to the surgical delivery'[10] of the child. This award was made on the basis of the state's interest in the unborn child which was found to outweigh the interests of the woman and her husband in protecting their privacy. There was little discussion of the issues involved. In practice the court's declarations were never put to the test of enforceability as the woman successfully gave birth on her own without returning to the hospital.

Little use has so far been made of criminal law in relation to harm caused by a woman to the foetus which she is carrying. A criminal action was raised in California against a woman who was alleged to have caused the death of her six-month-old baby by reason of her conduct prior to the birth.[11] Pamela Rae Stewart was arrested and charged under a California statute which makes it a crime for a parent to 'wilfully omit, without lawful excuse, to furnish necessary clothing, food, shelter or medical attendance, or other remedial care for his or her child'.[12] Ms Stewart was charged with having delayed in seeking medical attention when during pregnancy she began to haemorrhage; she had engaged in sexual intercourse with her husband and she had taken amphetamines and marijuana, all of which were against the advice of her doctor. The charges were later dismissed on the basis that Ms Stewart's failure to follow her doctor's advice was not illegal under the statute. Although this particular statute was incapable of a sufficiently wide interpretation to cover this specific situation, the possibility of further legislation was not ruled out. For the moment, however, it seems that development through the criminal law is less likely.

From the cases which have been considered it is clear that courts in several American states have gone some way towards recognising the legal rights of a foetus in relation to the woman who is carrying it. In these cases the interests of the foetus in proper development have been weighed against the interests of the woman in her own autonomy. In England there has been recognition of prenatal existence in relation to the subsequent care of a child but the courts have refused to recognise the foetus itself as having legal rights capable of protection.

Court-ordered Caesarians

The second type of situation which comes within the heading of maternal/foetal conflict is where, at the time of childbirth itself, the woman refuses to undergo medical treatment which is, in the opinion of the doctors and other medical staff, necessary to enable the live birth of the child. This aspect has been directly considered by an English court, albeit in a very unsatisfactory way, in the case of *Re S (adult: refusal of medical treatment)*.[13] On 12 October 1992, a UK court was asked for the first time to authorise an emergency Caesarian section on a pregnant woman against her wishes. Faced with this extreme example of an apparent conflict between the autonomy of a pregnant woman and the interests of a foetus, the court made its decision with what appears to have been remarkably little consideration, the judgement occupying less than a page, and the decision being reached in a matter of minutes.

A health authority sought permission for the surgeons and staff of a hospital to perform an emergency Caesarian section on a female patient who had been admitted to the hospital. The woman, who was six days beyond the expected date of birth, had been admitted to the hospital with ruptured membranes and in spontaneous labour. The medical personnel involved in the case were of the clear opinion that a Caesarian was essential to save the woman's life and that it was the only way in which the baby could be born alive. The woman and her husband were 'born-again Christians' and, on the basis of her religious beliefs, the woman was refusing consent to the operation. In her refusal, she had the clear support of her husband. Evidence was given by the surgeon in charge of the patient, in the hearing before Sir Stephen Brown P., to the effect that the situation for both mother and unborn child was 'desperately serious'.[14] While the judgement is so short as to make it almost impossible to discern the processes of thought which the judge employed, it is clear that he was caught up in the emergency atmosphere of the operating theatre. It was a 'life and death situation'[15] allowing 'minutes rather than hours'[16] for consideration of the major issues at stake.

In the judgement, the relative importance of the beliefs of the woman and the medical evidence is clear, with the woman being accorded one short sentence, whereas the surgeon secures a complete paragraph. The most that can be said for the woman and her husband is that they 'are clearly quite sincere in their beliefs'.[17] The words of the surgeon are, however, evidence which is in its nature emphatic and indisputable. The doctor says that 'it is absolutely the case that the baby cannot be born alive if a Caesarian operation is not carried out'[18] and who is a judge (far less a mother) to question that? Convinced by this evidence and by the pressing need for haste, a declarator was granted after a short hearing, to the effect that the hospital and its staff could perform a Caesarian and any necessary consequential treatment despite the patient's refusal to consent. This was done on the basis that it was in the vital interests of the patient and her unborn child.

In giving his decision, the judge is almost as dismissive of the law as he is of the woman. He believes that there is some American authority on the matter and he thinks that, if this case had arisen in the United States, it is likely that the courts would have granted a declaration in the hospital's favour. As far as English law is concerned, there is no direct authority, although passing reference is made to *Re T (adult: refusal of medical treatment)*.[19] In this decision of Lord Donaldson M.R. it had been stated that a competent adult was free to refuse to give consent to medical treatment. A possible exception was left open, however, with respect to the situation where refusal to consent might prevent the birth of a viable foetus. With an incredible lack of reasoned and considered opinion, Sir Stephen Brown in *Re S* adopted this exception.

In his opinion, he referred vaguely to American authority, citing the decision in *Re AC*.[20] This case concerned a woman, Angela Carder, who had been diagnosed as having cancer at the age of 13. Aged 27, and during a period of remission, she married and shortly thereafter became pregnant. Twenty-five weeks into the pregnancy she was informed she had an inoperable lung tumour and there was discussion as to her own care and that of the foetus. She agreed to palliative treatment aimed at extending her life until the 28th week, by which time there would be a better chance of the foetus being born alive and healthy. In deciding on this course of treatment, her concerns were to give the foetus a better chance of survival and also to protect her own comfort. A week later it became clear that the woman was unlikely to survive until the 28th week and a trial court was convened within the hospital to consider how the hospital should treat the patient. The court was asked to consider whether the hospital could perform a Caesarian section on the woman in view of the fact that, at $26^{1}/_{2}$ weeks, the foetus was viable. The woman was by this time heavily sedated and having great difficulty in communicating. A number of attempts were made by medical personnel to explain the proceedings to her and to ask her whether she wanted the baby to be born and whether she would consent to a Caesarian. The judge did not speak to her. It was unclear as to whether or not she would consent. Her mother was opposed to surgery on the basis that her daughter wanted to live long enough to hold the baby. At the final attempt to seek her consent, the woman responded to the effect that she did not want the surgery to be performed. There was medical evidence to the effect that she appeared to be alert and to understand what was happening.

This evidence was before the court, together with a medical opinion that the woman would not live for more than 48 hours and that the foetus had a 50–60 per cent chance of survival if delivered immediately by Caesarian. On this basis the court ordered that a Caesarian section should be carried out. The child died within two hours of the operation; the mother within two days.

At the hearings of the trial court, the views of the woman and her lack of consent – or apparent lack of consent – were almost totally disregarded. The decision was made on the basis of a weighing up of the chances of survival of both parties. The hospital argued that the foetus had a 50–60 per cent chance of survival if the Caesarian was performed quickly. The foetus was viable and therefore the state had an interest in protecting the potentiality of life. This was enough to allow the court to authorise the section, despite the fact that the mother did not consent and the operation was likely to hasten her death. Thus, for the court in this case, consent was a minor issue, with the viability of the foetus and the state's interest in its life being the primary consideration. This decision was appealed twice after the woman's death and was overturned by the Court of Appeals.[21]

It might be argued that *Re AC* was not a clear case of conflict as there was some uncertainty surrounding the woman's lack of consent. She had apparently previously given her consent to a Caesarian and there was some doubt as to her ability to understand and respond, owing to sedation. In the case of *Jefferson*,[22] as we have seen, there was no such doubt surrounding the woman's refusal of consent. Here both the woman and her husband refused consent, on religious grounds, to a Caesarian which the doctors said was essential. The court disregarded her lack of consent and found in favour of the foetus, emphasising in its decision the importance of the state's interest in protecting the life of a viable foetus.

It can be seen from these decisions that courts in both America[23] and the United Kingdom have been willing to ignore the wishes of a pregnant woman and to allow hospitals to carry out major surgery. While recognising the fundamental right of competent individuals to refuse consent to treatment, they have been prepared to ignore this refusal in favour of the interests of the foetus. In so doing they appear to recognise the foetus as having enforceable legal rights. As with the cases relating to conduct during pregnancy, these decisions are similarly lacking in their discussion of fundamental issues. In the face of emergency and overwhelmed by the emotion of the situation, the courts are willing to disregard the legal inconsistencies which result from their decisions. Although the case law in the United Kingdom is extremely limited, it does indicate some legal recognition of the foetus by the courts. The legal status of the foetus and its rights in relation to the mother are, however, ill-defined and this lack of definition creates a considerable area of uncertainty around the position of the pregnant woman. The majority of women will wish to act in the best interests of the foetus, but in order for them to do so with any certainty there must be adequate definition of their respective rights.

How should we approach the issues which have been raised? We can proceed in two different ways. On the one hand, we can continue within the confines of the conflict model, defining and clarifying the rights of the woman and the foetus. Recognising that in various situations there may be a conflict between the interests of the woman and those of the foetus, we can consider methods of resolving or dealing with this conflict. Alternatively, we can proceed by questioning the use of a conflict-based model, investigating instead the position of woman and foetus within a wider context.

A Conflict Defined

The construction of a conflict between woman and foetus requires the recognition of each as having legal rights. If the situation is perceived as a conflict of interests or a case of competing rights of woman and foetus, the judge, if he or she is to be the arbiter, must develop some legal method for dealing with the conflict and for deciding in favour of one or other of the parties. In order to reach such a decision the legal rights of both parties must be considered. Although the specific situations which the courts are being asked to deal with are new, the legal concepts on which they tend (or pretend) to rely are well established. A criticism which can be made is that the courts are adapting well-known concepts in a hurried manner without fully considering the effect of their application. Two legal concepts which have been used are the duty of care and consent to medical treatment and it could be argued that these concepts should be developed further for use in relation to maternal/foetal conflicts.

Duty of Care to the Foetus

If a mother owes a duty of care to her child not to cause it harm then why cannot this duty be extended to cover her unborn child? It is well established that a parent owes a duty of care to his or her child. What must now be considered is whether or not this duty can be extended backwards beyond the moment of birth. Does a pregnant woman owe a duty of care to her foetus? For many pregnant women the idea of harming the foetus which she is carrying would seem unthinkable. Morally, a society may consider that a pregnant woman is responsible for the well-being and development of her foetus. However, it is a significant step to transform these generally held beliefs into a clear and actionable legal duty.

The right of a child to sue his or her mother in respect of prenatal harm has been recognised in some US states. In *Grodin* v. *Grodin*,[24] for example, in which the court in Michigan held admissible a claim for compensation by a child against his mother for allegedly using an antibiotic during pregnancy which was argued to have resulted in the child being born with discoloured teeth. Can a child in the United Kingdom currently recover compensation for prenatal harm? The law in England and Scotland is the same to the extent that it is essential that there be a live birth before compensation can be sought. Thus neither legal system allows for wrongful death claims. Thereafter, however, the position is somewhat different with, it appears, a greater potential in Scotland for a claim against the mother than in England. In both jurisdictions, a survey of the common law was carried out in the early 1970s,[25] resulting in England in the Congenital Disabilities (Civil Liability) Act 1976 and in no change in the law in Scotland.

The English legislation provides that a child may sue a third party for damages in respect of injuries sustained while *in utero*, but specifically excludes the possibility of an action against the mother.[26] The only exception is where the child has been injured by the negligence of the mother in a car accident.[27] In that situation it was decided that claims should be admissible largely on the basis of the availability of insurance. Such an action against the mother can be seen primarily as benefiting the family financially, whereas in other situations a similar action may disrupt family relationships.

In Scots law, the possibility of a claim by a child against his or her mother in respect of prenatal injuries appears to be possible, although not yet tested.[28] It is clear in Scots law that a child can sue a third party in negligence in respect of prenatal harm, as happened in *Hamilton* v. *Fife Health Board*.[29] In this case, parents sought damages for loss of society in respect of the death of their child, three days after birth, owing to injuries suffered by the child *in utero*, allegedly as a result of the negligence of the doctors. The case was based on s.1(1) of the Damages (Scotland) Act 1976 which allows for a relative to recover damages which would have been owed to a person who has died 'in consequence of personal injuries suffered by him as a result of an act or omission of another person'. On appeal to the Inner House of the Court of Session, the court considered the meaning of the phrase, 'personal injuries sustained by him', and in particular whether this could include prenatal injuries. There was general agreement that this phrase could include personal injuries sustained in the womb, although there was no legal status to claim damages until the birth of the child. Although in this particular case the court seemed to accept that a duty of care was owed by the doctors to the foetus, there was little consideration of the wider concepts of the nature and extent of this duty. Similarly, there was no consideration of the possibility of a duty of care being owed by a pregnant woman to the foetus.

If a mother is to be held liable in damages to her child, there are several issues which should be considered and clarified. There are technical difficulties and there are also considerations of policy. If there is a duty of care owed to a foetus, at what point in time does this duty arise? This question has attracted little judicial attention: an omission which is perhaps not surprising considering the difficult philosophical and moral debates to which it gives rise. Traditionally, both Scots and English law have granted legal personality at the time of birth.[30] Had the child in *Hamilton*, for example, never been born alive, the parents would have had no right of action. The doctors' negligence would still have physically harmed the foetus, but the legal personality which founds the legal right to claim damages would never have been attained. The decision in *Hamilton* seems to make a distinction between existence and legal personality, with Lord McCluskey stating that there were 'injuries to his person although not to his legal persona'.[31] By recognising the existence of the foetus in the womb, the court was able to take account of prenatal harm while delaying attribution of legal personality until the moment of birth. Even within *Hamilton* there was a difference of opinion as to when the 'personal injuries' were 'sustained'. Lord McCluskey was of the opinion that the harm was sustained at the time of the negligence and endured until the point of birth, when it became actionable.[32] Lord Caplan argued that the legal harm was not sustained until the moment of birth, at which point the child also obtained legal status.[33]

If a duty of care is owed to a foetus then it is vital to know when the duty arises. In *Hamilton* the negligence occurred very shortly before the birth and the court declined to comment on whether it would have awarded damages in respect of negligent acts at a much earlier stage in the pregnancy. Even if most women would willingly accept that they should take reasonable precautions to protect the development of the foetus, it is difficult to know how early a woman needs to commence such precautions. The living child has obvious needs which can be identified by the mother but the needs of the foetus are to an increasing extent the domain of the doctor. Rapid developments in medical knowledge and techniques have focused attention on the impact of, for example, diet, health and environment on the foetus and have highlighted the particular importance of the period prior to conception. If a mother is to be held liable for prenatal injury to her child, could her liability extend as far back as conception or beyond?

The extension of a duty of care owed by the pregnant woman to the foetus gives rise to a number of problems. In addition to the technical legal problems in defining how far back the duty of care should extend, extension of the duty of care also has significant impact on the autonomy of the woman. To what extent, if at all, should the woman's freedom be curtailed? It has been argued that if a woman chooses to conceive and to carry a foetus to term then she should accept responsibility towards the foetus. This responsibility might arise at the point when abortion is no longer legally available. Thereafter she is being asked to do nothing more than she will be legally required to do in relation to her living child. Or is she? It appears from several of the decisions that she is being asked to do more than is ever demanded of one living person for another. The courts will not, for example, order an individual to undergo surgery for the benefit of another living individual even where it is necessary to save that person's life.

In most actions arising from personal injuries, establishing causation is a significant problem. Medical negligence cases in particular are notoriously difficult. There may be a risk, owing to the close and obvious connection between woman and foetus, of causation being presumed to a much greater extent than in other cases where the link is less evident. It would be all too easy to blame the mother for harm while ignoring less accessible, but perhaps equally responsible, sources.

Enabling a child to sue his or her mother for damages arising from prenatal harm has significant implications for family relationships, for the personal autonomy of women and also for the role of women within society. It also requires clarification of the standard of care which the woman must attain and in particular the stage of development at which the duty of care emerges. If children are to be allowed to raise such actions against their mothers, these issues should be considered in advance.

Consent

In confronting instances of maternal/foetal conflict, a second area of the law which has been used by the courts is that of consent to medical treatment. Cases concerning surgical intervention in relation to childbirth have been considered in terms of consent to medical treatment. They have been treated as an exception to the rule that a competent individual may refuse consent to medical treatment even where such refusal is not regarded, in medical opinion, as being in his or her interests. It is well established that medical treatment without consent is unlawful.[34] Problems have arisen in cases where an individual is refusing consent to treatment which is seen by the medical profession as being necessary for the preservation of the individual's life. The legal position is clear, however, that where the individual is legally competent, then he or she can choose to refuse such treatment. This was confirmed by the Court of Appeal in *Re T (adult: refusal of medical treatment)*.[35] In this case, an adult woman refused consent to a blood transfusion which was regarded as being necessary to save her life. The hospital sought a declaration to the effect that it was not unlawful for them to administer the transfusion despite the lack of consent because it was in her best interests. Although in this particular instance the transfusion was held not to have been unlawful on the basis that the patient was not in a physical or mental condition in which she could make such a decision, the court confirmed that, in general, 'an adult patient ... who suffers from no mental incapacity, has an absolute right to choose whether to consent to medical treatment'.[36] Lord Donaldson did, however, leave one potential gap in this rule, to the effect that 'the only possible qualification is a case in which the choice may lead to the death of a viable foetus'.[37]

It was on this 'possible qualification' that Sir Stephen Brown founded his decision in *Re S*.[38] What justification can be given, however, for overriding a woman's refusal to consent? It must be argued that there is some greater interest to be protected than the woman's interest in controlling her own body. What is this interest? Is it the interest of the foetus or is it the interest of the state: the public interest? Or is it the interest of the woman herself as defined by her medical protectors?[39]

Looking at the short opinion in *Re S* it is difficult to determine whose interests the judge was protecting. Authority to perform the operation was, however, granted as being 'in the vital interests of the patient and her unborn child'.[40] In the atmosphere of emergency this may sound convincing but on closer inspection the legal basis for this decision is uncertain. If the interests of the woman and the child are looked at separately, do they justify the declarator? The operation was authorised in the interests of the woman. First, it is difficult to accept that the declarator furthered the woman's interests. In a literal medical sense it may have been in her interests, as otherwise medical opinion suggested that she would die. From her personal point of view, it could not be described as being in her interests as she was strongly opposed to the operation. Second, the courts have refused to authorise life-saving surgery where there is no consent. If the court in *Re S* has accepted that an individual's interest in living outweighs his or her interest in personal autonomy, then that is inconsistent with established precedent. Such paternalism has been rejected in cases not involving a pregnant woman.[41] It would seem therefore that the operation could not be authorised in the interests of the woman alone where she had competently refused to consent.

Can it be argued that the declarator was justified as being in the interests of the foetus? It is arguable that it is better to be born than not to be born, but what of the quality of life of the child and its relationship with its mother following such a traumatic birth? Leaving aside moral arguments, there is again a legal problem in that to order the operation on the basis of the interests of the foetus is to recognise that a foetus has legally enforceable rights. This is at odds with the court's refusals in *D* v. *Berkshire County Council* and *Re F* to recognise the foetus as a legal person with enforceable rights.

Neither the woman's interests nor those of the foetus, looked at separately, are of sufficient weight, yet the conjunction of the two is put forward as justification for the decision. The magical unity of mother and child is capable of transforming the legal rules.

A further argument for overriding the woman's refusal to consent, which is not specifically dealt with in *Re S* but which features in several US cases, relates to the interest of the state or the public interest. What exactly is the public interest? Is it an interest in protecting the life of the unborn foetus? Is it an interest in securing the birth of healthy children? Frequent reference has been made to this vague but powerful notion, but with little detailed consideration of its content.

If, in the situation of maternal/foetal conflict, exceptions are to be permitted to the basic rule laid down in *Re T*, there must first be clear definition of the rights of the parties involved. Having defined these rights there should be consideration of how they are to be weighed in relation to each other. If a foetus has a right to life at the expense of another person, it is a remarkable right, in that it is superior to any legal right which the foetus will later have as a child.[42] It seems incongruous that the potential non-birth of a viable foetus is regarded as an exceptional circumstance which will justify the overriding of a refusal of consent, whereas the death of a living individual is not.

It is also surprising that the judge in *Re S*, in coming to this conclusion, cited as authority *Re AC* which on appeal upheld the principle of consent. It is difficult to avoid the conclusion that the judge in *Re S* was overcome by the emotion of the moment. He clearly sought support in the decision of *Re AC* but it must be assumed that he knew only of the original hearing – also conducted in the atmosphere of an emergency ward – and not of the much more calm and reasoned opinion of the appeal court. The Court of Appeals in *Re AC*, perhaps with the benefit of reflection long after both mother and child had died, returned quite firmly to the rational application of the law. The trial court had been wrong to decide the case on the basis of a conflict between woman and foetus. The Court of Appeals reaffirmed the rule that a competent individual is free to consent or to refuse consent to medical treatment and that the hospital and the law should respect the individual's choice. Where the individual was incompetent, the practice of substituted judgement should be used, whereby the court must attempt to discover what the individual would have wished had she or he been capable of choice. In making this substituted judgement, the court should have regard to the individual's previously expressed wishes, his or her personal beliefs and the views of his or her family. Wherever possible a decision should be made on the basis of the individual's life as a whole and not solely in the context of the immediate situation. The court left open the possibility that there may be exceptional circumstances in which refusal to consent could be overridden, but it made clear that the circumstances in *Re AC* had not fallen into this category. The question remains as to what these circumstances could be, if indeed such potential for an exception should be retained. If exceptions are to be made, their limits should be considered carefully in advance and not decided by a single judge in the heat of the moment.

In the use by the courts of duty of care and consent as methods of resolving maternal/foetal conflict it is clear that there are many unconsidered and unanswered issues. The hurried judgements suggest a frantic attempt to find some legal base for what is in effect a moral and personal decision. If the courts are to continue, and perhaps to increase, their involvement in the resolution of such disputes, there is an urgent need for greater consideration and clarification of the legal rules which they are to apply.

A Conflict Defused

The questions which are posed in the situation of conflict seem irresolvable. It may be, however, that by defining and refining legal elements of the conflict model, a set of concepts could be formulated by which the courts could adjudicate between mother and foetus.[43] A delictual/tortious duty of care, and an amended version of consent to medical treatment, might provide ways of regulating conflicts between pregnant woman and foetus. It might be argued that this is just another development of existing well established law.

Alternatively, it is submitted that the issues involved are much more complex than the easy label of maternal/foetal conflict suggests. This concise title contains a number of images and perceptions which should be challenged. It is misleading in many ways, none more so than in its suggestion that there is in fact a clear-cut dichotomy between mother and child. Instead of seeking to resolve maternal/foetal conflicts by defining more clearly the individual legal rights of the pregnant woman and the foetus, should we not question the construction of these so-called conflicts? This is an area of life, law and medicine which gives rise to dilemmas, some of which, it might be argued, are of our own making. We may struggle to resolve the conflict by resorting to legal adjudication, whereas we could instead reconsider the construction of the conflict. The conflict is presented as woman or child, all or nothing, life or death: a model of polarisation which contributes to the legal dilemma.

In this emotive context, the power of words is considerable. While the terms 'mother' and 'baby' have a comfortable and familiar sound, it should be recognised that we are in fact dealing with a pregnant woman and a foetus or embryo. When does a woman become a mother? A woman becomes a mother when she has a child and therefore the term maternal/foetal is a misnomer in that the child has not yet been born. While 'pregnant woman/foetal conflict' lacks symmetry it is a more accurate description and one which avoids the social perceptions of motherhood. A mother is defined in terms of her child. Mothers act for the good of their children; mothers make sacrifices, but a woman need not submit herself to these social constraints. It has been argued that parenting does not begin at birth but perhaps at the point when legal abortion is no longer available. At that point a woman has chosen to accept the responsibilities of motherhood. Most women will want to act in a way which is conducive to the healthy development of the foetus and it seems sensible to encourage education, counselling and care prior to birth which might help the woman to carry to term and to deliver a healthy child. To define the pregnant woman in terms of motherhood, however, contributes to the impression that, as an individual, she has become invisible.

The strongest image to emerge from the phrase 'maternal/foetal conflict' is that of the conflict, but where is this conflict of which the courts are told? The words are shocking in that they suggest a rejection of the expected mother and child relationship. Who are these women who refuse to accept their proper role? There may be women who deliberately choose to harm their foetus, but these are not the women who appear in the reported cases. Angela Carder is perhaps the most obvious example: she gave as one of her reasons for refusing a Caesarian section her concern that the foetus was not viable or that it would be born with severe disability. In *Re S* we can assume that the woman believed, in terms of her religion, that she was acting in the best interest of her foetus. These women are not fighting against their foetuses, they are in fact fighting for what they think is best.

It might, of course, be argued that certain beliefs are personal – for example, religious beliefs – and cannot be imposed on others. Or it might be argued that certain personal views or fears are so obviously ridiculous that they can be discounted. Where a woman acts in accordance with such opinions it should, however, be recognised that she is acting in what she considers to be her best interests and those of her foetus. To suggest that she is in conflict with her foetus is to misrepresent her intention. A woman who is seen as denying her foetus the possibility of life or of damaging its health is unlikely to receive the understanding of those who have the power to control or overrule her wishes. A woman, and in particular a mother, who is perceived as exercising her selfish rights is unlikely to win.

The conflict in many cases is not between woman and foetus but between woman and doctor. That, it might be argued, is a fairer fight; a fight which the woman might sometimes win. In the emotive terms of a struggle with her unborn child she stands little chance. In the few reported cases, the judges appear to defer to the superior knowledge of the doctors. Decisions are taken on the basis of medical judgements. 'Interests' are defined in terms of medical health. There is little recognition of emotional well-being. The adversarial attitude which emerges from the enforced Caesarian cases suggests a failure of communication. While woman and doctor may both be acting in the best interests of the foetus, there is a lack of agreement as to what those interests are. When the doctor seeks legal authority in 'the best interests' it is based on the assumption that those interests are as defined in clinical judgement. That displays an arrogance and a lack of understanding of the woman's life.

A conflict model tends to focus on the moment of emergency. The definition by the doctors of the situation as an emergency places extreme pressure on the judge to make an immediate decision. Caught up in the atmosphere of all or nothing, life or death, judges abandon all thoughts of legal reasoning and feel compelled to make heroic decisions. In many cases it should not be necessary to make decisions in such situations of hospital drama. Unforeseen crises may arise, but in many of the cases the problem has arisen because of the woman's personal views or beliefs, which could be ascertained at a much earlier stage in the pregnancy, thus allowing time for discussion, counselling and planning in a much calmer environment. Hospital ethics committees may provide a more suitable forum for the discussion and resolution of uncertainties as to how to treat.

There is some evidence of a rejection of the conflict model in favour of a greater level of communication and understanding between the doctor and the woman. This can be seen in the guidelines issued following *Re S* by the Royal College of Obstetricians and Gynaecologists. The guidelines focus on the common end of pregnancy and childbirth as being the entry of another individual into society. There is recognition of the respective roles of woman and doctor in this process and of their responsibilities.[44] Their tone represents a positive and co-operative approach. Where there is an apparent conflict, attempts to resolve it should be made by means of communication between the doctor and the woman, with the involvement of her family where appropriate. The emphasis is on both doctor and woman trying to explain and to understand each other's position. The doctor is reminded that the medical evidence on which he or she relies is 'seldom infallible' and that ultimately the choice of the woman should be respected.

To present these situations as maternal/foetal conflicts is to see them in isolation. The woman whose lifestyle is blamed for damage to her foetus may be bearing the responsibility for conditions which are not entirely within her control. An unhealthy environment, a dangerous job, an abusive partner[45] – these may be factors in the woman's lifestyle and yet, by concentrating on her as the obvious cause of harm, we may simply be finding an easy scapegoat. That is not to say that women should not be encouraged and assisted to provide the most sympathetic environment possible for the foetus, but by the law focusing on the very obvious link between woman and foetus there is a danger of blaming her for harm for which the responsibility should be shared. The conflict model, in particular in relation to surgical intervention, presents the court with an immediate conflict, a snapshot of the woman's life taken out of context.

Pregnancy and childbirth do not exist in isolation. They are events in a series of relationships – personal relationships, relationships between women and the medical profession, relationships between women and society – and, as with all relationships, they are based on communication. The conflict model stifles communication. In the presentation of the conflict the loudest voice, and sometimes the only voice, is that of the doctor. The foetus cannot speak and the woman is often not heard. In a dispute each side is closed to the words of the other.

The context of emergency provides no time for talking. As with medicine and law, communication will doubtless prove inadequate to resolve each dilemma, but it may in the process contribute to a better understanding of the interests of all those involved.

Notes

1   Owing to the lack of case law within England and Scotland it is difficult to discuss developments in terms of two separate jurisdictions. Where there are specific developments and differences within either system these will be identified, but the main comparison will be between the United Kingdom and the United States.
2   [1987] 1 A11 ER 20.
3   [1992] 4 A11 ER 671.
4   [1987] 1 A11 ER 20.
5   For discussion of the relevant statutory provision in Scotland, see A.B. Wilkinson and K.McK. Norrie, *Parent and Child*, Edinburgh: W. Green and Son, 1993, pp.116–18.
6   Children and Young Persons Act, s.1(2)(*a*).
7   [1987] 1 A11 ER 20, at p.28.
8   [1988] 2 A11 ER 193.
9   274 SE 2d 457 (Ga, 1981).
10 Ibid., at p.459.
11 For a discussion of this case, see D. Johnsen, 'A New Threat to Pregnant Women's Autonomy', 17 Hastings Center Report (1987), p.33. For a general discussion see S.A.M. McLean, *Women and Foetuses: Whose Rights?*, in Paper delivered to Royal College of Physicians and Surgeons.
12 Cal. Penal Code 270 (West Supp. 1986).
13 [1992] 4 A11 ER 671. For a discussion of how a similar issue might be treated under Scots law, see Wilkinson and Norrie, *Parent and Child*, pp.113–14.
14 Ibid., at p.672.
15 Ibid.
16 Ibid.
17 Ibid.
18 Ibid.
19 [1992] 4 A11 ER 649.
20 See note 12.
21 See discussion below.
22 274 SE 2d 457 (Ga, 1981).
23 For a discussion of court-ordered Caesarians in US states, see V.Kolder, J.Gallagher and M.Parsons, 'Court-Ordered Obstetrical Interventions', *The New England Journal of Medicine*, (1987), 1192.
24 301 NW 2d 869 (Mich, 1981).
25 Law Com., *Report on Injuries to Unborn Children* (1974); Scot. Law Com., *Report on Liability for Antenatal Injury* (1973).
26 Section 1(1).
27 Section 2.
28 For a discussion of the law, see Wilkinson and Norrie, *Parent and Child*, pp.101–4.
29 1993 SLT 624.
30 There is a discussion of 'personhood' in J.E.S.Fortin, 'Legal Protection for the Unborn Child', MLR (1988), 54.
31 1993 SLT 624, at p.632.
32 Ibid., at p.629.

33 Ibid., at p.632.
34 In Scots law it is assault and in English law, battery.
35 [1992] 4 A11 ER 649. For further discussion, see Chapter 3.
36 [1992] 4 A11 ER 649, at p.652.
37 Ibid., at p.653.
38 [1992] 4 A11 ER 671, at p.672.
39 For a discussion of the case, see K.Stern, 'Court-Ordered Caesarian Sections: In Whose Interests?', MLR (1993), 238.
40 [1992] 4 A11 ER 671, at p.672.
41 See, for example, *Re T*, above.
42 Neither Scots nor English law imposes any duty to rescue. See also *McFall* v. *Shimp* 10 Pa D & C (1978).
43 See, for an example of a model for resolving conflicts, A.M.Noble-Allgire, 'Court Ordered Cesarean Sections: A Judicial Standard for Resolving the Conflict between Fetal Interests and Maternal Rights', *The Journal of Legal Medicine* **10**, (1989), 211.
44 There is an interesting discussion of the concept of antenatal responsibilities by H.Draper in 'Women, Forced Caesarians and Antenatal Responsibilities', Feminist Legal Research Unit, University of Liverpool, Working Paper No.1, 1993.
45 There was evidence to suggest, for example, that Pamela Rae Stewart had been physically abused by her husband.

6 Wrongful Life and Wrongful Birth

PATRICIA M.A. BEAUMONT

Parents may seek to avoid the birth of a child for many reasons, including physical problems (for example, a further birth may be detrimental to the mother's health or the parents may have a genetic disease which the child might inherit) and social factors (such as wishing to avoid further burdening an already overcrowded planet, or being unable to afford further children without depriving the existing family). Failure to achieve this goal can either produce a healthy child, or one which is less than perfect and either way the parents may wish to be compensated for the damage which has been done to them by the arrival of a child, healthy or not, which they did not want. The child itself may also wish to be compensated, where it has been born damaged, for being forced to endure an often pain-filled, unpleasant existence.

Distinguishing Prenatal Injury From Wrongful Birth and Life Actions

Before considering wrongful birth and life actions it should be borne in mind that, although whatever agent has caused the damage to the child in a wrongful birth or life action has done so before birth, these actions are quite distinct from those for prenatal injury. The essence of prenatal injury claims is that the child, or his parents, allege that his injury was caused by a third party, for example a negligent motorist, prior to his birth.

The shift in attitude in the United States towards prenatal injury suits provides a useful study, since there have been many cases there, but few in the United Kingdom. Initially, a plaintiff injured before birth had no right of action. The first relevant case seems to have been *Dietrich v. Inhabitants of Northampton*,[1] where Oliver Wendell Holmes J., writing for the court, held that the foetus was not an independent person with standing to sue, basing this assertion mainly on the fact that the child was a part of the mother and not a separate legal entity when the damage was inflicted. One of the first instances where it was suggested that the action be allowed was the dissenting judgement of Boggs J. in *Allaire* v. *St. Luke's Hospital*,[2] where he stated that 'It is but natural justice that such an infant, if born alive, should be allowed to maintain an action in the courts for injuries so wrongly committed upon its person while so in the womb of the mother.'[3]

The action was first actually recognised in *Bonbrest* v. *Kotz et al*,[4] where the courts agreed with the dissent in Allaire and damages were awarded. The judgement was influenced by a decision in Canada a few years before (*Montreal Tramways* v. *Léveillé*[5]) which had held that when a child, not actually born at the time of the accident, was subsequently born alive it would have all the rights of action which it would have had if actually in existence at the time of the accident to the mother. As a result of *Bonbrest* all American courts since 1946 have held that a child can recover damages for prenatal injury. Some cases have even allowed recovery for damage which occurred before conception, the first being *Jorgensen* v. *Meade Johnson Laboratories, Inc*,[6] where the mother took birth control pills prior to conception which altered her chromosomal make-up to such an extent that she gave birth to twins with Down's Syndrome and the US Court of Appeals considered that a cause of action did lie. Similarly, in *Renslow* v. *Mennonite Hospital*,[7] the mother received the wrong type of blood several years before the defendant was conceived. This resulted in the child's brain, nervous system and several other organs being damaged due to haemolytic disease. In finding a duty on the part of the defender, the court emphasised the foreseeability of the injury to the child.

The position at common law was unclear until the cases of *B* v. *Islington Health Authority*[8] and *De Martell* v. *Merton and Sutton Health Authority*,[9] both of which concluded that the defendants were liable in tort to the plaintiffs for injuries inflicted prenatally. ('B' became *Burton* v. *Islington Health Authority* and the cases were jointly appealed[10] and the appeals rejected.) However, by the time these cases were heard the absence of case law had already led to the passing of the Congenital Disabilities (Civil Liability) Act 1976 which, having come into force on 22 July 1976, applies to all births after 21 July 1976 (the children in *Burton* and *De Martell* had been born before that date, therefore the statute did not apply) and under which the defendant is liable to the child only if liable to the parent in respect of the act causing the injury. This means that the child's action is totally derivative from rights owing to the parents; if no duty is owed to them, the child cannot sue.

There is an interesting distinction here with Scots law which, since it is civilian in its origins, has a tradition of working from principle rather than from precedent, as is the tendency in England. The Scottish Law Commission, in its Report on Liability for Antenatal Injury,[11] concluded that, by applying existing principles of law, and notwithstanding an absence of authority pointing in any direction, the Scottish courts would admit the right of a child who has been born alive to recover damages for antenatal injury: 'although there is no express Scottish decision on the point, a right to reparation would, on existing principles, be accorded by Scots law to a child for harm wrongfully occasioned to it while in its mother's womb, provided it was born alive'.[12] So, unlike the English position, the right is not derivative. It is the child's own right and the parents' behaviour (for example, knowingly undertaking a risk) is irrelevant. It would seem, at first glance, therefore that there would be no problem if a child in Scotland sought to sue its mother if she was the person who had inflicted the injuries.

A relevant case has subsequently occurred in Scotland (*Hamilton* v. *Fife Health Board*[13]) where injuries were inflicted on a child, in the course of its birth, from which it subsequently died. It was held that 'once the foetus ceases on birth to be a foetus and becomes a person there is a concurrence of injuria and damnum and the newly born child had a right to sue the person whose breach of duty has resulted in the child's loss. The coming into existence of that right to sue does not depend upon the application of any fiction. It depends upon the neighbourhood doctrine of *Donoghue* v. *Stevenson*.'[14,15] It is interesting to note that one requirement before a child can sue is that it must be born alive. Only the parents can sue where prenatal injuries have caused a still birth; the infant's estate cannot do so. Somewhat oddly, it might, therefore, be less expensive to inflict fatal injuries upon a foetus from which it dies, rather than merely to damage it.

The major distinction between prenatal injuries as just discussed and wrongful birth or wrongful life actions is that the defendant in the latter cases did not cause the damage from which the foetus, when born, suffers. Rather, these injuries will have been caused by some genetic defect, or illness, such as the mother becoming infected with rubella in the early stages of pregnancy. As these actions have developed, various terminologies have been used to describe them, usually based on the factual circumstances prevailing. When the action is being raised by the parents and where the child has been born healthy, 'wrongful pregnancy' tends to be the term used. This relates to an unplanned conception which has occurred as the result of another's negligence (such as where a birth control prescription was negligently filled with tranquillisers[16]). 'Wrongful conception' is the term used specifically where a negligently performed sterilisation has resulted in the conception.[17] Where the child has been born damaged in some predictable way, the claim by the parents is one for 'wrongful birth'. That is, had they been correctly advised or had the appropriate tests been correctly performed, the child would never have been born. When the action is being raised by a child which has been born with handicaps then the action is one for 'wrongful life': had the defendant not been negligent, the plaintiff child would never have been born.

Wrongful Birth

The history of the development of these types of action in the United Kingdom has been dealt with elsewhere;[18] it is sufficient here to say that the position of the *parents* in relation to unwanted children in the United Kingdom is now clear: an action can be raised and compensation will be awarded in meritorious cases. This has come about despite extensive judicial attempts to deny such actions, based on notions of public policy. It is worth looking at some of these policy-based objections, since many of them are also used to deny the rights of a child involved in a wrongful life action. A typical example was *Udale* v. *Bloomsbury Area Health Authority*,[19] where Jupp J. was of the view that 'on the grounds of public policy the plaintiff's claims ...should not be allowed'.[20] The factors which he took into account included the undesirability of the child discovering that his birth was a mistake; a plaintiff who loved and cared for her child would get little damages, as opposed to one who was bitter about the birth; medical men would be under pressure to advise abortions; and it is the assumption in our culture that a child is a blessing. Jupp J. asserted that there 'should be rejoicing, not dismay, that the surgeon's mistake bestowed the gift of life on the child'.[21] The arguments against these assumptions are self-evident and were enunciated in *Thake and Another* v. *Maurice*[22] by Peter Pain J.,[23] who quoted *Sherlock* v. *Stillwater Clinic*[24] to illustrate the US position and then, before considering and rejecting the points raised in *Udale*, decided that 'In these circumstances I have to make up my mind on first principles.'[25] Surely this is, on the whole, what judges are supposed to do, leaving policy decisions to parliament? Pearson J. pointed out in *Public Health Trust* v. *Brown*,[26] 'I am confident that the majority recognises that any decision based upon a notion of public policy is one about which reasonable persons may disagree' and he considered that judges should be more 'trusted as interpreters of the law than as expounders of what is called public policy'.[27] The policy of the state, as reflected in the lawfulness of abortion and sterilisation, is to recognise that a healthy baby does not evoke in all parties concerned the rejoicing assumed by Jupp J. in *Udale*. The child may have cause to rejoice, but not necessarily the parents confronted with yet another mouth to feed. A healthy baby is not always a blessing and the policy of the state is to provide the widest freedom of choice to plan a family and, if this planning goes wrong, to provide for abortion where the circumstances permit it.[28] As summarised in *Sherlock* v. *Stillwater Clinic*,[29] 'The use of various birth control methods by millions of Americans demonstrates an acceptance of the family-planning concept as an integral aspect of the modern marital relationship, so that today it must be acknowledged that the time-honoured command "be fruitful and multiply" has not only lost contemporary significance to a growing number of potential parents but is contrary to public policies embodied in the statutes encouraging family planning.'[30]

The kind of policy-based reasons put forward in the extensive US catalogue of cases in an attempt to justify rejection of birth-related actions (many of which reasons have been adopted subsequently in the English cases) have included the following:

1   *The sanctity of life and the desirability of humans procreating.* As was said in *Cockrum* v. *Baumgartner*,[31] 'the benefit of life should not be outweighed by the expense of supporting it. Respect for life and the rights proceeding from it are at the heart of our legal system.'[32]

2   *No 'injury' has been sustained by the parents.* This head is, of course, associated with the previous notion, that the bestowal of life on a child is always a blessing and never a detriment. It can either be raised to thwart an action at the outset – no injury was sustained by the pursuer so there is no cause of action – or it can go towards mitigation of the damages finally awarded. In any negligence action courts will often have to weigh up the damage caused and balance that against any benefits gained and the sum subsequently awarded will depend on the extent to which these elements outweigh each other. For example, an abortion performed only because the foetus was believed to be damaged may fail. If a healthy child was then born it is unlikely that the parents would be regarded as having been damaged, a healthy child having been born where a defective one was anticipated.

One issue which this raises is, should the parents be under a duty to mitigate their damage, assuming that it is possible to do so? (It may not be so if, for example, the pregnancy was too far advanced to permit a legal abortion and that was the only method of 'mitigation' available.) In *Emeh* v. *Kensington, Chelsea and Fulham Area Health Authority*,[33] it was held at first instance by Park J. that the plaintiff's failure to seek an abortion amounted to a *novus actus interveniens* which eclipsed the defender's negligence: 'her own unacceptable reasons for not seeking an abortion have convinced me that, in truth, she elected to allow the pregnancy to continue because she wanted to bear another child, and from that time onwards her pregnancy was not unwanted.'[34] However, on appeal[35] it was questioned whether the plaintiff's conduct was so unreasonable as to eclipse the defendant's wrongdoing. It was felt that the degree of unreasonable conduct would have to be extremely high and 'Save in the most exceptional circumstances, I cannot think it right that the court should ever declare it unreasonable for a woman to decline to have an abortion'.[36] It will be interesting to see, in the future, just what circumstances will be considered exceptional enough for the courts to hold it right that a woman should be expected to have an abortion.

3   *The risk of fraudulent claims.* Where the claim relates to the birth of a normal healthy child, the court may have difficulty in deciding whether the parents truly did not intend to have the child. For example, in *Gold* v. *Haringey Health Authority*,[37] the parents went on to have another child after the birth of the one which was allegedly unwanted. It is unlikely that this factor could be invoked in the situation where a severely disabled child has been born: how does one fake the symptoms of Down's Syndrome? The aspect of fraudulence could arise where the parents, with the aid of hindsight, claim that they would have aborted the child, when in fact this is not so. It should be borne in mind that the evidence of the parents, even when given in good faith and with all honesty, may be somewhat coloured. As was said of the mother in *Gregory* v. *Pembrokeshire Health Authority*,[38] 'the objectivity of an honest witness can fail in circumstances of stress and it serves as a warning to me that I must not regard Mrs Gregory's evidence as paramount and outweighing all the other evidence if that evidence is to the contrary'.[39] Doctors here had failed to tell an expectant mother (with a family history of Down's Syndrome) that an amniocentesis had not produced sufficient cultures to determine if the child had Down's Syndrome, which it did. The court considered that the doctors were not liable for the costs of bringing up the child because the mother had failed to prove that she would have had an abortion if the negligence had not occurred.

4   *Damages.* Initially there was great reluctance to allow parents to recover more than the damages directly associated with the pregnancy, delivery and any subsequent resterilisation, if the initial failure of such was what had led to the birth. However, it is now settled that defendants will be liable for all reasonable expenses incurred in the education and upkeep of the unplanned child and it has even been suggested that, if the child's siblings had been sent to expensive boarding schools, a very substantial claim for the educational costs of the child of a reasonably wealthy family might have to be met.[40]

The scope for judges to impose their own personal sentiments on parties to an action by describing it as public policy would seem to be unduly wide. Whether the birth of an unwanted, although healthy, child to a particular family is a blessing could be open to proof by the leading of expert evidence to that effect by the relevant social scientists in the fields involved. To decide a case on the basis of pronouncements such as that of Ognall J. in *Jones* v. *Berkshire Area Health Authority*[41] is unfair.

There he evinced surprise that the law allowed a mother to claim damages for the 'blessing' of a healthy child and justified his attitude by stating: 'Certain it is that those who are afflicted with a handicapped child or who long desperately to have a child at all and are denied that good fortune would regard an award for this sort of contingency with a measure of astonishment.'[42] Why should the judge's assumptions about the sentiments of these unfortunate people be of any relevance? No doubt expert evidence could be led to establish that individuals who have suffered such a misfortune might tend to take a biased view of the plaintiffs' situation in finding themselves with a healthy, but unwanted, child. On the other hand, however, it could equally be said that a single parent who has little in the way of financial resources, and is living in poor conditions with a very large number of children might view with envy those with no children, a comfortable lifestyle and few material worries. They may base this opinion on their own experience: that bringing up children is not the idyllic pastime child- and baby-oriented magazines would have the public believe. Although evidence which might be led to justify either element of this, or any similar argument, could never be conclusive (research on these types of subject is presumably continuous), at least statements such as Ognall J.'s, instead of arising as they currently do from persons with no expertise, could be properly led in evidence and thereby opened to adversarial examination and, if appropriate, would be discredited. Why should the beliefs and opinions of what is, in effect, a layman (with all of the inherent prejudices which everyone possesses) be used as a basis upon which to decide what principles of law are applicable in any given case? By allowing cases to be decided on the untutored speculations of judges, the law puts itself into a position where decisions become a matter of pot luck. Contrast the views taken by Jupp J. in *Udale* and Peter Pain J. in *Thake*. Only a year had passed between the two judgements, during which time it would seem that no earth-shattering changes had occurred in English society which could be said to account for so-called 'public policy' in the former case not allowing parts of the pursuer's claim, yet not preventing a claim in the latter case. Jupp J. paid particular heed to the undesirability of a child discovering that its birth had been publicly declared a mistake by the court; Mrs Udale would get little in damages because her joy at the birth would offset any financial disadvantages; medical men would be under subconscious pressure to encourage abortions; and finally it is assumed that the birth of a child is always a blessing. Peter Pain J., on the other hand, was able to counter these assertions by considering that the child had been warmly received by the family and in the future, when she came to consider the judgement, she would welcome it as having made life easier for her family. The joy the parents felt was of their own making and therefore the claims for the costs of the child's support and for the birth remained. So far as doctors feeling pressurised into advising abortion is concerned, in view of the divisions within the medical profession this argument had little force. Finally, the assumption that the birth of a child is always a blessing may have been part of our culture in the past, but was not an assumption that could be made today.

Perhaps more heed should be paid in general to the dictum of Lord Scarman in *McLoughlin* v. *O'Brian*,[43] where he stated:

> Policy considerations will have to be weighed; but the objective of the judges is the formulation of principle. And, if principle inexorably requires a decision which entails a degree of policy risk, the court's function is to adjudicate according to principle, leaving policy curtailment to the judgement of Parliament. Here lies the true role of the two law-making institutions in our constitution. By concentrating on principle the judges can keep the common law alive, flexible and consistent, and can keep the legal system clear of policy problems which neither they, nor the forensic process which it is their duty to operate, are equipped to resolve. If principle leads to results which are thought to be socially unacceptable, Parliament can legislate to draw a line or map out a new path.[44]

Legislation is the course which has been adopted in some parts of the United States so as to avoid these types of judicial wanderings,[45] and a fairly typical example is to be found in Utah: 'A cause of action shall not arise, and damages shall not be awarded, on behalf of any person, based on the claim that but for the act or omission of another, a person would not have been permitted to have been born alive but would have been aborted.'[46] There has been a judicial 'test' of such laws in Minnesota, in *Hickman* v. *Group Health Plan, Inc*,[47] where the Supreme Court upheld as constitutional a statutory ban on wrongful birth/life actions.

There have been even fewer Scottish cases than English, but the view of the Scottish courts seems also to be that there are no grounds to prevent damages being awarded where a child is born as a result of the negligence of another. In *Janice Allan* v. *Greater Glasgow Health Board*,[48] Lord Cameron considered the leading English cases[49] and concluded that there was no reason not to award damages for the pain, suffering and so on associated with childbirth and also could find no general bar to claiming child-rearing costs under the ordinary principles of law in Scotland.

Wrongful Life

Although, as has just been seen, the position with respect to actions raised by the parents is now settled, the same is not the case where the child itself raises the action. The essence of the parents' claim is that they were damaged by the infliction of something which they did not want; the child's claim is that, but for the negligence of the defendant, it would not have to live the unpleasant life that has been inflicted upon it. No claim is being made that the defendant is responsible for having caused the child's injuries (as is the claim put forward in a prenatal injury case[50]), but rather that he is responsible for the child having to endure life in its injured state. Had the parents been adequately informed of the child's condition, they could have aborted it. From the child's viewpoint this would mean that it was not burdened with a life afflicted by the disabilities of which it is complaining.

Children raising these actions have invariably been born suffering from physical and/or mental handicap. Attempts were made in the past in the United States by healthy children to claim that their status in life was such that they would be better off not having been born. The first of these, *Zepeda* v. *Zepeda*,[51] concerned a child, born illegitimate, suing its father on the basis that it would be better not to have been born than to endure life as a bastard. This case, which would better be called 'dissatisfied life', and others like it,[52] have received no sympathy from the courts.

As with wrongful birth actions, there is a considerably longer history of wrongful life actions in the United States than in the United Kingdom, a history which has been described elsewhere.[53] For the most part the actions have been unsuccessful[54] for substantially the same policy-based reasons put forward for initially refusing to acknowledge wrongful birth actions.[55] There have, however, been a few successful cases, the first being *Curlender* v. *Bio-Science Laboratories*.[56] The plaintiff's parents had consulted the defendants to arrange genetic tests to ascertain if they were carriers of Tay-Sachs disease. These tests were allegedly negligently performed and, in reliance on the erroneous information, the parents had the plaintiff, who was born afflicted with the disease. The court allowed the action, dismissing the 'floodgates' argument and also trying the case on legal principles and not 'metaphysics': 'The concept of public policy has played an important role in this developing field of law. Public policy, as perceived by most courts, has been utilised as the basis for denying recovery;... dissents have emphasised that considerations of public policy should include regard for social welfare as affected by careful genetic counselling and medical procedures.'[57] Both general and special damages were awarded and the court even suggested that punitive damages could be awarded if malice, fraud or oppression on the defendant's part could be proved.[58] However, the scope of the action was subsequently limited in *Turpin* v. *Sortini*,[59] where the specialist defendant assured parents that their daughter's hearing was normal, whereas she was actually stone-deaf. Partly as a result of these reassurances, they had a second daughter, found to be similarly afflicted. Special damages were allowed to cover various specific medical expenses, but not general damages for pain, suffering and so on. It would seem, however, that '*Curlender* was, and remains, the prevailing law of California'.[60] These cases were followed in Washington state in *Harbeson* v. *Parke-Davies Inc*,[61] which analysed the wrongful life action within the traditional tort framework, found that the defendant's negligence had caused the plaintiff's injuries and awarded special damages, but again not general damages, on the ground that valuation between life and non-life was inestimable. In 1984, the state of New Jersey became the third to recognise the action, in *Procanik by Procanik* v. *Cillo*.[62]

Despite the above cases it would appear that judicial attitudes to this type of action are still heavily weighted against them. In *Bruggeman* v. *Schimke*,[63] the court considered that actions for wrongful life were not being increasingly recognised (as was asserted by the plaintiff's counsel) and any notion that there was a legal right to be dead, rather than alive with disabilities, was contrary to the laws of the state.

The only relevant English case has been *McKay* v. *Essex Area Health Authority*,[64] where the court refused to acknowledge that the child had a right to bring an action for wrongful life for reasons similar to those put forward regularly in many American cases. The court could not accept that a duty of care to the foetus could involve a legal obligation to terminate its existence.[65] It also considered that the action would make further inroads into the notion of the sanctity of human life, which would be contrary to public policy,[66] and finally, they regarded the difficulties of assessing damages as overwhelming – how could a judge compare 'afterlife' or 'non-existence' with the injured child's life?[67]

The court in *McKay* was influenced by the Congenital Disabilities (Civil Liability) Act 1976 which it considered deprived any child born on or after 22 July 1976 of a wrongful life cause of action[68] and therefore concluded that the case raised no point of general public importance. For example, Ackner, L.J. considered that the wording of s.1(2)(*b*) meant that a child could have no right of action for wrongful life.[69] However, an alternative view has been put forward that a claim for wrongful life would still be sustainable at common law because 'the doctor's liability does not arise "in respect of disabilities" themselves, since he had no part in their cause or effect. His liability arises solely due to his failure to advise on the unborn child's potential quality of life, in the light of those disabilities'.[70]

As increasing emphasis is placed on the quality of life which an individual leads, so the question will often arise as to when the burdens imposed by a person's condition become so great as to outweigh any benefits which being alive has to offer. One way of answering this question is to consider briefly decisions which have been taken in cases where the person is alive, but wishes to achieve death – death being seen as preferable to existence in the prevailing condition. An individual has a right to self-determination and this can include refusing to consent to treatment perceived as being, according to the patient's or his representative's perceptions, futile. It can be futile either in the sense that the patient is dying and no treatment is going to prevent this, or futile in the sense that the patient's quality of life is so poor that they would rather not be burdened with such an existence. An example of the latter can be found in *Bouvia* v. *Superior Court*.[71] Elizabeth Bouvia was a quadriplegic, totally unable to care for herself, and she had to rely on others to wash, feed, turn her and help with all bodily functions. She had to lie flat in bed, she suffered from degenerative and severely crippling arthritis and was in continual pain to the extent that a tube permanently attached to her chest administered periodic doses of morphine which relieved some of the pain. Against her will, a nasogastric tube had been inserted which would probably keep her alive for 15 to 20 years, and the court considered that it was not the policy of the state to inflict such an ordeal upon anyone. It was, therefore, held that her right to refuse medical treatment entitled her to the immediate removal of the nasogastric tube. As was stated by Lord Keith in the UK case of *Airedale NHS Trust* v. *Bland*,[72] 'it is unlawful, so as to constitute both a tort and the crime of battery, to administer medical treatment to an adult, who is conscious and of sound mind, without consent. Such a person is completely at liberty to decline to undergo treatment, even if the result of his doing so will be that he will die.'[73]

It seems incongruous, then, that it is possible to make a choice between existence and non-existence by refusing to undergo treatment, yet this choice is refused to those who assert that they have been deprived of the opportunity of making this choice (albeit by proxy) by preferring not to have been born. If it is permissible to prefer death (non-existence) and exercise this preference by refusing treatment, with legal remedies available to back up attempts to thwart the exercise of this choice, why should it not also be permissible to prefer non-existence (abortion) and, since exercising this preference by choosing to be aborted rather than born has been denied the child, why should it not seek compensation?

In the case of a foetus this choice would, of course, have to be exercised by proxy, just as it is in the case of a comatose adult. When presented with a dilemma such as that posed by Tony Bland, the court was prepared to concede that, where you have a permanently insensate being with no cognitive capacity, 'it is difficult, if not impossible, to make any relevant comparison between continued existence and the absence of it ... it must be a matter of complete indifference whether he lives or dies'.[74] The courts, in cases concerning discontinuation of medical treatment, are prepared to compare existence and non-existence (that is, death) and guess that it is better not to exist, yet with wrongful life cases one of the major grounds for refusing to recognise the actions is that the distinction between existence and non-existence cannot be measured. As was stated in *McKay v. Essex AHA*,[75] 'The court then has to compare the state of the plaintiff with non-existence, of which the court can know nothing; this I regard as an impossible task',[76] and even if they could measure it, 'It is basic to the human condition to seek life and to hold on to it however heavily burdened. ...Our felt intuition of human nature tells us he would almost surely choose life with defects against no life at all. For the living there is hope, but for the dead there is none.'[77]

Effectively, the courts in the Bland type of case are prepared to concede that it may be better not to exist, yet they are denying that this may be so by rejecting wrongful life actions. Children involved in wrongful life actions are the only ones who cannot decide, it would appear, that they would like their lives terminated (when still a foetus); that is, that they would prefer to have been aborted than to enter upon a life with whatever handicaps they have. The next nearest category to them is the defective neonate who may, again on the judgement of proxy decision-makers, have his or her life terminated. What underlies decisions concerning whether or not to terminate the life of a neonate, or any other person, is what it is perceived will be their 'quality of life' should the available treatment be utilised. In the case of severely damaged, and often dying, children the courts will order whatever treatment is in the child's best interests, weighing up the adverse effects of treatment against any advantages which may be forthcoming. Where there is any doubt as to the outcome of this balancing, it would appear that the child will be given the benefit of the doubt and the treatment ordered. As Dunn L.J. said in *Re B (a minor)(wardship: medical treatment)*,[78] 'the court's first and paramount consideration is the welfare of this unhappy little baby ... There is no evidence at all as to the quality of life which the child may expect. ... the child should be put into the same position as any other mongol child.'[79]

As opposed to this type of case where there is uncertainty as to the outcome, or to the type of case where there will be clear benefit from the treatment, there will always be cases where all treatment is expected to be futile. In analysing the 'best interests of the infant' the President's Commission Report, 'Deciding to Forego Life-Sustaining Treatment',[80] stated: 'Clearly futile therapies. When there is no therapy that can benefit an infant, as in anencephaly or certain severe cardiac deformities, a decision by surrogates and providers not to try predictably futile endeavours is ethically and legally justifiable. Such therapies do not help the child, are sometimes painful for the infant (and probably distressing to the parents), and offer no reasonable probability of saving life for a substantial period.'[81]

If these are good enough reasons for allowing the non-treatment of a neonate, an actual live child, knowing that this will inevitably lead to its death, could similar criteria not be used when assessing whether a child involved in a wrongful life suit, whilst still only a foetus, should have been aborted? If the answer is that he does not fall within the category where, if a neonate, his life would be preserved, then surely he could have grounds for claiming that he would have been better off not being born and consequently justified in raising an action when he is born? After all, as Lord Donaldson M.R. stated in *Re J (a minor)(wardship: medical treatment)*,[82] 'What is in issue in these cases is not a right to impose death, but a right to choose a course of action which will fail to avert death. ... the choice is that of the parents or court if, by reason of his age, the child cannot make the choice and it is a choice which must be made solely *on behalf* of the child and in what the court or parents conscientiously believe to be his best interests'.[83] Where a child would have been aborted before being born with handicaps which would bring him or her within the above category, but owing to the negligence of a health care provider a successful abortion has not been performed, surely he or she has been damaged? If there are 'extreme cases in which the court is entitled to say: "The life which this treatment would prolong would be so cruel as to be intolerable" ... the court is entitled in the best interests of the child to say that deliberate steps should not be taken artificially to prolong its miserable life span.'[84] In other words, if parents or courts, can, on behalf of a live child, decide that it would be better off not continuing to live then surely, on the basis of s.1(1)(*d*) of the Abortion Act 1967, they can also make that same decision on behalf of a foetus which if born 'would suffer from such physical and mental abnormalities as to be seriously handicapped'. If the child, via the parents, is thwarted in its attempt not to be introduced to an often pain-filled existence, why should it not successfully sue? After all, a competent adult is allowed to refuse life-saving treatment if he chooses;[85] neonates can have such decisions made on their behalf (as on occasion can other incompetent patients), so why should a foetus, which in the eyes of the law is not even a human being (with all of the rights accruing to such), be the only form of (quasi) human life being denied this opportunity? If more attention was paid to the interests of the foetus in relation to the working of the Abortion Act, instead of basing the right to an abortion solely on the well-being of the mother or of any existing family, there might not be such a problem. The mother may seek to avoid the encumbrance of a defective child by ensuring it is not born; why should not the subject of the defects be able to avoid such encumbrances also? The child, when it is born alive, is the one who must live with the deformities; the parents can alleviate the daily pressure on themselves by employing help or putting the child into care; and eventually (depending upon the likely duration of the child's life), the parents could predecease the child – and all the while the child continues to live with its handicaps, day in and day out.

By denying the right to a wrongful life action the courts are under-mining the general principle that individuals have the right to control their own destinies. Those faced with a poor quality of life are allowed to choose death, yet a plaintiff who is claiming wrongful life is not allowed to assert that he would have preferred death (by means of being aborted). There seems no logical reason why the courts cannot use the same criteria which they use when deciding whether to permit the ter-mination of life-sustaining treatment to decide if a wrongful life pursuer has such a poor quality of life that he or she would be better off never having been born.

It has been stated in the United States that allowing a claim based on a failure to abort would be against the basic principle of tort law which is to protect the plaintiff from wrongs, and the greatest wrong is to cause another person's death.[86] Related to this is one reason exten-sively proposed for denying wrongful life actions: that it undermines the notion of the sanctity of life. 'To impose such a duty [that is, abortion] towards the child would, in my opinion, make a further inroad on the sanctity of human life which would be contrary to public policy. It would mean regarding the life of a handicapped child as not only less valuable than the life of a normal child, but so much less valuable that it is not worth preserving.'[87] Surely this lesser value is already placed on such lives by regarding them as prime targets in the abortion legislation? Also, need such laden language as 'valuable' have been used? The life may not be worth preserving because it is so painful and grossly unpleasant – that is what makes it less valuable.

It could be said that, if the argument is followed to its logical conclusion, the child in a wrongful life action should not be asking for damages, but should be asking to be killed, as, in effect was Elizabeth Bouvia when she sought to have her nasogastric tube removed. Death, and not compensation, would seem to be the obvious remedy. However, a parallel could be drawn here with cases such as *Emeh*.[88] Just as it would be generally unreasonable to expect a woman to have a pregnancy terminated and she can therefore be compensated for the burden of an unwanted child, so it could also be said that it is generally unreason-able to expect a person to have his or her life terminated and therefore that person should be compensated for the unwanted burden of living a life in an afflicted state. So, since there is logically no obligation on the child to seek death (just as there is no obligation on a woman to abort), there would seem to be no reason to deny a remedy in a wrongful life action.

In conclusion, actions which involved damage to a foetus were initially rejected by the judiciary but, with the exception of wrongful life actions, this attitude has largely changed. Actions brought by the parents, whether in relation to prenatal injury or to wrongful birth, are now largely accepted as valid causes of action, having initially been rejected on the grounds that they were against public policy. These notions of public policy seem to have been very far-reaching, and in cases such as *Udale* and *Thake* quite contradictory: what one judge regarded as being against public policy was not viewed thus by all of his contemporaries. Actions brought by children are still frowned on, again largely for reasons of public policy based primarily on the notion that life with disabilities is better than no life at all. There seems some inconsistency between this attitude and that taken towards severely damaged individuals who can succeed in having medical treatment discontinued, knowing that this will lead to their death. No life, that is death, is seen in situations such as the *Bland* type of case as better than living with certain kinds of disability. Logically, in order to maintain some consistency of approach, any patient in need of medical treatment should be denied the right to make any sort of measurement between life and death, as is the wrongful life pursuer, and should be compelled to undergo treatment. It could be that judges should avoid basing decisions on what they perceive to be policy: instead of making policy statements, they could perhaps leave the formulation of such to Parliament.

Notes

1   138 Mass. 14 (1884).
2   56 NE 638 (1900).
3   Ibid., at p.642.
4   65 F Supp. 138 (DDC 1946).
5   [1933] 4 DLR 337.
6   483 F 2d 237 (1973).
7   367 NE 2d 1250 (lll 1977).
8   [1991] 1 QB 638.
9   [1992] 3 A11 ER 820.
10 [1992] 3 A11 ER 833.
11 Scot Law Com. No.30, (1973) Cmnd. 5371.
12 Ibid., at para.19.
13 1993 SLT 624 [1993] 4 Med LR 201.
14 [1993] 4 Med LR 201 at p.206, per Lord McCluskey.
15 The parties brought a further action based on Mrs Hamilton's personal injuries and the death of the child; it was dismissed, however, being time-barred by the Prescription and Limitation (Scotland) Act 1973: as yet unreported decision of TG Coutts Q.C., sitting as temporary judge, 27 January 1995.
16 *Troppi* v. *Scarfe* 186 NW 2d 511 (Mich 1971).
17 *Emeh* v. *Kensington, Chelsea and Fulham Area Health Authority* [1985] QB 1012.
18 B. Dickens, 'Wrongful birth and life, wrongful death before birth, and wrongful law', in S.A.M. McLean (ed.), *Legal Issues in Human Reproduction*; Aldershot: Gower Publishing Company Limited, 1989. C.R. Symmons, 'Policy factors in actions for wrongful birth', MLR **50**, (1987), 269.

19   [1983] 2 A11 ER 522.
20   Ibid., at p.531.
21   Ibid., at p.531.
22   [1984] 2 A11 ER 513.
23   Ibid., at p.526.
24   Ibid., at p.524.
25   Ibid., at p.526.
26   388 So 2d 1084 (1980).
27   Ibid., at p.1086.
28   For example, within the terms of the Abortion Act 1967 or the Human Fertilisation and Embryology Act 1990.
29   260 NW 2d 169.
30   At p.175, per Rogosheske J.
31   447 NE 2d 385.
32   Ibid., at p.389.
33   (1983) *The Times*, 3 January.
34   Ibid.
35   [1984] 3 A11 ER 1044.
36   Ibid., at p.1053, per Slade L.J.
37   [1987] 2 A11 ER 888.
38   [1989] 1 Med LR 81.
39   Ibid., at p.86, per Rougier J.
40   *Allen* v. *Bloomsbury Health Authority* [1993] 1 A11 ER 651.
41   Unreported. Transcript 84/NJ/5283, 2 July, 1986.
42   Quoted in *Gold* v. *Haringey Health Authority* [1987] 2 A11 ER 888, per Lloyd J. at p.890.
43   [1982] 2 A11 ER 298.
44   Ibid., at p.310.
45   For example, South Dakota (S.D. Codified Laws Ann. §21-55-2) or Missouri (Miss. Stat. Ann. §188.130).
46   Utah Code Ann. §78-11-24.
47   396 NW 2d 10 (1986).
48   Unreported. Court of Session: Outer House, 25 November 1993.
49   For example, *Udale, Emeh, Thake*.
50   For further discussion, see above, p.100.
51   190 NE 2d 849.
52   *Williams* v. *State* 223 NE 2d 343.
53   T.J. Dawe, 'Wrongful Life: Time for a "Day in Court"', Ohio State LJ, **51**, (1990), 473.
54   For example, *Gleitman* v. *Cosgrove* 227 A 2d 689 (1967).
55   For further discussion see above, p.103.
56   106 Cal. App. 3d 811.
57   Ibid., at p.826.
58   Ibid., at p.831.
59   643 P 2d 954.
60   Ibid., at p.966, per Mosk J. dissenting.
61   656 P 2d 483.
62   478 A 2d 755.
63   718 P 2d 635 (Kan 1986).
64   [1982] 2 A11 ER 771 (CA).
65   Ibid., at p.781.
66   Ibid., at p.781.
67   Ibid., at p.782.
68   Mary McKay was born on 15 August 1975.

69 [1982] 1 A11 ER 771 (CA), at p.786.
70 J.E.S. Fortin, 'Is the "Wrongful Life" Action Really Dead?', JSWL (1987), 306.
71 (1986) 225 Cal Rptr 297 (Cal.CA).
72 [1993] 1 A11 ER 821 and [1993] 4 Med LR 39.
73 [1993] 4 Med LR 39, at p.54.
74 Ibid., at p.55, per Lord Keith.
75 See above, note 64.
76 Ibid., at p.790, per Griffiths L.J.
77 See above, note 54.
78 [1981] 1 WLR 1421 (CA).
79 Ibid., at p.1424.
80 President's Commission for the Study of Ethical Problems in Medicine and Biomedical and Behavioral Research, US Government Printing Office, 1983.
81 Ibid., at pp.217–23.
82 [1990] 2 Med LR 67.
83 Ibid., at p.71.
84 Ibid., at p.76.
85 *Re T (adult: refusal of medical treatment)* [1992] 4 A11 ER 649, at pp.652–3, per Lord Donaldson M.R.
86 *Stewart* v. *Long Island College Hospital* 296 NYS 2d 41 (1968).
87 See McKay, note 64 above, at p.781, per Stephenson L.J.
88 See note 17, above.

7 Contemporary Issues in Organ Transplantation

J.K. MASON, *University of Edinburgh*

The majority of contemporary issues in transplantation therapy stem from the single problem which has beset the programme since its inception – the gap between the demand for and the availability of transplantable organs.[1] Despite the fact that some 70 per cent of British people say they would donate their organs if needed, many have an inherent distrust of transplantation.[2] This goes deeper than the fear of death and dying. Transplantation is not seen as being wholly beneficent but is, rather, a procedure that is clouded by misfortune. The apocryphal surgeon complaining that the use of seat-belts in cars ruins his supply of organs and the parent expressing delight that a heart donor has been found for his child bring us face to face with hard reality. This non-specific antipathy lies at the heart of the problem. Several specific reasons for the shortage of organs have, however, been canvassed in the past and, although it may appear *déjà vu*, these will be reconsidered briefly.[3]

The Shortage of Organs

The Role of the Coroner or Procurator Fiscal

First, there is the statutory role of the coroner or procurator Fiscal.[4] Although the removal of healthy organs from a cadaver can rarely have an irremediable effect on the autopsy following violent death, such is the nature of the adversarial system of criminal justice and so great is the importance of unfettered evidence in criminal cases that there must be sympathy for the medico-legal authority who vetoes organ donation following deaths involving suspected homicide. In a comparatively recent study, which included 16 dead patients who were medically suitable as organ donors but were unused,[5] intervention by the coroner was found to be a commoner cause of failure to donate (eight cases) than was refusal of consent by relatives (five cases). All eight cases, however, resulted in criminal charges being brought against another person and this may have influenced the outcome. Some wastage may be due to misunderstanding on the part of coroners' officers who often believe that the fact that a patient has died while being ventilated dictates that the death be reported, whereas it is the *reason* for ventilation which should determine the issue. The practical answer to most legal objections to cadaver donation lies in the coroner's or fiscal's pathologist attending the donor operation, but this tactic seems to be employed only in Scotland. There is a subtle difference between the Human Tissue Act, s.1(5) – which, in effect, states that authority for donation in any case in which there may be an inquest, or in which the coroner may require an autopsy, must not be given except with the consent of the coroner – and s.1(9) which states that donation will not be authorised in any case where the procurator fiscal has objected to removal of organs. 'Mistakes' are rare in statutes; the difference in emphasis may well be deliberate and reflect the tendency for Scots law to leave doctoring to the doctors whenever that is possible.

Reluctance on the Part of Medical Staff

Much has been made of the suspected resistance to donation on the part of those responsible for the clinical care of the potential donor. This may be the result of basic misunderstanding on their part;[6] there must also be some reluctance to burden grieving relatives with further demands. On the other side of the coin, the intensive care unit staff often find it difficult to alter their approach, having just lost a patient despite heroic resuscitative measures.[7] Furthermore, maintaining a donor in a condition to provide viable organs requires intensive efforts from overworked staff.[8] In point of fact, this last difficulty is a rare cause of loss of organs, although the pressures are bound to increase as multi-organ donation becomes more commonplace.

The Search for a Remedy

Administrative Aspects

Various strategies designed to overcome these difficulties are being evolved. The most significant has been the increasingly widespread appointments of transplant coordinators responsible for liaison at regional and hospital levels. Working closely with the United Kingdom Transplant Support Service,[9] they are not only able to contact suitable recipient teams rapidly – thus shortening the time between death and procurement and, at the same time, increasing the number of organs harvested from a single donor[10] – but they also form the major link between the intensive care unit, the surgical teams involved and the relatives. The recently bereaved are more likely to respond to an experienced former nursing sister than they are to already harassed junior medical staff.

Organisation at hospital level is now so sophisticated that the introduction of 'required request' legislation, as developed widely in the United States,[11] can now be regarded as a dead issue. In this system, the clinician in charge of a suitable donor is legally bound to put the issue of organ donation to the next of kin. This was once regarded as a very good route to increased organ procurement.[12] There have, however, always been doubts. The requirement interferes grossly with clinical freedom[13] and any legislation would have to include a clause admitting 'professional privilege'; moreover, while legislation can cover what must be said, it cannot cover *how* it is said. It is well to leave matters in the capable hands of the transplant coordinators.

There has been considerable debate in the past as to the practical value of centralised registers of potential transplant donors. The UK government has now grasped the nettle and has established a new NHS Organ Donor Register which will be closely tied to applications for driving licences and which will be administered by the Driver and Vehicle Licensing Agency.[14] The register will be held by the United Kingdom Transplant Support Service Authority alongside the national database of those waiting for donor organs. One can foresee all the teething problems commonly associated with any bureaucratic enterprise; nevertheless, the initiative must be applauded.

Extending the Organ-donor Pool

Effort is currently being concentrated on establishing a wider source of organs than the intensive care unit, notably including those who die in the casualty department or in the medical wards as a result of cerebrovascular accidents. The less controversial of these procedures involves the use of 'non-heart beating' or 'asystolic' donors. Effectively, this represents a return to the early, pre-brain death, days of transplantation, but with additional cold perfusion of the organs *in situ*. The process applies only to the transplantation of kidneys, and the majority of transplant units derive a substantial increase in donations from the procedure.[15] The warm ischaemic time is reduced to less than 25 minutes, while the cold ischaemic time is unchanged. The results are not as good as those from beating-heart donors – graft failure and morbidity are more common – but they are acceptable.[16] Some ethico-legal concern lies in the fact that cold perfusion must often be undertaken without express consultation with the next of kin. In Varty's study, the protocol was advertised in the local press and no objections were raised; the problem of consent by the relatives is discussed in general terms below. Some surprise was caused recently when the Danish Council of Ethics rejected the concept of brain-stem death,[17] and beating-heart donation is not available, for instance, in Japan.[18] *In situ* perfusion may prove to be a particularly useful procedure where such opposition exists.

The practice of 'elective ventilation' is a far more controversial way of extending the source of organs beyond the intensive care unit (ICU) and into the medical and geriatric wards. The procedure[19] involves, first, that the proposed donor must be in the terminal phase of deep coma due, mainly, to an intracerebral vascular event; second, that the patient is a medically suitable organ donor; third, that the patient is transferred from the ward to the ICU for the management of organ donation; and, fourth, that the consent of the appropriate relatives to the management plan is obtained. It is difficult to establish from the published results, or from the analysis of New *et al.*,[20] whether the patients are transferred to the ICU before or after 'terminal' respiratory failure. The distinction is of some significance as, in the former, we would be dealing with the ethics of terminal care while, in the latter, we would be in the realm of reanimation and with a different set of moral problems. Ancillary evidence[21] indicates that the former situation prevails and the remainder of the discussion is based on that premise.

While its objective is irreproachable, the protocol lays a minefield of legal, practical and ethical problems. It is well established in law that no-one can consent to treatment on behalf of an incompetent adult – and this includes the next of kin. The practitioner may lawfully give non-consensual treatment in accordance with his clinical judgement but its legality depends, in turn, on its being considered to be in the patient's best interests.[22] There is no way in which invasive non-consensual treatment of a dying and incurable patient can be regarded as being in his or her best interests; it follows that elective ventilation must involve an assault or trespass to the person. Looked at from the civil law aspect, it is true that a right of action could pass to the executors but, the patient having died, the major source of compensation – in the form of solatium – would have died also; moreover, any action raised by the next of kin themselves – say, in respect of affronted sensibilities – would have been vitiated by their agreement to the procedure. In this respect, the Human Tissue Act 1961, s.1(2) empowers the relatives to agree to or refuse permission for organ donation only after the death of the donor; there is no suggestion that the statute fundamentally alters their inability to *consent* to treatment of the living even though it is directed to the same end.

The 'best interests' principle must also apply to the ethical parameters. It cannot be in the patient's interest to prolong his dying by invasive medicine. We can be doing him no good – and we *may* be doing him harm. Looked at in this way, there can be no starker example of using a patient as a means and offending a basic Kantian imperative. This is not to say that the process is *necessarily* unethical, but it does mean that a large proportion of philosophers must have grave doubts on the issue. In practice, medical ethics are usually better founded on utilitarian principles, which are satisfied by the provision of 21 life-saving organs at the expense of the somewhat dubious rights to autonomy of eight insensate, moribund patients.[23] The recent judgements in *Bland*[24] and *S*[25] suggest that the courts, if asked, would support such a balancing act. Nonetheless, there is a sense of unease as to the underlying morality of elective ventilation; there may be no 'slippery slope' at present – but the ingredients are there.

The possibility must also be considered that the criminal law may be infringed in so far as an assault by way of medical invasion of the body is decriminalised only on the grounds that it is for the patient's good; the question is, however, probably of academic interest only. The practical problems are of more immediate importance. There is concern for the consequent 'misuse' of the ICU – which is there to save lives rather than to prepare for death – and the possible denial of scarce therapeutic resources to needy patients. It is impossible to generalise about such matters which depend on the individual circumstances and on agreement between the intensivists and the transplant surgeons. All would accept that the therapeutic role of the ICU is paramount and that no person being electively ventilated should come between the emergency patient and his or her treatment.

It is prognosis, however, that raises the gravest doubts as to the validity of the process. It is true that all of Feest's reported cases went smoothly according to plan but this may not necessarily always be so. Routh[26] has pinpointed three possible untoward outcomes: the patient may develop some other condition while under intensive care, such as sepsis, which invalidates him as a donor; the patient may recover sufficiently to be discharged from hospital; or the patient may stabilise in the persistent vegetative state. It is this last possibility which raises the greatest fears and it is, probably, the least unlikely of the three scenarios to develop. The production of a persistent vegetative state in a person who was close to a peaceful natural death could only be described as a clinical disaster which, if publicised, could be catastrophically detrimental to the whole transplantation programme. It could also have serious legal consequences. While it might be argued that the saving of a life was a benefit irrespective of the quality of life achieved, the attitudes of the courts to the persistent vegetative state as expressed in *Bland* and *S*[27] indicate that it is improbable that they would accept such a proposition. The likely repercussions from such an occurrence must raise doubts as to whether the eventual advantages of elective ventilation justify the risks involved.

Beyond that, this discussion is not intended to pass judgement on the procedure. The pioneers have been at pains to ensure its acceptance by all concerned and there is no intended criticism in what has been said. Nonetheless, the practice has now attracted the attention of the news media[28] and it seems that the doubts expressed above as to the legality of the procedure have been confirmed.[29] A national study of its effects on organ procurement has been aborted and the main protagonists of the method have suspended their practice. It is widely argued that the current statute law is biased towards the interests of the donor at the expense of the recipient. There is little likelihood of its being changed in the foreseeable future, but it needs to be clarified in the light of modern experience.

Age and Transplantation

The age of suitable donors has steadily increased, along with technical advances in intensive care and transplantation, thus increasing the organ pool. Corneas can be donated by 90-year-old persons, kidneys, at least up to the age of 70 and other organs up to the age of 50. As a quid pro quo, previous limitations on the age of recipients have been greatly mitigated. Certainly, resuscitation of any type is contra-indicated in some elderly patients – particularly those suffering from severe neurological defect.[30] But, apart from such conditions, acceptable discrimination on grounds of age must depend upon prognosis: given an estimated five-year therapeutic gain, there is no reason why the enjoyment of those years by a 20-year-old should not be equally available to a competent 70-year-old.[31]

The Persistent Vegetative State

But, if severely neurologically compromised patients are beyond the limits of life-sustaining treatment, could not such persons be available as beating-heart donors by reason of their state of cognitive death? The movement towards the recognition of neocortical or cerebral death as death in its popular and legal sense is active[32] and, although it was developed on philosophical principles, it has been directed towards the practical field of transplantation. This trend should be resisted. On general grounds, death must be regarded as an absolute. Whether one defines it in cerebral or cardiorespiratory terms, cessation of respiration is an integral part of the diagnosis; patients in the persistent vegetative state (PVS) are breathing of their own volition – they may be insensate but they are not dead. Many other arguments can be raised against the use of the PVS patients as donors.[33] These include the difficulties of definitive diagnosis, which will be minimised in the future, and the 'slippery slope' argument, which can be contained, at least at a logical level. But the most cogent reason for not combining PVS and transplantation is that the public simply would not understand the rationale; the end result would be deleterious to the programme as a whole.[34] Finally, there is no doubt that to use a patient in PVS as a donor would be unlawful in the United Kingdom, where the court, which must be consulted in virtually all apposite cases, cannot authorise a deliberate lethal action but can only sanction withdrawal of treatment.[35] Patients in PVS cannot and should not be looked upon as possibly ancillary to the donor pool, at least not until they are dead or until Parliament decrees otherwise.

Education, Incentives or Enforcement?

Parliament is extremely unlikely to and, indeed, there are no indications that it wants to alter the current law in any significant way. For this reason, any discussion of introducing a 'contracting out' system of organ donation – under which the organs of a dead person are deemed to be available for transplantation unless contrary instructions have been given – is sterile. As a member of the government has said:

> We must accept that nobody has a right to anybody else's organs. If something untoward happens, our organs may be of value to someone else but that should be the result of an altruistic decision about how we want our bodies to be used when we die. It should not be as a result of a right of the recipient. We must make that philosophic approach clear and accept it as the basis on which we encourage organ donorship. It is our responsibility to make such a decision and to ensure that our friends and relatives are aware of our views. It is the responsibility of the living whose organs may be of use to someone else; it is not anyone else's job to claim the organs.[36]

This seems as firm a statement as is likely to be found. Moreover, although the system apparently works well where it is in operation, especially in Belgium, Austria and, more recently, France, it is probable that the British public would not be prepared to accept such a radical alteration to our concepts of personal privacy at the present time. In the absence of legislation, there are three main routes to improvement in the supply of cadaver organs: education, the introduction of incentives, or greater use of the law as it stands.

Education

Education of the public – who are a heterogeneous crowd – is not easy. The use of the news/entertainment media is expensive and organ donation should not be singled out as a disproportionate recipient of such public funds. One route to the public conscience could be through the general practitioner's surgery with posters encouraging patients to register their agreement to donate in their G.P.'s files.[37] It is easy to foresee an adverse public reaction to recording patients' intentions in hospital notes; but there is a world of difference between, on the one hand, being asked one's views on organ donation while consulting a doctor for a relatively minor complaint and, on the other, being asked the same question on admission to hospital for major surgery.[38] It is true that G.P.'s notes are rarely available in hospital; yet it is still easier for the admissions officer to ask the question, 'Have you registered with your G.P.?' than 'Will you register now?' Prospective consent might be improved if the advantages of multi-organ donation were stressed: the concept of enhanced positive life-gain should be more attractive to the waverer; there is, however, no empirical evidence to this effect and it is equally possible that many who would happily donate, say, their kidneys would rebel at the prospect of 'being gutted'.

One group which is rarely selected as a special target is that of solicitors. A simple agreement to donate one's organs after death does not carry the same difficulties as does the advanced therapeutic directive or 'living will'; a statement to that effect in one's will would, however, clearly satisfy the conditions of the Human Tissue Act 1961, s.1(1) and would be readily available to executors in the event of admission to the intensive care unit; it is suggested that solicitors should be encouraged to incorporate such a statement of intention in all wills as a matter of routine.[39]

All surveys of organ procurement comment on the need for the medical staff to be better informed. This should extend to the whole profession, including general practitioners, those in accident and emergency departments and junior hospital staff. Since the latter take many of the emergency decisions, education should be incorporated at undergraduate level – possibly in the community medicine module.

Incentives

The question of incentives is far more controversial. The transplant world has always prized its dependence upon altruism: 'A shift into any form of commercialism ... holds the potential of threatening the entire spiritual structure upon which organ transplantation is based at present.'[40] But, the ideal having failed, one has to ask whether there is not room for an alternative approach. If altruism proves inadequate, might not inducement succeed?

In the end, it is a matter of balancing the practical benefit against the sacrifice of moral principle involved. There can be no argument if the latter is seen as an absolute but it is hard to maintain such a premise – there is no irrefutable reason why the treatable sick should be condemned to die in pursuit of a principle which is largely inspired by the medical profession itself[41] and which has no more than minority public support, at least in the United States. Inducement need not be in monetary terms. As long ago as 1976, it was suggested that relatives might be fairly induced to consent to donation by, say, having a hospital bed named after the deceased[42] and, today, the most popular options, in addition to the payment of a standard amount of money, include preferred status in the event of the consenter's future therapeutic need, payment of funeral expenses, payment to a charity and assistance with a life insurance policy.[43] Altruism could be retained under such a scheme, in so far as no relative would be compelled to accept inducement, but the most important safeguard would be that no inducement should be allowed to pass by way of a third party between named donors and recipients, for it is blatant commercialism which is immoral. Any transactions would have to be through a statutory body – say, a restructured Unrelated Live Transplant Regulatory Authority (see below) – thus ensuring that any recompense was standard and reasonable and that there was no discrimination based on the recipient's financial status. Finally, while many would decry such comparisons, it is fair to say that the cost of five year survival with end-stage renal disease treated by dialysis is some four to five times that following successful renal grafting;[44] it follows that the government could afford to offer incentives for cadaver donation and still be justified on economic grounds, *provided that to do so did, in fact, result in increased procurement.*

All in all, the use of controlled incentives as a means of improving the supply of organs might be less morally suspect than appears at first glance; the final analysis rests on the unknown answer to the question, would it achieve its objective?[45]

Implementation of the Existing Law

Lastly in this section, we should consider the current state of enforcement or use of the law as it stands, a matter which is likely to be just as controversial. The Human Tissue Act 1961, s.1(1) states:

> When a person ... in writing at any time ... has expressed a request that his body or any specified part of his body be used after his death for therapeutic purposes ... the person lawfully in possession of his body after his

death may ... authorise the removal from the body of any part or, as the case may be, the specified part, for use in accordance with the request.

Two questions arise from this: who is lawfully in possession of the body, and what is the status of the organ donor card? As to the former, there is no doubt that the word 'possession' in the section infers physical possession: that is, the lawful possessor is the hospital authority[46] or, otherwise, the owner of the property in which the body rightly lies. As to the latter, it is difficult to see how a signed organ donor card can be anything other than an 'expression of request in writing'. The Act says nothing as to approval by the next of kin and there is no space on the donor card for a countersignature. From any view, the next of kin have no right of veto of the deceased's expressed wishes which can be validly stated on the current donor card.[47] Confusion arose as early as 1973 as the result of an unfortunate exchange in the House of Commons following a previous maverick opinion obtained by the Medical Defence Union which was very poorly presented and discussed.[48] This had a profound influence on the medical profession at the time which has been passed on through generations of students; moreover, personal experience strongly suggests that the general public believe the organ donor card to have no legal standing.[49] As a result, it is now standard practice to seek the concurrence of the relatives even when s.1(1) has been satisfied and to accept a veto when one is given.[50]

It is easy to understand the reluctance of a transplant coordinator to add to the distress of the recently bereaved and of the transplant and ICU teams by engaging in controversy; to bow to the wishes of the next of kin may be the easy way, but is it logical to do so? Medical jurisprudence is dominated by the concept of the autonomy of the competent adult patient who can ethically and legally accept or refuse treatment even though this may be against the wishes of his or her relatives – or, indeed, against reason. How, then, can we justify denial of the patient's final expression of autonomy simply because he or she is now dead? The answer lies in a retreat to utilitarianism, which most people would be thankful to accept.

Evidence as to how great an impact strict adherence to the law would have on organ procurement is conflicting; it would probably not be very great, given the current relatively low rate of 'opting in'. Nonetheless, it is scarcely reasonable to lament the shortage of organs with one breath and to abrogate the law which was specifically designed to avoid that situation with the next – certainly a case can be made for utilising whatever power the law provides. It might be argued that the resultant confrontation would act to the overall detriment of the programme, but this would not necessarily be so. Most people now understand and approve the principle of self-determination; put in this way, any opposition on the part of relatives to the expressed wishes of the deceased would probably be moderated.[51] Secondly, perhaps the majority of us have a respect for the law as a controlling influence on our lives. And, thirdly, relatives – and, particularly, spouses – might well feel nothing but a sense of relief when presented with a fait accompli and a release from decision making.[52] In the end, however, the justification of any law enforcement campaign in terms of additional organ retrieval would depend on a proportionate increase in the number of those completing a donor organ card or its equivalent.

Living Donation

The supply of organs could be significantly increased by the free use of living donors. At present, live donation is limited, in practice, to that of kidneys or portions of the pancreas, but the field is rapidly enlarging to include lobes of the liver[53] and of the lung. These last procedures can be regarded as experimental or innovative and, as a consequence, may require special ethical consideration.[54] They may also raise interesting legal complications, and this applies especially to segmental liver donation. It has been suggested that, since liver tissue regenerates quite readily,[55] segments of liver could be regarded as tissue similar to bone marrow and, accordingly, be free from the controls applied to organ transplantation.[56] For reasons of space, however, such arguments will not be pursued and the remainder of this section will be confined to living donation of a kidney.

Currently, some 5 per cent of renal transplants undertaken in the United Kingdom involve living donors, and the proportion has fallen since 1987.[57] The practice is now regulated by the Human Organ Transplants Act 1989; the question arises whether the Act, which was introduced almost as an emergency measure, has been positively restrictive of living donation. The main thrust of the Act is to criminalise the sale or purchase of human organs, whether these be obtained from a dead or a live body. Its terms are strict and, in contrast to the rather analogous legislation in the Surrogacy Arrangements Act 1985, the principals involved in any such contract are subject to prosecution as well as any third party entrepreneur. Proof that living organs were being sold in quantity before 1989 – and that this accounts in part for the dramatic fall in numbers of live transplants at the turn of the decade – would obviously be hard to obtain. The proposition is so unlikely, however, that it can be disregarded.[58] Moreover, the purchase of organs from living donors is equally prohibited in the United States where, by contrast, the number of living donations has increased *pari passu* with the number of cadaver donations. Even so, the converse proposition, that the supply of organs would be materially increased if financial incentives for live donation were permitted, remains and must be considered when any review of improved organ procurement is undertaken.

Unproven Reasons for Restriction

We should, first, eliminate the invalid reasons for statutory control of living donation. Foremost among these is danger to the donor, which must be accepted as being very slight. In the perioperative period, it should be no more than is that of any elective major surgical operation.[59] As regards the donor's future health, very few pathological renal conditions are unilateral: only trauma to the remaining kidney stands out as a significant hazard. While there is some disagreement in the literature, recent studies confirm the normal prognosis for living kidney donors.[60] Pragmatically, so long as unrestricted related donation is allowable, the hazards must lie within the parameters of legally acceptable self-inflicted injury;[61] moreover, the dangers do not deter donors in those countries where, for religious and/or economic reasons, cadaver donation is rare.[62]

Second, the possibility of ill-considered compatibility and consequent rejection of transplanted organs if widespread trafficking is allowed is unlikely to be an important consideration. There is no reason why donors and recipients should not be matched in the living as well as in the cadaver state – indeed, the urgency of the situation is virtually eliminated in the former. Moreover, modern immunosuppressant therapy has revolutionised graft rejection[63] and, in practice, the spread of relationships within which unrestricted living donation is permissible in the United Kingdom is so wide as to suggest that those responsible for the regulations were more concerned with intrafamilial altruism than with scientific principles.[64]

Generally Accepted Reasons for Restriction

Some other reasons must be found for prohibition of the sale of organs – a prohibition which is well-nigh universal.[65] Much of the opposition is inchoate and attributable to what is popularly, and expressively, known as the 'yuk factor'. In the end, this crystallises into two main fears, those of excessive commercialism and of exploitation. Commercialism – that is, the interposition of a third party as broker – as related to the disposal of human body parts is generally abhorrent. Yet it is clear that it can be contained without a total ban on financial inducement or advantage.[66] There is little reason to fear commercialism so long as any financial transaction is conducted through a body such as the Unrelated Live Transplant Regulatory Authority in the same way as has been suggested above in the case of cadaver organs. In practice, there is nothing to stop a British national paying for an organ implant outside Great Britain, an arrangement which would result in a privately arranged operation which falls to be followed up within the National Health Service.[67] In an article written before the publication of the 1989 Act, it was suggested that the risk of trafficking in organs could be met by action against those who undertake procurement on a commercial basis[68] – and this remains true today.

Effectively, therefore, we are left with the problem of exploitation, the concept of which has been so well publicised as to be scarcely worth repetition. In an unregulated commercial setting, the majority of recipients would certainly be rich and the majority of donors would, equally certainly, be poor. But this is not, of itself, a reason for outlawing the practice altogether. There is no reason why a government-controlled agency should not be the purchaser of organs which it could distribute on the basis of need;[69] what Bonomini[70] has called 'the only really unethical side of living donor transplantation' would be automatically removed. And, if it is still said that this would not eliminate exploitation of the poor, are there not grounds for asking why we should prevent a poor person realising his or her assets? The reasons for doing this may be wholly altruistic. What is the difference between donating a kidney to one's daughter for treatment of her renal condition – which would be laudable – and selling one's kidney elsewhere so as to facilitate treatment of her non-renal disease – which is condemned?[71] Coming closer to the core of the argument, how is it that we can approve the principle of autonomy to the extent that we insist on a person's right to refuse life-sustaining treatment and yet, at the same time, endorse a form of paternalism which prevents him saving another life for a reasonable recompense? We cannot plead the dangers of donation and, in any event, we do little to prevent the incompetent and impoverished boxer sustaining certain brain damage in a mismatched contest. Finally, it is said that consent to surgery cannot be voluntary and unfettered against a background of poverty and potential reward; but it cannot be denied that the pressures to consent within a familial environment could be as great as those imposed by economic need.

Fundamentally, the objections to payment or, if it be preferred, 'rewarded gifting' for organ donation are based on the fear of the floodgates[72] – a fear which we might all share. But this is based on an unregulated system. There is no reason why we should not consider the possibilities of *regulated* rewarded donation, as opposed to its total rejection – and this might well be acceptable both to the public and to health carers.[73] If we are to fear the floodgates, we should equally fear that 'As long as there are adequate safeguards, any ethical or legal fastidiousness demanding that donation be only gratuitous could condemn the sick'.[74] Condemnation of financial recompense for live donation of organs is virtually total in the Western world,[75] but it is difficult to establish a logical basis for what is, essentially, a gut reaction. The basic question is, how much do we want to improve the transplant service? It is, at least, arguable that, given an effective programme of rewarded donation deployed by a government health agency, 'Deficits in organ supplies would disappear [and] the free, unregulated market would atrophy'.[76]

Xenotransplantation

Xenotransplantation – or the use of animal organs for human treatment – represents the last potential resource from which to fill the gap between demand and supply. Only a few years ago, the procedure would have been regarded as science fiction and its actual practice a matter of suspect morality;[77] it is doubtful if one should now be so dismissive. Advances in immunosuppression are revolutionising transplantation therapy and at least 23 humans have received organs from animals.[78] One patient has survived for 98 days and another lived for 70 days, apparently without tissue rejection.[79] While it is doubtful if such results should be regarded as successes, they do seem to herald an advance in organ transplant techniques. Once again, however, serious ethical dilemmas are exposed.

At the practical level, primates are difficult to breed in captivity and many species are dying out in the wild. In effect, it is only baboons that could provide a reservoir of organs and these are not very satisfactory for transplantation into man. On the higher plane, we have to ask ourselves whether the use of animals in this way is morally justifiable. The philosophical attack on speciesism is gaining momentum[80] and is likely to attract its greatest support when primates – which are most closely related to man – are involved. Antipathy to their use as organ providers is amplified in that man receives no other general benefit from their killing; we cannot plead that we use the apes for food and, thereby, justify their use as organ donors. A concerted attempt to raise primates for the specific purpose of transplantation might well not succeed in its objective and would provoke opposition, not only from animal activists (it is noteworthy that at least one potential xenografter withdrew from the field because he became too fond of his organ donor).[81]

Many of these objections are minimised in the case of farm animals, which have been bred for centuries for human consumption. Attention has recently focused on the pig – an animal which has surprising anatomical and physiological affinity with man – as a ready supply of organs.[82] In ordinary circumstances, pig tissue is immediately rejected by the human host; recent advances in genetic engineering do, however, raise the strong possibility that transgenic pigs, whose tissues would be resistant to the human immune reaction, could be of clinical use.[83]

That outcome is, currently, years away and this is, perhaps, just as well from the point of view of the medical ethicist. Given an infinite supply of useable organs, one can foresee a steady replacement of the human body as individual human organs fail in the ageing process; the only limiting factor would be descent of the patient into total dementia. Moreover, since the National Health Service would be unable to accept a financial responsibility of enormous proportions, longevity would become the prerogative of the rich. Such a prospect is scarcely inviting.

Transplantation of Ovarian Tissue

The use of both oocytes and ovarian tissue from living and dead donors has been the subject of a public consultation document and subsequent report issued by the Human Fertilisation and Embryology Authority (HFEA).[84] We are concerned in this section only with the donation of ovarian *tissue* from the living or dead adult for therapeutic purposes. The use of foetal ovarian tissue raises specific issues of its own, while the donation of individual ova is a very different process which is controlled by the Human Fertilisation and Embryology Act 1990.

It is important to distinguish the possible uses to which explanted ovarian tissue could be put (Consultation Document, para.13). The main purpose would be its maintenance *in vitro* and the subsequent maturation and harvesting of ova for donation. The alternative, and far less probable, use would be its transplantation into an anovular woman, thus allowing her to conceive and implant embryos in the normal way despite the fact that the ova involved were genetically distinct. Unlikely as this scenario may sound, it could become the method of choice for the treatment of certain forms of infertility if the problems of rejection could be overcome to such an extent that the full-term birth rate was substantially better – and less onerous – than that achieved by existing methods involving embryo transfer.[85] The first of these uses is a matter of assisted reproduction, which is not the subject of this Chapter. The latter involves transplantation procedures, and further discussion is directed only to this futuristic concept.

It is a moot point whether the Authority, which is responsible for licensing treatment using the eggs of another woman,[86] is also responsible for treatment involving the potential eggs present in ovarian tissue. Common sense would say that it was. However, the Authority cannot have sole responsibility for controlling the grafting of ovarian tissue; as things stand, any licenses granted for the use of such transplanted tissue would have to accord with the Human Tissue Act 1961 in respect of cadavers or the Human Organ Transplants Act 1989 in the case of living donation. Thus the use of ovarian *tissue* occupies a unique statutory position.

Living donation introduces very little statutory conflict save as to counselling. In the event of related donation, counselling would be required under the Human Fertilisation and Embryology Act 1990 Act, s.13(6) but would not be necessary under the 1989 Act. Few would deny that the conditions of ovarian tissue donation are so distinctive that the strict attitude of the 1990 Act should apply. Counselling is obligatory under both statutes in the case of unrelated live donation.[87]

More difficulty arises in the case of cadaver donation, where the issue of consent looms large. The essential difference between ovarian and any other form of organ donation is that, in the former, the woman is doing more than replacing a defective organ – she is also passing on her genetic material, possibly *ad infinitum*. Consent to donation is, therefore, of an entirely different quality and is covered inadequately by the Human Tissue Act 1961. A request that one's generative organs be used after one's death should be specific and separate from any other request; if this proposition is accepted, it entails, at least, a modification of the current donor card which should, for reasons given below, also include the consent of the woman's living parents. HFEA has also decided that the age for valid consent should be 18 years (Report, para.19) and this seems right; since donation after death cannot conceivably be regarded as medical treatment of the deceased, the requirement cannot conflict with the provisions of the Family Law Reform Act 1969, s.8[88] – and the concept of the *'Gillick-*competent' minor[89] has caused enough confusion in medical jurisprudence without adding to it unnecessarily.

However, the genes of the woman's parents are also being passed on and they, therefore, have a major interest in the disposition of their daughter's ovaries. In these circumstances, it seems only right that they should be specifically nominated as persons to be given the opportunity to object to donation. And, as a corollary, the inherent power of the hospital administrator – as the person in lawful possession of the body – to authorise removal of tissue if he cannot contact a suitable relative should be withdrawn in the case of generative organs. A question still remains as to whether the counselling regulations contained in the Human Fertilisation and Embryology Act 1990 should apply by proxy to those not objecting to cadaver donation of ovarian tissue; logically, this should be so but, in practice, it would place an additional, and considerable, burden on the transplant coordinator.

Stress has been laid on the effects of assisted reproduction on the resulting child or children in the 1990 Act and this figures prominently in both the consultation document and the report of HFEA. Unless treatment has been provided on the grounds of genetic abnormality, the need to inform a child of his or her unusual genetic parentage seems even less urgent in the somewhat bizarre conditions envisaged here than it is in the more probable event of ovum or embryo donation.[90]

In fact, some of the points made above have been pre-empted in the HFEA report. Thus, at least for the time being, the Authority will not condone the use of cadaver ovarian tissue for treatment purposes; this is not because of any objection in principle: the caution stems from the currently unknown effect such conception may have on any prospective children (Report, para.19). Live donation is acceptable to HFEA, but the circumstances in which transplantation of tissue so obtained would be justifiable are very rare. No doubt this particular discussion is, again, one for the 21st century.

Other Aspects of Transplantation

The Neonate

Transplantation therapy is widely needed in the neonatal period and early infancy, and major procedures, such as cardiac and hepatic replacement, are especially in demand. The supply–demand shortfall is particularly acute as small children are rarely killed accidentally; other potential donors arise from birth mishaps and criminal activity. Their availability is, therefore, capricious and some 20 per cent of children requiring liver transplantation die while awaiting the operation.[91] Attempts to improve the situation include the use of reduced size grafts – which, effectively, can be done only at the expense of graft availability for adults – and the inclusion of live persons as segmental donors. The problems here are largely of a technical nature and are beyond the scope of this chapter. The major ethical and legal issues concern the use of anencephalic infants as donors. These comprise what might be seen as an ethical morass which merits a chapter on its own. Only the briefest summary will be attempted here.

Simplistically, the anencephalic neonate is comparable to the adult in the persistent vegetative state whom we have already discarded as a potential organ donor. No matter how hard it may be argued that the definition of death should be amended so as to include anencephaly,[92] the current situation is that death cannot be certified in the presence of a functioning brain-stem.[93] Tests for brain death are notoriously suspect in the neonate and may be impossible in the case of the anencephalic.[94] It follows that only cardiorespiratory death is available as a diagnostic criterion in the latter, and present practice is that 'organs for transplantation can be removed from anencephalic infants when ... spontaneous respiration has ceased'.[95] This, however, takes no account of the fact that neonatal tissues are particularly sensitive to hypoxia. At the very least, therefore, there will be a powerful temptation to minimise the diagnostic apnoeic period prior to reoxygenation in order to preserve the individual organs. There are other technical difficulties: many organs will be too immature for use, there is evidence that organs from anencephalics do not function as well as those taken from anatomically normal neonates and it is doubtful whether the eventual harvest would make any appreciable difference to the neonatal organ pool.[96] Finally, we must come to terms with the ethical implications of women prolonging their pregnancies with known anencephalic foetuses in order to stock that pool. For these, and other, reasons, I have concluded elsewhere that, for the present, the ethical and practical costs are too high to support the use of anencephalics as organ donors, although future improvements in techniques may serve to tip the balance the other way.[97]

The Foetus as a Tissue Donor

The use of the foetus as an organ donor is, in practice, hypothetical. In so far as the donated organs must be 'viable', the foetus itself must be of sufficient maturity to be capable of being born alive. It follows that the prospective foetal donor must be either a still birth – in which case the organs are unlikely to be usable – or it must die of a non-hypoxic condition in the process of a premature birth. This must be very rare and, in effect, the term 'foetal organ donor' is a misnomer for 'neonatal organ donor'.

Far more ethical and practical importance attaches to the foetus as a tissue donor and, for present purposes, discussion will be limited to cerebral and ovarian tissue. The common denominator here is that the tissues either must or may be immature to be of value. Foetal tissue donation is, therefore, tightly bound to abortion, a circumstance which makes it anathema to a sizeable minority of the public. An abortion may derive either from a natural miscarriage or from a medical termination of pregnancy. Since the former is often associated with genetic abnormality, foetal ovarian tissue can only be used with safety when obtained from the latter and it is noteworthy that over 3 per cent of the responses to the HFEA Consultation Document (which considered foetal as well as adult donation) were in the form of petitions, signed by over 10000 people, which were clearly organised by the anti-abortion lobby. Is this basic reason for objection justified?

With the possible exception of intrafamilial donation, when it is just imaginable that a young girl might be induced to become pregnant in order to treat an ageing relative,[98] the danger of 'foetus farming' for the express purpose of providing donor tissue is negligible. There could be no shortage of material in the light of some 170000 legal abortions already performed annually in Great Britain, and a similar figure will recur regardless of the needs of transplant recipients. Thus the ethical argument can be condensed into the question of how far it is right to derive some good from what many would see as an intrinsic evil. The arguments are finely balanced and it is surprising how the same analogies can be used to support each side.[99] In the end, I support the view that it is ethically acceptable to make the best of a bad job, given that one has no complicity in the bad job itself. It is also to be remembered that the definition of a good or bad job is a matter for the individual. There is no obligation on anyone to practise foetal tissue transplantation; rather, the obligation is not to ban a procedure because a number – even a substantial number – would opt out if asked. Even so, it could well be said that such a procedure should be approved only as a last resort, when less contentious methods have failed. It has to be accepted, however, that were it to be shown that foetal implants of non-generative material were therapeutically useful, the demand could not be met from natural miscarriages and ectopic pregnancies.[100]

The use of tissues derived from natural miscarriage can rightly be compared with their use following the accidental death of an adult. The same cannot be said in respect of elective abortion and there is considerable force in the argument that foetal tissue transplantation following that process tends to reduce the status of a potential human being to that of a pharmaceutical preparation. There is a need for a balancing act: do the advantages of using foetal materials outweigh the moral unease which it generates or, put even more simply, is the operation worth doing from the therapeutic standpoint?

The use of foetal brain cells in the treatment of neurological disease has run a chequered course. Originally introduced for the treatment of idiopathic Parkinson's disease, it was suggested and used in Parkinsonism of other cause,[101] in Alzheimer's disease and, indeed, a tendency developed to consider the treatment in any form of degenerative cerebral disease. It was mainly this escalation, together with an innate feeling that the procedure was inadequately researched, that prompted both medical professionals and politicians to call for a halt or, at least, for marking time.[102] These calls seem to have been heeded and very little has been heard of foetal brain implants in the last few years. In point of fact, reported results indicated doubtful therapeutic benefit. Moreover, the procedure highlights a unique medico-jurisprudential problem in that, since the foetal brain cells must be viable, it follows that the foetus is not 'brain-dead'. It is easy to say: 'But a 12-week foetus was never alive'; nevertheless, it is, perhaps, this feature which stimulates greatest antipathy in the public mind. As things stand, it is extremely doubtful if foetal brain implant therapy passes the balancing test.

That test cannot be applied in the case of foetal ovarian implants because the process has never been used. It is possible that foetal ovarian tissue could be implanted in an infertile woman and would grow and produce mature ova – but it certainly seems improbable. And, of course, the major ethical hurdle of consent, including that of the foetus's father, would need to be overcome in these unusual circumstances. In practice, any potential problem has been pre-empted: not only does HFEA not consider the use of foetal ovarian tissue in treatment to be acceptable (Report, para.4), but the process is now unlawful following the passage of the Criminal Justice and Public Order Act 1994. The proposition that 'No person shall, for the purpose of providing fertility services for any woman, use female germ cells taken or derived from an embryo or foetus or use embryos created by using such cells' was passed by an overwhelming majority in Parliament and is incorporated in s.156 of the 1994 Act.[103]

Conclusion

Transplantation has been with us for more than a quarter of a century and it could be expected that the legal and ethical furrows would have been ironed out by now. Instead, it provides an object lesson. Medical technology advances inexorably and it does so in an ambience of rapidly changing societal values. It is the function of the law to interpret and to reflect public attitudes but, inevitably, it lags behind. There is an urgent need for the piecemeal legislation in the field of organ transplantation, much of which has been introduced as panic measures, to be consolidated in a coherent and logical set of principles. But, even if that were done, it might still be outdated within a decade.

Notes

1   This has been the subject of a recent major research project from which many of the statistics quoted have been derived: B. New, M. Solomon, R. Dingwall, and J. McHale, *A Question of Give and Take*, London: King's Fund Institute, 1994.
2   A recent Swedish study indicated, somewhat surprisingly, that, while some 85 per cent of the public would consent to autopsy examination, only 39 per cent would consent to donation of organs by a close relative: M. Sanners, 'Attitudes towards Organ Donation, Autopsy and Dissection', paper presented at 10th World Congress in Medical Law, Jerusalem 28 August – 1 September 1994 (referred to in later footnotes as 'Jerusalem').
3   New *et al.* (note 1 above) have analysed the UK and Eurotransplant figures and report that, in 1992, nearly 15 000 patients were waiting for renal transplants, 938 for hearts and 344 for livers.
4   Human Tissue Act 1961, ss.1(5) and 1(9).
5   A. Bodenham, J.C. Berridge and G.R. Park, 'Brain Stem Death and Organ Donation', *Brit Med J*, **299** (1989), 1009. The role of the coroner or medical examiner may be more significant in the United States: C.L. Jaynes and J.W. Springer, 'Decreasing the Organ Donor Shortage by Increasing Communication between Coroner, Medical Examiners and Organ Procurement Organizations', *Amer J Forens Med Path*, **15** (1994), 156.

6   A.J. Wing and R.W.S. Chang, 'Non-heart Beating Donors as a Source of Kidneys', *Brit Med J*, **308** (1994), 549.

7   R.E. Wakeford and R. Stepney, 'Obstacles to Organ Donation', *Brit J Surg*, **76** (1989), 435.

8   W.B. Ross, 'Increasing Organ Donation – A Review', *Scott Med J*, **34** (1989), 451; N.J. Odom, 'Organ Donation', *Brit Med J*, **300** (1990), 1571.

9   See, *inter alia*, United Kingdom Transplant Support Service Authority Regulations 1991 (S I 1991/408); Human Organ Transplants (Supply of Information) Regulations 1989 (S I 1989/2108).

10 The logistics are all-important. In one study of a few years ago, half of those having permission for multi-organ donation had only the kidneys removed: D. Gentleman, J. Easton and B. Jennet, 'Brain Death and Organ Donation in a Neurosurgical Unit: Audit of Recent Practice', *Brit Med J*, **301** (1990), 1203.

11 Public Law 99-509 9318.

12 R.M.R. Taylor and J.H. Salaman, 'The Obligation to Ask for Organs', *Lancet*, **1** (1988), 985; S. Gore, C.J. Hinds and A.J. Rutherford, 'Organ Donation from Intensive Care Units in England: First Report', *Brit Med J*, **299** (1989), 1193.

13 S.J. Youngner, 'Brain Death and Organ Procurement: Some Vexing Problems Remain', *Dialysis Transplant*, **19** (1990), 12.

14 Department of Health Press Release 94/447, 6 October 1994.

15 For example, T.J.M. Ruers, J.P.A.M. Vroeman and G. Koostra, 'Non-heart Beating Donors: A Successful Contribution to Organ Procurement', *Transplant Proc*, **18** (1986), 408; K. Varty, K.S. Veitch, J.D.T. Morgan *et al.*, 'Response to Organ Shortage: Kidney Retrieval Programme Using Non-heart Beating Donors', *Brit Med J*, **308** (1994), 575.

16 A.O. Phillips, S.A. Snowden, A.N. Hillis and M. Bewick, 'Renal Grafts from Non-heart Beating Donors', *Brit Med J*, **308** (1994), 575. The surgeons were, however, using rapid cooling *after* procurement rather than *in situ* cooling.

17 B.A. Rix, 'Danish Ethics Council Rejects Brain Death as the Criterion of Death', *J Med Ethics*, **16** (1990), 5.

18 M. Yamauchi, 'Waiting for Japanese Transplants', *Brit Med J*, **303** (1991), 266.

19 T.G. Feest, H.N. Riad, C.H. Collins *et al.*, 'Protocol for Increasing Organ Donation after Cerebrovascular Deaths in a District General Hospital', *Lancet*, **335** (1990), 1133. See also M.A.M. Salih, I. Harvey, S. Frankel *et al.*, 'Potential Availability of Cadaver Organs for Transplantation', *Brit Med J*, **302** (1991), 1053.

20 Note 1 above, at 55.

21 C.H. Collins, 'Elective Ventilation for Organ Donation – The Case in Favour', *Care Crit Ill*, **8** (1992), 57.

22 *Re T (adult: refusal of medical treatment)* (1992) 9 BMLR 46, per Lord Donaldson, at 50.

23 Results taken from Collins (note 21, above).

24 *Airedale NHS Trust* v. *Bland* (1993) 12 BMLR 64 (withdrawal of alimentation).

25 *Frenchay Healthcare NHS Trust* v. *S* (1994) 17 BMLR 156 (non-replacement of gastrostomy tube).

26 G. Routh, 'Elective Ventilation for Organ Donation – The Case Against', *Care Crit Ill*, **8** (1992), 60.

27 See notes 24 and 25, above.

28 *The Mail on Sunday*, 9 October 1994, p.1.

29 See S. Ramsay, 'UK Organ-retrieval Scheme Deemed Illegal', *Lancet*, **344** (1944), 1081.

30 See, for example, L. Doyal and D. Wilsher, 'Withholding and Withdrawing Life Sustaining Treatment from Elderly People: Towards Formal Guidelines', *Brit Med J*, **308** (1994), 1689.

31 It may be that the elderly do, in fact, accept organ grafts better than the young: R.J. Tesi, E.A. Elkhammas, E.A. Davies *et al.*, 'Renal Transplantation in Older People', *Lancet*, **343** (1994), 461.

32 R.J. Devettere, 'Neocortical Death and Human Death', *Law Med Hlth Care*, **18** (1990), 96.

33 J. Downie, 'The Biology of the Persistent Vegetative State: Legal, Ethical and Philosophical Implications for Transplantation', *Transplant Proc* (1990), 995.

34 The British Medical Association recommends that patients in PVS should not at present be considered as potential organ or tissue donors: *Guidelines for the Management of the Persistent Vegetative State* (1993), para.9.

35 *Practice Note* (1994) 2 A11 ER 413.

36 Official Reports, HC, 28 March 1991, vol.188, col.1142, per Stephen Dorrell.

37 This proposal already attracts support from general practitioners: R. Vautrey, 'Increasing the Number of Organ Donations', *Brit Med J*, **308** (1994), 1512. Patients registering with a general practitioner will now be able to send their donor wishes to the NHS Organ Donor Register via the local FHSAs (Family Health Service Authorities): see note 14, above.

38 Doubts are expressed, however, as to the extent of public resistance: R.M.R. Taylor, 'Opting In or Out of Organ Donation', *Brit Med J*, **305** (1992), 1380. See also the views of Wakeford and Stepney (note 7 above).

39 Both the Human Tissue Act 1961 and the Anatomy Act 1984 run counter to the common law principle that a man cannot dispose of his dead body by will.

40 F.T. Rapaport, 'Progress in Organ Procurement: The Non Heart-beating Cadaver Donor and Other Issues in Transplantation', *Transplant Proc*, **23** (1991), 2699.

41 I. Davies, 'Live Donation of Human Body Parts: A Case for Negotiability?', *Med-leg J*, **59** (1991), 100.

42 J.S. Pliskin, 'Cadaveric Kidneys for Transplantation: Is there a Need for More?', *J Forensic Sci*, **21** (1976), 83.

43 D.P. Kittur, M.M. Hogan, V.K. Thukral *et al.*, 'Incentives for Organ Donation?', *Lancet*, **338** (1991), 1441.

44 C. Green, *Recent Progress in Organ Transplantation*, Oxford: The Medical Group (UK) Ltd, 1990, p.7.

45 For arguments in favour of incentives, see T.G. Peters, 'Life or Death: The Issue of Payment for Cadaveric Organ Donation', *J Amer Med Ass*, **265** (1991), 1302; G.P. Smith, 'Market and Non-market Mechanisms for Procuring Human and Cadaveric Organs: When the Price is Right', *Med Law Internat*, **1** (1993), 17. Those of opposing view include E.D. Pellegrino, 'Families' Self-interest and the Cadaver's Organs: What Price Consent?', *J Amer Med Ass*, **265** (1991), 1305; R.W. Evans, 'Incentives for Organ Donation', *Lancet*, **339** (1992), 185.

46 This is clearly to be inferred, *inter alia*, from s.1(6) which specifically denies the power to authorise removal to the funeral director. See also DHSS Circular HM (61)98 and Lord Edmund Davies, speaking in an extrajudicial capacity: 'A Legal Look at Transplants', *Proc R Soc Med*, **62** (1969), 633.

47 The same applies to the voluntary certificate now included in the driving licence.

48 P.H. Addison, 'Human Tissue Act', *Brit Med J*, **1** (1968), 516. The early discussions of the issues are very well summarised by Legal Correspondent, 'Kidney Donors and the Law', *Brit Med J*, **2** (1973), 360.

49 This impression is based, in part, on an unfortunate participation in a 'popular' television production where this interpretation went unchallenged by both the audience and the presenters.

50 The same applies in the United States, even though the donor card there is a legally binding document: A. Spital, 'The Shortage of Organs for Transplantation', *New Engl J Med*, **325** (1991), 1243. By contrast, there is no power of veto in, say, France.

51 For the United States, see D.L. Manninen and R.W. Evans, 'Public Attitudes and Behavior Regarding Organ Donation', *J Amer Med Ass*, **253** (1985), 3111.

52 This might, however, not be so. V. Parsons and E. Matthewman, 'Ethical and Legal Aspects of Organ Donation', Jerusalem, 1994 report that 72 per cent of relatives would find it abhorrent not to be given the opportunity to withhold consent; 16 per cent would have preferred to be left out and the remainder were indifferent.

53 This might even become the optimum treatment of hepatic incompetence in children: G. McBride, 'Living Liver Donor', *Brit Med J*, **299** (1989), 1417.

54 P.A. Singer, M. Siegler, P.F. Whitington *et al.*, 'Ethics of Liver Transplantation with Living Donors', *New Engl J Med*, **321** (1989), 620; L.R. Shaw, J.D. Miller, A.S. Slutsky *et al.*, 'Ethics of Lung Transplantation with Live Donors', *Lancet*, **338** (1991), 678.

55 S. Kawasaki, M. Makuuchi, S. Ishizone *et al.*, 'Liver Regeneration in Recipients and Donors after Transplantation', *Lancet*, **339** (1992), 580.

56 B. Dickens, 'Organ Segment Transplantation: Legal and Ethical Issues', Jerusalem, 1994. This might apply in the United Kingdom where the Human Organ Transplants Act 1989, s.7 defines an organ as any part of a human body consisting of a structured arrangement of tissues which, *if wholly removed*, cannot be replicated by the body (my emphasis). This might be said to do no more than define a liver and to have no relevance to a segment of liver.

57 The source is New *et al.* (note 1, above) where the years 1985–7 are compared with 1990–92. The authors do not, however, comment on any possible effect of the 1989 Act.

58 See also Unrelated Live Transplant Regulatory Authority, *Annual Report 1990/91* (1992).

59 The same low risk factor could not be attributed to living liver donation. See Singer *et al.* (note 54 above).

60 J.S. Najarian, B.M. Chaters, L.E. McHugh and R.J. Matas, '20 Years or More of Follow-up of Living Kidney Donors', *Lancet*, **340** (1992), 807; V. Bonomini 'Ethical Aspects of Living Donation', *Transplant Proc*, **23** (1991), 2497.

61 *Attorney-General's Reference (No 6 Of 1980)* [1981] 2 A11 ER 1057.

62 J. Nudeshima, 'Obstacles to Brain Death and Organ Transplantation in Japan', *Lancet*, **338** (1991), 1063; J. Bignall, 'Kidneys: Buy or Die', *Lancet*, **342** (1993), 45.

63 For a full review, see J.F. Burdick, J. Diethelm, J.S. Thompson *et al.*, 'Organ Sharing – Present Realities and Future Possibilities', *Transplantation*, **51** (1991), 287.

64 See the Human Organ Transplants (Establishment of Relationship) Regulations 1989 (S I 1989/2107) which regard uncles and aunts of the half blood as being antigenically 'related'.

65 A. Dorozynski, 'Europe Condemns Sale of Organs', *Brit Med J*, **307** (1993), 756. The sale of organs is now illegal even in India (Transplantation of Human Organs Act 1994). See G. Nandan, 'India Outlaws Trade in Human Organs', *Brit Med J*, **308** (1994), 1657.

66 See, for example, the Surrogacy Arrangements Act 1985, under which the payment of legitimate expenses between the principals is not criminalised.

67 J. Odum, P.B. Rylance and M.A. Jackson, 'From Wolverhampton to Bombay', *Lancet*, **343** (1994), 734. It is, however, probable that the principals involved in the practice commit an offence under the Human Organ Transplants Act 1989, s.1(1)(a).

68 M. Evans, 'Organ Donations should not be Restricted to Relatives', *J Med Ethics*, **15** (1989), 17.

69 See the persuasive article by J. Harvey, 'Paying Organ Donors', *J Med Ethics*, **16** (1990), 117.

70 See note 60, above.

71 J.K. Mason, 'Legal Aspects of Organ Donation', in C. Dyer (ed.), *Doctors, Patients and the Law*, Oxford: Blackwell, 1992, ch.7.

72   Which could extend even so far as criminal provision of organs: see A.S. Daar, 'Ethical Issues – A Middle East Perspective', *Transplant Proc,* **21** (1989), 1402.
73   See A. Guttmann and R.D. Guttmann, 'Attitudes of Health Care Professionals and the Public towards the Sale of Kidneys for Transplantation', *JMed Ethics,* **19** (1993), 148; J.P. Wight, 'Ethics, Commerce and Kidneys', *Brit Med J,* **303** (1991), 110.
74   Davies, note 41, above.
75   World Health Organisation, *Human Organ Transplantation,* Geneva, 1991. For the opposing view, see Bignall, note 62 above, quoting K.C. Reddy, 'Should Paid Organ Donation Be Banned in India? To Buy or Let Die!', *Nat Med J India,* **6** (1993), 137. It will be interesting to see how the outlawing of paid living donation affects the mortality from end-stage renal disease in India where there is no adequate dialysis or cadaver transplant back-up.
76   R.A. Sells, 'Commerce in Human Organs: A Global Review', *Dialysis Transplant,* **19** (1990), 10.
77   L.J. Hubbard, 'The Baby Fae Case', *Med Law,* **6** (1987), 385.
78   N. Nuttall, 'Surgeons Transplant Baboon's Liver into Hepatitis Patient', *The Times,* 30 June 1992, p.4.
79   T.E. Starzl, J. Fung, A. Tzakis *et al.,* 'Baboon-to-human Liver Transplantation', *Lancet,* **341** (1993), 65.
80   See, for example, P. Singer and T. Regan (eds), *Animal Rights and Human Obligations,* Bookvale: Prentice Hall, 1988.
81   Hubbard, note 77, above.
82   Pig heart valves are already widely used in human therapy and porcine insulin has long been used for the treatment of diabetes.
83   D. White and J. Wallwork, 'Xenografting: Probability, Possibility or Pipe Dream?', *Lancet,* **342** (1993), 879; A. James, 'Transplants with Transgenic Pig Organs?', *Lancet,* **342** (1993), 45.
84   Human Fertilisation and Embryology Authority, *Donated Ovarian Tissue in Embryo Research and Assisted Conception,* Public Consultation Document (January 1994), Report (July 1994).
85   Currently an overall rate of 12.7 per cent per treatment cycle: Human Fertilisation and Embryology Authority, *Third Annual Report* (1994).
86   Human Fertilisation and Embryology Act 1990, s.4(1)(*b*).
87   Human Organ Transplants (Unrelated Persons) Regulations 1989 (S I 1989/2480), r.1(*e*).
88   Though it is uncertain whether one could say the same in Scotland, where the comparable Age of Legal Capacity (Scotland) Act 1991, s.2(4) refers to consent by a minor to 'any medical procedure'.
89   *Gillick* v. *West Norfolk and Wisbech AHA* [1985] 3 A11 ER 402, which established the right of the mature and understanding minor aged less than 16 years to consent to medical procedures.
90   See J.K. Mason and R.A. McCall Smith, *Law and Medical Ethics,* 4th edn, London: Butterworths, 1994, p.57 for discussion.
91   A. Salt, G. Noble-Jamieson, N.D. Barnes *et al.,* 'Liver Transplantation in 100 Children', *Brit Med J,* **304** (1992), 416.
92   R.M. Veatch, *Death, Dying and the Biological Revolution,* New Haven: Yale University Press, 1989; *J Thanatol,* **3** (1975), 13.
93   For legal discussion – and rejection of a special definition of death – see the US case, *Re TACP* 609 So 2d 588 (Fla, 1992).
94   J.R. Solaman, 'Anencephalic Organ Donors', *Brit Med J,* **298** (1989), 622.
95   *Report of the Working Party of the Conference of Royal Medical Colleges and their Faculties in the United Kingdom on Organ Transplantation in Neonates* (1988).

96 W.F. May, 'Brain Death: Anencephalics and Aborted Fetuses', *Transplant Proc,* **22** (1990), 985.

97 J.K. Mason and R.A. McCall Smith, *Law and Medical Ethics,* (note 90, above), pp.307ff.

98 There might, therefore, be a case for proscribing intrafamilial donation.

99 For a short debate, see J.A. Robertson, 'The Ethical Acceptability of Fetal Tissue Transplants', *Transplant Proc,* **22** (1990), 1025; K. Nolan, 'The Use of Embryo or Fetus in Transplantation: What There Is to Lose', *Transplant Proc,* **22** (1990), 1028.

100 J. Roberts, 'Bush's Fetal Tissue Plans Unrealistic', *Brit Med J,* **305** (1992), 440.

101 Editorial Comment, 'Parkinson's Disease: One Illness or Many Syndromes?', *Lancet,* **339** (1992), 1263.

102 *Lancet,* **1** (1988), 1087. A moratorium was imposed in the United States during the Reagan administration in 1988 but this was mainly inspired by the abortion debate.

103 The British Medical Association approved this policy.

8 Transplantation and the 'Nearly Dead': The Case of Elective Ventilation

SHEILA A.M. MCLEAN

It is an accepted fact of contemporary society that organ transplantation programmes hold out great hope for those whose lives would otherwise be lost prematurely. It is also true, however, that the effectiveness of these programmes is hampered by a significant shortfall of available organs. Since the passing of the Human Tissue Act 1961 in the UK, the transplantation picture has changed dramatically. More, and multiple, organs can now be recycled for life-saving purposes, the public is considerably better informed about the value of transplantation surgery, and yet we continue to find a not insubstantial number of people dying every year because organs cannot be found for them. We are better able to match organs, we have more sophisticated drugs to counter possible organ rejection, we have a sophisticated system of transplant coordinators, and educational programmes continue to exhort people to carry donor cards, yet lives are needlessly lost. Writing in 1990, Gentleman et al.[1] noted that 'In the United Kingdom more patients with renal failure are considered suitable for transplantation than in other countries, but there are fewer cadaver donations in Britain than in most European countries'.[2] In the same year, Feest et al.[3] made the point that, although renal transplantation has increased, the waiting list has increased even faster. And the problem continues to grow.

This situation contains within it its own paradoxes. On the one hand, when asked, members of the community will generally endorse the policy of transplantation (70 per cent in a Gallup Poll in 1989,[4] for example) whilst, on the other, they seem to show a certain reluctance to be proactive in supporting it, for example by filling in and carrying

143

organ donor cards. The reasons for this are not entirely clear. Some people, of course, have religious objections to transplantation but they would be unlikely to show up in opinion polls as being positive about the programme, so we can probably discount their impact on the difference between stated attitude and actual practice. However, it is possible to speculate on other reasons for this dissonance. It is one thing to declare oneself prepared to be altruistic and another actually to do something about it. Moreover, given the tradition in the United Kingdom of clinical freedom, and of assuming that doctors will act as they see fit in the circumstances that apply, it may be that individuals do not feel it to be necessary to make any advance declaration of intent, since, in the long run, doctors will do as they choose. Equally, many remain dubious about the definition of brain-stem death, and fear that doctors are merely using a redefinition of death as a mechanism for taking their organs, or those of their loved ones, when they are not 'really dead'. And, of course, it may be that the problems inherent in the Human Tissue Act itself, discussed elsewhere in this volume,[5] play a significant part in the shortfall between supply and demand of organs. The recent government proposals to establish a central register may go some way towards remedying that situation, but will this move be enough? Although those who genuinely have a strong commitment to the programme will doubtless welcome it, those who currently claim to be positive, but who actually fear becoming a donor, will have an opportunity not to register. And since the register will represent a more accurate picture of who will and will not consent, this may have the effect of reducing rather than expanding the numbers of organs available. On a pragmatic level, therefore, many people feel that there is an urgent need to reform our current legal position in order to make more organs available and satisfy the aims of the transplantation programme.

Before considering whether or not this is an absolute good, it might be wise to run quickly through the options most commonly mooted. These may take a number of forms, but need only scant mention here since they are discussed at greater length elsewhere.[6] It should also be noted that, given the context of this chapter, it is not intended to consider the position of live organ transplantation. One characteristic which it is said underpins a 'good' system of organ transplantation is its voluntariness. This is an important point which will be returned to later in relation to 'elective' ventilation, but it is also a philosophy which militates against one of the more commonly supported modifications to our law: namely, the process of 'opting out'. This kind of scheme, which operates in some other countries, continues to receive no real support. Donation, it is argued, should be just that – an act of conscious altruism. We have no legal obligation to rescue,[7] maybe not even a moral one, and to require us to register our refusal to rescue is thought by many to be unreasonably intrusive. In any event, the evidence suggests that opting out schemes do not necessarily have the benefits which they were expected to have.

Equally, we could use the American model of required request, but again this has not proved to be an unalloyed success, and it shares some of the same problems as the first option. Since it *requires* clinicians to make a request in appropriate circumstances, it also has the additional problem that it is thought to be insensitive. Indeed, it may be that it could generate antagonism rather than cooperation from relatives who have so recently confronted bereavement, and doubtless it is extremely difficult for medical staff to carry out.

One option which would prove helpful and would not affect the voluntary nature of the programme is, of course, that we could make better use of the system we currently have. Over the years, reports have suggested that there are a number of reasons for the shortage of organs which are independent of the potential donors and their families.[8] Most significantly, the presumption has been that a main contributory factor has been that doctors are reluctant to ask relatives for authority and that relatives are likely to refuse in the moment of their grief. Were this, in fact, the case, then it would go some considerable way to explaining why apparently usable organs are discarded with the body of the deceased. However, there is some evidence that – even if this were once true – it is no longer actually the case. Gentleman *et al.*[9] suggest that, from their study and others which have been carried out, the request rate is actually high and refusal rates are relatively low. As they say, 'The belief that the main reason for losing potential donors is the failure to ask relatives to consent is no longer sustainable'.[10]

This is a significant finding. Over the years, doctors have arguably misinterpreted the Human Tissue Act and have requested relatives' permission even where the law has not actually required it. In part, this has been an explicable misinterpretation, on two counts. First, the terms of the Act cannot be described as crystal-clear. Even in the presence of a written statement of intent by the deceased, the person 'lawfully in possession of the body' *may* remove the organs, not *must*.[11] This seems to suggest that the advance statement of the potential donor is by no means binding. In addition, doubts about who is 'lawfully in possession'[12] of the body may mean that the clinician is infinitely more comfortable if consent has been obtained from those most immediately linked to the donor: namely, the remaining relatives. While the human need to do this is intelligible, it was never legally required where an advance statement had been competently made, but it seems likely that it influenced the number of organs available for transplantation. Rather than putting themselves and families through such an additionally traumatic event, it may be that doctors simply avoided the issue altogether, since after all their professional and emotional commitment was to the immediate patient and not to potential recipients of that patient's organs. That doctors are now apparently more willing to request consent should expand the pool of organs available, assuming that Gentleman et al.[13] are also correct in their assertion about relatives' apparent willingness to authorise donation.

Even if all of this is true, however, we cannot escape the reality, which is that we still do not have enough organs to meet needs. So, if this shortfall continues, why should it be the case? We have the doctors ready, willing and able to undertake the surgery, we have people dying with usable organs and we apparently have a compliant public. Why then is the programme so strapped? Commentators have suggested some significant practical changes which could be made and which would undoubtedly affect the availability of organs. In some cases, for example, some donors are lost because the tests for brain-stem death are not carried out.[14] Some evidence was that '26% of patients identified as possibly brain dead did not have formal tests of brain stem function'.[15] Although 'there were sometimes good reasons for not testing for brain death ... others have speculated that negative attitudes to transplantation and resource restraints in donor intensive care units may also contribute'.[16]

In addition, they note that not all available organs are used. Again, their view is that the reasons for this are pragmatic rather than based on principle: either the transplant team arrived too late or resource constraints in recipient units meant that the offer had to be rejected. Rectification of this problem is, of course, feasible by the injection of additional funding and other forms of resourcing. Now, it may be that the provision of increased funding is practically unlikely, but it is theoretically possible and a cause to be fought for if we really do value the life-giving programme of organ donation. Intensive care facilities are undoubtedly expensive, but not as expensive as the social, human and financial costs to those whose lives are on the line when the transplant programme lets them down, and through them to the community.

Salih et al[17] identified a further problem, namely, who is considered as a suitable donor. Their evidence highlights the fact that the attitude of relatives to the provision of consent may be in part based on the age of the individual whose organs are being requested. In their survey they found that consent was most readily obtained in respect of patients in the age range 50–69, yet, 'According to current practice, this age group is the least likely to be transferred to intensive care facilities, and hence, less likely to be considered as potential organ donors'.[18]

One conclusion that can be reached from this is that a way of facilitating the programme would be via a radical rethinking of the judgements made by doctors themselves. Doctors do not work in a value-free vacuum, and make judgements and assumptions about benefits in the same way as anyone else does. The doctor, for example, pressed for intensive care beds may be unlikely to seek aggressively to rescue the older patient (indeed, may actively fail to make that move) on the basis of one set of constraints – those of a perceived more pressing need for someone else to gain access to available facilities where the length or quality of their life looks likely to be better than the older person who has suffered irremediable or substantial damage. But that decision has an impact on the work of other doctors – the transplant surgeons. All that this does is to point to the often unnoticed inter-relationship between *all* clinicians, no matter which area of medicine is their specialism. It also highlights the complexities generated by the practical inability to take an overview, a problem which is shared by the law. But at the clinical level, the fact that transplantation, particularly of certain organs, can truly be claimed as one of medicine's successes must render the shortage of organs particularly frustrating – a frustration which seems to be shared by the public.

Although clinical success and anecdotal evidence of public support are not in themselves sufficient to justify the aggressive pursuit of any programme, they do go some way towards validating the claim that organ transplantation is seen as a 'good' thing. In addition, and widening the area of concern somewhat, we would likely agree that saving life is in any event inherently valuable. However, there are also possible competing values which need to be addressed and which will be considered below. What does seem clear is that, assuming that we are morally, ethically and legally satisfied with the means used to secure the benefits of a successful organ transplantation programme, there are few, if any, obstacles to endorsing and seeking to facilitate it. However, even if we assume that the structural difficulties can be resolved – that money will be pushed into this part of the health service, that we will have better information about who agrees to donate, that doctors will ask relatives only when required to do so and relatives will consent – the question remains, would we be able to meet the need for organs? If this Utopia came about, the answer might be that we would no longer need to debate ways of solving the problem of organ shortage: the problem would have disappeared. But, of course, we know that Utopia is a fantasy, and that the seemingly endless round of debate, strategies and agonising will be likely to continue for some time.

One consequence of this is that alternative means of 'harvesting' organs are increasingly sought. For many, the existing strategies are in themselves controversial, and any new scheme proposed is likely to be even more so. Any method of acquiring organs for transplantation challenges value systems by exposing the tensions between respect for the dead and for the living. But few, if any, have generated so much concern as the practice of 'elective' ventilation. This practice, described by Feest *et al.*,[19] involves ventilating someone afer they have 'had a respiratory arrest'[20] – in other words, reanimation for the exclusive purpose of removing organs. As Salih *et al.* put it, 'Organ donation has generally been justified in terms of better and longer lives for the recipients. A policy of elective ventilation may call into public question the necessary means to this end, and it is not yet clear that a public debate on this issue would endorse this move.'[21]

The purpose of this chapter is to address the ethical and legal implications of following such a practice, and to stimulate just such a debate. It is not designed to encourage or discourage 'elective' ventilation, but rather seeks to assess whether or not, and in what circumstances, a case could be made which would shift the current presumptions about 'elective' ventilation and facilitate informed debate about its merits and demerits. This will be undertaken in the light of general law and ethics rather than merely those which relate directly to organ transplantation. This is necessary because, as was mentioned above, law often seems to develop in a vacuum, and this can blind us to options and alternatives which may – even if only theoretically – be worthy of exploration.

The discussion will focus on four main areas. The first concerns the relationship between the individual, medical ethics and the value systems which underpin our society. The second will concern the extent to which, and the ways in which, individuals can make disposal decisions about what can and cannot be done with their own bodies. The third will focus on the nature of the choices which people can make and the fourth will address the relevance of the concept of 'best interests' as a guiding principle in medical care.

Individual and Medical Ethics

A fundamental cornerstone of Western liberal democracies is the philosophy which accords a moral primacy to the individual. The Kantian[22] philosophy that people should never be used as a means, provides one obvious – and difficult to defeat – argument *against* treating individuals as a useful collection of organs. Respect for the individual demands that he or she should be valued for what he/she is and not what uses he/she may have. In a sense, of course, strict adherence to this philosophy would potentially rule out all organ donations (unless specifically consented to by the donor), since the respect that is due is due to us as members of the species *homo sapiens* and can reasonably be expected to extend to respect for the corpse of that species. However, this ethic is not generally called into service to prohibit organ transplants, in particular where the removal of the organ is endorsed or requested by the donor. Respect for persons, therefore, also includes respect for their choices, and nothing in this ethic prohibits people from making decisions themselves about the use to which their body may be put. (There may, of course, be other considerations which *do* affect rights of disposition, and these will be considered below.)

From the perspective of the individual, then, there is nothing which Kant has said which precludes the donation of an organ from being respectful of the donor. If this is so, then it is so in any situation, or under any scheme, which is based on consent. Indeed, respecting a competent request may be an essential concomitant of this philosophy, and arguably should be endorsed by the law. As Wolf[23] has said in a slightly different context: 'The law is about human beings. And the law governing the termination of life-sustaining treatment is about a particularly human matter – how people come to their death, and how we treat those nearing the end. It is about choosing between a society that honors our preferences, embeddedness in relationships, and control of our bodies, or a society that leaves us stranded, defenseless, and imprisoned at the end.'[24]

The ethics of individual respect, therefore, if anything might be said to liberate individuals to make a wide range of choices about the disposal of their bodies, at least in the abstract. Equally, however, the individual when a patient is subject to the tradition of medical ethics.[25] The principles said to underlie medical ethics are fundamentally individualistic. In other words, they require the doctor to address the individual patient and not to concern him/herself with other patients in reaching decisions about treatment. Again, therefore, the doctor, in deciding what should be done, should have no concern for what might benefit other patients, a view endorsed in the House of Lords in the case of *Airedale NHS Trust* v. *Bland*[26] and in the Report of the House of Lords Select Committee on Medical Ethics.[27] Nor should the law or the doctor reach a decision based on the scarcity of resources[28] – a particularly important caveat in the light of what has been said about the shortage of available donor organs.

The principles of medical ethics – particularly beneficence and non-maleficence – seem to be breached when the doctor's concern shifts from the immediate patient's welfare and focuses on the welfare of other patients. The tradition of medical ethics is dominated by the doctor–patient relationship: in other words, it is highly individualised and requires that doctors concern themselves with the individual patient in front of them. The presumption that this is the optimal clinical relationship is again one that is hard to defeat, and it too poses a potential threat to the practice of transplantation. For this reason, medical ethics require that the doctors seeking to harvest organs should be different from those involved in the care of the patient.

For the moment what we seem to have is an impasse. In terms of both our social ethics and our medical ethics, we are prohibited from considerations which are extraneous to the individual patient in the care of the individual clinician. As has been said, although this might seem to put an ethical block on transplantation programmes, this has not been the case, although it does reflect why some people are hostile to the programme itself. To this extent, there is nothing specific to 'elective' ventilation here. Rather, this extremely brief animadversion to certain ethical perspectives becomes of interest when combined with the other considerations which will be addressed by this chapter.

Making Health Care Decisions

Central to the lawfulness of transplantation programmes has been said to be the question of consent. Most particularly, ethical objections may disappear where the consent given is that of the individual donor, rather than his or her relatives. Despite the interpretational problems of the Human Tissue Act, it seems clear that the person 'lawfully in possession of the body' would act lawfully if they respected an advance statement from the deceased as to the use of their organs. In a way, this kind of declaration is an equivalent to the advance directive or 'living will', whose status in law has been considerably less than clear.[29] But the advance directive plays a significant role in what follows. If we concede that ethical principles permit the use of parts of the human body, and we agree that this is particularly acceptable when the individual donor has consented, then there may be a valuable role to be played by the advance directive in reaching a conclusion about 'elective' ventilation. But before considering this specifically, it is worth reminding ourselves briefly of what an advance directive is. This is considered extensively elsewhere in this volume,[30] but merits some comment here.

Kuczewski puts it thus: 'the living will expresses the values by which one lives and is committed to living. It encodes the desire for treatment and a death in accordance with one's commitment to these values. Thus, the living will is an expression of the vision of the good in accordance with which one lives his or her life.'[31] The value of advance health care statements has now been accepted by the House of Lords Select Committee on Medical Ethics,[32] the British Medical Association[33] and most recently the Law Commission.[34] This recognition follows a perceptible shift in the attitude of UK courts towards the kinds of decisions which individuals when competent may make about future health care.[35]

It is now universally accepted that, barring unusual circumstances, the sane adult has the right to refuse treatment even where it is life-saving. In the case of *Airedale NHS Trust* v. *Bland*,[36] it was also said *obiter* that, had Anthony Bland made an advance statement of what he would have wished, this should have been persuasive on his treating physicians and would have contributed significantly to the evaluation of what was or was not lawful.[37] The case of *Re C*[38] extended the rights of the individual to make advance decisions – decisions which come into effect when the individual is no longer competent to express a choice.

Recognition of the value of advance directives by the House of Lords Select Committee[39] opened the door to a final statement as to their legal weight. Whilst not recommending legislation, and not supporting the view that they should be binding on clinicians,[40] the House of Lords commended their development, suggesting that codes of ethics should be drawn up by the relevant medical bodies.[41] In a sense, this brought the UK position closer to that in a number of other jurisdictions, such as the United States, where 'Advance directives in their many variations continue to be the preferred solution to treatment decisions for incompetent patients. Recommended by most medical ethicists and advisory bodies, they have achieved judicial or legislative recognition in more than forty states.'[42]

The House of Lords Report has now been followed by recommendations from the Law Commission,[43] who – interestingly, and in the view of this author, thankfully – have proposed a draft bill which would consolidate and define the scope and effectiveness of these directives. The Law Commission report takes account of 'an almost unanimous view that patients should be enabled and encouraged to exercise genuine choice about treatments and procedures'.[44] Now, traditionally, advance directives have been seen as useful primarily to ensure that treatment which the individual does *not* want cannot be provided. Some forms of directive, notably those carried by Jehovah's Witnesses, have been recognised for some considerable time and are generally deemed to be binding on clinicians.[45] But the advance directive need not be a negative statement only. And it is here that its relevance to 'elective' ventilation becomes clear.

So far, we can conclude two important things: first, that there is no fundamental ethical objection to the use of body parts, particularly when directed by the donor; second, that people are entitled to make decisions about what treatment should be given or not in the event of their lapsing into incompetence. The question is, need that entitlement be confined to decisions about what treatment they do not want? The Law Commission recognises that this is too narrow a definition, noting that, when an advance decision has been made, there is a 'further important distinction ... to be drawn between the legal effect of a decision *in favour* of a particular (or all) treatment and a decision *against* such treatment'.[46] *Ex hypothesi*, therefore, the decision could be that some things *should* be done rather than merely demanding that other things are *not* done. From the point of view of 'elective' ventilation, therefore, there is a theoretical window of opportunity provided by the recognition that individuals can proactively require certain forms of treatment.

However, this is not unproblematic. Although individuals can competently refuse treatment, they cannot oblige a doctor – even when they are competent – to treat against the doctor's clinical judgement.[47] No advance directive could change that position, since the directive cannot render lawful something which is otherwise unlawful. There are two parts to this conclusion. Even if a patient chose to make a directive stating his/her wish to be ventilated in appropriate circumstances for the purposes of removing organs, this statement would be no more binding on a doctor than would any other. Second, and most significantly for these purposes, if the treatment which they sought was *in any event* unlawful, then clearly the directive would have no force at all. This, then, raises one of the most problematic aspects of the whole question. We agree that people can consent to something in advance, but are there limits to what it is that consent can be given for? The answer, of course, is yes, and that this is so might suggest that as a strategy 'elective' ventilation is doomed to be consigned to the medical dustbin. The rest of this chapter will question whether or not this is a necessary conclusion.

What Can be Consented to?

The individual who seeks to offer advance consent (which seems to be lawful) to specific treatment is nonetheless bound by the general rules concerning what can and cannot be consented to. Thus it is accepted in Scots law that the consent of the victim, except where consent is central to the crime, for example in the case of rape, does not remove criminal liability from the perpetrator, since what is critical is the intention of the assailant.[48] This, of course, excludes common situations such as certain contact sports. In England, the position was put thus: 'it can be taken as a starting point that it is an essential element of an assault that the act is done contrary to the will and without the consent of the victim; and it is doubtless for this reason that the burden lies on the prosecution to negative consent. Ordinarily, then, if the victim consents, the assailant is not guilty.'[49]

However, as Lord Mustill pointed out in *R* v. *Brown*,[50] 'There are ... objections to a general theory of consent and violence. Thus, for example, it is too simple to speak only of consent, for it comes in various sorts.'[51] Consent may be specific, general or relatively speculative. What is important, therefore, is the points at which agreement is nullified by factors which might broadly equate to policy considerations. As Lord Slynn said in the same case: 'I accept that consent cannot be said simply to be a defence to any act which one person does to another. A line has to be drawn as to what can and as to what cannot be the subject of consent.'[52]

The question, then, is whether or not that line does or should include consent to ventilation for the purposes of organ donation. There are a number of possible arguments which might suggest that 'elective' ventilation could fall within the category of lawfully consented to treatment. Analysis of the law highlights the criteria which the courts have felt to be important indicators of the role played by consent in decriminalising behaviour which would otherwise prima facie have amounted to assault. In *Attorney General's Reference (No 6 of 1980)*,[53] Lord Lane saw the answer as being 'that it is not in the public interest that people should try to cause, or should cause, each other actual bodily harm for no good reason'.[54] Or as Lord Jauncey put it in *R v. Brown*,[55] 'the infliction of bodily harm without good reason is unlawful and ... the consent of the victim is irrelevant'.[56]

There are two ways in which criminal liability might flow from 'elective' ventilation. The first relates to the ventilation itself, and the second to the subsequent removal of organs. At first sight, the doctor who ventilates someone without the intention of benefiting them commits an assault. If this is to be challenged by the availability of consent in the form of an advance directive, one or more of the exceptions to the general rule must exist. In this case, the question would be, is the assault undertaken for 'no good reason'? If the *reason* is important, then it is arguable that the facilitation of a programme which has public support and which confers enormous benefits on individuals and the community is, on the contrary, a very good reason to translate what would otherwise be an indefensible harm into an act capable of being rendered lawful by consent.

A second matter raised concerns the extent to which consent is, in any event, central to the issue or merely forms one part of the reasons which provide a defence. Again, this is relevant for ventilation. If the programme itself is legitimate, and the consent is real, then it may fit a slightly different theoretical perspective offered by Lord Mustill. As he says,

> when one examines the situations which are said to found such a theory [concerning consent and violence] it is seen that the idea of consent as the foundation of a defence has in many cases been forced on to the theory, whereas in reality the reason why the perpetrator of the harm is not liable is not because of the recipient's consent, but because the perpetrator has acted in a situation where the consent of the recipient forms one, but only one, of the elements which make the act legitimate.[57]

Translated into the situation of 'elective' ventilation, are there any other factors which might make the 'assault' legitimate? Again, we might refer to the 'good' of the donation of organs and to the respect which honouring the desire to be altruistic shows for the individual potential donor. These things would certainly render the act ethically defensible, even if there remains some legal doubt.

So what, if anything, can we add to the scales which might finalise the debate? We have already conceded that donation of organs is a 'good' thing and that there is a need to fill the shortfall between supply and demand. It has been agreed that respect for persons is a fundamental value, and that its fulfilment is a goal worthy of attainment. In addition, the power of the individual to make an advance statement of consent or refusal has been given legal standing and is based on sound ethical principles. But even taken together, these may not be sufficient justi-fication for accepting a policy of 'elective' ventilation as ethical or lawful. However, there is one further card held by the proponent of 'elective' ventilation and that is the context in which the activity is carried out: namely, that it is done by doctors in a medical setting. Much of medical practice, and certainly all surgery, would amount to an assault were it not for the elements peculiar to the practice of medicine. Indeed, some surgery would amount to an extremely severe form of assault, but, as Lord Mustill says, even where it is 'well on the upper side of the critical level',[58] it can be 'legitimate if performed in accordance with good medical practice and with the consent of the patient'.[59]

It may well be that – assuming prior consent – ventilating an individual is not, therefore, in itself unlawful or unethical. However, what of the actual removal of the organs? Arguably, removing an organ, such as a kidney, which is not essential for survival is covered by the above. But doctors will also want hearts, livers and so on – organs whose removal actively kills the individual. This is, of course, a much more problem-atic situation since killing is generally reckoned to be a crime in any circumstances which fall outside very narrow excuses, such as self-defence. Therefore, even if consent plays a part in ventilation, it is accepted that it is not a defence to killing, even where the intention is benign, as it is generally assumed would be the case in the medical setting.[60]

Given this, there is only one possible way around the problem. Unfortunately, it is not a solution which commended itself to the House of Lords Select Committee.[61] Simply put, it concerns the acts/omissions doctrine. This doctrine indicates that we are liable for our acts but not for our failure to act. However, it is also accepted that when there is a pre-existing duty of care, as there clearly is in the medical setting, then omissions are as culpable as acts.[62] Nonetheless, although this last is a statement of the doctrine as it should be applied, the law has not followed the logic of this in every medical case. In cases concerning handicapped neonates, for example, failing to save life has not generally been sanctioned either by the civil[63] or the criminal[64] law. In other cases, it has been held permissible to withhold or withdraw treatment, even by redefining treatment to include nutrition and hydration,[65] so as to allow death to occur. Arguably, therefore, if it is right that an omission to save life does not render a doctor liable, and given that his/her omissions theoretically have the same standing as his/her acts, the act which results in death is equivalent to the omission which has the same, intended outcome. In fact, it could be said to be ethically disingenuous to maintain this distinction. Moreover, we cannot justify its maintenance on the basis of an adherence to the sanctity of life, since the outcome in each case is death. In these situations, therefore, it is a distinction without a difference. Its endorsement by the House of Lords Select Committee was doubtless predicated on their reluctance to sanction active voluntary euthanasia,[66] but this approach has had unfortunate consequences in the area of 'elective' ventilation. Taking a broader perspective might have led to a different conclusion, or at least might have further opened the debate.

The question remains, therefore, if consent is a significant, but not sole, determinant of bringing an act which would otherwise be unlawful within the framework of legitimacy, what is the additional factor at work? Again, Lord Mustill gives the answer: 'The answer must in my opinion be that proper medical treatment, for which actual or deemed consent is a prerequisite, is in a category of its own.'[67] Of course, a critical word here is 'proper' in relation to medical treatment, but since no-one has suggested that organ transplantation is improper, we might legitimately conclude that this statement can apply to a predictive donation of organs by means of 'elective' ventilation. The significance of context here should, if anything, reinforce the argument that the distinction between act and omission is no longer tenable in this setting. Thus, arguably, both the (consented to) ventilation and the (consented to) removal of organs could be rendered lawful.

There remains, however, one further subtlety which relates to the propriety of the treatment envisaged by this argument. 'Proper' medical treatment is generally taken to be that which is in the 'best interests' of the patieint, yet elective ventilation is clearly only in the interests of someone other than the individual – or is it?

'Best Interests'

Generally, the law says clearly that nothing which is not in the patient's best interests can be done. This means that to impose any treatment which is not in the best interests of the individual patient is to commit the crime of battery or assault and the tort of trespass to the person, or in Scotland a civil or criminal assault. In other words, it is unlawful at civil law and a criminal offence. In the case of 'elective' ventilation, therefore, the answer seems clear: it must in these terms be unlawful.

No apparent benefit is derived by the individual patient – indeed, none is intended.

This conclusion is at first sight reinforced by addressing ourselves to the question of 'best interests'. It is now widely accepted that this test is the one most commonly applied when treatment decisions are being scrutinised.[68] Traditionally, this has been judged in line with the tests developed by our courts over the years and in accordance also with the test enunciated in the case of *Bolam* v. *Friern Hospital Management Committee*,[69] which holds doctors to be acting appropriately when they act in accordance with a responsible body of medical opinion. But it has also taken on a wider meaning than the merely medical. As the Law Commission has said: 'it is one thing to say that "best interests" are the test, and quite another to say that "best interests" are to be judged by what a responsible body of medical opinion would consider acceptable ... a test developed to deal with matters of clinical judgement is not necessarily the most appropriate one to use in circumstances where the balancing of other interests may be required'.[70] So we accept that the judgements being made extend beyond clinical expertise, and must take account of other value systems too. But it is still assumed that no amount of sophistry can define intrusively maintaining 'life' for the benefit of others as being in conjunction with a 'best interests' test. At least this is so given our current understanding of 'best interests'.

Unlike their counterparts elsewhere,[71] British courts remain in thrall to the notion that best interests is the correct test to use when judging the quality of decisions taken on behalf of another person. Even if an advance directive stipulating consent to 'elective' ventilation were to be in existence, the proposals of the Law Commission would seem to indicate that the triggering of the terms of the directive should always take account of the 'best interests' of the person concerned.[72] Ventilation for these purposes, and removal of organs, if viewed from a traditional perspective surely cannot fit into this concept. The person ventilated may, for example, suffer a deterioration into persistent vegetative or other state.[73] The removal of organs (even those which are not immediately necessary to preserve life) fulfils no interest of the donor, or at least not in terms of physical health. There are two possible responses to this. Persons undergoing ventilation can scarcely be worse off in PVS than they currently are, and now that our law in respect of the management of such states has been clarified, we know that they need not survive in such a condition indefinitely.[74] Furthermore, to assume that no interests of the donor are served is to mistake the nature of 'best interests'.

Although British courts have tended to assume that the relevant indicators are physical, might it not be argued that the individual's best interests are both continuing and satisfied when proper respect is paid to their competently expressed wish to benefit others by a short extension of existence? The Law Commission puts the conundrum as follows:

Anything done in relation to the health care of a person who lacks capacity to make his or her own decision about that matter must be (1) reasonable and (2) in the best interests of that person. In deciding what is in his or her best interests regard must be had to four listed matters, namely:
(1) the ascertainable past and present wishes and feelings of the person, and the factors he or she would consider,
(2) the need to permit and encourage the person to participate,
(3) the views of other appropriate people, and
(4) the availability of an effective less restrictive option.[75]

In terms of this argument, (1) and (2) have been dealt with. Equally, the reasonableness condition can be met if what is 'reasonable' is defined widely rather than narrowly. The third consideration might be met by consultation with relatives or others who are intimate with the individual, although arguably this would be entirely unnecessary (even if humane) were an advance directive in existence. The fourth criterion might suggest that 'elective' ventilation should be seen only as a last resort in a transplantation programme, but does not rule it out completely.

If this is accepted, and is added to the points already made, then an advance statement in favour of 'elective' ventilation would not fall foul of the Law Commission's statement that 'We have now recommended that reasonable treatment which is in a person's best interests will be lawful. Advance consent to *other* sorts of treatment would not, however, have the effect of rendering them lawful.'[76]

Conclusions

This brief analysis of the four issues postulated as being central to the dilemma of 'elective' ventilation might, perhaps surprisingly, form the basis of a re-evaluation of the ethics and law involved. Indeed, it will be noticed that, in describing the practice which was undertaken in the hospital pioneering it, the word 'elective' has been set in quotation marks throughout this chapter. The reason for this is that, in its original form, even though the consent of relatives was sought and obtained, it could not properly be described as truly elective. The one individual who could elect was never in a position so to do. Yet the use of advance declarations of wishes could render the ventilation truly elective – not by the doctor or the relatives, but by the person most intimately concerned, the prospective donor. Obviously, such a choice would need to be made in full knowledge of the implications and consequences of the decision, but this is not uncommon in medical practice.

In any event, even taking a Kantian perspective does not, it has been suggested, preclude my voluntary entry into such a programme, and other things being equal, it might in fact positively endorse it. The principles of medical ethics equally do not inevitably conflict with a doctor following my wishes. In so doing the doctor is acting beneficently (in terms of respecting my desire to be altruistic). The additional principles of respect for autonomy and justice are also satisfied when my wishes are vindicated and others benefit from this. This does not challenge the doctor's commitment to attend only to me without concern for other patients. Rather, the concern for others is an integral part of what I, and not the doctor, seek.

Equally, there is little remaining doubt that I may make a valid advance directive which, even if not binding on my doctors, should at least be persuasive. Of course, for some there may be concern about the combination of advance directive and organ donor authorisation. As one commentator said: 'much effort has been expended over the past 20 years to separate the issues of organ donation and treatment decisions in the public's mind, since the main reason people do not sign organ-donor cards is that they believe doctors might "do something to me before I am really dead." Tying organ donation to treatment refusals that might lead to death only heightens this concern and is likely to lead people to use neither form.'[77] This is, of course, a matter of concern, but it also misses the point.

The form of advance directive which would trigger truly elective ventilation is a positive and not a negative one. Indeed, it presumes that something *will* be done when you are not 'really dead'. The whole point of its relation to elective ventilation would be that people are making a choice for a particular kind of death – not simply permitting it to happen, but proactively acknowledging, as even our courts have done, that death in some cases may be preferable to continued existence, and making the form of that death less futile, thereby perhaps providing comfort rather than generating fear. The knowledge that I may make such a gift may serve as a positive thought throughout my competent life, since its vindication reflects values which are important to me. As has been said: 'What seems to have been overlooked until now is the recognition that advance directives are syllogisms that ask for medical conclusions. One premise is a not-yet-existent future medical condition or event; the conclusion is the treatment the person does or does not want, at least given today's range of possible options. *What is lacking in the syllogism is the other important universal premise: the values that underlie and inform any such decision*'[78] (emphasis added).

Unsurprisingly, the most difficult part of the argument that suggests reconsideration of the lawfulness of elective ventilation relates to the question of the impact of consent on behaviour which at first sight seems clearly to be unlawful. In what has gone before, the main area of interest was in posing the question as to whether or not an advance exercise of my rights to dispose of my own body would be sufficient to legalise the behaviour of those who acted upon my expressed wishes. A tentative conclusion was that – in line with other aspects of the law – this might well be possible. This, of course, was also contingent on one other consideration. The assumption underlying the argument has been that the act of ventilation is an assault, but one to which I can consent, and secondly that the removal of organs also constitutes an assault, to which perhaps I may not consent in a manner which renders the doctor non-liable. The argument here has been that my consent, when coupled with the other contextual and ethical factors, could render the doctor non-liable using existing principles of law. This position would be reinforced by one further step, and that is the casting out once and for all of the notion that there is, in the clinical setting, a difference between an act and an omission.

The behaviour of my doctor in *acting* on my expressed wishes is little, if any, different from the doctor's adherence to my refusal of treatment. Yet we have no difficulty with the latter (except in circumstances where we have reason to believe that my attitude may have changed). Why, then is this not equally applicable to elective ventilation? If we can recognise the possibility that my attitude to treatment refusal is acceptable, there are no good reasons to assume that the same could not be true merely because the *nature* of my expressed wishes is different. After all, the outcome – that is, my death – is the same however it is achieved and the clinician is fully aware of this in carrying out these wishes.

Finally, attention was turned to the question of 'best interests'. If it is possible to accept that I may believe that my interests are served by having my wishes in this respect vindicated, then this test poses no serious threat to the practice of elective ventilation. And it has been argued that it does not stretch the credibility of this concept to encapsulate within it my gift to others.

Thus, although for the moment it seems that opinion is clear that elective ventilation is unlawful, there may be arguments which would suggest that, in the right climate and with the requisite will, re-analysis would render it acceptable in certain circumstances. Elective ventilation may be a special case to be considered on all of its merits and not simply as a knee-jerk reaction to the shortage of organs. As has been said, 'In effect, either all or almost all the instances of the consensual infliction of violence are special. They have been in the past, and will continue to be in the future, the subject of special treatment by the law.'[79]

It may be that some legal clarification is required, possibly by legislative intervention, but ultimately we must return to the initial questions. In an ideal world, we would not need to address this issue, but this does not make it a bad question, nor does it make any attempt to explore its ethical and legal feasibility merely an unlovely attempt to disguise pragmatics under a veil of theory, however plausible or implausible. Some of the arguments for elective ventilation are acceptable in themselves and all of them would remain as valid as they are, or might be, even if there was no shortage of organs for donation. As to the legal response, we would do well to bear in mind the words of Lord Mustill. As he says, 'the state should interfere with the rights of an individual to live his or her life as he or she may choose no more than is necessary to ensure a proper balance between the special interests of the individual and the general interests of the individuals who together comprise the population at large'.[80]

Notes

1   D. Gentleman, J. Easton and B. Jennett, 'Brain death and organ donation in a neurological unit: audit of recent practice', *BMJ*, **301**, 24 Nov 1990, 1203.
2   At 1203.
3   T.G. Feest, *et al.*, 'Protocol for increasing organ donation after cerebrovascular deaths in a district general hospital', *Lancet*, **335**, (1990), 1133.
4   Quoted by Feest *et al.*, 'Protocol', at 1135.
5   See Chapter 7.
6   Ibid.
7   See *Report of the Select Committee on Medical Ethics* (HL Paper 21-I), London, HMSO, 1994, at p.19, para.68: 'Unlike many foreign legal codes, which contain "easy rescue" provisions, English law is such that, in the absence of a specific duty, a person commits no offence if he fails to save the life of another, although he could easily do so with no undue risk to himself.'
8   Conference of the Medical Royal Colleges and their Faculties in the UK, working paper, '*Report of the Working Party on the supply of donor organs for transplantation'*, London, 1987.
9   'Brain death', note 1, above.
10   At 1205–6.
11   Human Tissue Act 1961, s.1(1).
12   For discussion, see P.D.G. Skegg, *Law, Ethics and Medicine*, 2nd edn, Oxford, Oxford University Press, 1984.
13   'Brain death', note 1, above, at 1204: 'the English survey and a recent report from Cambridge both showed a request rate of 96%, and in Glasgow it was 88%. Refusal rates in these three studies were 30%, 10% and 30%, respectively.'
14   Gentleman *et al.*, 'Brain death', note 1, above, at 1205.
15   Ibid.
16   Ibid.
17   M.A.M. Salih *et al.*, 'Potential availability of cadaver organs for transplantation', *BMJ*, **302**, 4 May 1991, 1053.
18   Ibid., at 1055.
19   'Protocol'.
20   Ibid., at 1135.
21   'Potential availability', note 17, above, at 1065.
22   Cf. I. Kant, 'Duties Towards the Body in Regard to Life', *Lectures in Ethics*, reprinted in J. Donnelly (ed.), *Suicide: Right or Wrong?*, New York, Prometheus, 1990.

23 S.M. Wolf, 'Nancy Beth Cruzan: In No Voice At All', vol.20, no.1, *Hastings Center Report* (1990) at p.38.
24 Ibid., at 41.
25 The principles of medical ethics are generally taken to be beneficence, non-malefi-cence, justice and autonomy.
26 [1993] 1 A11 ER 821.
27 Cited in note 7, above.
28 See comments in the House of Lords Select Committee *Report*, for example at p.23, para.89.
29 Cf. *Airedale NHS Trust* v. *Bland*, Report of the House of Lords Select Committee on Medical Ethics: S.A.M. McLean, 'Advance Directives: Legal and Ethical Considerations', in N. Pace and S.A.M. McLean (eds), *Law and Ethics in Intensive Care*, Oxford, Oxford University Press, in press; D. Morgan, 'Odysseus and the Binding Directive: Only a Cautionary Tale?', *Legal Studies*, **14**, (1994), 411.
30 See chapter 10.
31 M.G. Kuczewski, 'Whose Will Is It Anyway? A Discussion of Advance Directives, Personal Identity and Consensus in Medical Ethics', *Bioethics*, **8**, (1),(1994) 27 at 35.
32 Cited in note 7, above.
33 BMA Statement on Advance Directives, January 1994.
34 The Law Commission (LAW COM No 231) *Mental Incapacity, Item 9 of the Fourth Programme of Law Reform: Mentally Incapacitated Adults*, London, HMSO, 1995.
35 Cf. *Airedale NHS Trust* v. *Bland*; *Re C (adult: refusal of treatment)* [1994] 1 WLR 290.
36 See note 26, above.
37 Cf. the judgements of Lords Keith and Goff.
38 See note 35, above.
39 Cited in note 7, above.
40 Cf. *Report*, p.54, para.265.
41 Ibid; c.f. also p.55, paras.266 and 267.
42 J. Robertson, 'Second Thoughts on Living Wills', vol. 21, no.6, *Hastings Center Report*, (1991) at p.6.
43 See note 34, above.
44 *Mental Incapacity*, at p.66.
45 See, for example, the Canadian case of *Mallette* v. *Shulman et al.* [1991] 2 Med. LR 162.
46 *Mental Incapacity*, at p.65.
47 Law Commission, *Mental Incapacity*, at p.67–8, para.5.6: 'It is quite clear that the law will not "second guess" a doctor who has formed a reasonable and respon-sible clinical judgement that a particular form of treatment is not called for because it would be futile or inappropriate. No document signed by a patient in advance can overrule such a judgment.'
48 *Smart* v. *HMA* 1975 SLT 65.
49 Per Lord Lane, *Attorney General's Reference (No 6 of 1980)* [1981] 1 QB 715, at p.718.
50 [1994] 1 AC 212.
51 At p.259.
52 At p.279.
53 Cited in note 49, above.
54 At 719.
55 See note 50, above.
56 At p.243.
57 In *R* v. *Brown*, at 259.
58 Ibid., at 258–9.
59 Ibid.
60 Cf. *R* v. *Cox* (1992) 12 BMLR 48.

61   *Report*: see particularly p.19, paras. 68–79.
62   Cf. *Report*, particularly p.19, paras. 68 and 72.
63   Cf. *Re B*.
64   *R* v. *Arthur*, The Times, 5 November 1981.
65   Cf. *Airedale NHS Trust* v. *Bland*.
66   *Report*: see pp.48–49, paras. 236–241.
67   In *R* v. *Brown*, at 266.
68   Cf. *Re F (mental patient: sterilisation)* [1990] 2 AC 1; see also the *House of Lords Select Committee on Medical Ethics, Report*, p.36, paras. 164–8.
69   [1957] 1 A11 ER.
70   Law Commission Consultation Paper no. 119, *Mentally Incapacitated Adults and Decision-Making: An Overview*, 1981, p.33, para. 2.24.
71   Other jurisdictions, such as the United States and Canada, often use the 'substituted judgement' test, which attempts to assess what the individual would have wanted had they had the opportunity of making their own statement. This, for example, was the test used in *Cruzan* v. *Director, Missouri Dept. of Health* 110 S.Ct. 2841 (1990).
72   *Mentally Incapacitated Adults*, at p.672.
73   Although Feest *et al.*, 'Protocol', found no evidence of this happening; see also, more recently, M. Riad and A. Nicholls, 'Elective Ventilation of Potential Organ Donors', *BMJ*, **310**, 18 March 1995.
74   Cf. *Airedale NHS Trust* v. *Bland*.
75   *Mentally Incapacitated Adults*, at p.68.
76   *Mentally Incapacitated Adults*, at p.70.
77   *New England J. of Medicine*, April 1991, 1212.
78   P. Lambert, J. McI. Gibson and P. Nathanson, 'The Values History: An Innovation in Surrogate Medical Decision-Making', *Law, Medicine and Health Care*, **18**(3), (Fall, 1990), at 210.
79   Per Lord Mustill in *R* v. *Brown*, at 259.
80   Ibid., at 273.

9 Reason, Law and Medicine: Anencephalics as Organ Donors

JOHN PORTER

It is widely supposed that any philosophical contribution to medical ethics must consist in proffering arguments supporting one side or the other in some dispute. The philosophical task would be discharged through its presentation and defence of a rationale favouring one or other of the protagonists. However, this assumption concerning the nature of philosophical discussion is controversial and an alternative role for philosophical thought is urged by some.[1] This consists in standing back from the dispute itself and becoming clearer about how the dispute itself is pictured by the protagonists – seeking to become clearer about 'the self-image' of the dispute the protagonists have and subjecting the characterisation of the dispute to critical examination. That critical examination may result not in a declaration of support for one side or the other in the dispute but in a realisation that the dispute itself is misconceived.

Anencephalics are severely impaired. Both cerebral hemispheres are missing and there is little brain function above the brain-stem. Most anencephalics are stillborn but, it is said, between 25 and 45 per cent are live births.[2] Circulatory and respiratory functions are performed naturally. Thus anencephalics are not dead either according to what has been called the 'traditional' criterion of death – the irreversible cessation of cardiopulmonary function – or the newer criterion of 'death of the whole brain' – loss of all function in the cerebral hemispheres (the brain cortex or higher brain) and loss of all function in the brain-stem (the vegetative or lower brain).

163

Some 40 per cent of infants born alive survive for 24 hours. Of these one out of three will live for three days and one in 20 to at least seven days.[3] It has been said:

> If a significant percentage of these infants born alive could be utilized as organ sources, a major supply of neonatal organs would become available.[4] Theoretically, a single anencephalic infant with healthy thoracic and abdominal organs could supply vital organs to save the lives of two other infants (one needing a heart and another a liver) and enhance the lives of several others (who need kidneys, corneas and various transplantable tissues).[5]

Anencephalics, considered as beings from whom organs might be taken for transplantation purposes, are problematic for what has been called 'the dead donor' rule: non-consenting patients must be dead before removal of their organs. Anencephalics do not generally meet current legal criteria for being dead. They are typically born with some or all of their brain-stem functions intact. They are incapable of consenting and have no present or future interest that is served by saving the life of the recipient, related or not.[6]

Most anencephalics die within a few days of birth. Cardiorespiratory arrest, with poor perfusion of vital organs, is said to be 'the life-ending event',[7] rendering the heart, liver and kidneys unsuitable for transplantation. For medical and legal reasons, brain death must occur prior to cardiorespiratory collapse if removal of organs is to proceed under current law. If existing law is to be complied with, the acquisition of organs for transplantation purposes from anencephalics requires sophisticated medical techniques: vigorous life support, including mechanical ventilation in anticipation of brain-stem death, procedures which themselves have occasioned ethical concern.[8]

In consequence, there has been much discussion aimed at changing the current law to make it easier to obtain suitable organs from anencephalics. It is the character of that discussion which this chapter seeks to address, in the light of the opening remarks. Those who seek amendment to the law must, if they are rational agents, have some conception of what in the current legal position they find unacceptable and some conception of how the considerations they advance show the unacceptability of that position. This contribution will discuss the nature of the dialogue between law and medicine on the matter of organ transplantation from anencephalics to suitable donors. No arguments will be put forward for retaining or changing the law, although the discussion does suggest it embodies nothing ethically unsound. Rather the argument pays attention to the matter of how the empirical information medicine possesses can properly be brought into relation with the law.

The legal position, at least in Scotland, is unequivocal: if organs are removed from an anencephalic for whatever purpose by procedures which cause the death of the brain-stem the relevant surgeon is rendered liable to a charge of murder.[9] The physical condition of the anencephalic may vary somewhat; but there seems to be a general consensus that the anencephalic, in virtue of physical abnormalities of various kinds, neither has, nor will have, 'higher cortical functions'. These 'higher cortical functions', again according to a general consensus, are required for the possession of characteristic human psychological and sentient capacities. It should, of course, be mentioned, that many higher cortical functions are missing from those in comas and in what is called 'a persistent vegetative state'. Consequently, considerations which pertain to anencephalics might conceivably be extended to include these other cases.[10]

One way of bringing into focus the topic of this contribution is to ask of those who seek an amendment to the law what, if the law were changed in accordance with their wishes, they would take themselves to be doing in the problematic cases.[11] There are, I think, two ways of picturing this. First, it might be conceded to the law that the killing of an anencephalic is a homicide like any other, but what would be being sought, in the light of particular circumstances, was a legal dispensation to kill. This might be thought of as akin to, although not identical with, the special dispensation given to police and security forces to kill in particular circumstances.[12]

It is expedient to comment very briefly upon this first line of argument. First, it is widely assumed in the literature that, if a moral justification for seeing a right to kill is sought, that justification must be on utilitarian grounds – roughly, the greater good will be served by permitting the killing. This seems to me *prima facie* a quite unwarranted assumption. Without further argument it seems implausible. For example, most are prepared to concede a right to kill in cases of self-defence; but it is here wildly implausible to suppose that a justification would be sought by appeal to utilitarian considerations. Or again, necessity is sometimes thought of as conferring a moral right to omit to take steps to preserve another's life. I have in mind here cases where the consequences of preserving your life will involve the loss of my life but where you offer no threat to me. Utilitarianism is again *prima facie* the wrong place to look for an understanding of such a view. But, however a defence of the right to take life might properly be sought, there does not seem to be overwhelming evidence of the utilitarian calculations having properly been done. Indeed, the utilitarian benefits, it has been suggested,[13] are really quite minimal, while the utilitarian costs do not seem to have been calculated at all. Nor does there seem much prospect of a justification being found in terms of necessity. It does not seem unjust to conclude that serious work on providing a moral justification for conferring a right to kill has yet to be undertaken.

The second way is to bring the medical facts into critical relation with the law by taking them to provide evidence, perhaps conclusive evidence, that the position embodied in the law is without rational foundation. On this second view of the matter, those urging a change in the law would not take themselves to be asking for a special dispensation to kill. They would not concede to the law the soundness of treating the killing of an anencephalic as homicide. Their 'self-image' would, rather, be that of those asking for an unsound legal taxonomy to be adjusted: killing an anencephalic 'really' is not to be classified as a homicide. They would, further, take the physical facts in their possession as providing the 'grounds' for such a view. Roughly, their view would be: because the physical facts are as they are, this demonstrates the unsoundness of the current legal taxonomy.

This second view must, of course, have some conception of what is being done when organs are removed from anencephalics in the problematic cases and, moreover, it must, to be rational, hold that what *is* being done has not the moral status of a homicide. Coupled with the role that the physical evidence plays in such thinking we arrive at the idea that there is a moral difference between procedures performed on an anencephalic and killing properly classified as a homicide and that the physical evidence medicine possesses is sufficient to establish that this difference exists.

This second view itself might be sustained in two quite different ways. On the one hand, it might be conceded that something is killed but that the killing is not properly classified as a homicide. On the other, it might not be conceded that any killing takes place at all, since nothing is alive save a functioning brain-stem. Either view would, of course, charge the law with embodying a faulty moral taxonomy. Either view would take itself to support this charge by appeal to the physical facts. Thus either view holds that current law embodies a taxonomy of homicide which is vulnerable to correction in the light of physical evidence, evidence which, in the case of an anencephalic, is possessed.

This account of the nature of the discussion of the moral propriety of removing organs from anencephalics for transplantation is flawed. It is flawed in its conception of what *must* be involved in the legal taxonomy of homicide. In particular, it will be argued, it is mistaken in holding that legal taxonomy *must* be vulnerable to correction in the light of the evidence that medicine possesses. The remainder of this chapter will argue this case with reference only to the distinction between homicide and killings of other kinds of things. Therefore it will address only the idea that killing an anencephalic is not properly to be seen as a homicide. The demands of space are such that the idea that there really is no killing at all cannot be directly addressed. But the line of thought which will be developed in this chapter might profitably be applied there also.

The view under consideration is, then, that the law is irrational on the grounds that, although there is a killing, what is killed is not something which warrants considering the killing as liable to a charge of murder. The law, as it stands, recognises certain killings as inappropriately regarded as liable to a charge of murder – the killing of animals, for example. There may be restrictions imposed on such killings (they should be humane, they should not be gratuitous, and so forth) and, one might suppose, similar restrictions would be imposed on the killing of an anencephalic for transplantation purposes. The physical condition of the anencephalic is such that it is, as it were, wrongly categorised by the law as something the killing of which attracts liability to a charge of murder. If a legal difference is drawn between the killing of one kind of thing and the killing of another, a difference exemplified in the different charges thought relevant, this must be because there is thought to be an empirical difference involved in the respective killings. The physical condition of the anencephalic is taken to be the kind of evidence relevant to determining the legal category into which the killing should fall, the charge being that it is located in the wrong category. This line of thinking directly involves issues discussed within moral philosophy concerning the rationality or otherwise of the difference drawn between killing animals and killing humans. One party holds that the moral difference we undoubtedly draw is without rational foundation as animals and humans equally have what are called 'interests' (a notion itself explained in terms of the capacities for suffering pain and distress and for gaining want satisfaction) and it is that capacity which, in some sense, 'explains' why killing human beings is wrong. *A fortiori* it will 'explain' why killing animals is wrong. Others wish to stress that, in killing human beings, generally speaking we are killing what are called 'persons', beings with certain characteristic psychological capacities and abilities, and it is this which 'explains' why killing human beings is wrong and which permits us to draw a moral distinction between killing animals and killing humans.

The physical condition of the anencephalic, however, is such that it cannot be said to have 'interests' in the relevant sense,[14] nor can it be said to be a 'person' in the relevant quasi-technical sense; so that we may consider the view that it is irrational to treat killing an anencephalic as even a possible murder without discussion of the relevant merits of the two views described above. For either position would sustain the same conclusion. But both the positions described above make a common assumption, namely that, if a moral difference between killing one kind of thing and killing another is to be rationally sustained, some empirical difference must be found between the two cases, an empirical difference which warrants drawing the moral difference. It is this assumption which will be discussed below and argued to be an unwarranted assumption which misrepresents what is involved in drawing a moral difference between killing one kind of thing and killing another.

It is important to remind ourselves that, sometimes when there is talk of there being 'a difference', we do not take ourselves to be *judging* that there is a difference, a judgement liable to correction in the light of further information. For example, when it is said that, if one person is five feet tall and another is six feet tall, these people differ in height, we should not take ourselves to be making a judgement concerning their respective heights which was capable of being corrected in the light of further information about the relevant individuals. There is a contrast here with judging of two people that they differ in height. For here we do take ourselves to be speaking in such way that what we say may be shown to be untrue in the light of measurement of the relevant individuals. When, however, we wish to speak of someone who is five feet tall and another six feet tall differing in height, we take ourselves to be speaking of what Wittgenstein called 'the grammar' of the expression 'differing in height'.[15] It is, of course, true that, if one person is five feet tall and another six feet tall, they differ in height: but that is because the expression 'differing in height' is applied in these circumstances. We could imagine our way of speaking here addressed to a child learning to use the expression 'differing in height'.

In consequence, it would be an error to think that, just because we wish to speak in terms of there being a difference, a moral difference, between one case and another, we must take ourselves to be speaking in such a way that what we say is open to correction in the light of further information. *A fortiori*, it would be an error to think that, just because there is talk of a difference, a moral difference, between killing one kind of thing and killing something of another kind, the talk is of something open to correction in the light of further information, perhaps information concerning the psychological capacities of the respective beings.

An associated error would be to think that, just because there is talk of a difference, a moral difference, an understanding of what is being said may be exhibited in thinking one is making a contribution to moral discussion by looking for 'the difference' or demonstrating that there really is no 'difference'. Someone who thought that they could engage in conversation with those who talk of there being a difference in height between someone who is five feet tall and someone who is six feet tall by suggesting that further investigation of the respective individuals would be of assistance would transparently fail to understand what it meant to speak of 'a difference in height' here. Without further consideration, misunderstanding of a similar kind might be shown by someone who thought an investigation of psychological or physical capacities was relevant to what is being spoken of when there is talk of a moral difference between killing one kind of thing and killing another.

Of course, our talk of moral differences is sometimes thought of as talk which does introduce judgements capable of correction in the light of further information. Someone might hold that it was morally improper to consider cases in which they had a personal interest but morally proper for them to consider cases in which they did not. They might further hold of some particular case that it was proper for them to consider it, believing their interests were not involved, and of another that they could not hear it because their interests were. Of course, the judgement here that there was a moral difference might be mistaken. It would make sense here for someone to talk in terms of having made a mistake if it could be shown that his or her interests really were involved.

So now the crucial question becomes, how should we understand our talk of there being 'a moral difference' between killing one kind of thing and killing another? Should such talk be assimilated to talk concerning 'the grammar' of an expression (what it means to speak of 'a moral difference') as talk of there being a difference in height between someone five feet and someone six feet tall is talk concerning the expression 'a difference in height'? Or should such talk be assimilated to the *judgement* that one person differs in height from another, where we think of what we are doing as capable of correction in the light of further information.

These questions can only be answered by reminding ourselves of the circumstances in which there is talk of 'a moral difference' between killing one kind of thing and killing another. Most of us are prepared to draw a moral difference between the slaughter of an animal and the slaughter of a human being. We do not consider that abattoirs are places where terrible moral wrongs are done. But we would consider it morally appalling if prisoners in jails were systematically killed. We do not consider the humane killing of a terminally ill animal to be a matter of considerable moral weight. But we do think that euthanasia deserves deep moral consideration. We do not consider the expedient of gassing unwelcome numbers of rats to be a matter which should weigh heavily on our moral conscience. But the gassing of our enemies in war is a matter of profound moral repugnance. We react differently, in these and other ways, to the killing of humans and the killing of animals.

It is not our concern to endorse or criticise these responses. Rather, we offer reminders of (some of) the circumstances in which there is talk of 'there being a moral difference' between killing an animal and killing a human being. Whilst talk of 'a moral difference' between killing humans and killing animals is familiar, we should also mention that it is common to draw a difference, a moral difference, between the killing of a child and the killing of an adult. The former is commonly considered morally worse than the latter. Likewise, it is common to draw a moral difference between the killing of someone mentally retarded and the killing of someone of normal human intelligence, again the former being thought morally worse than the latter. Along with these distinctions go others. Hitting women is thought worse than hitting men; hitting children is thought worse than either. Again attention is being drawn here to another set of cases in which there is talk of 'a moral difference'.

The philosophical significance in offering reminders of circumstances in which the expression 'a moral difference' is used is held to rest in the fact that it is only through paying attention to the use a form of words has amongst those who do use the expression that an account of understanding the meaning of that form of words can be given. For, according to one philosophical view of what understanding consists in, it consists precisely in a capacity to operate with the relevant form of words. Here it is important to stress what is to be included in 'a use of a form of words', in particular that this is not to be accounted for merely in a grasp of the circumstances in which a given form of words is held to be appropriate.

An illustration may assist in making this clear. Suppose a group of individuals who, when asked to measure the length of a table, unravel a tape-measure and proceed to lay it carefully against the table, accurately reading off from the measure the relevant figure. Generally, we may suppose, when asked to measure the length of something, they go through the relevant procedures in the proper manner and accurately announce the results of so doing. We might suppose also that the individuals know that if the tape reads 'two metres' then if someone asks 'is the table three metres long?' they should answer in the negative. They are also capable of reasoning: 'if the table is two metres long, then it is not three metres long'; 'capable of reasoning' here meaning they know that if the sentence 'the table is two metres long expresses a truth then the sentence 'the table is three metres long' does not. In short, these individuals are capable of using a tape-measure and correctly reading from it the result and are aware of interrelations between sentences used to express those results. However, these individuals are quite unaware of the connexion between such procedures with the tape-measure and other aspects of life. For example, let us say they do not understand what relationship there is between using the measure and buying furniture. They do not understand that knowing what figures appear after carefully laying the tape can be used to tell whether another table will fit where the original table stands. Or they are quite unmoved if, after careful laying of the tape against the table at time t1 and careful laying at time t2, the results are quite different (the table having been surreptitiously replaced in the interim). They might, perhaps, respond to a query as to how that could be with blank astonishment; or, if told that their second result could not be correct, they might merely check the second reading again, not seeing any connexion between that result and the one taken earlier. Let us say that they have no conception that something's length is thought of as fixed, save that the thing has shrunk. If these were the reactions of the imagined individuals, despite their prowess with the tape and despite their possessing skills in understanding the relationships between sentences expressing the results of measurement, we should be disinclined to credit them with the conception of measurement and of length with which we credit ourselves. This description is very much like the description we would give of children playing at measuring things. As described, these individuals lack any conception of what might be called 'the significance', 'the point' of the procedures with the measuring tape. Their lack of comprehension of the connexions between those procedures and buying furniture, their unawareness that there is something requiring explanation if one measurement of something apparently unchanged fails to match another bout of operations with the tape, constitute what 'not seeing the significance', being unaware of 'the point' of the procedures amounts to. These differences between our lives with the words 'this is two metres long' and their lives with those words warrant describing them as lacking our conception of measurement and of length; warrant describing them as not understanding what (our conception) of measurement and length come to.

In this example, coming to accept that the individuals described do not possess our conception of measurement and length required paying attention to the differences in our life with the relevant words and their life with those words. And, in describing that difference, attention was paid to rather more than the capacity to come out with the sentence 'this is two metres long' when something was two metres long. Attention was also paid to reactions to connexions between the procedures with the tape and other aspects of life. In understanding what is involved in the notion of 'describing the circumstances in which an expression is used' what must be described are the characteristic reactions associated with those expressions if we are to come to an understanding of the sense of significance of them.

If, therefore, we are to understand talk of there being 'a moral difference' we shall need to pay attention to 'life with those words' if we are to understand what sense or significance talk of 'a moral difference' has. How is the talk of 'a moral difference' here to be taken? Do those who speak, for example, of 'a moral difference' between hitting a woman and hitting a man take themselves to be making a judgement which is susceptible of correction in the light of further information? Do such people need to be reminded that women feel pain, can be injured, dislike being hit, and all these to a degree no different than men? Are we to suppose that those who draw this 'moral difference' are ignorant of such facts and would come to see that there really had been no difference at all? And we might remind ourselves here that it can be thought there is a moral difference between hitting a woman and hitting a man from quite different perspectives. From one, hitting a woman is no different from hitting a dog; both need training in the ways to behave and physical violence has proved a useful means to that end. From the other, women are thought of as requiring protection from those aspects of life with which men are expected to deal. From the one perspective, it would be 'unmanly', 'ungentlemanly' to hit a woman, as it would be 'unmanly' to hold a child to physical account. From the other, it would be 'unmanly' not to 'chastise' a woman, as it would be a sign of weakness not to 'chastise' a dog. But from neither perspective is it plausible to suppose ignorance of the physical effects of violence upon women. When 'a moral difference' is spoken of here, it is spoken of in full knowledge of the physical effects that violence has. Indeed, a knowledge of the effects of violence forms a necessary part of the thinking of either perspective. As dogs can withstand a whipping, so can a woman. Or the wrong done to a woman in beating her is not to be accounted for in terms of the increased harm done to her, but in quite different terms.

Similarly, when people wish to speak of 'a moral difference' between assaulting a child and assaulting an adult, are we to suppose that they take themselves to be making a judgement susceptible to correction in the light of further information about children and adults? Suppose it turned out that children experience less pain than adults, their nervous systems being not yet fully developed; or that they experienced less fear, being more ignorant of what was fearful. Would such 'discoveries' show that 'the moral difference' was not as great as had been previously thought or even did not exist at all? Would it make sense to suppose that assaulting a child might not really be of much moral import, certainly not as important as had previously been thought? And, one wishes to say, those who think in terms of 'a moral difference' here do not characteristically account for 'the greater moral wrong' in terms of the greater amount of pain or distress that children suffer (characteristically, it is said that children are 'more resilient' than adults). Rather, it is accounted for in terms of 'betrayal of trust', 'loss of innocence', and so forth. Degrees of pain, suffering and distress need not figure in explication of 'the moral difference'. In these examples, misunderstanding of what talk of 'a moral difference' amounted to would be exemplified if it were thought further information concerning the psychological capacities of women and men, children and adults was of any relevance to 'the moral differences' spoken of.

'A moral difference' is also spoken of in connexion with the killing of animals and the killing of humans and something of the character of 'the difference' was described above. And, again, it seems quite wrong to take those who wish to speak of 'a moral difference' here to be expressing a judgement thought of as vulnerable to correction in the light of additional information concerning the psychological and other capacities of animals and humans. Finding out that some (adult) monkeys were more skilled than some (infant) humans would not be taken as relevant to 'the moral difference' between killing the one and killing the other. Discovering that horses suffered more 'distress' in war than battle-hardened humans would not cause those who draw 'the moral difference' to suppose they had found out that it was 'morally worse' to kill a horse than a human. 'The moral distinction' between putting down a terminally ill pet and killing a terminally ill relative turns not at all on the greater pain and distress caused by the latter. Indeed, in that regard, things might be quite the other way around. But still 'a moral distinction' will be drawn.

The general position being argued for here is, then, the following: that attention to the talk that there is with the expression 'a moral difference' shows that there are cases in which those who wish to speak of 'a moral difference' do not take themselves to be expressing something vulnerable to correction in the light of additional information concerning the capacities and capabilities of the subjects of the relevant cases once such case concerns the killing of humans and the killing of animals. Talk of 'a moral difference' between killing a human and killing an animal serves as a reminder of 'the grammar' of the expression 'a moral difference'. Talk here of 'a moral difference' is misconstrued if it is taken as expressive of a judgement thought to be vulnerable to further information concerning animals and humans. Further, one way of revealing that talk of 'a moral difference' has been misconstrued would be to suppose that, by giving information concerning the intellectual capacities of animals and humans, one might show that there 'really' was no moral difference.

This general position impinges on the argument in question in the following way: it would be a mistake to suppose that the legal conception of an anencephalic as someone who can be murdered is a position which must rest on mistaken views about the anencephalic's capacities and capabilities, views which medical science can demonstrate to be ill-founded. And it would equally be an error to think of the physical facts as providing reason to take the killing of an anencephalic as morally different from the killing of a neonate. This would be an error traceable to the view that holding to there being a moral difference between killing one kind of thing and killing another must be understood as expressive of a judgement vulnerable to correction in the light of information concerning psychological and other capacities. But this view, it has been argued, is mistaken. We do not cleave to the view that killing a dog differs morally from killing a child because we think dogs and children differ in psychological and other capacities. We should regard lighting a candle on the anniversary of a dog's death as sentimental,[16] and would begin to wonder what significance lighting a candle for a human's death would have for such a person. We might hold a funeral service for a child dead after two days but not for a dog dead after ten years. And this is not a difference we draw because we hold any mistaken views concerning the psychological capacities of infants and adult dogs. Rather, our idea is that the passing of human beings is something to be marked by a funeral, whilst the passing of animals is not. What it is for us to draw 'a moral difference' between the deaths of animals and the deaths of humans, we might say, is constituted by the very different reactions we display – the deaths of humans have a significance for us, marked by our social practices, that the deaths of animals do not. We do not have these different reactions because of commitment to views concerning animals and humans which are vulnerable to correction in the light of new information concerning animals and humans. Rather, there being a moral difference, what it is for there to be a moral difference is constituted by these differing reactions and consequences. We really do not need to be reminded that animals suffer pain, distress and fear, but we do perhaps need to be reminded that it is not the capacity for experiencing pain, distress and fear which is relevant to our finding the killing of an infant morally unacceptable. If it were, then deaths unaccompanied by pain, distress and fear should not strike us as unacceptable. We are not inclined to think that it was the failure to convince Jews that they were not going to their deaths which explains the horror of the gas-chambers. On the contrary, we are inclined to think that, had the deceit been successful, it would have been worse: the final humiliation. We can and should say that holding that the psychological incapacities of the anencephalic are sufficient to sustain the view that killing it morally differs from the killing of a neonate shows an inability to understand what it is to think the killing of a human being so morally terrible.

If the killing of an anencephalic, whatever the reasons, has not been shown to involve, on the law's part, moral misclassification, are we to conclude that there is no way in which morality might permit organ donation from an anencephalic other than ways already permitted? This conclusion is not warranted. The resources of the law and of morality allow for considerable complexity of thought. Two examples, from two directions, illustrate the point.

The first draws on some comments of Cora Diamond's in a discussion of animal rights,[17] a paper which has greatly influenced my discussion here. Diamond takes strong exception to arguments for animal rights which conclude that it is quite irrational to see nothing wrong in killing and eating animals for food but to see as quite wrong treating human beings in the same way. The arguments she has in mind are those which see the wrong in cannibalism as the violation of someone's interests, interests which animals share. She points out that we would consider it wrong to eat the flesh of those who have died from natural causes and that, if violation of interests is what matters, no-one could consider it wrong to eat the flesh of a cow obligingly struck by lightning. A discussion of the morality of eating animals cannot start from a discussion of interests but must start from an understanding of what is involved in such things as our not eating people. And that cannot be understood in terms of violation of interests.

She is then concerned to ask just how we could seek to show someone that they do have reason to treat animals better than they are now treated. She suggests that what is needed is the 'extension to animals of modes of thinking characteristic of our responses to human beings'.[18] She suggests, for example, that we might think of feeding birds in winter as something akin to charity, not a response to a moral demand that might be made on the birds' behalf. That is, if someone were to ask what reason they had to feed birds, we would not make an appeal to a recognition of their interests in being fed but might make an appeal to see them as fellow creatures. Or, if we wished to explain why we could not eat our pets, we might make appeal to the idea of a pet being a companion, and part of the conception of a companion is the conception of something that cannot be treated in that way. In much the same way, something could not be thought of as a pet if it were thought of as something for the stock-pot. In short, in considering how we might give reasons to someone to treat animals rather differently than they are currently treated, we should seek imaginatively to extend a range of concepts we already deploy in understanding our moral relations to human beings. The giving of reasons would take its starting point from the range of concepts in terms already deployed in our moral thought and talk. For our understanding of what it is to give moral reasons for action is constituted by what counts as the giving of reasons within that framework of thinking.

The second example is drawn from the decision in *Airedale NHS Trust* v *Bland*.[19] This too, might be looked upon as the exercise of legal imagination in the resolution of a difficult issue. The House of Lords was considering an appeal from a decision of the Court of Appeal, Civil Division, that physicians might lawfully discontinue all life-sustaining treatment and medical support measures designed to keep Anthony Bland alive in his existing persistent vegetative state, including the termination of ventilation, nutrition and hydration by artificial means, and that physicians might lawfully discontinue and thereafter need not furnish medical treatment to Anthony Bland except for the sole purpose of enabling him to end his life and die peacefully with the greatest dignity and the least of pain, suffering and distress.[20]

The court had to consider a submission from the official solicitor that the withdrawal of artificial feeding would constitute murder and, as such, could not be lawful. The court accepted that Anthony Bland was alive: his brain-stem was still functioning although all higher cortical activity had ceased. More importantly, the court considered that it had not the power to change the existing law of murder and could only apply the law as it stood to the undisputed facts of the case.[21] The court also accepted that there was in the case the *mens rea* for murder.[22] Anthony Bland was patently incapable of refusing treatment and had given no prior indication that he did not wish invasive treatment of the kind in question. The court also considered that any previous *parens patriae* jurisdiction it may have had was now expunged.[23] How, in these circumstances, could the court dismiss the appeal against the Court of Appeal decision as to the legality of discontinuing treatment?

It did so by arguing that the termination of hydration and nutrition by artificial means was an act of omission, not commission: the significance being that in English criminal law, if an act resulting in death is done without lawful excuse and with intent to kill, it is murder; but an omission to act with the same result and with the same intent is, in general, no offence at all, save for one general exception at common law, namely that a person may be criminally liable for the consequences of an omission if he or she stands in such a relation to the victim that he or she is under a duty to act. In this case, with the relevant *mens rea* it will be murder. Thus, having argued that termination of treatment would be an omission, it remained to argue that the physicians were under no duty to continue the treatment. Invasive treatment without consent would be lawful provided the patient's best interests were served by that treatment. But, in this case, the patient's medical condition was such that no improvement whatsoever could be contemplated. His best interests in being kept alive had, therefore, disappeared and the invasive treatment had no lawful foundation. The duty to continue with it had therefore disappeared and with that any liability to a charge of murder.[24]

Here is not the place to discuss all the elements of reasoning relied upon in reaching this decision. It serves, rather, as a reminder of how existing resources might be deployed to reach decisions seemingly beyond reach and it did so by making use of and imaginatively applying those existing resources. In like manner, I am suggesting, holding firmly to the view that no good reason has been given for supposing that killing an anencephalic differs morally from killing any other human being is not, thereby, to close the door on providing moral argument that would permit some of the procedures physicians seek. Whether it is possible to provide these arguments or not is not known, but, if it should be possible, it must be through the development of existing resources in moral reasoning, not by their replacement.

The discussion above warrants concluding that nothing emerges from recent discussion which provides compelling moral reason to alter the current position in law regarding the constraints on procedures pertaining to the acquisition of organs from anencephalics for transplantation purposes. In particular, the discussion suggest that attempts to replace 'the dead donor rule' with a 'violates no interests rule'[25] is not well motivated. Advocates of 'the dead donor rule' are, in the literature, distinguished from those seeking exemption from the criminal law on homicide through the creation of a legally recognised permission to kill anencephalics as 'a special category'. But this discrimination seems to turn on the latter being somewhat ad hoc in its selection of 'a special category', the former offering some kind of account of how membership of 'a special category' is acquired.[26] This category is generated by 'the lack of interests' the anencephalic has in virtue of its physical condition. As already noted above,[27] this sense of 'interests' already finds expression in law. It is, however, noteworthy that, in *Airedale NHS Trust* v. *Bland*, Anthony Bland was afforded the full protection of the criminal law despite his physical condition.

But this view of 'interests' finds expression in contrast with other views. Hoffman L.J., in considering a submission, is reported as follows:[28]

> I think that the fallacy in this argument is that it assumes that we have no interests except in those things of which we have conscious experience. But this does not accord with most people's intuitive feelings about their lives and deaths. At least a part of the reason why we honour the wishes of the dead about the distribution of their property is that we think it would wrong them not to do so, despite the fact that we believe that they will never know that their will has been ignored. Most people would like an honourable and dignified death and we think it wrong to dishonour their deaths, even when they are unconscious that this is happening. We pay respect to their dead bodies and to their memory because we think it an offence against the dead themselves if we do not.

Whether the term 'interests' has an application to patients lacking higher cortical function or not is of no major importance. What is of importance is this expression of the plain facts concerning our moral experience. We might take these words, to use terms taken from the discussion above, as reminders of 'the grammar' of our conception of 'a human being' – in these and other ways are human beings to be treated. The discussion above aims to provide some reasons for holding that this way of thinking and speaking really is not threatened by the findings of medicine. These ways of thinking and speaking are not shown to be irrational. And, of course, these ways of thinking and speaking are applicable to the anencephalic child as well as any other. Recognition of this by the law need not and, indeed, should not be seen as moral flotsam left behind by advances in medicine.

Notes

1   Cf. A. Maclean, *The Elimination of Morality: Reflections on Utilitarianism and Bioethics*, London/New York, Routledge, 1993

2   Cf. James W. Walters and Stephen Ashwal, 'Organ Prolongation in Anencephalic Infants: Ethical and Medical Issues', *Hastings Center Report* (October/November 1988), p. 19.

3   Cf. P.A. Baird and A.D. Sadovinich, 'Survival in Infants with Anencephaly', *Clinical Pediatrics*, **23** (1984), 268–71.

4   Cf. D. Alan Shewman, 'Anencephaly: Selected Medical Aspects', *Hastings Center Report* (October/November 1988) pp. 11–19 for a strongly dissenting opinion.

5   Walters and Ashwal, 'Organ Prolongation', p. 19.

6   Cf. Norman Fost, 'Organs from Anencephalic Infants: An Idea Whose Time Has Not Yet Come', *Hastings Center Report* (October/November 1988) pp. 5–10.

7   Ibid., p. 6.

8   Cf. Joyce Peabody, 'Loma Linda University's Protocol on Anencephalic Infants as Organ Donors', *BioLaw*, **2**(10) (January 1988), U: 763–9. Walters and Ashwal, 'Organ Prolongation', pp. 19–27.

9   What follows will concentrate on procedures which are held to cause death, but much of what is said might, with suitable adjustments, be applied to procedures less calamitous.

10 For a cautionary comment on this development, see Norman Fost, 'Organs from Anencephalic Infants', p. 8.

11 'Problematic cases' will exclude those cases in which organ transplantation takes place following death determined by cardiovascular criteria, a practice dating back to the early 1960s: see James W. Walters and Stephen Ashwal, 'Organ Prolongation', p. 19.

12 Cf. Michael R. Harrison, 'The Anencephalic Newborn as Organ Donor', *Hastings Center Report* 16:2 (April 1986), pp. 21–3; 'Organ Procurement for Children: The Anencephalic Fetus as Donor', *Lancet*, ii (13 December 1986), 1383–5.

13 D.Alan Shewman, 'Anencephaly'.

14 A sense of 'interests' which finds expression in *Airedale NHS Trust* v. *Bland* [1993] 1All ER 858 Lord Mustill, 894.

15 Cf. Ludwig Wittgenstein, *Philosophical Investigations*, trans. G.E.M. Anscombe, Oxford, 1968.

16 Cf. Raimond Gaita, 'The Personal in Ethics', in D.Z. Phillips and P. Winch (eds), *Wittgenstein: Attention to Particulars*, London, Macmillan, 1989, pp. 124–50.

17 Cf. Cora Diamond, 'Eating Meat and Eating People', *Philosophy*, **53**, (178), 465–79.

18 Ibid., 474.

19 Cf. note 14, above.

20 Ibid., per Lord Keith of Kinkel, at 859.

21 Ibid., per Lord Mustill, at 888.

22 Ibid., per Lord Browne-Wilkinson, at 880.

23 Ibid., per Lord Browne-Wilkinson, at 882.

24 Ibid., per Lord Mustill, at 894.

25 Cf. Norman Fost, 'Organs from Anencephalic Infants', 9; Arthur L. Caplan, 'Ethical Issues in the Use of Anencephalic Infants as a source of Organs and Tissues for Transplantation' (referred to in Fost as 'in press').

26 Cf. Norman Fost, 'Organs from Anencephalic Infants', 8–9.

27 Cf. p. 167 above.

28 Cf. *Airedale NHS Trust* v. *Bland*, Hoffman L.J. at 853–4.

10 Advance Directives/ Living Wills

CHRIS DOCKER

Introduction

There is a general consensus among medical ethicists[1-4] that favours patients being able to make their own decisions about health care, a consensus reflected by law;[5-7] but the practicality of how to ensure this in law is sometimes far from clear. Advance directives (ADs) are an attempt to implement this interest as regards refusal of medical treatments[8] should certain specific states of incompetence arise. Forms of incapacity might arise from physical illness or injury and include coma, persistent vegetative state (PVS),[9] dementia, heavy sedation, or the 'locked-in'[10] state.[11] Difficult decisions may need to be taken about whether the patient, if faced with little or no possibility of recovery, would have wanted measures that might only prolong a dying process to a possibly more painful conclusion than might be obtainable without active treatment.[12] Hence the advance instructions of the patient can serve many uses. Such instructions may be formalised into a written document.[13] In spite of popular support, and in some cases legislation, attempts to encourage the widespread use of advance directive documents in other jurisdictions have met with limited success; but if the solutions have not yet worked, the problems, brought on largely by medicine's increasing capacity to extend our lives into incapacity, are getting more acute. This chapter seeks to cover two aspects of advance directives: first the situation as it has developed, is now, and is likely to progress; and second what appear to be potential flaws in such documents and the possibility of overcoming them, with the underlying question being posed, to what extent can advance medical directives help patients to die in the way they wish?

Advance directives are likely to become increasingly common in the future. The House of Lords Select Committee on Medical Ethics[14] commended their development and recommended a code of practice that should 'encourage professionals to disseminate information about advance directives'.[15] We should ask what modifications might be desirable to maximise such documents' usefulness both to patients and to health care staff. To begin, the chapter draws on published research, legal precedent and the author's own examination of advance directives in different countries.

Definitions

Terminology is unclear in the United Kingdom, and the phrase 'living will' has often been used loosely or interchangeably with the phrases 'advance directive' or 'advance declaration'.[16,17] In other jurisdictions these terms are quite distinct. For instance, as Dworkin says,

> Every state in the United States now recognizes some form of advance directive: either *living wills* – documents stipulating that specified medical procedures should not be used to keep the signer alive in certain specified circumstances, or *health-care proxies* – documents appointing someone else to make life and death decisions for the signer when he no longer can.[18]

These definitions will be used, to make it quite clear when we are concerned with a living will instruction from the patient to the heath care team, and when what is meant is a proxy document in which the patient authorises a third person to instruct that health care team.[19,20]

Theory

Developments in medical technology over the past 50 years have dramatically altered the dying process and, in this respect, our society is radically different from the one contemplated by Locke, whose ideas have nevertheless so heavily influenced our social structures to this day.[21] Laws have tended to attempt accommodations within existing law rather than tackling from scratch the questions of euthanasia and dying. Severe problems can arise when new factors, such as a prolongation of life beyond any expectation of residual quality of life, are unaccounted for in the initial scheme of things, or in constitutions written or unwritten.

Whether one argues from a utilitarian point of view in order to maximise beneficial outcomes, along with John Stuart Mill, or with Kantian arguments based on autonomy, dignity and individual rights, the same conclusion can be reached, namely that, as long as they do not interfere with the liberty of others, people should be free to pursue their own good in their own way.[22] It is not difficult to recognise in each of us a desire to exercise control over our own destiny and to have a chance to finish our own 'work of art' in the manner of our own choosing. But we may need to free our older, rigid ways of thinking in order to satisfy the morality and values commonly held by our populace today. The immediacy of the task has been considerably highlighted in this generation by AIDS patients, all of whom may well face a distressing death, many of whom are well-educated and knowledgeable about the medical prognoses, and who, as a group, are extremely vocal about ascertaining and demanding their rights.[23] Demands for the right to die at the time and in the manner of one's own choosing continue to fuel public debate in the area of medical decisions at the end of life.[24,25] In such an atmosphere, finding solutions that will satisfy opposing factions can be far from easy.[26] Death is a very emotive subject, and the real question may not be about a right to die but, as Lord Donaldson said, about the 'right to choose how to live'.[27]

The argument is not advanced by inappropriate use of language, nor by allegiance to a particular philosophical doctrine. As Brody suggested:

> We cannot resolve these moral tensions by making one side of the tension disappear. Instead, we must learn to live with these tensions within a pluralistic society. This requires more reliance on negotiation, compromise, and practical reasoning, and less on abstract ethical theory.[28]

History

The phrase and idea of a living will first received serious attention in the late 1960s when Luis Kutner, in the *Indiana Law Review*, considered the case when a terminal patient had requested help in accelerating death. He observed,

> the current state of the law does not recognize the right of the victim to die if he so desires. He may be in a terminal state suffering from an incurable illness and literally forced to continue a life of pain and despair. Such a denial may well infringe on the individual's right of privacy.[29]

Following the case of Karen Quinlan,[30] California, in 1976, became the first state to pass legislation that directly addressed decision making on behalf of incompetent patients. The California Natural Death Act[31] allowed individuals, in certain circumstances, to plan in advance for their treatment at the end of life. The idea was substantially developed in the United States in the case of *Cruzan* v. *Director* (1990),[32] in which the 14th Amendment[33] was interpreted by the Supreme Court to imply that a competent person has a constitutionally protected liberty interest (rather than a fundamental right) in refusing unwanted medical treatment. O'Connor J., in her concurrence, entrusted the task of crafting appropriate procedures for safeguarding incompetents' liberty interests to the 'laboratory of the states' in the first instance.[34]

The Patient Self-Determination Act (PSDA)[35] went into effect in December 1991, and required health care providers (primarily hospitals, nursing homes and home health agencies) to give patients information about their rights to make advance directives under state law; the substance of the law governing advance directives is left to the states. The PSDA also requires care providers to have written institutional policies regarding advance directives and to document whether or not a patient has executed one.

Most states now have living will legislation and/or proxy legislation;[36] proxy legislation is largely based on, or similar to, the Uniform Power of Attorney Act (1982).[37] Although every state has a durable power of attorney (DPA) law that permits persons to designate someone to make decisions for them if they become incapacitated, the current trend is for states to enact additional proxy laws that specifically deal with health care. The original DPA laws were enacted primarily to permit the agent to make financial decisions, whereas the new durable power of attorney for health care (DPAHC) specifically deals with health care.[38]

While 'Advance planning fits well with dominant American values, such as individualism, self-reliance, and an active as opposed to a fatalistic outlook',[39] the fundamental ethical principles on which US laws are based are common to most Western countries and it is not surprising that legislation recognising one or both types of directive has also been enacted elsewhere. In Denmark,[40] living wills are widely available and registered by law at the State University Hospital. In Canada, there is legislation in Nova Scotia,[41] Quebec,[42] Manitoba[43] and Ontario,[44] with bills pending in other provinces. In Ontario, the Act had been preceded by the landmark case of *Malette* v. *Shulman* (1990),[45] in which the Court of Appeal had upheld a judgement giving a Jehovah's Witness damages, on the basis of assault, after a physician had proceeded with a blood transfusion in spite of a card that had been found in the plaintiff's purse directing that she not be given a transfusion under any circumstances. Although avoiding the issue of living wills directly, the same court later upheld the principle in another case, saying, 'A patient, in anticipation of circumstances wherein he or she may be unconscious or otherwise incapacitated and thus unable to contemporaneously express his or her wishes about a particular form of medical treatment, may specify in advance his or her refusal to consent to the proposed treatment. A doctor is not free to disregard such advance instructions, even in an emergency.'[46] Some provinces, however, such as Saskatchewan, have no legislation yet in place concerning either living wills or proxy empowerments.

In Australia there is also statutory provision of some kind in South Australia, Victoria and Northern Territory.[47] In the Netherlands, there was no legislation covering advance directives until the Act on the Medical Treatment of Patients[48] (passed in 1994), although written requests have been viewed sympathetically before that in an environment in which voluntary euthanasia has been tolerated within certain limits.[49]

In England the present legal position may be drawn from a number of cases. In the case of *Re T* [1992],[50] it was concluded that the woman in question, a Jehovah's Witness refusing a blood transfusion, had been lulled into a false sense of security by the hospital staff and had been misinformed as to the availability and effect of alternatives. The judge concluded that her refusal did not extend to the situation as it had developed, and granted an order for the transfusion. This highlights the necessity for *informed* refusal, and suggests that a properly informed refusal would have been binding.

In the case of *Airedale NHS Trust* v. *Bland* [1993],[51] the patient in question was in persistent vegetative state (PVS) following the collapse of the Hillsborough Football Stadium and had not made anything that could be construed as an advance directive. However, the Court of Appeal and the House of Lords, in their asides, both commented on aspects of the binding nature of advance directives. Health care staff could not overrule patient decisions by claiming such decisions were irrational: 'A medical practitioner must comply with clear instructions given by an adult of sound mind as to the treatment to be given or not given in certain circumstances, whether those instructions are rational or irrational',[52] said Sir Thomas Bingham in the Court of Appeal. The Appeal Court also concluded that, if Tony Bland had made a living will covering non-treatment in the event of PVS, the doctors could not only lawfully comply but would be acting unlawfully if they did not. Lord Butler-Sloss said that all counsel agreed that the right to reject treatment extends to deciding not to accept treatment in the future by way of an advance directive or 'living will'.[53] The Law Lords called for parliamentary clarification to avoid the necessity of leaving similar future decisions to the courts, and so the Select Committee on Medical Ethics[54] was set up.

Meanwhile the Law Commission, in its consultation paper on mentally incapacitated adults and decision making,[55] provisionally proposed, in accordance with what appeared to be the common law position, that a clearly established anticipatory decision should be as effective as the contemporaneous decision of the patient would be in the circumstances to which it is applicable.[56] In October 1993, however, the case of *Re C*[57] seemed to clarify the issue in case law. A man who was a chronic paranoid schizophrenic (known in the case simply as 'C'), had sought a court injunction restraining a hospital from amputating his gangrenous leg, even though such refusal of treatment might result in his death. The court was asked to determine the effect of a purported advance directive as to the future medical treatment, and the court agreed that a draft could be drawn up so as to reflect injunctive or declaratory relief through such a directive. A secondary and interesting aspect of the case was that the Court decided that, although C was mentally impaired, he was not impaired in a way that prevented him from sufficiently understanding the nature, purpose and effects of the treatment he wished to refuse.

Contrary to expectation, the Select Committee of the House of Lords failed to recommend statutory legislation to support even the power of those precisely worded advance directives which refuse specific medical treatments.[58] Since their report, much has been written about whether living wills are 'binding' in law in the United Kingdom;[59-62] the crux seems to be that, although a carefully worded living will may be decisive evidence in court, the conditions laid down by Lord Donaldson in *Re T*[63] must first have been satisfied and, unless and until that is established in any particular case, living wills are persuasive and informative documents but lacking the full weight of the law at the time that they are needed. Their current position as strong guidance documents, pending further recommendations by the Law Commission, was also outlined in Parliament's debate on the Select Committee's report, and Lord Walton reiterated the Committee's view that they 'should not be made legally binding'.[64]

In 1995, the Law Commission proposed a bill[65] that would clarify the legal status of advance directives. They recommended 'that an "advance refusal of treatment" should be defined as a refusal made by a person aged eighteen or over with the necessary capacity of any medical, surgical or dental treatment or other procedure and intended to have effect at any subsequent time when he or she may be without capacity to give or refuse consent'.[66] Validity is determined by capacity, not the document, and is presumed unless there is evidence to the contrary.[67] If an advance refusal is present, other justifications for proceeding with a treatment cease if the refusal applies to that treatment or procedure in the circumstances of the case.[68] While rather narrow, this at least saves having to interpret case law[69] at every turn. Authority to treat or not treat when there is not this clear applicability requires treatment to be in the patient's best interests, which are specifically defined to include regard to the 'ascertainable past and present wishes and feelings of the person and the factors he or she would consider'.[70] Given the difficulties of ascertaining all possible situations in advance, this might mean that an expression of wishes and a history of values, an option we shall presently examine, may be a more effective vehicle for projecting and enforcing patient autonomy into states of future incompetence than the traditional advance medical directive: whether treating against a specific medical refusal or against ascertainable wishes, the doctor would be liable to an action in damages for battery.

All this leads us to examine the probable wording of such documents and, having considered the question of the patient's right to make an advance directive and its present and potential effect in law, to ask to what extent such directives will assist the patient in achieving the type of death he or she desires to effectuate by such documents. First of all, let us look at living will directives, in which the patient makes an advance instruction addressed directly to the health care staff. After that, we will consider proxy directives.

Living Wills: Pros and Cons

On the plus side, living wills are considered to:

1 reassure the patient who fears continued application of life-sustaining technology;[71]
2 protect patient autonomy by extending it into a future incompetent state;[72]
3 provide guidance and legal protection for doctors;
4 reduce the emotional anguish to the patient's family members by relieving them of the obligation to make life-and-death decisions, or at least by assuring them that they are making the decision the patient would have wanted;
5 stimulate the doctor–patient dialogue and relationship;[73]
6 seek to avoid ambiguity, by allowing the patient to express wishes in precise detail.[74]

Arguments against living wills include the following:

1 sanctity of life considerations;[75]
2 the inflexibility of living wills or the difficulty of making an informed decision about a scenario that has yet to occur, and difficulties of interpretation;[76]
3 the possibility that the patient may change his or her mind (if patients' preferences are quite unstable, then carrying them forward into incompetence is harder to justify);[77]
4 the advent of new technology or treatments not envisaged by the living will;[78]
5 the danger that legislation may restrict patients' rights[79] (in the United States, some states only allow patients who are terminally ill to complete a binding advance directive);

6   the danger that a slippery slope may be precipitated by using advance directives as a justification to save health care resources or to bring undue influence to bear;[80]

7   the possibility that patients may not understand complex forms;[81]

8   patients may be unable to understand treatments or to distinguish therapeutic from palliative procedures;[82]

9   the possibility that legally executed directives may, in practice, be ignored;[83–88]

10 the fact that too few people sign them, even in the presence of supportive legislation;[89,90]

11 the fact that the document may not be easily available when needed;[91,92]

12 choices, even if informed and apparently in context, might in some cases be irrelevant to the patient's desired aim;

13 living wills may perhaps be a shortsighted and inadequate or incomplete response to the question of whether death can, in some situations, be preferable to life.

(the last two are less commonly listed, but I wish to propose them here as questions that need practical answers.)

There may also be perceived *barriers*[93] to completing living wills such as the following:

1   inability to write (for example, from arthritis or illiteracy);

2   a belief that a living will is unnecessary;

3   a fatalistic attitude;

4   a desire to leave the decision to doctors;

5   uncertainty about preferences;

6   a desire to discuss rather than document preferences or rely on previous discussions;

7   a desire to wait until a crisis arises;[94]

8   a desire to avoid thinking about preferences or living wills;

9   research by Stelter *et al.*[95] in 1992 also identified lengthy or complex forms as possible barriers (supporting the work of earlier commentators);[96]

10 lack of availability of forms;

11 lack of physician initiative.[97,98]

Space does not allow us to weigh up all the pros and cons in detail here, but given the likely increase of such documents into the area of medical law, we may examine the pitfalls which appear to have been largely ignored by many. By examining the weaknesses of such documents, future drafters may be able to formulate sensible improvements.

Living Wills: the Type of Forms Used

Simple v. Complex

Legal documents require precision, and the attempt to achieve this by use of medical terminology has been seductively easy. Most people would like to decline useless treatment, but it is the grey areas that cause health care staff concern. Would the patient have wanted to trade some extra life for unpleasant treatment in cases where the term 'recovery' might be considered arguable or ambiguous – if it involved, say, lasting paralysis or partial dementia?

Most trends are towards complex forms, rather than simple documents containing broad statements about avoiding heroic and useless treatment.[99] Many critics[100–102] have noted that often advance directives are too vague to be adequate guides to the patient's wishes. Phrases like 'meaningful quality of life' have been challenged in court as ambiguous.[103] This is perhaps the main factor that has led to what some commentators, including McLean, have described as the excessive medicalisation[104] of living will legislation. To have any legal weight, living wills must be fairly specific in what is being demanded by force of law. The British Medical Association has called for legislation to cater for therapy-specific directives.[105] A greater physician response to therapy-specific than to general-statement living wills has also been reported.[106] The medical model, with a spiralling glossary of terminology, seems a convenient language, but, as I hope to demonstrate, this in itself can generate very considerable problems.

Medical Models and Shortcomings

The Lords' Select Committee opined that 'it could well be impossible to give advance directives in general greater legal force without depriving patients of the benefit of the doctor's professional expertise'.[107] One can, however, argue that this is a problem that needs to be tackled rather than giving up the ghost on legislation to protect patient autonomy. Most living wills give a list of specific medical situations and a list of specific medical scenarios in which these treatments are to be withheld. Given the infinite range of medical situations which could arise, there is no possibility of making such lists and their interactions exhaustive. The situation can therefore occur where a form of treatment prohibited by the living will, although extending the patient's life, would have enabled the patient to experience a more peaceful dying than simple non-treatment might bring about.[108] In such cases, this would be the opposite of the effect desired at the time of making the living will.[109] Under present law, the living will in these circumstances could be overruled as 'not applicable in the circumstances' – if the patient was lucky – but this is a subjugation of patient autonomy in favour of beneficent paternalism; if the patient was less than lucky, the document might be followed to the letter. With or without supportive legislation, the medicalisation of the living will may, in some instances, reverse the real intent, which was to protect the autonomy of the patient in choosing a peaceful death. Most living wills, including those drafted by top lawyers, legislators and right-to-die societies, do not make allowance for this. Listing specific interventions in advance may not necessarily enhance self-determination or reduce uncertainty in the decision making. As expressed by Brett, 'the intervention-focussed directive runs the risk of promoting the selection or rejection of interventions because of their inherent characteristics, rather than as appropriate means to the ends that the patient would have wanted'.[110]

The trend is overwhelmingly towards this greater medicalisation of living wills, however. Living wills in America often run to several pages, with complex grids to refuse various treatments in various medical situations. This type of document is easier legally to enforce than generalised statements, and the trend continues.

Minimising the Shortcomings

One option is to embody careful legal phrasing in the living will to anticipate such possibilities as those just described. An example can be seen in the living will of the National Agency for Welfare and Health in Finland.[111] After the schedule which lists treatments refused and in what circumstances, it adds two qualifiers: it says, 'However, modes of treatment mentioned above may be applied for elimination or alleviation of serious symptoms'. Then it says, 'Giving intensive care to me is to be allowed only on the condition that reliable reasons for the possibility that this kind of treatment will have a result better than a merely short prolongation of life'. It thus provides *escape clauses* so that, if literal adherence to the living will and refusal of treatments mentioned therein would result in increased suffering, such adherence is overruled.

Another option is to supplement or replace the medicalised living will with a values history, a possibility that will be discussed later in this chapter.

Competence and Witnessing

The Finnish form also makes curious use of witnesses, who attest not only to the genuineness of the signature, but to the fact that they know the person well, and that the patient is of sound mind and fully understands the meaning expressed in the living will: an important point, when we consider that, to be truly valid, the patient must have understood the import of what was being signed. Adequate disclosure of information relies partly on the patient asking enough questions, and the involvement of the doctor at this stage is potentially beneficial in showing that anticipatory decisions are clearly established. This idea is also touched on in the Terrence Higgins Trust document, which has an optional box to indicate that the form has been discussed with a doctor.[112] While most legislation assumes that, in the absence of evidence to the contrary, a living will should be deemed valid and signed with full understanding, this does not go very far to meet the objection of possible abuse through coercion. Competence might also be increased and better established by use of accompanying vignettes to explain the medical situations to which the living will pertains. Further witnessing provisions have been considered by the Law Commission.[113]

Layout

Legally binding forms for use by lay people should be well designed, clear and straightforward. As Lord Donaldson said in the case of *Re T* (commenting on standard forms currently in use for refusal to accept a blood transfusion), the declaration by the patient of his decision with the full appreciation of the possible consequences should be 'emphasized by a different and larger typeface, by underlining, the employment of colour print or otherwise'.[114] Most attempts at living will documentation so far have been notable for their blandness, almost as if they were designed for lawyers and academics rather than lay members of the community who might have ailing health and poor eyesight. An exception has been the Terrence Higgins Trust form, which, although it has the drawback of being a lengthy and bulky document for inclusion in a person's medical records, nevertheless is notable for its imaginative use of the factors just mentioned.

Explanatory Language

Eloquent arguments for the use of the living will as a starting point for patient–doctor dialogue and understanding, as advanced by the BMA or by Nancy King in her excellent book, *Making Sense of Advance Directives*,[115] fall short when we consider that, in Britain's hard-pressed health service, the doctor may barely have the time to explain current medication, much less sit and explain as yet non-existent diseases, prognoses and life-saving treatments. It would seem that explanations as well as safeguards should be built into the living will paperwork itself, as has been done with a number of Canadian documents.[116] Some documents include descriptions of various medical states referred to in the document. Brett, on the other hand, considers that most of the problems of living wills could be solved by encouraging greater use of proxies,[117] but this approach, as will be demonstrated below, has its own problems.

Some Very Helpful and Very Unhelpful Refinements

The multiplicity of variations in living will documents raises questions of appropriate and inappropriate refinements. A Dutch document[118] has a customisable section where the declarant can specify his or her attitude by adding a personalised paragraph (sample paragraphs are included in the guidance notes). This falls midway between a medicalised graph and the 'values history' which will be examined presently. Pregnancy waivers,[119] indicating whether or not a refusal of treatment shall be overruled in the event that the incapacitated person is concurrently pregnant, may be very helpful if the declarant is of child-bearing age, but might invoke further problems unless there were prior statutory clarification.[120] There may also be a good rationale for specific illness modifications.[121] Refinements which have been subjected to much criticism include combining organ donor statements on the same form.[122] Similar complications could arise when attempts are made to cover several purposes in one document.

Ingenious legal refinements may have their own pitfalls. One Scottish living will,[123] for instance, suggests authenticating a signature by appending 'adopted as holograph' instead of using a witness; while providing prima facie evidence of a true signature and relieving the declarant of the need to find a witness, it might leave the signature more open to challenge than if it had been witnessed in the normal way.

In addition to absolving the health care team from civil liability in relation to following the living will's instructions, some directives add an element of polite gratitude. The Japanese living will, for instance, says 'I express my heartfelt thanks to all those concerned who faithfully realise my requests'. If we consider the amount of cooperation being asked for such an emotionally demanding task, the need for a firm doctor–patient relationship for anything to be achieved at all (this may include the willingness of the doctor to consider fully the text of the document) and the difficulty of framing a law that would be readily enforceable, perhaps the incorporation of such etiquette should not be dismissed as mere window dressing. It is perhaps not unconnected that, according to a 1991 survey, 93 per cent of Japanese doctors have supported the living will.[124]

Proxies

Rather than relying on the living will alone, an alternative or additional device is that of a proxy authorisation document, wherein a third party, designated in advance by the patient, can take the necessary health care decisions if the patient later becomes incompetent.

Scottish Proxy Provisions

Generally speaking in the United Kingdom, family members have no authority to make decisions for the incompetent patient. Although there are legal mechanisms to protect the *property* of the incapacitated person, there is no equivalent, for instance, to the US durable power of attorney for health care, whereby a third party can be authorised to make medical decisions on the patient's behalf. The agency which a person may create for the management of his or her affairs under the Powers of Attorney Act 1971 terminates upon the incompetence of the declarant, and provisions under the Enduring Powers of Attorney Act 1985 are basically for handling the financial affairs of the incapacitated person and it is unlikely that any court would extend these to handling refusal of treatment decisions.[125] One option (though perhaps not the best one) would be simply to extend such Acts to include provisions allowing an authorised proxy to make refusal of treatment decisions. The advance directive formerly issued by the Voluntary Euthanasia Society of Scotland made a proxy provision by way of tutor dative, in a form designed by Dr McCall-Smith of the Law Faculty of Edinburgh. In Scotland (though not in England) there is a convoluted mechanism whereby a person can nominate a third party, and an application can be made to the Court of Session for that person to be accorded the authority of a *tutor dative*.[126] There is a case of this vehicle being used to consent to the treatment of an incapacitated person,[127] but none where it has yet been used to refuse treatment. It could be argued that the powers of the tutor dative, while extending to a protection of the patient's best interests, could be challenged if a substituted judgement decision involving refusal of treatment seemed against the 'interests' of that patient. It may cause initial difficulties as this is an uncommon use of the powers of tutor dative and confusing to many lawyers. Furthermore, if the authority of the tutor dative is challenged it could prove a costly business.

Unauthorised Surrogates

In many cases the next of kin may be called for permission anyway, but this does not necessarily reflect the patient's wishes and has little foundation in law. As Lord Donaldson said in *Re T*:

> There seems to be a view in the medical profession that in emergency cir-
> cumstances the next of kin should be asked to consent on behalf of the
> patient and that, if possible, treatment should be postponed until that
> consent has been obtained. This is a misconception because the next of
> kin has no legal right either to consent or to refuse consent. This is not
> to say that it is an undesirable practice if the interests of the patient will

not be adversely affected by any consequential delay. I say this ... because contact with a next of kin may reveal that the patient has made an anticipatory choice which, if clearly established and applicable in the circumstances ... would bind the practitioner.[128]

One should perhaps note in passing that there are cases where treatment should definitely not be postponed merely to ask the next of kin, especially when there is no reason to believe that an advance refusal has been made. When a person has been diagnosed definitively as being in a *persistent* vegetative state, then further treatment is medically futile; but in the initial stages, when recovery (or partial recovery) may still be possible, immediate and aggressive treatment is indicated until the prognosis is more certain[129] – unless there has been a clear advance refusal. Advance directives, it could be argued, might be useful in these initial stages, as an indication of whether the patient would want to risk partial recovery. In the latter states of PVS, when recovery is no longer conceivable, guidelines for the discontinuation of futile medical treatment might be more appropriate than reliance on advance statements.

Trends Towards Proxy Legislation

There have been many proposals[130] favouring the introduction of proxy legislation; the trend in the United States is also towards increasing use of proxy legislation with the living will as the guidance-only vehicle.[131] The idea is an attractive one. It relieves the health care staff of any difficulties of interpreting a written document by enabling them to consult the proxy directly. It appeals to many patients who would rather trust the decision of a close relative or friend than attempt to posit complex advance medical instructions. Some parts of the United States and Australia use proxy legislation without any living will legislation. In Canada, Nova Scotia[132] and Quebec[133] have legislation permitting the use of proxy directives alone.

Basis and Theory of Proxy Decisions

Proxy decisions rely on a 'substituted judgement' standard. Lord Goff in *Airedale NHS* v. *Bland*[134] did not accept that the substituted judgement test is part of the law of England. It has been defined by Brett, for instance:

> The *substituted judgement* standard asks the surrogate to make the decision that the patient would have made in the particular situation. This standard is limited by the fact that the surrogate must know something about the patient's preferences, as expressed when the patient's decision-making capacity was intact. On the other hand, the *best interests* standard is

invoked when the patient's preferences were unknown. This standard, by definition, cannot apply to the patient's preferences. Instead it seeks the surrogate to choose the course of action that promotes the patient's interests according to a more impersonal standard (e.g. that which most reasonable persons would choose).[135]

This standard may not necessarily result in the same decision that a 'reasonable' body of medical opinion would have made; the latter decision-making process, sometimes known as the 'Bolam' test,[136] being one that, although heavily criticised,[137] is much used. A further problem is that the standards themselves are not always clearly defined. A more elaborate procedure based on a set of three tests was developed in the landmark case of *In re Conroy*.[138] This involved looking for unequivocal evidence of the patient's wishes in the first instance, failing which good evidence of such would be acceptable to withhold treatment if burdens of treatment outweighed benefits; finally, if there was no evidence at all of the patient's wishes, then treatment could be withheld if continuing with it would be inhumane.

Pros and Cons of Proxies

Briefly, the advantages of proxy documents are considered to be the following:

1   flexibility (unlike living wills), and the ability of the proxy to make contemporaneous decisions suited to changing circumstances;
2   they may be more accessible than a living will document, which might be held at another location;
3   several studies have shown that proxy delegation tends to be preferred by patients;[139,140]
4   the physical presence of an authorised proxy may be simpler for health care staff than written living will documents;
5   whereas a living will can stimulate doctor-patient dialogue, Annas suggests that designating a proxy 'gives us all the opportunity to confront our mortality and to determine who among our friends and relatives we want to make treatment decisions on our behalf when we are unable to make them ourselves'.[141]

Arguments against proxy documents include the following:

1   some people, especially elderly patients, may not have persons they can ask to be proxies, or may have difficulty choosing a proxy;[142]
2   proxies may be ignored: as one critical care nurse put it, the agent must act as a 'bodyguard';[143] the bottom line may be that often strangers – the medical personnel who happen to be on duty at the critical time – will make the crucial choices;[144]

3   proxies may not be emotionally capable of carrying out a patient's wishes. One commentator[145] concluded: 'of the proxies who do manage accurately to judge patients' wishes, less than two-thirds will be emotionally capable to carrying them out'. Relatives may 'answer with the fatal words, "Do everything," because they translate the question as a challenge to prove their love for and fidelity to this person';[146]

4   *most seriously*, several studies have demonstrated, by presenting vignettes to pairs of proxies and patients, that, although proxies and patients are confident that they understand each other, proxies may fare no better, or even worse than average, in predicting patient's wishes in particular situations.[147] Results have approached statistical significance[148] and cannot lightly be ignored. Emanuel,[149] combining data from various published researches, concluded that 'living wills and other written instructional directives can be relied on to represent a patient's wishes accurately, under good circumstances, in 46 to 84 per cent of decisions'. There might be different views on how acceptable or unacceptable such percentages are. This practical observation is, I believe, the major flaw to the attractiveness of the proxy option. Physicians fare little better at predicting patients' wishes, as demonstrated in a number of studies.[150] Where patients have completed both a living will and a proxy document, slightly better results may be observed.[151] But, unlike living wills prima facie, proxy directives leave room for ambiguity as to the patient's true wishes.

As there is a greater tendency for proxy delegation to be implemented, serious consideration needs to be given to overcoming this last problem.[152] One way might be by the use of vignettes attested to by both patient and proxy to ensure effective communication. This will be examined further under alternative approaches. In California, interviews between the patient and a trained counsellor are sometimes videoed and then used by the patient to introduce responsible dialogue with the proxy.[153] While this seems to have a good effect, it would be too time-consuming for mass application. Tomlinson[154] demonstrated an improved performance if proxies were reminded that they were to 'make the decision they believe the elderly person would want for themselves', study results showing that this simple measure was not a vain or merely symbolic measure. However, Hare *et al.*[155] still found agreement in only 70 per cent of cases, even when proxies were asked to base treatment decisions on this substituted judgement test.

Critics of the 'self-determination' basis of advance directives have argued that since 'it is not empirically obvious why interests in dignity, the financial well-being of one's family, bodily integrity, and so on, should be said to survive and be applicable to a person who either no longer exists or cannot cognize and presently appreciate these values'[156] one could instead favour interpreting advance directives as *embodiments of acts of will* rather than as evidence of preferences, in order that the advance directive will, in fact, be employed and given a substantial role in decision making. Whatever the philosophical arguments, it is easy to see that justification for following the advance wishes, even through a fallible proxy, could be reassuring to the declarant;[157] and even if the proxy will make an erroneous decision in attempting to apply a substituted judgement, the declarant has had the comfort of knowing that he or she chose the person who would make that decision, rather than leaving it up to a stranger.[158]

Other Approaches

Given that living wills and proxy vehicles have so many shortcomings, are there other viable options? Or should we concentrate on overcoming the limitations? Without mutely accepting or rejecting advance directives so far, it might be of benefit to consider other approaches. We will briefly look at the following:

1   combined use of living will and proxy documents;
2   use of vignettes to educate patients, their proxies and health care staff, and also to improve mutual understanding;
3   reassessment of the area of decision making;
4   use of a values history;
5   greater reliance on doctor–patient dialogue;
6   comprehensive legislation for choices in dying;
7   redefining death;
8   use of ethics committees;
9   continuous updating of medical records.

Combined Use of Living Will and Proxy Documents

Combined living will and proxy legislation seem to offer some hope. Research by Mower concluded that 'Therapy-specific ADs with a designated proxy, coupled with patient–physician discussions, furnish the most reliable medical ADs'.[159] This is *not* to suggest that they should necessarily be on the same document. A proxy's authority might be undermined by living will instructions open to different interpretations than the one accorded by the proxy.[160]

Use of Vignettes

In the medical model already considered, effective communication can be hampered at several levels. The patient first translates his or her *wants* into refusals of medical interventions that are to be triggered by certain medical conditions. Largely for medical accuracy within a framework of legal effectiveness, the terminology is then further strait-jacketed, often to the point of jargon. In the event that this type of advance directive is triggered it *may* be effective, or it may be rejected by con-comitant medical or legal factors. In some cases there may be genuine antagonism, but in other cases there may be a medical and legal bene-ficence that is simply unsure how to proceed, the *ethical* questions having been obscured beneath the medical model. When the advance directive misses its mark, it may prove impossible to reconstruct what the declarant's true intentions would have been for the situation that has arisen. In contrast, vignettes can be used to express the patient's values to the health care team or proxy, or to convey information to the patient about the patient's potential situation and options, without resorting to technical jargon. This need not mean slipping into gener-alities: in fact it can be linked to the question of trying to select the area of decision making more effectively.

Hare used vignettes to test patient–proxy agreement,[161] whilst Ouslander, after using a story-book format to convey the pros and cons of tube feeding, concluded that 'Advance-directive discussions about enteral tube feeding and other health care decisions, using under-standable hypothetical clinical vignettes that describe risks and benefits that might influence decisions, should be encouraged in the practice of geriatric medicine'.[162] He observes that vignettes may be 'useful not only in research and clinical care, but in teaching medical and other health care professional students how to use advance directives in practice'.[163]

The format and construction of vignettes may have its own particular problems, such as appropriate pitching of the reading level, taking into consideration such factors as whether the patient is healthy or sick, or whether wording is in the patient's own first language. These problems do not seem insurmountable and, if the scope of vignettes is not exag-gerated, they may prove to be an increasingly useful communication tool in areas that have (quite incorrectly) been considered 'medical'.

Reassessment of the Area of Decision Making

Ouslander *et al.* have addressed a very practical consideration:

> For the rapidly increasing number of people who will live into extreme old age with some degree of cognitive and/or physical impairment, certain types of decisions are probably more important to address in an advance directive than others. Decisions about cardiopulmonary resus-citation (CPR) among the old and frail geriatric population, especially in

nursing homes, may be viewed as moot because of the abysmal survival rate of [sic] CPR in this population. Decisions about enteral feeding, on the other hand, may be critical because more and more people are living to an age when self-feeding becomes problematic.[164]

Various types of tube feeding all confer considerable benefits and burdens, and decisions about their acceptability bear little uniformity with the patient population. There is possibly a greater need for advance decision making on such treatments than there is for the relatively uncontroversial decisions which involve refusal of most interventions in the event of terminal illness, severe dementia or irreversible coma. On a similar note, Gillick[165] and fellow researchers found that functional dependence or, in healthy subjects, even age alone, were strong predicators of varied refusal patterns and suggested that both clinical practice and research in the field of advance directives should seek to define the goals of medical care for such circumstances.

Values History

A value-based directive, sometimes called a values history, may be easier to complete as it does not require knowledge of health problems or medical treatments. It allows the patient to delineate varying qualities of life situation that he or she would or would not consider acceptable. Schneiderman *et al.*'s study concluded that 'The brief general instruction component of the California DPAHC [durable power of attorney for health care] is not helpful in communicating patient wishes regarding specific life-saving procedures'.[166] Further examining the usefulness of various types of documents to patients, they observed that

> asking them to complete a checklist of procedures may direct attention away from more important issues of values and goals. Nothing, of course, can substitute for thoughtful, timely, and, perhaps, repeated discussions recorded in detail in the patient's medical record[167] Unfortunately, the reality of medical practice makes it likely that such information will be overlooked ... we suggest that advance directive instruments should be developed that enable patients to express their wishes in terms of quality of life under varying clinical states ... The rationale is that patients are fully capable of knowing and expressing their wishes with respect to conditions under which they would prefer not to be kept alive and that physicians, through their training and experience, are best able to understand which treatments (or lack of treatments) best meet their patients' wishes.[168]

Overmedicalisation by way of a therapy-specific directive misses part of the problem, and can result in the goals being mistaken for the means. A values history relies on partnership: as Battin says, 'most patients do not have enough medical knowledge to foresee the consequences of refusing treatment on a selective basis; it is this that the physician must supply'.[169]

Dickens finds non-medicalised statements a way out of the simple v. complex dilemma of living will drafting:

> [There are] serious questions about the value of executing directives that specify great detail. Indeed, the more detailed an advance directive is, the more likely it is to vary from events that actually occur. It may be of more value for individuals to express themselves in their own terms, not in the medical jargon that health professionals use to write documents, and to address their personal goals, hopes and fears.[170]

A combined medical directive and values history has been suggested by some authors:

> Value-based directives may be easier for patients to complete, because they do not require a knowledge of health problems or medical treatments. However, preference-based directives may be easier for health care professionals to interpret and implement, because they provide more explicit directions regarding treatment. It is difficult to know how to balance these conflicting goals. Since values and preferences represent fundamentally different, but complementary, approaches, instruction directives should contain both these components.[171]

There is reason to agree with Schneiderman *et al.* that the values history may more accurately reflect patients' understanding and wishes; it could be a valuable guidance vehicle for proxies, but, without clarification of the law,[172] it seems it could also be lacking in legal force, being subject to interpretation by the health care staff, and the vagaries of acceptance and non-acceptance. Nevertheless, it would seem there should be considerable room for development of the values history, perhaps as a corollary to the advance directive.[173]

Reliance on Doctor-Patient Dialogue

This was the mainstream BMA view[174] for a while, although it may be changing now. Many medical commentators have urged that living wills should be advisory only,[175] or not subject to legal sanctions, without constitutional status,[176] or that their main use is to stimulate dialogue and understanding between doctor and patient. This seems to avoid the need for crucially accurate drafting, but fails to fully answer charges of paternalism, and, as has already been indicated, doctors are not as good as they think they are at knowing the wishes of their incompetent patients.[177] This does not negate the importance of the doctor–patient relationship,[178] and perhaps care should be taken in drafting documents so as not to undermine it. This could be done by greater use of non-confrontational formats, as evidenced by the Japanese or Terrence Higgins Trust documents.[179] The importance of language and choice of non-controversial terminology has been demonstrated both by semantic analysis[180] and by empirical study.[181]

Comprehensive Legislation for Choices in Dying

According to many commentators, living will legislation alone is a poor second best, brought about by failure to answer the underlying question of whether death can be preferable to life, which, of course, leads to the question of whether it is permissible to actively seek death. This is something that I would tend to favour personally. A comprehensive structural reform such as the Model Aid In Dying Act[182] could introduce permissive legislation to allow active euthanasia or physician-assisted suicide when applications met suitable criteria that had been developed from a comprehensive ethical framework. Advance directives and values histories could be supportive vehicles within such legislation. At present, refusal or acceptance of treatment are the *only* options open to a patient experiencing intractable suffering. Instead of asking whether the patient may validly want and expect death as a preferable alternative to continued life, non-treatment offers only a hypocritical response to medical failure.[183] This puts unrealistic pressures on advance directives as a vehicle for patient autonomy.

Suggestions of legislation or reform that would, under exceptional circumstances, allow assisted suicide or voluntary euthanasia evoke even more heated debate, however.[184] Given Parliament's reluctance to take a composite approach, some reformers may well wish to concentrate on the area of advance directives, where results seem more readily achievable.

Redefining Death

In *Auckland AHB* v. *Attorney General*, Thomas J. suggested:

> Whether or not ever-advancing technology and the maturity of thought which may be no more than the product of the passage of time will lead to a further revision of the moment when a person can be accounted dead is an open issue. That is as it should be. It will ultimately be for the medical profession, sensitive to the values of the community and alert to the requirements of the law, to decide whether the irretrievable destruction of nerve tissues which are imperative to breathing and heartbeat as are the 'tissues' which constitute the brain stem, require the definition of death to be revised.[185]

The fairly modern concept of 'brain death'[186] is not universal, but was developed to allow for modern technology. As Mason says,

> The standard medical definition of death is a permanent state of tissue anoxia and this is predetermined by the irreversible cessation of the cardiopulmonary system. In fact, in natural circumstances and provided you are watching the person, the moment of somatic death is very clear. Brain death follows inevitably from this and, in 99.9 per cent of cases, irreversible and complete failure of all the cerebral functions can be assumed – you do not test for brain death following natural death. The concept of brain death is necessary *only* when a permanent state of tissue anoxia is being *prevented* artificially.[187]

Mason points out that to ventilate someone who is brain dead is to 'oxygenate a cadaver'.[188] If the definition of death evolves to encompass patients such as Tony Bland or Nancy Cruzan, for whom tests had shown there was no brain tissue left that could conceivably restore cognition, then some situations, particularly less controversial ones, would no longer require a vehicle such as the advance directive for treatment to be stopped.

Use of Ethics Committees

Favoured by many commentators as a practical option to avoid going to the courts, use of ethics committees has been heavily criticised as being less satisfactory in practice, unable to reflect the wishes of patients and difficult to implement fairly.[189] A review of available literature highlights problems of how to reduce the liability of individual committee members by maintaining secrecy of records and other measures, which are more oriented towards health care staff than to patients.[190] Although fall-back positions are undoubtedly required (when, for instance, no advance directives have been made),[191] there may be more equitable steps to consider before the implementation of ethics committee powers.[192]

Continuous Updating of Records

Favoured by at least one hospice,[193] whose patients' prognoses are comparatively well known as a group, both to themselves and their health care staff, a day-to-day updating of medical records to indicate patients' individual wishes about particular treatments could, in limited circumstances, perhaps avoid the need for advance directives. Unfortunately, this is largely applicable only to certain groups of patients, rather than to patients generally, and needs a particular institutional policy.

Concluding Remarks

In concluding, I think Loewy expressed a fairly impartial view when he declared:

> On the whole, advance directives ... by producing some order in a legally chaotic situation, give some legal protection to physicians and hospitals. Giving such protection, if the shield of protection is used wisely and responsibly, may be an ethically good thing. It may, on the one hand, encourage physician communication and enable patient choice; but, on the other hand, the protection given by this law may be used by institutions and physicians to distance themselves all too easily from a particular patient's particular situation by taking refuge in a generic rule. Medicine does not want to throw out the baby of genuine and ethical caring with the bathwater of physician paternalism.[194]

But I would suggest to Loewy that the conceptual weaknesses of advance directives limit their usefulness. Incremental reforms such as advance directive legislation and improved documents may do some good, but until the challenge of a comprehensive approach to death, dying, letting die and assisting death can be developed, any system of advance directives may be biased, weighted towards those that can benefit from them, and fraught with difficulties needing much application to resolve successfully.

Notes

1 President's Commission for the Study of Ethical Problems in Medicine and Biomedical and Behavioural Research, *Deciding to Forego Life-Sustaining Treatment – A Report on the Ethical, Medical, and Legal Issues in Treatment Decisions*, New York, Concern for Dying, 1983, pp.43–5.
2 British Medical Association, *Medical Ethics Today*, London, British Medical Association 1992, p. 161: 'the Association confirms its commitment to the fundamental right of patients to accept or reject, through advance directives, treatment options offered to them'.
3 J. Stanley (ed.) 'Appleton International Conference: Developing Guidelines for Decisions to Forgo Life-Prolonging Medical Treatment', *Journal of Medical Ethics*, **18** (Supplement) (1992), 4; R. Downie, 'Limiting Treatment at the End of Life', *Voluntary Euthanasia Society of Scotland Newsletter*, January 1994, pp. 1–3.
4 It is not just religious factions that oppose such consensus, however, and we cannot minimise problems that may arise in a multicultural society. For instance, see E. Young and S. Jex, 'The Patient Self-Determination Act: Potential Ethical Quandaries and Benefits', *Cambridge Quarterly of Healthcare Ethics*, **2** (1992), p. 112: 'In many Chinese and Japanese communities, autonomy has different connotations. In these communities, *autonomy* is to be expressed by the family as a whole rather than by a single designated proxy ... Chinese, Japanese, Vietnamese, and Lebanese families ... have conspired to keep elderly patients in ignorance of their true diagnosis – principally out of respect.'

5   P. Ferguson, 'Criminal Omissions', *Journal of the Law Society of Scotland*, June 1983, 272: 'to impose a duty on a person to force help on an unwilling patient, for example, is unjustifiable'.

6   D. Giesen, 'Law and Ethical Dilemmas at Life's End (Ethical and Legal Framework)', in *Council of Europe Proceedings of the XXth Colloquy on European Law, Law and Moral Dilemmas Affecting Life and Death*, (A): Ethical and Legal Framework, 1990.

7   *Sidaway* v. *Bethlem Royal Hospital Governors and others* [1985] 1 All ER 643, 649 gives an example in case law, where Lord Scarman says, 'The existence of the patient's right to make his own decision, which may be seen as a basic human right protected by the common law, is the reason why a doctrine embodying a right of the patient to be informed of the risks of surgical treatment has been developed in some jurisdictions in the United States of America and has found favour with the Supreme Court of Canada.'

8   Typically, treatments specifically refused might include cardiopulmonary resuscitation, antibiotics, chemotherapy, dialysis, blood transfusion, enteral feeding or ventilator support. Generally, incompetent patients who have not signed living wills have neither consented nor refused, but the legal defence for giving them treatment is outlined in J. Mason and R. McCall-Smith, *Law and Medical Ethics*, London, Butterworths, 1987, pp. 142–5. Cf. G. Kimsma and E. Leeuwen, 'Dutch Euthanasia: Background, Practice and Present Justifications', *Cambridge Quarterly of Heathcare Ethics*, **2** (1993), 24: 'Within the law … passive euthanasia is self-contradictory because it concerns the omission of a treatment to which the patient has not consented.'

9   For a description and discussion of this state, see for instance: Medical Ethics Committee of the BMA, *Discussion Paper on Treatment of Patients in Persistent Vegetative State – Consultation Paper*, London, British Medical Association, September 1992. On attitudes to the vegetative state, see B. Jennet, *High Technology Medicine – Benefits and Burdens*, Oxford, Oxford University Press, 1986, p. 147 (Table 5.4).

10   *Auckland Area Health Board Attorney General, New Zealand High Court* (1993) 4 Med LR 239 provides a relevant example and explanation of this state. It is characterised by a situation in which the brain is unable to communicate with the body or vice versa, and can be distinguished from brain death or persistent vegetative state.

11   Forms of incompetency due to minority or when the incompetent person has never been competent are not applicable here.

12   The problems affect a growing number: P. Webber, P. Fox and D. Burnette, 'Living Alone with Alzheimer's Disease: Effects on Health and Social Service Utilization Patterns', *Gerontologist*, **34**(1) (1994), p. 8: 'The prevalence of Alzheimer's disease is estimated at 3.75 million cases in 1990, representing slightly over 10% of the total population aged 65 or older; nine million Alzheimer's disease cases are projected by the year 2040 … The estimated prevalence of severe dementia for persons aged 85 or older (the oldest old) is much higher, ranging from 25 to 45% … [USA].' For illustrative examples of incompetence, see Age Concern Institute of Gerontology Centre of Medical Law and Ethics, *The Living Will: Consent to Treatment at the End of Life – A Working Party Report*, London, Edward Arnold, 1988, pp. 87–8. See also Cogen *et al.*, below, note 71.

13   For examples of such documents from the United States, see Choice in Dying, Inc., *Refusal of Treatment Legislation – A State by State Compilation of Enacted and Model Statutes*, and updates, New York, Choice in Dying, 1991. For examples of such documents from other countries, see C. Docker (ed.), *Collected Living Wills*, Edinburgh: VESS, 1993.

14   House of Lords, *Report of the Select Committee on Medical Ethics*, London, HMSO, 1994: 'Volume I – Report' (HL Paper 21–I); 'Volume II – Oral Evidence' (HL Paper 21–II); 'Volume III – Written Evidence' (HL Paper 21–III).

15   House of Lords (HL Paper 21–I), above, note 14, paras, 263–6.

16 British Medical Association, *BMA Statement on Advance Directives*, November 1992, p.2; House of Lords (HL Paper 21–I), above, note 14, para. 27.

17 C. Schlyter, *Advance Directives and AIDS – An Empirical Study of the Interest in Living Wills and Proxy Decision Making in the Context of HIV/AIDS Care*, London, Centre of Medical Law & Ethics, 1992, p.3.

18 R. Dworkin, *Life's Dominion – An Argument about Abortion and Euthanasia*, London, Harper Collins, 1993, p.180. Similar, though fuller, definitions are given in M. Brazier, *Medicine, Patients and the Law*, London, Penguin, 1992, pp. 457–8.

19 For a fuller justification of the use of the term 'living will' as opposed to 'advance directive' see J. Fox, 'Professional Acceptance of Living Wills to be Encouraged', *British Journal of Nursing*, **3**(5), (1994), 203. See also House of Lords (HL Paper 21–III), above, note 14, at pp. 265–6; Annas, below, note 29, at 1210.

20 In relation to the phrases 'living will' and 'advance directive' the Law Commission pointed out subsequently that 'A disadvantage of both these terms is that they concentrate attention on the existence and terms of a piece of paper': The Law Commission, *Mental Incapacity (Law Com No 231)*, London, HMSO, 1995, p. 65.

21 Dworkin, above, note 18, at p. 195; B. Russell, *History of Western Philosophy*, London, George Allen & Unwin, 1940, pp. 628–72.

22 This is not to say that Kant and Hume themselves might not equally have argued the opposite with regards to refusal of treatment. See, however, I. Kant, 'Duties towards the Body in Regard to Life', *Lectures in Ethics*, reprinted in J. Donnelly (ed.), *Suicide: Right or Wrong?*, New York, Prometheus, 1990, pp. 47–55; and J. Mill, 'On Liberty' (quoted and discussed in R. Campbell and D. Collinson, *Ending Lives*, Oxford, Basil Blackwell, 1988, pp. 40–44).

23 Schlyter, above, note 17, at p. 24; G. Kolata, 'AIDS Patients Seek Solace in Suicide, but Many Find Uncertainty', *New York Times* 14 June 1994; R. Ogden, *Euthanasia, Assisted Suicide & AIDS*, British Columbia, Perreault/Goedman Publishing, 1994.

24 Talk of rights often tends to polarise issues that are already confrontational. Arguably imprecise use of the language in phrases such as 'a right to die' has been ably called into question by both advocates and opponents of living wills. See J. Fletcher, 'The Right to Choose When to Die', *Hemlock Quarterly*, January 1989, p.3; L. Kass, 'Is There a Right to Die?' *Hastings Center Report* (Jan.–Feb. 1993) pp. 34–43; P. Miller, 'Death With Dignity and the Right to Die: Sometimes Doctors Have a Duty to Hasten Death', *Journal of Medical Ethics*, **13** (1987), 81–5.

25 For an introductory and concise examination of the use of rights-based language in morality, law and political rhetoric, see R. Brandt 'The Concept of a Moral Right and Its Function', *Journal of Philosophy*, **80** (1983), 29–45; C. Palley, *The United Kingdom and Human Rights*, London, Sweet & Maxwell, 1991, especially 'Human Rights Talk – Rhetoric and Enforcement Devices', pp. 71–78.

26 Since how we view the facts is crucial to any conclusions we reach, significant progress may be achieved by striving for changes in the perception of familiar data. The difficulties of applying this approach (developed by Thomas Khun, *Structure of Scientific Revolutions*, Chicago, University of Chicago Press, 1970) to social dilemmas are to be found in the lack of agreed paradigms; the anomalies disclosed by quantitative study are a powerful impetus to theory construction, however; see S. Thornstrom, 'Quantitative Methods in History', in S. Lipset and R. Hofstadter (eds), *Sociology and History Methods*, New York, Basic Books, 1968.

27 *In re T. (adult: refusal of treatment)* WLR 6 [1992] 782, 786. Consider also Y. Kamisar, 'Are Laws Against Assisted Suicide Unconstitutional?', *Hastings Center Report*, **23**(3) (1993), p. 33: 'Many proponents of the "right to die" are quick to point out that the "sanctity of life" is not an absolute or unqualified value (and they are right), but they are slow to realize that the same is true of the "right to die".' Also C. Wells, 'Patients, Consent and Criminal Law', *Journal of Social Welfare & Family Law*, **1** (1994), 70.

28 H. Brody, 'Assisted Death – A Compassionate Response to a Medical Failure', *New England Journal of Medicine*, **327**(19) (1992), 1384. See Also A. Brooks, 'Dignity and Cost-Effectiveness: A Rejection of the Utilitarian Approach to Death', *Journal of Medical Ethics*, **10**, (1992), 148: 'it is the failure to respect the intellectual integrity of other moral approaches and to understand the levels on which these differ fundamentally from the utilitarian approach that generates much of the heat in ethical controversy within the profession, whilst failing to illuminate the issues clearly'.

29 L. Kutner, *Indiana Law Journal*, **44** (1969), 539–54. See also G. Annas, 'The Health Care Proxy and the Living Will', *New England Journal of Medicine*, **324**(17) (1991), 1210.

30 *In re Karen Quinlan* 70 N.J. 10, 355 A2d 647 (1976) (a young woman in PVS).

31 California Natural Death Act, CAL. Health & Safety Code 7185–7195 (West Supp. 1989).

32 *Cruzan* v. *Director, Missouri Dept of Health*, 111 L.Ed.2d 224, 110 S. Ct. 2841, 58 U.S.L.W. 4916 (U.S., June 26, 1990) (25-year-old woman in PVS following a car accident).

33 Which states, 'nor shall any State deprive any person of life, *liberty*, or property, without due process of law' (my emphasis).

34 *Cruzan*, above, note 32.

35 Patient Self-Determination Act U.S.C.A. 1395cc & 1396a, 4206–4207, 4751, Omnibus Budget Reconciliation Act of 1990, P.L:. 101–508 (101ST Cong. 2nd Sess. Nov. 5, 1990) (West Supp., 1991).

36 State legislation is collected in Choice in Dying, above, note 13.

37 Uniform Power of Attorney Act, 8 Uniform Laws Annotated 74 (1982).

38 Annas, above, note 29, at 1211, suggests that among the more responsible attempts at drafting a DPAHC is that of New York, drafted by the New York State Task Force on Life and the Law.

39 B. Logue, *Last Rights: Death Control and the Elderly in America*, Oxford, Maxwell Macmillan, 1993, p. 159.

40 *Law No. 351 of 14 May 1992 Amending the Law on the Practice of Medicine (Provisions concerning information and consent) (Loventide 1992, Part A, 16 May 1992, No. 66 P.1361 Den.92.31); and Order No. 782 of 18 September 1992 on Living Wills. (Loventide, 1992, Part A, 29 September 1992, No. 130, pp. 3591–3592 (Den.92.34).* The problems of implementation, whether in the United States, Denmark, or prospectively in the United Kingdom, cannot be adequately dealt with in this short chapter, but some of the difficulty of the task can be construed from the fact that, although 45 000 Danes registered within a few months of the living wills system being initiated, only one or two doctors are consulting the register each week, *British Medical Journal*, **306** (1993), 414–15.

41 Nova Scotia: Medical Consent Act, RSNS 1989, c 279.

42 Quebec: Public Curator Act, SQ 1989, c 54.

43 Manitoba: Health Care Directives Act, Statutes of Manitoba 1992, c 33 (the first statute in Canada to deal directly with living wills).

44 Ontario: Consent to Treatment Act (1992), c 30.

45 *Malette* v. *Shulman* (1991), 2 Med LR 162.

46 *Fleming* v. *Reid* (1991) 82 DLR (4th) 298, 310.

47 South Australia: Natural Death Act 1983; Victoria: Medical Treatment Act 1988, subsequently amended by The Medical Treatment (Enduring Power of Attorney) Act 1990 (Vic); Northern Territory: Natural Death Act 1988 (NT).

48 *British Medical Journal*, **308** (1994), 616. The new Patients' Rights Law in the Netherlands now legally obliges doctors to honour living wills.

49 P. Maas, J. Delden and L. Pijnenborg, 'Euthanasia and other Medical Decisions Concerning the End of Life – An investigation performed upon request of the

Commission of Inquiry into the Medical Practice concerning Euthanasia', in *Health Policy*, vol. 22/1 & 2 Special Issue, Amsterdam, Elsevier, 1992. Table 8.4 (p. 82) shows percentages of written advance directives present in decisions to withdraw or withhold treatment.

50 *Re T*, above, note 27, at 783.

51 *Airedale NHS Trust* v. *Bland* [1993] WLR 316 [1993] 1 All ER 821.

52 Ibid., 1 All ER, 835.

53 Ibid., 1 All ER, 843.

54 Chaired by Lord Walton. See House of Lords (HL Paper 21–I), above, note 14.

55 Law Commission, *Consultation Paper No 129, Mentally Incapacitated Adults and Decision-Making – Medical Treatment and Research*, London, HMSO, 1993, p. 33.

56 Cf. *Cruzan*, above, note 32, where the court required 'clear and convincing evidence' of the incompetent's earlier wishes.

57 *Re C* [1994] 1 FLR 31.

58 House of Lords (HL Paper 21–I), above, note 14, para. 264: 'we conclude that legislation for advance directives generally is unnecessary. Doctors are increasingly recognising their ethical obligation to comply with advance directives. The development of case law is moving in the same direction ... Adequate protection for doctors exists in terms of the current law and in trends in medical practice.'

59 Medical and Dental Defence Union of Scotland, 'Living Wills', *Summons*, (Spring 1994), 2.

60 D. Jeffrey, 'Active Euthanasia – Time for a Decision', *British Journal of General Practice*, **44** (1994), 136–8.

61 S. Meredith 'A Testament of Intent', *Law Society Gazette*, **91**(15) (1994), 26–8.

62 British Medical Association, *BMA Statement on Advance Directives* (January 1994 revision), London, BMA, 1994, pp. 2–3; and later, A. Sommerville, 'Euthanasia: Why It Is Still Unacceptable', *BMA News Review* (May 1994), 26.

63 *Re T*, above, note 27, at 787: 'an anticipatory choice which, if clearly established and applicable in the circumstances – two major "ifs" – would bind the practitioner'. See also Lord Donaldson's summary, ibid., at 799. Also Law Commission, above, note 55, p. 32: 'The BMA was concerned about the patient who is inadequately informed, but it appears to us that directives given in such circumstances would not be "applicable" in the circumstances about which the patient had not been adequately informed.'

64 *Hansard*, 9 May 1994, p. 1349. Direct questions to the government for clarification on the legal position are made at p. 1384, and replied to at p. 1408.

65 The Law Commission, *Mental Incapacity Bill* (draft): see above, note 20.

66 Ibid., para 5.16.

67 Ibid., para 5.30.

68 Ibid., para 5.20.

69 *Re T*, above, note 63.

70 The Law Commission, *Mental Capacity Bill*: See above, note 20, para 5.7.

71 It has often been suggested that patients unduly fear unnecessary treatment: British Medical Association, *Euthanasia*, London: BMA, 1988, p. 21. For arguments against, see G. Cogen, B. Patterson, S. Chavin *et al.*, 'Surrogate Decision-Maker Preferences for Medical Care of Severely Demented Nursing Home Patients', *Archives of Internal Medicine*, **152** (1992), 1885–8, 1887: 'Hospital level services including ICU stays and mechanical ventilation can reverse concurrent acute illnesses but have no beneficial effect on the underlying dementia and are frequently associated with superimposed delirium that exacerbates patient discomfort.'

72 L. Emanuel, E. Emanuel, J. Stoeckle, L. Hummel and M. Barry, 'Advance Directives: Stability of Patients' Treatment Choices', *Archives of Internal Medicine*, **154** (1994), 209: 'The common assumption justifying the use of advance directives is that a

patient's prior expression of treatment choices accurately represents his or her future choices, that is, they are stable over time.' Emanuel *et al.*'s study demonstrates some empirical evidence for this, without tackling the philosophical questions of extending autonomy into a future state of incompetence.

73   Although this is a common argument (see for instance, King, below, note 115) it is unsupported by at least one study: J. Virmani, J. Schneiderman and R. Kaplan, 'Relationship of Advance Directives to Physician–Patient Communication', *Archives of Internal Medicine*, **154** (1994), 909: 'Despite public enthusiasm for the use of advance directives and great efforts to promote them, we found little evidence that these documents are associated with enhanced communication between patients and physicians about end-of-life treatment decisions.'

74   Note that it cannot be assumed that most people have similar preferences. See M. Heap, R. Munglani, J. Klinck and A. Males, 'Elderly Patients' Preferences Concerning Life-Support Treatment', *Anaesthesia*, **48** (1993), 1031: 'Elderly patients faced with a life threatening illness are a heterogeneous group. They have widely differing preferences for treatment and there are few external guides to these preferences.'

75   Sanctity of life arguments are used both for and against living wills and are discussed as an 'unhelpful argument' in I. Kennedy and A. Grubb, *Medical Law: Text with Materials*, 2nd ed, London, Butterworths, 1994, pp. 1197–9. See also Dworkin, above, note 18, at p. 238: 'People who want an early, peaceful death for themselves or their relatives are not rejecting or denigrating the sanctity of life; on the contrary, they believe that a quicker death shows more respect for life than a protracted one.' See also Kamisar, above, note 27. For sanctity of life arguments in the Christian tradition, see, for instance, 'Memorandum by the Linacre Centre for Health Care Ethics: Sanctity of Life and Autonomy', in House of Lords (HL Paper 21–III), above, note 14, pp. 156–63; 'Memorandum by the House of Bishops of the Church of England and the Catholic Bishops' Conference of England and Wales', ibid., p. 113. For a comprehensive overview of religious attitudes, see G. Larue, *Euthanasia and Religion – A Survey of the Attitudes of World Religions to the Right-to-Die*, Los Angeles, Hemlock, 1985.

76   See, for instance, Young and Jex, above, note 4 at 109; also B. Dickens, 'A Response to the Papers of Molloy and Colleagues (Canada) and Cranford (United States) on Advance Directives', *Humane Medicine*, **9**(1) (1993), 80: 'The application of these theoretical responses within hypothetical scenarios to the actual events that occur is a matter of conjecture and speculation.'

77   Emanual *et al.*, above, note 72, at 212: 'Stability was moderate among patients who did not complete high school and was greater among patients with a higher education.' One Dutch advance directive (which also includes a euthanasia provision) additionally contains a risk-acceptance clause. Nederlandse Vereniging voor Vrijwillige Euthanasie (NVVE), *Declaration of Euthanasia/Refusal of Treatment*, Amsterdam, NVVE: 'I have made and signed this declaration of will after thorough deliberation and of my own free will. It shall remain in force irrespective of the time that has elapsed. I hereby deliberately accept the risk that I may no longer be able to revoke my declaration of will if I am in the condition referred to at 1, in order to exclude a risk which is greater to me, namely that I should continue living in circumstances that are not acceptable to me' (translation of NVVE), in C. Docker (ed.), *Collected Living Wills*, Edinburgh: VESS, 1993, at pp. 107–115.

78   British Medical Association, above, note 2, at p. 162. 'The possibility of patients inadvertently misdirecting their doctors by an inadequate appreciation of the circumstances or of the evolution of new treatments led the Association to recommend strongly that advance directives should not be legally binding on doctors.' See also Annas, above, note 29.

79 G. Annas, 'When Procedures Limit Rights: From Quinlan to Conroy', *Hastings Center Report*, 24–6 April 1985; G. Rodriguez, 'An Opposing View. Routine Discussion of Advance Health Care Directives: Are We Ready?', *Journal of Family Practice*, **31**(6) (1990), 657.

80 The 'slippery slope' argument is generally misused. See J. Burgess, 'The Great Slippery Slope Argument', *Journal of Medical Ethics*, **18** (1993), 169: 'Although there are slippery slope arguments that are sound and convincing, typical formulations of the Nazi-invoking argument are found to be seriously deficient both in logical rigour and in the social history and psychology required as a scholarly under-pinning'; and 173: 'those who offer the Great Argument seem to be entirely ignorant of the vast technical literature on slippery slopes and related phenomena now available'. Some rational cost allocation considerations are given in C. Chambers, J. Diamond, R. Perkel and L. Lasch, 'Relationship of Advance Directives to Hospital Charges in a Medicare Population', *Archives of Internal Medicine*, **154** (1994), 541: 'During discussions of advance directions, patients often opt to limit the extent of care they desire in certain situations. Although the most appropri-ate setting for developing advance directives is not clear, the results of this study imply that an enormous cost saving to society may be realized if such discussions take place, while, at the same time, autonomous patient choice will be respected.'

81 W. Diamond, J. Jernigan, R. Moseley *et al.*, 'Decision-Making Ability and Advance Directive Preferences in Nursing Home Patients and Proxies', *Gerontologist*, **29**(5) (1989), 626: 'Discrepancies between patients' stated preferences and responses to the AD form should alert providers to possible confusion or lack of comprehen-sion. Presenting the AD alone without interview and discussion may elicit inaccurate preferences. Future research might experiment with a simplified form, as well as one that specifies various options'. Dangers of complexity apply similarly to proxy documents: Annas, above, note 29, at 1211: 'Some Massachusetts attorneys, for example, have already drafted a 13-page, single-spaced proxy form that is all but unintelligible to non-lawyers.'

82 M. Gillick, K. Hesse and N. Mazzapica, 'Medical Technology at the End of Life – What Would Physicians and Nurses Want for Themselves?', *Archives of Internal Medicine*, **153**, (1993), 2542–7: 'nurses and physicians had higher [treatment] refusal rates … clinical experience affects preferences. This suggest that individuals who complete advance directives do so in the absence of adequate information.'

83 T. Fried, M. Stein, P. O'Sullivan, D Brock and D. Novack, 'Limits of Patient Autonomy – Physician Attitudes and Practices Regarding Life-Sustaining Treatments and Euthanasia', *Archives of Internal Medicine*, **153** (1993), 722, in a study of 392 physicians, found that 'Physicians value the concept of patient autonomy but place it in the context of other ethical and legal concerns and do not always accept specific actions derived from this principle'; and at 726: 'although respon-dents believe that the principle of patient autonomy should *usually* be complied with, other concerns can determine how a physician will act'.

84 Rodriguez, above, note 79, at 656: 'Hospital do not routinely enquire about their [living wills'] existence when important medical decisions are being made.' See also M. Danis, L. Southerland, J. Garrett *et al.* 'A Prospective Study of Advance Directives for Life-Sustaining Care', *New England Journal of Medicine*, **324**(13) (1991), 882: 'In an analysis of 96 outcome events (hospitalization or death in the nursing home), care was consistent with previously expressed wishes 75 percent of the time; however, the presence of the written advance directive in the medical record did not facilitate consistency … The effectiveness of written advance directives is limited by inattention to them and by decisions to place priority on considerations other than the patient's autonomy.'

85 D. Molloy, C. Harrison, M. Farrugia and A. Cunje, 'The Canadian Experience with Advance Treatment Directives', *Humane Medicine*, **9**(1) (1993), 72: 'Surveys of the

attitudes of physicians and nurses to health care directives show support for their use; still, when confronted with them, a significant proportion of these professionals ignore the written directives and provide care incompatible with patients' choices.'

86 Logue, above, note 39, at pp. 160–63.

87 N. Kaplan, 'Health Care Agent's Authority Nullified by Living Will that Forgot to Mention Reversible, Secondary Conditions', *National Academy of Elder Law Attorneys Quarterly*, Fall 1992, 3–5.

88 Annas, above, note 29, at 1210, points out that in the United States generally there is no penalty if health care providers do not honour living wills.

89 N. Zweibel and C. Cassel, 'Treatment Choices at the End of Life: A Comparison of Decisions by Older Patients and Their Physician-Selected Proxies', *Gerontologist*, **29**(5) (1989), 615: 'The proportion of respondents having written a living will varied from 4% in the study population reported in this research (Cassel & Zweibel, 1987) to 15% in a telephone survey of a random sample of adults conducted by the American Medical Association (*Wall Street Journal*, 1988), to 17.5% in a sample of older research volunteers (High, 1988).'

90 J. Hare, C. Pratt and C. Nelson, 'Agreement between Patients and Their Self-Selected Surrogates on Difficult Medical Decisions', *Archives of Internal Medicine*, **152** (1992), 1049–54.

91 L. Emanuel and E. Emanuel, 'Decisions at the End of Life Guided by Communities of Patients', *Hastings Center Report* (Sept–Oct. 1993), p. 6.

92 British Medical Association, above, note 2, at p. 162: to facilitate the accessibility of the document, 'The BMA suggest that patients who have drafted an advance directive carry a card indicating that fact as well as lodging a copy with their doctor.'

93 Sam M. and P. Singer, 'Canadian Outpatients and Advance Directives: Poor Knowledge and Little Experience but Positive Attitudes', *Canadian Medical Association Journal*, **148**(9) (1993), 1497–1502.

94 J. Puma, D. Orentlicher and R. Moss, 'Advance Directives on Admission: Clinical Implications and Analysis of the Patient Self-Determination Act of 1990', *Journal of the American Medical Association*, **266**(3) (1991), 402.

95 K. Stelter, B. Elliott and C. Bruno, 'Living Will Completion in Older Adults', *Archives of Internal Medicine*, **152** (1992), 954–9. However, well-structured forms that are otherwise justifiable should not be entirely dismissed because *some* people find the complexity disproportionate to the level of decision making they wish to exert at a particular time; a general-statement AD may be preferred, but followed up by a detailed one at a later date perhaps.

96 M. Battin, 'The Least Worse Death', *Hastings Center Report* (April 1983), pp. 13–16.

97 L. Emanuel, M. Barry, J. Stoeckle *et al.*, 'Advance Directives for Medical Care – A Case for Greater Use', *New England Journal of Medicine*, **324**(13) (1991), 889–95. This study concluded that advance directives require physician initiative and that 'the empirical case in favor of planning for medical care with a comprehensive document is already strong enough to warrant recommending that physicians initiate routine discussion of planning with their patients'.

98 J. Saultz, 'Routine Discussion of Advance Health Care Directives: Are We Ready? – An Affirmative View', *Journal of Family Practice*, **31**(6) (1990), 653–9. Saultz suggests, 'Perhaps the two most important reasons why advance directives are not discussed more frequently are physicians' lack of knowledge about the outcome of medical interventions and lack of skill in counselling patients. A contrary view is presented in a more recent study, D. High, 'Advance Directives and the Elderly: A Study of Intervention Strategies to Increase Use', *Gerontologist*, **33**(3) (1993) 347: 'The reasons for the low rate of use of advance directives among US citizens, especially older Americans, are more complicated than a lack of information and a lack of encouragement from health care professionals.'

99 T. Klosterman, 'Analysis of Health Care Directive Legislation in the United States', unpublished study, 1992.

100 Logue, above, note 39, at p. 162.

101 E. Kluge, 'A Guide to Living Wills', *Last Rights* (Oct.–Nov. 1992), 14–18.

102 J. Leonard-Taitz, 'Euthanasia, The Right to Die and the Law in South Africa', *Medicine & Law*, 11 (1992), 597–601.

103 Kaplan, above, note 87.

104 S. McLean, interviewed in 'The Law, the Courts and the Interests of the Dying Patient', *Voluntary Euthanasia Society of Scotland Newsletter*, January 1994, 12–13.

105 'There Should be Limited Legislation on Advance Directives', *British Medical Journal* (Medicopolitical Digest), 308 (1994), 276–7. 'The BMA council has endorsed the Law Commission's new proposals for limited legislation on advance directives. The commission wants legislation to be introduced to cater, for example, for explicit refusal of treatment on the lines of Jehovah's Witnesses' no blood directives but not for advance directives which outline in general terms a patient's wishes about non-treatment and the circumstances in which they are to apply.'

106 W. Mower and L. Barraff, 'Advance Directives – Effect of Type of Directive on Physicians' Therapeutic Decisions', *Archives of Internal Medicine*, 153 (1993), 375–81.

107 House of Lords (Paper HL–I), above, note 14, at para. 264.

108 Battin, above, note 96, gives one detailed example. Another can be found in: L. Schneiderman and J. Arras, 'Counselling Patients to Counsel Physicians on Future Health Care in the Event of Patient Incompetence', *Annals of Internal Medicine*, 102 (1985), 697. See also M. Battin, *The Least Worst Death – Essays in Bioethics on the End of Life*, Oxford, Oxford University Press, 1994, p. 34.

109 A notable exception is when the advance directive is made on religious grounds rather than to avoid suffering, as is the case with a Jehovah's Witness's 'no blood' directive.

110 A. Brett, 'Limitations of Listing Specific Medical Interventions in Advance Directives', *Journal of the American Medical Association*, 266(6) (1991), 826. For a recent example of the 'checklist' or 'laundry list' approach, see Anon., *Do-it-yourself . . . Power of Attorney & Living Will*, London: Law Pack Publishing Ltd, 1994.

111 P. Kokkonen, *Living Will*, Helsinki: National Agency for Welfare and Health, 1992. This is not mere hair-splitting: a not-applicable-in-the-circumstances ruling might achieve the same result as an autonomy-based escape clause in many instances, but would fail in cases where the refusal was based on principle or firm conviction.

112 Living will document of the Terrence Higgins Trust and King's College London reproduced in Kennedy and Grubb, above, note 75, at pp. 1365–8. See also A. Holt and S. Viinikka, 'Living Wills', *Legal Action*, April 1994, 9; and British Medical Association, above, note 2, at p. 161.

113 Law Commission, above, note 55, at p. 36. For a fuller examination of the ethical issues involved in ascertaining competence, see J. Kilner, *Who Lives? Who Dies? – Ethical Criteria in Patient Selection*, London, Yale University Press, 1990, pp. 169–74.

114 *Re T*, above, note 27, at 798.

115 N. King, *Making Sense of Advance Directives*, Amsterdam, Kluwer Academic, 1991.

116 The Center for Bioethics, University of Toronto, provides an example in its living will document.

117 Brett, above, note 110.

118 NVVE, above, note 77.

119 *In Re T*, above, note 27, at 786, Lord Donaldson suggested the only possible qualification to a competent adult's right to refuse treatment is a case where the choice might lead to the death of a viable foetus. In the United States, prohibitions currently in some states against living wills allowing a pregnant women to refuse treatment are considered potentially unconstitutional: *Roe v. Wade* (1973)

410 US 113, 35 L Ed 2d 147, 93 S Ct, 705, 148, upheld a woman's right to decide whether to terminate a pregnancy up to and after the end of the first trimester until the point at which the foetus became viable, and this was upheld in *Planned Parenthood of Southeastern Pennsylvania* v *Casey*, 120 L Ed 2d 674, 687, which declared: 'viability marks the earliest point at which the State's interest in fetal life is constitutionally adequate to justify a legislative ban on nontherapeutic abortions'. See, against this, Age Concern Institute of Gerontology, above, note 12, at p. 60: 'If a living will comes into operation in relation to a woman who is pregnant, any instruction to forego life-sustaining treatment should be regarded as invalid during the course of the pregnancy.'

120 The Law Commission recommend a presumption in favour of preserving life unless the question is specifically addressed in the advance refusal of treatment (above, note 20, at para. 5.26), but says, 'We do not, however, accept that a woman's right to determine the sorts of bodily interference which she will tolerate somehow evaporates as soon as she becomes pregnant' (ibid., para 5.25).

121 N. MacDonald, A. Sommerville and C. Docker, 'The BMA Interview', *Voluntary Euthanasia Society of Scotland Newsletter*, Sept. 1993, 12–15. The BMA representatives suggested 'looking at a cohort of patients who have similar characteristics, and then at a particular style or form that might be useful to them. The idea is underpinned by saying that patients who have a particular disease may be better informed as to their particular prognoses and treatments than a healthy declarant, and so possibly be able to made a responsible decision.'

122 Annas, above, note 29.

123 The living will document formerly issued by the Voluntary Euthanasia Society of Scotland (VESS) in J.K. Mason and R.A. McCall Smith, *Law and Medical Ethics*, 4th ed., Edinburgh, Butterworths, 1994, pp. 439–40. VESS withdrew the document in 1995 in favour of that reproduced in A. Barr, J. Biggar, A. Dalgleish and H. Stevens, *Drafting Wills in Scotland*, Edinburgh, Butterworths, 1994, pp. 97–100.

124 T. Oki, 'Opening Declaration', *The Living Will in the World: The 9th International Conference of the World Federation of Right to Die Societies: Participants' Lectures*, Tokyo, Japan Society for Dying with Dignity, 1994.

125 Age Concern Institute of Gerontology, above, note 12, at p. 49; Brazier, above, note 18, at p. 458.

126 British Medical Association, above, note 2, at p. 18.

127 *Usher Petitioner* (1989) discussed in A. Ward, 'Tutors to Adults: Developments', *Scots Law Times*, (1992), 325–9.

128 *Re T*, above, note 27, at 787.

129 British Medical Association, above, note 9.

130 M. Gilhooly, 'Memorandum by Scottish Action on Dementia – Living Wills and Proxy Directives', in *House of Lords* (HL Paper 21–III), above, note 14, at p. 230; Brett, above, note 110. See also below, note 152.

131 Klosterman, above, note 99.

132 Medical Consent Act, RSNS 1989, c 279.

133 Public Curator Act, SQ 1989, c 54.

134 Above, note 51, All ER 872.

135 Brett, above, note 110. For a fuller examination of substituted judgement see C. Lowy, 'The Doctrine of Substituted Judgement in Medical Decision Making', *Bioethics*, **2**(1) (1988), 15–21. The best interests standard was examined at length in *Airedale NHS Trust*, above, note 51, and summed up in Kennedy and Grubb, above, note 75, at p. 1225: 'Thus, for these judges, the task was to endorse "best interests" as the test generally but then immediately to try to find a way to avoid what they saw as its implications in the case. The way they chose was to say that in a case of PVS the law need not proceed to weigh the various interests of the

patient because the patient by being permanently insensate *has no interests*. In particular, the patient has no interest in treatment being continued.'

136 *Bolam* v, *Friern Hospital Management Committee* [1975] 1 WLR 582 held that 'a doctor who had acted in accordance with a practice accepted at the time as proper by a responsible body of medical opinion skilled in the form of treatment in question was not guilty of negligence merely because there was a body of competent professional opinion which might adopt a different technique'.

137 *Airedale Trust NHS* v. *Bland*, above, note 51; at 895, Lord Musthill says, 'I venture to feel some reservations about the application of the principle of civil liability in negligence laid down in *Bolam* v. *Friern Hospital Management Committee* [1957] I WLR 582 to decisions on "best interest" in a field dominated by the criminal law. I accept without difficulty that this principle applies to the ascertainment of the medical raw material such as diagnosis, prognosis and appraisal of the patient's cognitive functions. Beyond this point, however, it may be said that the declaration is ethical, not medical, and that there is no reason in logic why on such a decision the opinions of doctors should be decisive.'

138 *In re Conroy*, 98 NJ 321, 486 A2d 1209 (1985). The tests are elaborated on more fully in Giesen, above, note 6, and an excellent comparison of the relevant tests is made in J. Crowley, 'To Be or Not to Be: Examining the Right to Die', *Journal of Legislation of Notre Dame Law School*, **18**(2) (1992), 347–55.

139 High, above, note 98, at 348: 'The data suggest that serious attention needs to be given to understanding elderly people's overwhelming preference for family surrogates.'

140 Sam and Singer, above, note 93.

141 Annas, above, note 29, p. 1213.

142 J. Roe, M. Goldstein, K. Massy and D. Pascoe, 'Durable Power of Attorney for Health Care: A Survey of Senior Center Participants', *Archives of Internal Medicine*, **152** (1992), 292: 'the most frequent reasons for not executing a durable power of attorney for health care were: lack of awareness of the form, procrastination, and difficulty choosing a proxy'.

143 Logue, above, note 39, at p. 163.

144 Ibid., at p. 165.

145 Emanuel and Emanuel, above, note 91.

146 J. Bresnahan, 'Medical Futility or the Denial of Death?', *Cambridge Quarterly of Healthcare Ethics*, **2** (1993), 215.

147 J. Lynne and J. Teno, 'After the Patient Self-Determination Act – The Need for Empirical Research on Formal Advance Directives', *Hastings Center Report* (Jan.–Feb. 1993) p. 21: 'A flurry of articles has documented that surrogates (next of kin, usually) err substantially in predicting patient preferences.' For a similar overview, see E. Emanuel and L. Emanuel, 'Proxy Decision Making for Incompetent Patients – An Ethical and Empirical Analysis', *Journal of the American Medical Association*, **267**(15) (1992), 2067–71.

148 Zweibel and Cassel, above, note 89.

149 Emanuel and Emanuel, above, note 91, at p. 7

150 J. Ouslander, A. Tymchuk and B. Rahbar, 'Health Care Decisions Among Elderly Long-term Care Residents and their Potential Proxies', *Archives of Internal Medicine*, **149** (1989), 1367–72. Also A. Seckler, D. Meier, M. Mulvihill *et al.*, 'Substituted Judgement: How Accurate Are Proxy Predictions?', *Annals of Internal Medicine*, **115**(2) (1991), 92: 'Although patients predicted that both their physicians (90%) and family members (87%) would accurately predict their wishes, neither family members nor physicians, in fact, were able to accurately predict patients' wishes', and at 95: physicians did no better than chance alone in predicting the wishes of their patients'.

151 Zweibel and Cassel, above, note 89.

152   The Law Commission recommend a 'Continuing Power of Attorney' (above, note 20, Part VII), but pay scant attention to any inability of the donee to make decisions 'in the best interests' of the donor. A simple modification could have called for consideration of some form of values history document as an indication that the donee had some guiding information on the best interests of the donor.

153   Hemlock of Northern California operates this scheme.

154   T. Tomlinson, K. Howe, M. Notman and D. Rossmiller, 'An Empirical Study of Proxy Consent for Elderly Persons', *Gerontologist*, **30**(1) (1990), 54–64.

155   J. Hare, C. Pratt and C. Nelson, 'Agreement between Patients and Their Self-Selected Surrogates on Difficult Medical Decisions', *Archives of Internal Medicine*, **152** (1992), 1049–54.

156   M. Kuczewski, 'Whose Will is it Anyway? A Discussion of Advance Directives, Personal Identity, and Consensus in Medical Ethics', *Bioethics*, **8**(1) (1994), 37, and generally for a number of philosophical constructs relating to questions of autonomy and future incompetence.

157   H. Kuhse, *The Sanctity of Life Doctrine in Medicine – A Critique*, Oxford, Clarendon Press, 1987, pp. 218–19.

158   J. Menikoff, 'Beyond Advance Directives – Health Care Surrogate Laws', *New England Journal of Medicine*, **327**(16) (1992), 1165–6. Some options involving giving legal authority to the highest person on a statutory list of relatives, providing a back-up in the absence of a nominated proxy, are developed for instance in Alberta Law Reform Institute, *Advance Directives and Substitute Decision-Making in Personal Health Care, Report for Discussion No. 11*, Edmonton, Alberta, 1991, pp. 1 and 39–42. See Loewy, below, note 194, at 1975, for a contrary viewpoint.

159   Mower, above, note 106, at 381.

160   Kaplan, above, note 87, at 4.

161   Hare *et al.*, above, note 155, at 1051.

162   J. Ouslander, A. Tymchuk and M. Krynski, 'Decisions about Enteral Tube Feeding among the Elderly', *Journal of the American Geriatrics Society*, **41** (1993), 70. The idea is further developed in M. Krynski, A. Tymchuk and J. Ouslander, 'How Informed Can Consent Be? New Light on Comprehension Among Elderly People Making Decisions About Enteral Tube Feeding', *Gerontologist*, **34**(1) (1994), 36.

163   Ouslander *et al.*, above, note 162, at 74.

164   Ibid. at 73.

165   Gillick *et al.*, above, note 82, at 2547.

166   L. Schneiderman, R. Pearlman, R. Kaplan, J. Anderson and E. Rosenberg, 'Relationship of General Advance Directive Instructions To Specific Life-Sustaining Treatment Preferences in Patients with Serious Illness', *Archives of Internal Medicine*, **152** (1992), 2114. This paper also includes an excellent example of a values history, the Durable Power of Attorney from Seattle Veterans Affairs Medical Center, University of Washington. Further use of non-medicalised hypothetical scenario questions is found in M. Lee and L. Ganzini, 'The Effect of Recovery From Depression on Preferences for Life-Sustaining Therapy in Older Patients', *Journal of Gerontology*, **49**(1) (1994), M16 and M21. For a very extensive values history, with a rather different scope, see P. Lambert, J. Gibson and P. Nathanson, 'The Values History: An Innovation in Surrogate Medical Decision-Making', *Law, Medicine & Health Care*, **18**(3) (1990), 202–12.

167   This continual updating approach has been tried at Milestone House Hospice, Edinburgh, which cares for patients with AIDS.

168   Schneiderman *et al.*, above, note 166, at 2120.

169   Battin, above, note 96, at pp. 15–16. See also J. Roe, M. Goldstein, J. Massey and D. Pascoe, 'Durable Power of Attorney for Health Care: A Survey of Senior Center Participants', *Archives of Internal Medicine*, **152** (1992), 295: 'A clear indication of the patient's goals for therapy is probably more important than an exhaustive

checklist; the latter may indicate preferences that change with slight changes in the medical situation,' But note N. Christakis and D. Asch, 'Biases in How Physicians Choose to Withdraw Life Support', *Lancet*, **342** (1993), 645: 'Should, therefore, advance directives be drafted to specify how life support could be withdrawn? We think not: rather than seek such specificity physicians should focus on the underlying goals.' While supporting goal-oriented over therapy-oriented directives, Christakis and Asch found that some clinicians are biased when they choose how to withdraw life support and that they should re-evaluate their practices, since such biases 'may represent impediments to rational and compassionate decision making in critical care' (at 642).

170 Dickens, above, note 76, at 80.

171 Advance Directives Seminar Group, 'Advance Directives: Are they an advance?' *Canadian Medical Association Journal*, **146**(2) (1992), 129.

172 Some clarification might be provided by the scope of 'best interests' considered in *Mental Capacity Bill*, note 70, above.

173 For an example of a combined document, see Barr *et al.*, above, note 123.

174 British Medical Association, *BMA Statement on Advance Directives*, London, BMA, November 1992, and January 1994 revision.

175 Declaration of the Standing Committee of Doctors of the EC on living wills/advance directives (adopted Cascais, 12–13 Nov. 1993), *CP 93/83 final-EN*; R. Fisher and E. Meslin, 'Should living wills be legalized?', *Canadian Medical Association Journal*, **142**(1) (1990), 26.

176 J. Robertson, 'Second Thoughts on Living Wills', *Hastings Center Report* (Nov.–Dec. 1991), 8–9.

177 Ouslander *et al.*, above, note 150, at 1371: 'of particular concern is the high rate of disagreement between the physicians and their elderly patients'.

178 S. McLean, *A Patient's Right to Know – Information Disclosure, the Doctor and the Law*, Aldershot, Dartmouth, 1989: generally, for an analysis of the relationship in its legal and ethical context; p. 5: 'Recognizing the significance of communication between doctor and patient is a fundamental step in generating a therapeutic atmosphere of respecting the rights of the individual patient.' Reliance on professional judgement, and examination of its viability as an area for reform, is examined in Alberta Law Reform Institute, above, note 158, at pp. 19–20.

179 Japan Society for Dying with Dignity living will document, Tokyo; and the Terrence Higgins Trust document, above, note 112.

180 M. Battin, 'Assisted Suicide: Can We Learn Anything from Germany?', *Hastings Center Report* (March–April 1992), pp. 47–9.

181 Euthanasia Research and Guidance Organization, *What's in a Word? – The results of a Roper Poll of Americans on how they view the importance of language in the debate over the right to choose to die*, Oregon, ERGO, 1994.

182 Model Aid-in-Dying Act, 75 Iowa Law Rev. 139–215 (1989). Some commentators have suggested that statutory change is unnecessary. See I. Kennedy, *The Upjohn Lecture*, 25 April 1994 at the Royal Society, London, p. 4: 'All I mean is that the doctor's conduct be so described that it may be subsumed within the range of conducts which are already permitted by law. Put shortly, the courts should decide as follows: that, in certain specified and carefully defined circumstances, the concept of treating a patient for dying, already well recognized by the law in the context, for example, of the severely handicapped child, should extend to the administration of that which in the context of doctor-assisted suicide will kill the patient. Against this, see S. McLean and G. Maher, *Medicine, Morals and the Law*, Aldershot, Gower, 1983, p. 76: 'What is clear is that merely by permitting decisions about life and death to be taken by those whose role deals with such issues most often, i.e. the doctor, will not resolve the problem, but will merely involve us in yet more convoluted attempts to rationalise our behaviour in so doing.' For

examples of the inadequacy of non-treatment options, see *R* v. *Cox* [1992] 12 BMLR, 48 (Doctor tried for attempted murder for administering a lethal dose to a dying patient): '"Five minutes of peace", he said, "is not very much but it was all Dr Cox could give, and he gave it."', per Ognall, J.; or *Rodriguez* v. *British Columbia* [1993] 3 SCR 519, para 18, (ALS sufferer seeks assisted suicide as a constitutional right): 'Although palliative care may be available to ease the pain and other physical discomfort which she will experience, the appellant fears the sedating effects of such drugs and argues, in any event, that they will not prevent the psychological and emotional distress which will result from being in a situation of utter dependence and loss of dignity' (Sopinka, J.).

183 J. Savulescu, 'Treatment Limitation Decisions under Uncertainty: The Value of Subsequent Euthanasia', *Bioethics*, **8**(1) (1994), 49. This is not necessarily an argument for liberalisation. Savulescu concludes by saying, at 72: 'Paradoxically, it is only with the possibility of an offer of death that we can rationally save more worthwhile lives.' The lack of legislation is also seen as undermining the doctor–patient relationship. B. Ward and P. Tate, 'Attitudes among NHS doctors to requests for euthanasia', *British Medical Journal*, **308** (1994), 1334: 'the current law on euthanasia is not satisfactory for patients. Patients may be aware that, although they may request active euthanasia, doctors cannot provide it legally; indeed, to raise this issue may be thought to compromise their relationship with the doctor. Conversely, remaining silent may also affect this relationship. A doctor may think that he or she cannot raise the issue for personal, professional, or legal reasons, and so communication between doctors and patients may be blocked.'

184 For a fuller examination of possible steps towards comprehensive legislation, see J. Mason, 'One Step at a Time', and C. Docker, 'The Way Forward?', *in Death, Dying and the Law*, S. McLean (ed.), Aldershot, Dartmouth, 1996.

185 *Auckland Health Board*, above, note 10, at 246.

186 For a summary of brain death and accepted tests, see British Medical Association, above, note 71; or Canadian Medical Association, 'Guidelines for the Diagnosis of Brain Death', *Canadian Medical Association Journal*, **136** (1987), 200A–200B.

187 J. Mason, 'Definitional Issues and Life and Death: The Contribution of Science, Law and Ethics', in *Law and Moral Dilemmas Affecting Life and Death: Council of Europe Proceedings of the 20th Colloquy on European Law*, 1990.

188 Ibid.

189. For more on ethics committees see, for instance, B. Lo, 'Behind Closed Doors: Promises and Pitfalls of Ethics Committees', *New England Journal of Medicine*, **317**(1) (1987) 46–50.

190 Ibid., at 48.

191 J. Menikoff, 'Beyond Advance Directives – Health Care Surrogate Laws', *New England Journal of Medicine*, **327**(16) (1992), 1165: 'A statute that designates a "backup" surrogate decision maker attempts, in effect, to make the world of living wills more like the world of ordinary wills.'

192 For instance, see Emanuel and Emanuel, above, note 91.

193 Milestone House, Edinburgh. See C. Docker and G. Sprigge, Report on 'To Treat or Not to Treat? Dilemmas Posed by the Hopelessly Ill – International Conference of the Royal Society of Edinburgh', in *Voluntary Euthanasia Society of Scotland Newsletter*, April 1993, 17–18.

194 E. Loewy, 'Advance Directives and Surrogate Laws – Ethical Instruments or Moral Cop-out?', *Archives of Internal Medicine*, **152**, (1992), 1973–6.

11 Confidentiality and the Human Genome Project: A Prophecy for Conflict?

IONA JANE BROWN AND
PHILIPPA GANNON

Introduction

The Human Genome Project,[1] in increasing our knowledge about the nature of DNA, will augment current capacities for testing and eventually treating genetic diseases. Genetic testing has the potential to reveal information pertinent to those who have not actually been tested. In this chapter we intend to demonstrate that the application of genetic knowledge will raise important issues in the area of confidentiality. We will analyse the nature of the duty of confidentiality owed by the doctor to his patient and illustrate that conflicts may occur between a doctor's duty to his patient and his duty to society.

Genetics, Genetic Testing and Human Health

The impact of genetic technology and knowledge is comprehensive, as demonstrated by widespread discussion in areas as diverse as gene therapy, intellectual property and genetic discrimination. Medical genetics,[2] as a branch of modern medicine, has witnessed tremendous advances during the past decade. The Human Genome Project – the international attempt to map and sequence the human genome – in providing further invaluable knowledge about the whole nature and basis of genetic disorders will undoubtedly magnify the role, potential and application of genetics in our society. It has even been predicted that 'the new genetical anatomy will transform medicine and mitigate

215

human suffering in the twenty-first century'.[3] It is interesting to note that, as 'improvements in living standards and advances in medicine have led to a gradual decline in the incidence of nutritional deficiencies and infectious diseases in childhood ... others have been uncovered which are largely, or even entirely, genetically determined'.[4] To fail to use the knowledge generated by the genome projects would be absurd. However, the information is not without disadvantages. It is the blatant dilemma that genetic information simultaneously reveals information that relates to others whilst also revealing the essence of ourselves that is particularly problematic. Genetic information can never exist in a vacuum, as 'There are ripples from genetic testing that don't have analogues in most other kinds of medical testing'.[5] It is the possibility of genetic information revealing apposite information about other people, more often than not individuals who did not consent to the genetic test, that attracts attention here.

It has been estimated that there are more than 4000 identified genetic defects.[6] Genetic conditions usually manifest themselves during childhood[7] and are ultimately life-threatening, cures being elusive owing to a present limited understanding of the nature and function of genes. The desire to eliminate certain traits is understandable[8] and the Human Genome Project will undoubtedly help to achieve this goal. At the outset we distinguish the implications of genetic technology for, on the one hand, people now alive who are inflicted with genetic conditions and, on the other, future generations. The nature of genetic testing is such that it is possible to obtain sensitive genetic information before a person is born. Whilst genetic conditions usually arise as the result of hereditary factors, it is imperative not to ignore the fact that genetic disorders may arise independently; for example, Down's Syndrome is a genetic condition that is not inherited. Questions are thus raised regarding informed consent, abortion and wrongful life/birth actions. For those who are the carriers of or afflicted with a genetic illness, differing considerations, for example confidentiality and compulsory screening, may be more pertinent.

Genetic disorders adopt a multitude of guises but are traditionally divided into three categories.[9] First, disorders due to changes in single genes, for example Huntington's Chorea.[10] Single gene defects can be further classified into dominant, recessive and X-linked inheritance patterns, terms which refer to the arrangement and probability of inheriting a genetic defect.[11] Second, there are polygenic disorders, that is disorders which occur as the result of the arrangement, absence or interaction of more than one gene. Knowledge about polygenic disorders is currently limited because of infinite gene combinations and environmental factors; most manifestations of cancer have been observed as having an inherited genetic basis which can be triggered by social factors, for example radiation.[12] Finally, there are chromosomal disorders (rearrangement of chromosomes): for example, Down's Syndrome or Turner's Syndrome.[13]

It is important to distinguish between the concept of being afflicted with a genetic disorder and being the carrier of a defective gene.[14] If a person is a carrier of a defective gene although they are not personally troubled by the genetic disorder, there is a strong possibility that they may transmit the disease to their offspring. If a person is afflicted with a disorder they manifest the symptoms, either from birth or during the course of life. This distinction is best illustrated by an example: if an individual is a carrier of the cystic fibrosis (CF) gene there is a high probability that he or she may transmit the gene to their offspring, but he or she will never suffer from the symptoms of CF. Conversely, if an individual is afflicted with CF, they will have the symptoms from birth. It is submitted that confusion in the exact nature and manifestation of genetic disorders has led to draconian or inappropriate considerations, as witnessed in America with sickle cell anaemia in the black population during the first part of this century.[15]

Genetic information has the potential to influence choices about reproduction, health or lifestyle. In the absence of a cure for the majority of genetic disorders, prospective parents at risk of transmitting genetic disease may have the option to make use of the new reproductive technologies.[16] However, it is submitted that using the gametes of others is merely circumventing the problem of genetic disease, as tampering with the germ line is strictly prohibited by law in most countries. The current trend, in the absence of genetic cures, is undoubtedly towards aborting the foetus if a genetic disorder is identified,[17] so, 'Genetic disease can at least be prevented if it cannot be cured'.[18] We submit that, for those already alive, the ultimate goal of genetics will be to enable us to gain an increased knowledge of multifactorial conditions. Thus it will be possible to identify triggering factors in lifestyles which may be avoided, for example certain foods or toxic hazards in the workplace. Again, genetic tests may serve to give an early detection of conditions such as breast cancer, thereby enabling the patient to embark on vital early screening programmes and so prevent the cancer from spreading.

Despite enormous advances in medical genetics, at present it is not possible to test for all genetic disorders. Moreover, the testing which is possible is not straightforward: 'Genetic testing is not a single technology. Rather it refers to a broad range of methods for gauging the presence, absence or activity of genes in cells.'[19] Chromosome testing remains the easiest technique, often performed during amniocentesis and chorionic villus sampling and is therefore associated with pregnancy. Certain tests developed to detect genetic disorders remain at an unsophisticated level, necessitating the cooperation of other blood relatives. For example, the ability to test for Huntington's Disease is often perceived as a landmark in the science of genetics. Yet, such tests require medical information from other members of the family. This is because 'at the present time there is no method to test a single blood sample for the presence or absence of HD. DNA samples are needed from numerous relatives in order for predictive testing to be informative'.[20]

The Concept of Confidentiality

The relationship between doctor and patient is based upon and necessitates mutual trust; in order to be correct in his diagnosis, the doctor has to assume and trust that the patient is disclosing all facts relevant to his or her condition. The patient likewise trusts that the doctor will respect the knowledge to which he has been made a party and not disclose it to others.[21] 'The principle of confidentiality, like the law of battery, is as old as medical practice,'[22] yet a precise definition of confidentiality within the medical context is difficult to ascertain. We would take it to involve an implied promise on the part of the doctor not to disclose voluntarily medical information gained in the course of his relationship with a particular patient.

'It is universally accepted that a doctor owes a duty of confidence in respect of information concerning his patient which he acquires in his capacity as a doctor.'[23] The main justifications for preserving confidentiality between a doctor and his patient rest upon deontological and consequentialist theories.[24] Deontologists, in appealing to intuition, would argue that confidentiality should be respected as part of the general principle of patient autonomy. Consequentialists regard confidentiality as a necessary prerequisite to obtaining full and frank disclosure from the patient, thus ensuring the identification and treatment of disease. This aspect was judicially recognised by Rose J. in the case of *X* v. *Y*:[25] 'In the long run, preservation of confidentiality is the only way of securing public health; otherwise doctors will be discredited as a source of education, for future individual patients will not come forward if doctors are going to squeal on them.' Confidentiality concerns the medical profession in a threefold manner.

Law and Confidentiality

The obligation of confidentiality may exist as an implied term of a contract or where there is no established contract between doctor and patient.[26] In certain circumstances the courts will sanction an action to restrict a breach of confidence. In order to do so the information must be confidential in nature, have been imparted in circumstances that impose an obligation not to disclose without consent, and finally, if it is in the public interest, to protect the confidential nature of the information.[27] If these conditions are satisfied, it is clear from decided cases that the patient can approach the court to restrict the disclosure of confidential medical information about himself by his doctor. Indeed, the courts have been willing to grant injunctions where necessary to prevent a threatened disclosure of confidential medical information.[28] However, the question has to be posed as to what extent damages, if available, can ever compensate a person when disclosure of personal and intimate information has already occurred.[29]

Professional Recognition

The medical profession's recognition of the duty of confidentiality is evidenced in numerous professional codes.[30] Professional sanctions are important, especially in the United Kingdom where, owing to the high costs of litigation, it may not be feasible for most to take legal action against members of the medical profession. In the United Kingdom, breach of the provisions contained in the General Medical Council's (GMC) *Professional Conduct and Discipline: Fitness to Practice* ('The Blue Book') could lead to a finding of professional misconduct against a particular doctor; furthermore, a finding by the Professional Conduct Committee of 'serious professional misconduct' could have serious implications for a doctor's career. However, there is no effective remedy for the aggrieved patient who might be forced to pursue a civil action to recover damages.[31] The judiciary has also demonstrated a propensity to take such codes, and subsequent professional judgements, as important guidelines when making decisions on medical matters in negligence and breach of confidence actions.[32]

Moral Considerations

Notwithstanding legal and professional sanctions, the individual doctor may consider himself to be under a moral obligation to maintain a confidential relationship between himself and his patient. It is difficult to define what exactly constitutes a moral obligation. Gillon[33] has described two conditions necessary to create a moral duty of confidentiality: 'one person must undertake – that is, explicitly or implicitly promise – not to disclose another's secrets and that other person must disclose to the first person information that he considers to be secret'. This obligation may in some circumstances be stricter than the law or that required by the medical profession itself. In the case of *Hunter* v. *Mann*,[34] a doctor who treated two people involved in a road accident refused to supply the names of his patients to the police on the basis that such information was confidential. The court disagreed and stated that the doctor was under a legal obligation to give this information, so implying that the moral obligation which the doctor felt he owed to the patient was stricter than the actual legal requirement.

Despite such widespread recognition, confidentiality has never been regarded in the United Kingdom as an absolute principle, by either the law or by the medical profession.[35] Recognised derogations exist, which either enable or require a doctor to disclose confidential information.[36] If the doctor operates within these derogations he will secure immunity from professional sanctions or legal liability. These exceptions are as follows: where the patient or legal adviser gives consent; where it is in the patient's best interest or undesirable on medical grounds to seek such consent; for the purposes of medical research; and where required by the legal process. Moreover, both the law and the medical profession recognise that a doctor may be justified in disclosing confidential information about his patient if in doing so he is averting serious harm to others. This is due to the fact that, whilst a doctor has a relationship of trust with the patient, his relationship with society is also based upon trust:[37] the so-called 'public-interest' exception to a breach of confidentiality. However, as Giesen and McLean recently stated, 'The doctor's ethical commitments to do good and to do no harm may, in these circumstances, conflict with the duty of confidentiality which he owes to his patients'.[38]

If we consider the fact that an additional role and aim of the doctor is to prevent suffering and to improve public health, it is understandable that confidentiality can never be regarded as an absolute. Yet, 'The doctor's overriding duty to society represents what is arguably the most controversial permissible exception to the rules of confidentiality in so far as it rests on subjective definitions'.[39] It is the grounds of averting serious harm to others which, it has been suggested, might be used to justify disclosing confidential genetic information about a patient to his or her relatives and thereby avoid the doctor's attracting legal and professional sanctions. In accepting that a doctor may be justified occasionally in breaching patient confidentiality, we must consider whether genetic information will come within the 'public interest exception'; Ngwena and Chadwick have commented that it 'is apparent from decided cases that the public interest exception can be invoked to protect an open rather than closed category of interests of which the physical and mental health of an identified individual or class of subjects is but one'.[40]

Our concern is that, in the attempt to eliminate genetic disease in the 'public interest', a situation may arise whereby individual autonomy is sacrificed for the common good. This is, we believe, perilous because of the eugenic implications and the subsequent pressure placed on pregnant women, who may be condemned by society for breeding imperfect babies.[41] Similar fears have been expressed by Mason and McCall Smith, who state, 'while the prevention of genetic disease may well be seen as admirable community medicine, there are difficulties when the principles are applied to the individual'.[42] Arguably, if it becomes accepted that prevention of genetic illness is in the 'public interest', negative perceptions of disability will increase and may result in a self-fulfilling prophecy. That is, those who are born with any sort of disability will encounter great hostility and prejudice by society. Furthermore, the birth of any disabled child will automatically be avoided. The extent to which the law will take into account moral viewpoints regarding genetic information, however, remains to be seen.

The 'public interest' defence, developed by the courts and recognised by the medical profession, has to date been largely framed in terms of preventing harm from violent individuals. However, knowledge generated through the study of genetics illustrates that violence is not the only harm from which the public can be protected. In a society which values self-sufficiency, efficient use of resources and minimisation of cost of health care recourses there are many who would argue that there is a public interest in preventing genetic disease.[43] In a climate in which individuals are increasingly regarded as responsible for their health and that of their children, to seek genetic information may soon be regarded, not merely as an option, but as an obligation.

Genetics and Relatives

It is ironic that, in an age when the extended family occupies a less significant role in people's lives, genetics has made such radical inroads in medicine, science and related technologies. This irony is due to the fact that genetics, as the study of inheritance and hereditary patterns, occasionally necessitates the cooperation of the family unit in order to interpret data via linkage analysis or family studies. Information pertaining to other family members may be discovered with the consent and participation of the relative, or may become apparent owing to the inherent fact that genetic conditions and genes run in families. The impact of genetics will have a significant bearing upon confidentiality within the doctor–patient relationship. Information pertaining to others will be discovered, thereby raising dilemmas of a legal and professional nature. Suter recently encapsulated this dilemma: 'when genetic testing of one person can benefit another family member, privacy and autonomy interests of the former may collide with the relative's interests protecting her health or planning her future'.[44] The problem facing the doctor is therefore to establish when certain individuals can establish a positive right to be informed of a particular genetic trait disclosed by a relative's test, or a negative right not to have personal genetic information disclosed. The use of the language of rights is problematic. In relation to genetic information, we believe that rights fall into two distinct categories: the right to claim access to information and proprietary rights of ownership of information. We are not concerned with a 'property right' per se, that is the physical ownership of medical records and information contained therein,[45] but rather with the extent to which a person can claim a legitimate interest in genetic information. Therefore, for the purposes of our discussion, we regard rights in this context as equating to the notion of a 'claim right' to gain access to genetic information which may have been obtained from another.

We submit that genetic information is distinct from medical information per se as 'most genetic information concerning an individual is personal in the sense that others will not become aware of it simply by observing the phenotype'.[46] Moreover, genetic information enables us to determine the very essence of a person and not his experience.[47] That is, information that is independent from personal decisions and social influences, for example diet and lifestyle. The possibility of this information determining 'undesirable' traits in individuals or condoning or justifying certain actions towards others – that is, discrimination – is very real.[48] We believe that genetic information, by its nature, necessitates confidential treatment. It is important that such data are not abused or disclosed to those who cannot establish a legitimate right to have access to such information. Do other family members have such a legitimate right? It can be convincingly argued that genetic information should not be seen as being only of relevance to the person who has undergone testing, as genetics implies community of family information and so an individual may find it more difficult to claim sole rights to such information.[49] The problem facing the doctor is therefore that personal information may not only be solely relevant to that person.

The crux of the problem lies in attempting to reconcile the notion of a doctor's duty of confidentiality to his patient and his role in furthering the good of public health medicine. On the one hand, it is necessary to recognise individuals as autonomous moral agents, who should be free to make decisions regarding their own health care. However, when these autonomous agents make decisions that may prove detrimental to the health of others, problems arise. This is especially so when omitting to provide relatives with information interferes with their autonomy by restricting their present and future life choices and decisions.[50]

We must remember that a third party may be well aware of their risk of genetic disease and may have chosen for one reason or another not to undergo testing. To force unrequested genetic information upon such a person could be viewed as disrespect for their autonomy. The practical and ethical problems of a doctor or third party forcing unsolicited and perhaps unwanted information onto a genetically related individual are considerable. It must not be assumed that, simply by having such information available, there is a duty to use and disclose it to those who may benefit from the information. We agree with Pullen that, 'if individuals have a right to counselling and testing if they so wish, then in a free society they must also have the right to decide not to participate'.[51] Interesting as such discussions may be, we are not concerned with the impact that such information may have on the emotional state of such a person. Rather this work examines the extent to which a doctor may be justified in breaching patient confidentiality in order to inform another person of a genetic diagnosis.

Can it be maintained that a doctor owes a positive obligation to those on whom he holds genetic information to inform them of this information, when this may prevent harm to them or their unborn offspring? At the outset we must be clear on the difference between a discretion to inform relatives of genetic disease and a duty to do so. If the doctor has a discretion he may be entitled to breach confidentiality in certain defined circumstances, set by the law, the medical profession or both. Obviously whenever the doctor exercises his discretion he must be prepared to justify his decision, and if found to have made such a decision incorrectly will be liable to sanction either by the courts or by his professional body. In contrast, if the doctor is under a duty to disclose information and he fails in this duty, resulting in harm to a third party, he may well find himself liable in negligence for any reasonably foreseeable harm which he did not seek to prevent. Consequently, a failure by a doctor to inform others of genetic information may possibly be construed as negligent behaviour. What we must consider is whether or not the court is likely to accept that the public interest in warning an individual at risk of genetic disease outweighs the public interest in maintaining patient confidentiality. Consider the following hypothetical example:

A pregnant woman (A) consults her doctor and after agreeing to amniocentesis discovers that her foetus is affected by Cystic Fibrosis (CF).[52] CF is a particularly cruel genetic disorder, the symptoms of which include progressive lung disorder and destruction of the pancreatic tissue.[53] Children born with this disorder have a life expectancy of 27 years, need daily physiotherapy to prevent the congestion of liquid in the lungs, and are dependent throughout life on antibiotics and enzyme supplements. Owing to the nature of genetics, there is a high probability that A's blood relatives may also carry the CF gene and may also pass the CF gene to their offspring.[54] A has two sisters (B and C), each of childbearing age. B is also a patient of the same doctor as A. C is not. The doctor clearly is placed in a difficult position. The knowledge made available to him through the use of genetic tests has revealed information not only about the patient who consented to being tested but also about genetically related third parties, who may be unaware that their relative has undergone such testing and that such testing may reveal that they personally carry a gene defect. Is the doctor under any obligation to disclose to B or C their increased risk of carrying the CF gene and so enable the parties to participate in screening programmes? This scenario raises questions of a legal, professional and moral nature and is more complicated if B or C are either pregnant or attempting pregnancy, as the doctor may owe a duty to a person who is not born: the so-called 'wrongful life' and 'wrongful birth' actions.[55] This is due to the fact that, if an individual is contemplating starting a family, being aware of this risk may have a considerable impact on their financial and emotional future.

To establish the doctor's legal and professional duties and to determine whether the doctor is justified in breaching confidentiality we must examine the exact nature of the relationship between the doctor with both B and C. It is significant to note that in relation to B the doctor has assumed responsibility regarding her health due to the fact that she is also his patient. However, as regards patient C he has no direct relationship and this may well have implications should he breach confidence with his original patient A.

Disclosure to a Person Who is Also a Patient

Is the doctor justified, legally and/or professionally, in using his knowledge of A's condition to advise patient B to undertake screening for CF? Obviously it is possible that the test could be suggested to B without disclosing that A also is a carrier of the condition, and provided that B consents to the test there will be no breach of confidentiality. Medicine is a continual learning profession and we believe that there is no difference between a doctor becoming aware of genetic information via a relative and current practice that doctors advance their knowledge of disease via the observation of patients. For example, is there any difference in a doctor advising B of the opportunity to have a genetic test and a doctor advising a pregnant Jewish woman to undertake screening for Tay-Sachs disease? In both instances we submit, the doctor is utilising the knowledge he has gained in the course of his profession. Admittedly, the information in the first instance has been gained in the course of diagnosing another individual, but it can be argued that 'in genetics the true patient is a family with a shared genetic heritage. Family members have a moral obligation to share genetic information with each other.'[56]

If the patient does not consent to testing, however, or questions the need for testing, the situation is problematic. Can the doctor inform B that his reason for proposing the test was that A, or even a 'relative' had tested positive to CF? It is interesting at this stage to draw an analogy to AIDS and HIV. It is commonly argued that a doctor is justified in breaching a patient's confidentiality in order to warn someone who is also a patient of their risk of being infected with the HIV virus.[57] For example, Brazier suggests, 'When the doctor reasonably foresees that non-disclosure poses a real risk of physical harm to a third party he should be free to warn that person, especially if that person too is a patient'.[58] We would apply this reasoning to genetics. Therefore, despite discovering information in the course of treating another patient, the doctor could use this information to benefit B. We recognise that this is a very subjective decision and state of affairs; the doctor is in a position to determine whether he will disclose the information, and, moreover, what constitutes a risk to health will vary according to the nature of the genetic disease.

For example, informing a woman that she is a carrier of CF after she has had a hysterectomy would seem to offer little practical benefit to her. However, if the woman already has children there is a possibility they may also be carriers of CF, which may have implications for their decision whether or not to have children. Informing B of her carrier status would perhaps lead the doctor to conclude, or even urge, that she should impart this knowledge to her own offspring. The question arises, however, as to the extent to which the health of future generations should concern the doctor. We argue that, if an obligation was imposed upon doctors to consider disclosing information that may affect the health of future generations, this would also have implications for the whole of society. For example, if an individual had knowledge about the harmful effects of nuclear energy on future generations, would he be obliged to inform the whole of society who would undoubtedly be affected? We believe that the doctor owes a duty to B alone to inform her of her position and so enable her to make her own reproductive choices. We would go as far as to say that, even if B were unable to conceive, she should still be informed of her CF carrier status because patients are entitled to be fully informed of medical information, even if the doctor considers there is no benefit to the patient. To conclude this part of the discussion, we believe that, if the doctor breached confidentiality in order to inform patient B of her increased risk of genetic disease, it would be very unlikely that either the courts or the GMC would take the view that the doctor's duty to his patient could never justify breaching another's confidentiality in order to warn of such a risk. The doctor not only owes a duty of confidentiality to A; he also has an obligation to use his medical knowledge and experience to benefit patient B.

Moreover, given that a special relationship exists between the doctor and B, we would suggest that the doctor is under a legal duty to inform

B, as his patient, of her increased risk of genetic disease, and to fail to do so would be negligent, because there is the established duty of care, there is a foreseeable risk, and the doctor has the ability to take steps to minimise or eliminate that risk.[59] For example, in discovering the information from A, it would perhaps be an understandable reaction for B to ask why the doctor did not make the facts at issue clear to her. It is possible that, in the absence of clear guidelines on confidentiality and genetics, the doctor will consequently err on the side of caution and disclose the genetic information, thus further eroding the principle of confidentiality.

Disclosure to a Third Party Who is Not the Doctor's Patient

If in the course of testing a patient the doctor becomes aware that a genetically related third party who is not his patient is also at risk of genetic disease or of being a carrier of a defective gene, then he may wish to know whether he is justified in disclosing this increased risk to the third party and thus breaching confidentiality to his patient. In such circumstances the first option would perhaps be to persuade the patient to discuss the matter with their relative. The British Medical Association (BMA) has expressed the view that a breach of confidentiality might be justified, depending on the 'severity of the disorder and the implications for other family members'.[60] Furthermore, the Nuffield Council on Bioethics[61] notes that genetic information should be communicated to other family members and that health professionals should seek to persuade individuals, where necessary, to disclose such information. If, however, the individual refuses to disclose the information, they recommend, 'In such exceptional circumstances the individual's desire for confidentiality may be overridden'.[62] Despite criticism,[63] the recommendations of this report will obviously be highly influential on those in the medical profession.

Persuading a patient to inform their relative of the genetic information revealed to them is not, however, always an ideal situation. This information may be completely unexpected and the relationship within the family may not be cordial.[64] Moreover, the absence of professional support and counselling has the potential to increase the shock of receiving the unexpected information. For example, Pullen argues that 'there will be a marked reaction to the discovery that there is an illness in the family and that members are at risk. There will be grief for the loss of normality and the threat of illness.'[65] Consequently, some have argued that the doctor is justified in passing information to the doctor of the person he believes to be at risk, thus leaving it up to the particular doctor to use such information to benefit his patient.[66] Although this might seem preferable to directly informing a person who is not the doctor's patient, the end result is the same: confidentiality has been breached.

Would a doctor be justified in breaching confidentiality by virtue of the 'public interest' defence in preventing/recognising possible harm to a third party? In order to evaluate the probable interpretation of this situation by the UK courts, we must look to analogous cases where the doctor has been held justified in overriding patient confidentiality in the interests of a third party. The most important case in this area is *W v. Egdell*.[67] Here a patient convicted of murdering five people sought transfer to a regional secure unit as a step towards eventual release. He engaged Dr Egdell to prepare a mental health report on him for his case review by the Mental Health Tribunal. The report recommended strongly against his transfer, noting that he was still a dangerous man, with little real insight into his mental condition. W's solicitors withdrew the application for his discharge but did not pass on the report to either the tribunal or the hospital. Dr Egdell then disclosed the report to the hospital authorities and the Home Secretary without W's consent. The Court of Appeal held that in this instance the public interest in maintaining confidentiality was outweighed by the public interest in maintaining public safety. For the purpose of our discussion, we draw attention to the fact that to justify disclosure it was necessary to identify a real risk of danger to the public of serious harm; furthermore, disclosure was only acceptable if made to the relevant authorities. In a subsequent case, *R v. Crozier*,[68] a psychiatrist called by the accused passed his report to counsel for the crown. Yet again the Court of Appeal considered there to be a stronger public interest in disclosing the psychiatrist's views than in the duty of confidentiality owed to the appellant. On the basis of these two cases it would seem that a doctor may be justified in breaching patient confidentiality if he has a reasonable belief that, if he does not do so, there is a real risk of serious harm to the public. In the context of genetics, it is necessary to pose two questions: first, will the public interest include the interest of an identifiable individual, and second, do genetic disorders constitute a 'serious harm' to the public?

We first consider the question of whether the risk of harm must be to the public in general or whether it can include risk to an identified individual. Jones[69] submits that, even when danger is merely directed at a single individual, the public interest in protecting that individual from physical harm will justify disclosure. This was illustrated in the case of *Re C (a minor) (medical treatment)*[70] where medical confidentiality was breached on the grounds that disclosure was justified in assessing the suitability of a woman to look after her child. The 'public interest' in ensuring the child's safety and welfare outweighed the doctor's duty to preserve the mother's confidentiality. In this case, harm was being directed by a specific person at a recognised individual who was sub-

sequently endangered by that specific person. This decision highlighted the fact that the 'public interest' can be interpreted to cover a
single individual. We therefore consider that the 'public interest' could
be afforded a narrow interpretation to encompass the interests of an
identifiable individual at risk of genetic disease.

Turning to the question as to the scope and degree of harm necessary
to invoke the public interest exception, we appreciate that it is difficult
to interpret genetic disorders as constituting harm, mainly because there
is no direct threat from a third party. Moreover, Ngwena and Chadwick[71]
draw attention to the fact that, 'for the great majority of genetic disease,
other than palliative measures, there is no curative or prophylactic
therapy which the third party at risk can take'. Again, in a situation
where a person is a carrier of a gene, there is no harm as such which
can be prevented, and being made aware of one's carrier status may
make no difference to the individual's health[72] and may offer nothing
but despair.[73] The risk will be to that person's offspring, a problem which
we will explore later. However, the problem will arise in the future when
it becomes possible to test for late onset and mutifactorial defects, thus
allowing a person to adopt a particular course of action or lifestyle, for
example diet, which may have an effect upon the progress of their
condition. While currently in its infancy, gene therapy may become an
increasingly available option.[74] Thus, in the future, failure to inform a
person of their genetic status could constitute 'serious harm' if being
made aware of the potential harm could have averted or alleviated the
condition. We would submit that in these situations a doctor would
be legally, morally and professionally justified in breaching confidence
and disclosing the information to the relative.

Is There a Legal Duty to Inform a Third Party Who is Not a Patient of the Doctor?

We believe that a doctor in the United Kingdom currently has no legal
duty of care towards C because she is a third party who is not his patient.
If a doctor fails to warn a third party of a genetic risk he cannot be
negligent for any ensuing 'damage'. This is due to the fact that the law
only requires positive preventive action when there is a special relationship between the parties or when the danger was caused by one
of them. This point was raised in *Yuen Kun Yeu* v. *Attorney-General of
Hong Kong*,[75] where it was stressed that 'foreseeability of harm is a
necessary ingredient of a [proximity] relationship, but it is not the only
one. Otherwise there would be liability in negligence on the part of one
who sees another about to walk over a cliff with his head in the air,
and forbears to shout a warning.'

Can it be argued that, simply because a doctor possesses genetic information, a special relationship is created between the doctor and the third party – that is, in having access to sensitive and important information the doctor automatically assumes a special relationship with the relative to whom this information relates and by virtue of this is obliged to warn that person of this fact? Consider the US case of *Tarasoff*,[76] in which the duty of a psychiatrist to warn an identified victim of possible harm by the psychiatrist's patient was established. This was despite the fact that the psychiatrist had referred his patient's intentions to the police. In *Tarasoff* the crucial factor was that the psychiatrist had particular knowledge to ascertain that his patient would kill the victim. It was maintained by the court that a special relationship existed between not only the psychiatrist and the patient/killer but between the psychiatrist and the victim. It was decided that 'the relationship between the psychiatrist and his patient means that the former becomes sufficiently involved to assume a degree of responsibility for the safety of an identified party whom the doctor knows is endangered by the patient'. The result was that, once a therapist determines that a patient poses a serious threat to others, 'he incurs an obligation to use reasonable care to protect the intended victim against such danger'.[77] The court in *Tarasoff* therefore balanced the breach of confidentiality against the 'harm', that is the direct threat to life, 'implying that the duty to warn only exists if the harm in failing to disclose endangers another's life'.[78]

If we apply the reasoning adopted in *Tarasoff* to our hypothetical situation, it is possible to deduce an identifiable victim, that is patient C. However, we would question whether there is an actual relationship between the doctor and C such that would establish a duty of care. We submit that UK courts would continue not to follow the reasoning adopted in *Tarasoff*. Norrie states that, in the United Kingdom, 'foreseeability is not enough to create a duty of care where the danger has not been caused by the person foreseeing it'.[79] Moreover, 'a person who has not created a danger in the first place cannot be forced to do anything to prevent that danger from hurting anyone ... There is no "Good Samaritan" principle in our law.'[80] If a legal duty were to be established, how would we ever be able to determine the scope of such a duty? For example, if the doctor is aware that there also exists a sister (D), currently living in Australia, would he be obliged to conduct an independent search in Australia to inform her? In the context of genetics we conclude that no special relationship exists between a doctor and someone who is not his patient such that would impose a legal or professional duty on the doctor to disclose genetic information.[81] In the context of the hypothetical example, we conclude that the doctor would be justified in breaching the confidential relationship he has established with his original patient, A, in order that C may be made aware of any increased risk of having or being the carrier of a genetic disease. The doctor is, however, under no legal duty to impart such information.

The Position of the Unborn Child

A dilemma to be resolved is whether the public interest defence would cover a breach of confidentiality to prevent harm to a person not yet born. This situation might arise if a doctor found out that someone who was not his patient was at a high risk of carrying the gene for CF. For example, if patient C were already two months pregnant or trying to conceive, informing her of her risk of carrying the CF gene would enable her to take a genetic test to affirm her carrier status and perhaps to consider abortion in the early stages of her pregnancy.[82] The courts have already accepted that in certain circumstances an action in negligence may lie against a genetic counsellor in failing to disclose abnormality in the foetus or the risk of genetic disease. It must be stressed that this duty is owed to the parents of the child, who are able to claim damages in respect of distress occasioned by the existence of the defect in the child and the extra costs entailed in bringing up the child.[83] These 'wrongful birth' actions[84] demonstrate that the courts that recognise genetic illness, where it might have been prevented, may occasion damages payable to those who were denied the opportunity to prevent it.

We would agree with Brazier[85] when she postulates that a genetic counsellor may be justified in breaching patient confidentiality where there is a risk of passing a genetic disease to yet unborn offspring. Clearly in this situation it is conceivable that the court will regard the 'public interest' as being wide enough in scope to encompass an interest in preventing the birth of 'damaged' children.[86] In arguing this we make no judgement on the morality of this decision or the implications which this may have for the handicapped or society in general. We merely indicate a belief that the courts would be unlikely to find against a doctor who breached confidentiality in such an instance. In summary, we consider that, on the basis of cases relating to genetic disease, the courts or the medical profession would be unlikely to condemn a doctor who exercised his discretion and breached his patient's confidence to prevent genetic illness in those not yet born. We would note, however, that this in no way imposes a legal obligation to inform.

Possession of genetic information undoubtedly places a burden upon the doctor. However, if this burden is too severe, attracting legal and professional sanctions for failure to disclose his knowledge to those establishing a right to be informed, the doctor may err on the side of caution and breach confidentiality to the patient who has requested genetic tests on a regular basis. The doctor therefore may be seen to have a very wide discretion: if he breaks confidence he will be justified and will attract neither legal liability nor professional sanctions; if he does not choose to breach confidence it is highly unlikely that he will attract the above sanctions for failure to do so.

In the situation postulated here, some of the potential problems might have been alleviated if the doctor had made his position known at the outset. If when consulted by A he explained that the results of her genetic test would provide information on B, also a patient, and that the doctor might find it necessary to inform the other sister of her risk (if there proved to be one). A might then decide whether or not to take the test[87] and might discuss the implications of the test with her relatives prior to being tested. Alternatively, A might feel morally obliged to pass on such information herself, thus totally avoiding the doctor's involvement in disclosure. In fact it is interesting to speculate to what extent A is morally obliged to include family members in her decision to take genetic tests or, indeed, to respect the views of those members who wish to remain ignorant of genetic facts.

Conclusion

The debate about recognising confidentiality is 'the assessment of whether more harm is done by occasionally breaching confidentiality or by always respecting it regardless of the consequences'.[88] Genetic testing clearly challenges established principles of confidentiality because individuals are able to obtain sensitive information that relates to themselves and other people. The current problems will increase as more information is generated by the Human Genome Project. At present genetic testing is conducted in a piecemeal fashion, either during pregnancy or on those who are already aware of their likelihood of developing a genetic disorder. As more people are able to establish a right to be informed about genetic information, we should be cautious of making further inroads into the principle of confidentiality. Perhaps, instead, we could pre-empt this problem by encouraging genetic screening programmes, coupled with positive legislation to prevent genetic discrimination outside the medical context. Genetic testing should be a decision for the patient and it is the patient and the patient's family who should be faced with the dilemma outlined above, rather than the individual doctor. Any other option has the potential to destroy the notion of confidentiality or to resurrect paternalism.

Notes

1 For comprehensive information concerning the Human Genome Project, see T. Wilkie, *Perilous Knowledge: The Human Genome Project and its Implications*, London, Faber & Faber, 1993; and D. Kelves and I. Hood (eds), *The Code of Codes Scientific and Social Issues in The Human Genome Project*, Cambridge, Mass., Harvard University Press, 1992.

2   Medical genetics has been described as 'the part of human genetics concerned with the role of genes in illness': Nuffield Council on Bioethics, *Genetic Screening; Ethical Issues*, London, 1993, at 2.3.

3   T. Wilkie *Perilous Knowledge*, p. 1

4   Ian M. Pullen, 'Patients, families and genetic information', in Elaine Sutherland and Alexander McCall Smith (eds), *Family Rights: Family Law and Medical Advance*, Edinburgh, Edinburgh University Press, 1990, p. 42.

5   John Rennie, 'Grading the Gene Tests', *Scientific America*, June 1994, at 72, quoting Arthur Caplan, a bioethicist at the University of Minnesota.

6   M.P. Sawicki *et al.*, 'Human Genome Project', *The American Journal of Surgery*, **165**, February 1993, 258–64. 'It is now estimated that gene defects underlie 3,000 to 4,000 different diseases, and this is before one considers polygenic etiologies or etiologies in which there is interaction between genes and environment' (Nancy S. Wexler, 'Disease Gene Identification: Ethical Considerations', *Hospital Practice*, October 1991, at 145).

7   'Currently, the proportion of childhood death attributable wholly or partly to genetic factors runs at about 59%' (J.K. Mason and R.A. McCall Smith, *Law and Medical Ethics*, London, Butterworths, 1994, p. 123).

8   'A common feature of genetic disorders is that they are often severe, sometimes lethal, and even to this day most often incurable and even untreatable. With advances in the treatment of infectious diseases and other childhood complaints, and improved general health care, there has been a significant decline in perinatal mortality and morbidity; the exception is when a genetic disease is involved. This means that genetic disease is apparently more important nowadays than hitherto' (M.J. Seller, 'Genetic Counselling' in Raanan Gillon (ed.), *Principles of Health Care Ethics*, London, John Wiley, 1994).

9   See J.K. Mason, and R.A. McCall Smith, *Law and Medical Ethics*, p. 123.

10 An individual with a family history of Huntington's Chorea, a disease of the central nervous system, has a 50 per cent chance of developing the disease. If the gene is present in their DNA there is nothing that person can do to prevent, or delay, the onset of the condition.

11 A dominant gene will dominate the chromosomal pairing, and result in the immediate or future development of the genetic disorder. A recessive condition only arises when two defective genes are inherited from both parents. X-Linked conditions usually occur in males, but both females and males can be carriers of the gene; an example is haemophilia.

12 See W. Bodmer and R. McKie, *The Book of Man The Quest to Discover Our Genetic Heritage*, London, Little, Brown and Company (UK) Ltd, 1994, ch. 6.

13 'In Down's Syndrome there is an extra (third) copy of chromosome 21 found in the cells of affected individuals ... In Turner's Syndrome, one of the X chromosomes in girls is missing. This type of disorder is not inherited but occurs during conception' (Nuffield Council on Bioethics, *Genetic Screening: Ethical Issues*, London, 1993, ch. 2, 2.6.

14 Note, however, that the two states are not mutually exclusive; that is, it is possible to be afflicted with a disorder and also to be a carrier of a disorder.

15 For a discussion of this point, see T. Wilkie, *Perilous Knowledge*, ch. 6.

16 For a discussion of reproductive issues, see, for example, S.A.M. McLean, 'The Right to Reproduce', in T. Campbell *et. al.* (eds), *Human Rights: From Rhetoric to Reality*, Oxford, Basil Blackwell, 1986.

17 B.K. Rothman, *The Tentative Pregnancy*, New York, W.W. Norton, 1993.

18 Charles Ngwena and Ruth Chadwick, 'Genetic Diagnostic Information The Duty of Confidentiality: Ethics and Law', *Medical Law International*, **1**, (1993), at 73.

19 John Rennie, 'Grading the Gene Tests', *Scientific America* (June 1994), at 68.

20 Letter from Marlene Hughes, *Journal of Medical Ethics*, **18** (1992), at 47.

21 'The law has long recognised that an obligation of confidence can arise out of particular relationships. Examples are the relationships of doctor and patient, priest and penitent, solicitor and client, banker and customer. The obligation may be imposed by an express or implied term in a contract but it may also exist independently of any contract on the basis of an independent equitable principle of confidence' (*A-G* v. *Guardian Newspapers (No 2)* 1988 3 All ER 545, 639, per lord Keith of Kinkell).

22 Norman Fost, 'Genetic Diagnosis and Treatment Ethical Considerations', *American Journal of Diseases in Children*, **137** (November 1993), at 1192.

23 Michael A. Jones, 'Medical confidentiality and the public interest', *Professional Negligence* (March 1990), at 16. See, in addition, Ian E. Thompson 'The Nature of Confidentiality', *Journal of Medical Ethics*, **5**, (1979), 57–64.

24 For a further discussion of this point, see C. Ngwena and R. Chadwick, 'Genetic Diagnostic Information', at 76.

25 *X* v. *Y* [1988] 2 All ER 648, 653.

26 For example, consider the fact that 'there is no legal contract between a National Health Service (NHS) doctor and her or his patient. The doctor's contract is with the relevant health authority and, accordingly, contractual rights and duties lie with the administration. Thus a patient is unable to rely on either express or implied contractual terms in such a case' (Harry Lesser and Zelda Pickup, 'Law, Ethics and Confidentiality', *Journal of Law and Society*, **17**(1), (Spring 1990), at 19).

27 See, for example, M. Brazier, *Medicine, Patients and the Law'*, London, Penguin Books, 1992, p. 46.

28 See *X* v. *Y* [1988] 2 All ER 414. Note, however, that the facts of this case involved a health authority claiming an injunction, as opposed to a particular patient.

29 Note that the Law Commission Report 110, *Breach of Confidence*, Cmnd 838, London, HMSO, 1981 at paragraph 6.106 recommended that damages be available for breach of confidence as the result of psychological suffering or embarrassment. This recommendation has not been adopted in the United Kingdom.

30 For example, the Hippocratic oath, the Declaration of Geneva (as amended at Sydney, 1968) and the International Code of Medical Ethics.

31 For a discussion of this point, see J.K. Mason and R.A. McCall Smith, *Law and Medical Ethics*, p. 168.

32 For example, in *W* v. *Edgell* [1990] 1 All ER 835, Sir Stephen Brown P. at 843 and Bingham L.J. at 849 both refer to the provisions of the GMC 'Blue Book'.

33 R. Gillon, 'Confidentiality', *British Medical Journal*, **291**, 7 December 1985, 1634–6.

34 *Hunter* v. *Mann* [1974] 1 QB 767.

35 Note, however, the position in France and Belgium, where confidentiality is regarded as absolute and is protected by the criminal code.

36 'Whilst the principle of confidence itself may be justified by utility, so may the exceptions to it, and a balancing act needs to be performed in each situation to discover whether utilitarian factors in favour of disclosure outweigh those in favour of confidentiality' (Harry Lesser and Zelda Pickup (1990), 'Law, Ethics and Confidentiality', at 20).

37 Kenneth M. Boyd, 'HIV Infection and AIDS; the ethics of medical confidentiality', *Journal of Medical Ethics*, **18**, (1992), 173–9.

38 Sheila A.M. McLean and Dieter Giesen, 'Legal and Ethical Considerations of the Human Genome Project', *Medical Law International*, **1** (1994) at 163.

39 J.K. Mason and R.A. McCall Smith, *Law And Medical Ethics*, p. 170.

40 C. Ngwena and R. Chadwick, 'Genetic Diagnostic Information', at 81.

41 'With the availability of genetic tests, bringing an affected child into the world could be construed by some as reproductive irresponsibility', L.A. Whittaker, 'The Implications of the Human Genome Project for Family Practice', in *The Journal of Family Practice*, **35**(3) (1992), at 296. See, in addition, J. Rennie, 'Grading the Gene

Tests', in *Scientific America*, June 1994, at 72, for a discussion of an American television personality suffering from ectrodactyly who was publicly criticised for having a baby.

42   J.K. Mason and R.A. McCall Smith, *Law and Medical Ethics*, p. 126.

43   Health care costs of treating individuals with genetic disease are usually high. For example, 'the average lifetime cost of caring for a CF sufferer will certainly exceed £200,000' (T. Wilkie, *Perilous Knowledge*, p. 118.)

44   Sonia M. Suter, 'Whose Genes Are These Anyway?: Familial Conflicts over Access to Genetic Information', *Michigan Law Review*, **9**, (June 1993), at 1855.

45   For discussion as to the extent to which it is possible to own medical records and knowledge, see I. Kennedy and A. Grubb, *Medical Law Text with Materials*, London, Butterworths, 1994, ch. 8.

46   Dennis Strouse, 'A Legal Research Agenda For the Human Genome Initiative', *Jurimetrics Journal*, **32**(2), (Winter 1992) 163.

47   In recent years criticism has been aired that 'biological determinism' – the tendency to view individuals in a biological capacity – ignores important social, psychological and theological influences on mankind. The Council for Science and Society noted that the genetic component of the common diseases of western society is not only likely to be extremely complex, but may be obscured entirely by the contribution of environmental and social conditions. Even supposing that a partial biochemical basis for, say, some mental illness could be found, we should beware of the hazards of reducing what is partly a social problem down to the individual, medical level' (Council for Science and Society, 'the Human Genome – Any Questions?' A discussion meeting organised by the Council for Science and Society, *Medico-Legal Journal* **59**(1), (Winter 1991), p. 43).

48   Consider, for example, the experience of sickle cell in America. Again, in Japan, 'a screening test for colour vision for all schoolchildren has long been conducted in a semi-compulsory manner at school. As a result of this screening, it is reported that some schools denied some of the colour-blind the chance of higher education and free choice of subjects, and that some companies in their employment policies discriminate against the colour-blind' (K. Takagi, 'Genetic Screening – Policy Making Aspects', in Z. Bankowski, and A.M. Capron (eds), *Genetics, Ethics and Human Values*, Geneva, The Council for International Organizations of Medical Sciences, 1991, p. 119).

49   For example, the Nuffield Council on Bioethics states, in *Genetic Screening: Ethical Issues*, at 5.6, '*In such clearly defined contexts* it may be appropriate to treat those family members as a "unit" and to place less emphasis on individual patient autonomy. This may not always be feasible, for example where blood relations have lost contact with each other, but even in such cases the individuals being screened should be made aware of the implications for their relations.'

50   See Dennis S. Karjala, 'A Legal Research Agenda For The Human Genome Initiative', *Jurimetrics Journal* **32**(2), (Winter, 1992), at 166.

51   Ian Pullen 'Patients, families and genetic information', at 45.

52   CF is a frequent genetic disorder that affects Western Caucasians: 'About one in twenty-five Caucasians carries a single abnormal gene for this condition but is not clinically affected' (N. Wexler, 'Clairvoyance and Caution: Repercussions from the Human Genome Project', in *The Code of Codes Scientific and Social Issues In The Human Genome Project*, 1992, p. 224).

53   The role of the pancreas is to produce enzymes to aid the digestion of food.

54   Cystic fibrosis is a recessive condition: 'in the case of a recessive disease, the responsible gene is failing to make a crucial protein. In carriers, one gene makes enough of this protein for normal function, and the other makes none ... Only when a person gets two faulty genes are they in a position in which no functional

protein is being made. They then suffer from symptoms due to the lack of that protein' (W. Bodmer and R. McKie, *The Book of Man*, p. 83).

55 See, *Salih* v. *Enfield Health Authority* [1990] 1 Med LR 333; *Gregory* v. *Pembrokeshire Health Authority* [1989] 1 Med LR 81; *McKay* v. *Essex Area Health Authority* [1982] QB 1166 [1982] 2 All ER 771, CA.

56 D.C. Wertz and J.C. Fletcher, 'Proposed: an international code of ethics for medical genetics', *Clinical Genetics*, **44** (1993), at 41.

57 This is because 'the need to control the spread of infection makes it vital that maintaining confidentiality should serve the common good as well as that of the individual patient' (K.M. Boyd, 'HIV infection and AIDS: the ethics of medical confidentiality', *Journal of Medical Ethics*, **18** (1992), 173).

58 M. Brazier, *Medicine, Patients and The Law*, p. 56.

59 However, to all intents and purposes, this is perhaps an academic point. As in all actions for medical negligence, compliance with a reasonable body of medical opinion exonerates a doctor from liability in negligence. See *Hunter* v. *Hanley* [1955] SC 200 and *Bolam* v. *Friern Hospital Management Committee* [1957] 2 All ER 118.

60 British Medical Association, *Our Genetic Future: the Science and Ethics of Genetic Technology*, Oxford, Oxford University Press, 1992, p. 201.

61 Nuffield Council on Bioethics, *Genetic Screening: Ethical Issues*, at 5.40.

62 Ibid., at 10.10.

63 R. Gillon, 'Ethics of Genetic Screening: The First Report on Bioethics', *Journal of Medical Ethics*, **20** (1994), 67–8.

64 The situation could become quite difficult. For example, in certain societies it is preferable for women to bear male heirs. However, if a woman is detected as carrying the haemophilia gene (which only affects males) there is a strong possibility of social abuse and stigma for a carrier.

65 Ian Pullen, 'Patients, families and genetic information', at 48.

66 'The information should be passed only to the general practitioner of the subject; he alone is able to assess the family situation in the light of all the background knowledge' J.K. Mason and R.A. McCall Smith, *Law and Medical Ethics*, p. 126.

67 *W* v *Egdell* [1990] 1 All ER 835.

68 *R* v. *Crozier* [1990] 8 BMLR 128.

69 Michael A. Jones, 'Medical Confidentiality and the Public Interest', in *Professional Negligence* (March, 1990), at 6.

70 *Re C (A Minor)* [1991] 7 BMLR 138.

71 C. Ngwena and R. Chadwick, 'Genetic Diagnostic Information', at 84.

72 For example, at present there is no available cure for Huntington's disease. Consequently, identifying a person's predisposition to this condition can neither prevent nor subsequently cure the disorder. In contrast, knowledge about diabetes enables the person at risk not only to modify their behaviour in an attempt to delay the onset of the disease, but, if diabetes develops, may lead to their using insulin injections to control the disease.

73 However, it can be argued that knowledge per se is useful in enabling a person to make relevant life decisions, plan their future and utilise the time that is available.

74 For further discussion about the potential and application of gene therapy, see W. Bodmer and R. McKie, *The Book of Man*, ch. 11, p. 208: 'there are several dozen gene therapy programmes aimed at correcting the worst excesses of a variety of serious ailments that are the outcome of those losing throws in the dice of life-inherited ailments, heart disease and cancer'.

75 *Yuen Kun Yeu* v. *Attorney-General of Hong Kong* [1988] AC 175, 192.

76 *Tarasoff* v. *Regents of the University of California* 529 P 2d 55 (Cal, 1974); 551 P 2d 334 (Cal, 1976).

77 Ibid.

78 Sonia M. Suter, 'Whose Genes are These Anyway?' at 1879.
79 Kenneth McK Norrie 'Medical Confidence: Conflicts of Duties', *Medicine, Science and the Law*, **24**(1) (1984), at 29.
80 Ibid., at 29.
81 In other jurisdictions, for example in the United States and Canada, it could be argued that a doctor is under a legal obligation to disclose genetic information which may prevent harm to someone who is not his patient. This would be by virtue of the developing 'duty to warn' principle and is especially pertinent in relation to multifactorial conditions. For a discussion, see Irwin Kleinman, 'Confidentiality and the duty to warn', *Canadian Medical Association Journal*, **149**(12), (1993), 1783–5; H.E. Emson, 'The duty to warn in the Canadian context', *Canadian Medical Association Journal*, **149**(12), (1993), 1781–2.
82 'Abortion for genetic indications is likely to be the least controversial reason for abortion' (Jeffrey R. Botkin, 'Ethical Issues in Human Genetic Technology', *Pediatrician*, **17**, (1990), at 104).
83 When a child is born with a genetic disorder the whole family can be affected both emotionally and financially because of the special care that is necessary for the child.
84 See, for example, *Salih* v. *Enfield Health Authority* [1990] 1 Med LR 333, and *Gregory* v. *Pembrokeshire Health Authority* [1989] 1 Med LR 81.
85 M. Brazier, *Medicine, Patients and The Law*, p. 250.
86 It is interesting to note that, in many countries, neonatal screening is performed to detect conditions such as galactosemia, phenylketonuria and congenital hypothyroidisms. This is due to the fact that early intervention can prevent the manifestation of the disease. See L.A. Whittaker, 'The Implications of The Human Genome Project for Family Practice'.
87 See Nuffield Council on Bioethics, *Genetic Screening: Ethical Issues*, at 5.6.
88 Michael A. Kottow, 'Medical Confidentiality: an intransigent and absolute obligation', *Journal of Medical Ethics*, **12**, (1986), 117–22. See K.M. Boyd, 'HIV infection and AIDS: the ethics of medical confidentiality', *Journal of Medical Ethics*, **18**, (1992), 173–9.

12 Biotechnology and Intellectual Property: A Marriage of Inconvenience?

GRAEME T. LAURIE

Introduction

Biotechnology has much to offer both humanity and medicine. The benefits which will accrue from recent advances and current research are extensive. These include the increased availability of diagnostic tests for genetic diseases and disorders, improvements in the quality and accuracy of such tests and the development of drugs and vaccines for the treatment of a number of conditions. From these advances a marked reduction in the number of sufferers will undoubtedly be witnessed and, perhaps one day, the eradication of debilitating diseases will be possible. Already it is possible to manufacture artificially substances which are produced by the human body. These can be used to treat individuals who cannot produce such substances naturally. Insulin – essential in the control of diabetes – was the first such 'man-made' substance to be developed and used in the treatment of patients.[1] In 1990, the first attempt was made to treat a human being with an inherited genetic disorder through the use of genetic engineering techniques.[2] The success of this procedure led to other attempts using similar techniques[3] and, in 1994, specialists at the Jones Institute for Reproductive Medicine at the Eastern Virginia Medical School successfully completed the first genetic testing for Tay-Sachs disease[4] to be carried out on an embryo *prior* to its implantation in the womb of its mother.[5]

These advances have far-reaching implications for the future of medicine and the provision of health care. It is undeniable that they bring considerable benefits to humanity. But what of the biotechnology industry? What benefit does it receive in return for that which it bestows on the community? It is estimated that the biotechnology industry spends upwards of $100 million annually in an attempt to secure profits and to recoup the expense of developing its products and processes.[6] This is done through the use of intellectual property law, primarily by obtaining patents.[7] This chapter examines the appropriateness of applying this area of law to the biotechnology industry as a means of providing financial reward, as well as a means of regulating the work of the industry. First, however, a brief account of the work of the biotechnology industry is given below.

Biotechnology

No universal definition of the term 'biotechnology' exists. Several common features can, however, be identified. An Expert Meeting of the World Intellectual Property Organisation (WIPO) has defined biotechnology as 'any technology that uses living entities, in particular animals, plants or microorganisms, or causes changes in them'.[8] The US Office of Technology Assessment considers that 'biotechnology, broadly defined, includes any technique that uses living organisms (or parts of living organisms) to make or modify products, to improve plants or animals, or to develop microorganisms for specific uses'.[9] From these definitions it is clear that, true to its Greek roots, the term 'biotechnology' is concerned with life.[10] More precisely, it is concerned with the application of various techniques in the manipulation of life with a view to creating new living organisms or products.

Briefly, there are currently three techniques used in the biotechnology industry for the manipulation of living organisms: tissue and cell culture technology, hybridoma technology and recombinant DNA technology (genetic engineering).

Tissue and Cell Culture

In 1951, a cell biologist in Baltimore, Maryland, Dr George Otto Gey, succeeded for the first time in growing human cells outside the body.[11] Previously, it had proved impossible to keep cells alive for any significant length of time.[12] By providing the cells with an appropriate medium in which to grow,[13] however, Dr Gey was able to establish the first 'cell line' from human matter.[14] What is more, this cell line had the property of immortality. That is, the cells continued to grow and divide indefinitely, providing a constant supply of source material.[15]

Since that time, many thousands of cell lines have been cultivated.[16] Their importance lies in their uniformity. Because all of the cells stem from a common ancestor they have the same genetic make-up. In this way scientists can carry out an accurate comparison of test results. In addition to being of interest per se, cell lines can act as tools in the study of general biological processes and can play a vital role in testing the potentially harmful effects of drugs or other compounds on human tissue. They are also of importance in the other techniques of biotechnology.

Hybridoma Technology

The Hybridoma Technique is concerned with two of the essential players in the human immune response: white blood cells and antibodies. White blood cells (in particular B cells) produce antibodies which work to fight off any attack by a foreign body (an antigen) in the human organism. Hybridoma technology has made possible the isolation and high yield of particular antibodies to facilitate useful study. As its name suggests, the hybridoma technique involves the fusion of two kinds of cells to form a hybrid cell with the characteristics of the combined cells. The two cells which are fused are B cells and tumour cells (myeloma). The B cell is injected with an antigen to provoke the response of antibody production and because the hybrid cell has the 'immortal' quality of a tumour cell, it will continue indefinitely in its production of the particular antibody, thereby producing a limitless supply. Such an antibody is called a monoclonal antibody.

Hybridomas have proved to be invaluable in immune system research. Monoclonal antibodies have also proved useful in genetic manipulation techniques and as reagents in diagnostic and testing kits.[17]

Recombinant DNA Technology

Recombinant DNA (rDNA) technology is more commonly referred to as genetic engineering. The processes and techniques involved in rDNA technology concern the manipulation of matter at the sub-cellular level. In this respect genetic engineering differs from its companion technologies.

Inside the heart of every cell is the blueprint of instructions which dictates the operation and function of the cell. This blueprint is contained in the form of an inordinately long string of molecules called deoxyribonucleic acid (DNA).[18] DNA takes the form of a 'double helix' – a twin-spined spiral – and is constructed from four simple chemicals (bases) which are represented by their initial letters: A, T, C and G.[19] These combine with each other to form the structure of the helix, always in the same order: A with T and C with G. A single human DNA molecule contains three billion 'bases'. An entire copy of the DNA molecule is found in every cell. Its function is to control the function of the cell. It does this through genes. Genes are sequences of DNA which 'code' for proteins; that is, the sequence activates amino acids to combine to form proteins which in turn cause the cell to perform a particular task.[20,21] In this way the ten million million cells which make up a human being are produced and function.

Genetic disorders occur when 'letters' in a gene sequence are misplaced or missing. For example, sickle-cell disease, which is one of the most common single gene defects in the world, is caused by one wrong letter in a sequence of bases which code for haemoglobin. The result of this is that those afflicted produce red blood cells which die prematurely and which have a tendency to clog in blood vessels, resulting in serious damage to the surrounding tissue.[22] The plethora of known genetic disorders is caused in a similar way. Clearly, the identification of 'dysfunctional' genes is the first step towards finding a cure for such conditions.

The discovery of naturally occurring enzymes in bacteria which 'cut' DNA sequences at specific base combinations proved to be the revolutionary turning point in the study of DNA.[23] This technique allows a particular fragment of DNA (usually a gene) to be isolated from the entire genome. Thereafter means are employed to replicate the molecule under scrutiny in sufficient quantities.[24] Since the first strands of recombinant DNA were created in 1971,[25] over 600 genes responsible for human genetic disorders have been identified.[26] As a result of these techniques tests for the detection of a variety of genetic disorders already exist. Drugs and vaccines have been developed using rDNA technology.[27] Genes themselves can be used as diagnostic tools and some can even serve as therapeutic agents.[28]

Intellectual Property

As has been stated,[29] the biotechnology industry spends vast sums of money every year seeking legal protection of its work.[30] Indeed, it is thought that the industry is particularly motivated by the attraction of patent protection.[31] There is, however, much wrong with the patent systems of the world. Yet a discussion of such problems is not the purpose of this chapter,[32] which will examine the problems which are specific to the biotechnology industry in seeking patent protection. These problems can be divided into two categories: practical and moral.

Practical Problems of Patent Protection

It might seem ironic to declare that the science of biotechnology and the law of intellectual property make uneasy bedfellows, given that they have identical aims: they seek to promote 'invention and the dissemination of new knowledge'.[33] Nevertheless, in practice, considerable problems have been encountered. To understand these it is first necessary to grasp the fundamentals of patent law.

Patent Law The philosophy underpinning the grant of a patent is simple. One who has created a novel 'invention' which is of perceived benefit to the wider community is rewarded by the grant of a monopoly to exploit his or her creation for a fixed period of time.[34] In return, the inventor must disclose details of the invention so that the community can make use of it on the expiry of the monopoly. In this way it is thought that several interests are served well. The inventor is rewarded for his or her industry, while the community is assured of some kind of benefit – albeit in the long term. Furthermore, it is believed that such a system is a source of encouragement to others to invent and innovate.[35]

Broadly speaking,[36] an application for the grant of a patent must satisfy four criteria: it must be 'new', it must involve an 'inventive step', it must have 'utility' and there must be adequate disclosure of the invention. In addition to such criteria, it is crucial that the application does not fall foul of one of the exceptions which exclude patentability. Under the European Patent Convention (EPC) these include discoveries, animal varieties and inventions which are immoral or contrary to 'ordre public'.[37]

The requirement of novelty exists to ensure that the public is not prejudiced by the grant of a patent over something which is already in the public domain.[38] The requirement is tested by an examination of current knowledge: the 'state of the art'. If this reveals that the invention has been 'anticipated' by the publication of its contents, in whole or in part, then no patent will be granted.[39] The notion of the 'state of the art' is also used in relation to the concept of 'inventive step'. Also known as obviousness, this criterion requires that the invention must not be obvious to a person skilled in the particular art.[40] In other words, the invention must not be an example of the normal progress of knowledge which does not exhibit particular skill or effort on the part of the inventor.[41] This is a particularly difficult criterion to satisfy because of its reliance on subjective views of witnesses (despite the 'objective' nature of the test) and the complex nature of the subject matter under examination. The third criterion of utility or 'industrial applicability' stresses the need for an invention to be of practical application or benefit to the community. It is unusual for biotechnological inventions to fail on this count.[42] Finally, inventors must provide adequate disclosure of their invention in the patent application in such a manner that allows repeatability: that is to say, that the invention can be reproduced by someone with the skills of a person versed in the particular art. This final criterion ensures that the inventor fulfils his or her obligation to make public their knowledge in return for the grant.

Each of these criteria is the subject of criticism in one form or another.[43] The problems encountered by the biotechnology industry, however, manifest themselves in a particularly acute form and fall mainly into two categories: the first relates to the problem of patenting 'products of nature'; the second problem arises from the disclosure requirement in patent law. The root cause of both of these problems is the subject matter of the work of biotechnology, namely life.

Products of nature/discoveries

The 'product of nature' doctrine has been described as 'one of the most pernicious sources of confusion and uncertainty as regards the patenting of biotechnological inventions'.[44] In essence, the doctrine has arisen from the conflation of three requirements for patentability: that an invention must be novel, that it must be non-obvious and that it must not be a mere 'discovery'. At a general level of abstraction the doctrine dictates that nothing which occurs in nature should be the subject of a patent application. Various justifications have been advanced for this proposition.[45] First, it is a paradigm example of the exclusion from patentability relating to discoveries. This exclusion dictates that it is inappropriate to offer a monopoly to someone who has merely 'stumbled' upon something which turns out to be important and/or useful. To do so would not be in keeping with the philosophy of the patent system which rewards skill, effort and endeavour.[46] Second, various jurisdictions around the world have excluded 'products of nature' for their own reasons. Historically, American case law took the view that the pre-existence of a substance precluded patentability on the grounds that it was not 'new'.[47] In this sense, nature seems to have been treated as a form of existing 'state-of-the-art'.[48] In Europe, early case law concerned with 'product of nature' cases concentrated on the question of whether or not the claimed invention was a result of a 'man-ufacture' by the inventor. That is, the question asked appeared to be a quasi-obviousness one: had there been an attempt to produce a substance or a product through endeavour rather than mere discovery?[49] Finally, an argument exists that 'products of nature' are the property of all mankind and as such should not fall to the ownership of any one individual or group of individuals.[50] This reflects a concern of a moral nature about the propriety of 'interfering with nature'. A moment's reflection will reveal that such a doctrine, strictly applied, would put an end to any chances of securing patent protection for biotechnology inventions: the role of the industry is to manipulate *naturally occurring* organisms. Fortunately for the biotechnology industry, the doctrine is not, in practice, applied in a strict manner. That is not to say, however, that it does not continue to cause problems for particular patent applications in this field.[51]

Essentially, the doctrine is applied selectively and in a haphazard fashion. There are two means by which the doctrine can be circumvented. An example of the rationale of the first is to be found in the Guidelines of Examination issued by the European Patent Office (EPO).[52] These state,

> To find a substance freely occurring in nature is ... mere discovery and therefore unpatentable. However, if a substance found in nature has first to be isolated from its surroundings and a process for obtaining it developed, that process if patentable. Moreover, if the substance can be properly characterised either by its structure, by the process by which it is obtained or by other parameters and it is 'new' in the sense of having no previously recognised existence, then the substance per se may be patentable.[53]

This passage emphasises several important features of this doctrine. First, it only affects applications for patents over naturally occurring substances per se.[54] A process or method to isolate, purify or produce a naturally occurring entity is patentable.[55] Second, it can be seen that a distinction is drawn between that which is *known* to pre-exist and that which is not. Only the former cannot be patented. These points demonstrate that it is not the mere pre-existence of the substance which justifies the existence of the doctrine.[56] Rather, provided sufficient effort is expended to 'characterise' a substance never before detected, a patent will be granted even if the substance has always existed in nature.[57] This suggests that the doctrine is more concerned with questions of novelty and obviousness than with the 'morality' of patenting products of nature.

The other means by which the effects of the 'product of nature' doctrine can be avoided is through the production of a synthesis of the substance in question. In this way a distinction is drawn between a patent for naturally occurring substances in their naturally occurring state (treated as little more than a discovery), and a patent for substances which, although existing in nature, possess qualities not found in their natural state.[58] Examples of this include the production of highly purified samples of naturally occurring substances such as human antibodies, insulin and interferon. The purity of samples enables scientists to carry out important research accurately and makes such substances far more amenable to development for use as therapeutic agents.[59] Such valuable forms of these substances do not exist in nature.

These means of evading the doctrine are not, however, particularly effective. Only rarely will someone working in the field of biotechnology discover a substance the existence of which was previously unknown. Overwhelmingly, biotechnological research involves a search for a substance known to exist which has displayed properties that promise substantial benefits – both social and financial – and which is therefore worth replicating.[60] Furthermore, as techniques of replication become more commonplace, and more and more substances are discovered with known useful properties, patent applications in this field may encounter problems because of obviousness. As Cook, Doyle and Jabbari have commented, 'nowadays ... the attitude is taken that if one knows that something which is naturally occurring is desirable it is then regarded as obvious to try to produce the material pure, or at least in a pharmaceutically useful form'.[61] A warning shot of this kind was fired by the English Court of Appeal in the important case of *Genentech Inc's Patent*,[62,63] which sent considerable shockwaves throughout the biotechnology industry.

Genentech Inc's Patent

Genentech applied for a patent, inter alia, over human tissue plasminogen activator (t-PA) which is a protein known to occur in very small quantities in human tissue. It plays a key role in dissolving blood clots and as such was perceived by Genentech to be an excellent therapeutic agent. Traditional methods of isolation had been ineffective in producing the protein in sufficient quantity, however, and Genentech had employed genetic engineering to identify the code for the protein t-PA and to synthesise it. At least five other research teams embarked on work towards the same end around the same time. Genentech won the race. Several objections were lodged to their patent application which included arguments that the product claims were merely claims to discoveries, and objections on the grounds of obviousness.

From the beginning, Genentech faced problems convincing the court of the patentability of their invention. Dillon L.J. took the view that the only thing which was new in the application was the data which described the DNA sequences of the protein t-PA.[64] However, as he indicated, 'by itself ... that discovery is merely a discovery and not an invention. The patentable invention, if there is one, must be found in the application of the discovery.'[65] In holding that the claims did not fail on the provisions of s.1(2) of the Patents Act 1977 (discoveries), he held that, 'they are not claims for the discovery of the sequences as such, but claims in relation to the practical application of the discovery in the production of human t-PA by recombinant DNA technology'.[66] In other words, he drew a distinction between patents for natural products per se and patents for the *use* of such products.[67] This distinction was affirmed by Purchas L.J. when he said, 'the authorities seem to support the proposition that, where the discovery is of a new substance, a patent can be claimed for that substance "however made" and will be valid as long as the specification discloses one method of manufacture, even if that method be not the most favoured one'.[68] However, Purchas drew a different conclusion from this to Dillon. He continued, 'this proposition does not apply, however, where, as in the case of t-PA, the discovery is merely part of the process by which a product already known to exist with properties already described can be manufactured. In the latter case the discovery can only form the basis of an invention limited to the method of producing the known artefact, ie-a process patent.'[69] In contrast to Dillon, Purchas L.J. held that Genentech's argument that it should be protected against any use of the sequence for t-PA was tantamount to a claim for the protection of the discovery as such and therefore unpatentable.[70] One can see how these judgements perpetuate the distinctions which embody the 'doctrine of products of nature'. What they do not do, however, is elaborate on these distinctions or offer any justification for them.[71]

Having dealt with the problem of discoveries, the court considered at great length the question of obviousness. Genentech's case failed substantially on this ground. It was the opinion of the court that, despite the tremendous effort and expense on the part of the company, everything they had done was unpatentable for lack of inventive step. It was known (and therefore obvious) that t-PA existed and had therapeutic qualities. It was known (and therefore obvious) that DNA sequences could be identified using existing genetic engineering techniques. Finally, it was known (and therefore obvious) that such techniques could produce human t-PA in desirable quantities and of sufficient purity. This was evidenced by the fact that five other teams had applied the same knowledge to achieving the same goal.

In the aftermath of this decision may parties speculated as to the success of future biotechnology patents in the United Kingdom.[72] Many were pessimistic. Recent decisions by the UK courts have done little to allay fears. *Chiron* v. *Organon Teknika* was delivered on 5 October 1993.[73] *Biogen* v. *Medeva plc* was decided on 4 November 1993.[74] Both cases involved patents for genetically engineered products concerning strains of the hepatitis virus. Both patents were held to be valid and to have been infringed. Chiron claimed, inter alia, a polypeptide in substantially isolated form and test kits for the detection of hepatitis C virus (HCV). Biogen sought protection for a vaccine for hepatitis B virus (HBV). Debate centred around questions of obviousness and sufficiency of disclosure. Aldous J. heard both cases and distinguished *Genentech Inc* in each. He held that the means employed by the patent holders to reach their chosen goals were not obvious and did not affect the validity of their patents. Despite the fact that competitors were also engaged in seeking out similar goals, the means employed by the interested parties were not substantially the same.[75] This was not so in *Genentech*. Commentators hailed these decisions as a 'boost for the biotech industry'.[76]

On 27 October 1994, the English Court of Appeal delivered the appeal judgement on *Biogen*.[77] Inter alia, the defendants' appeal succeeded because the court took the view that, given the business decision to invest the time and money in the relevant experiments, what the plaintiffs did was obvious to a person skilled in the art. It was stated:

> In cases such as the present, the analogy with a bet influences the language used ... and is compelling. The choice to place a bet on an entrant in a race represents an assessment whether the available odds are favourable or unfavourable. Bystanders may say that the entrant has no prospect of winning – the backer was 'out of his mind' to place the bet. But, if the choice is made to back that entrant, the obvious course to follow is to place a bet. If the entrant then wins, it would be wholly wrong to say that the backer had invented, or even discovered, a way to pick winners or to procure that the entrant won that or any other race. The analogy illustrates an unobvious decision which is not an invention ... Thus, on the plaintiffs' own evidence, what they did in 1978 [the date from which priority was claimed] was obvious *even though* no one else chose to do it. If they had been able to say that they had adopted some novel and non-obvious method, that would be different. It would also have been different if the resultant product had been something other than that which was to be expected if the experiment was successful. But both the methods used and the types of recombinant DNA molecule that would and did result from the use of those methods were obvious.[78] (emphasis added).

This most recent decision indicated that the problem of uncertainty will continue to beleaguer the biotechnology industry in the United Kingdom. What is more, none of these decisions changes anything about the 'product of nature' doctrine.

Given the above, considerable confusion continues in respect of the role of the doctrine of non-patentability of products of nature. In light of the subtle distinctions which have been drawn between various 'kinds' of product of nature, it would seem that the doctrine now only applies to defeat applications for patents for substances already existing in nature, and known to exist in nature, which are produced in essentially the same form as they are found in nature. It is not the pre-existence of the substance in and of itself that renders the substance unpatentable. Indeed, the importance which is attached to prior knowledge of the existence of the substance is simply an appeal to novelty. Similarly, to concentrate on the sufficiency of effort expended to obtain the substance is a concern with obviousness. If this is the case, then an application for a patent for such a substance will be defeated by these criteria in the course of the patent application, whether or not the doctrine exists. Why then retain the doctrine? The only justification which remains is that premissed on moral objections to exploiting or interfering with nature, yet the practice of patent offices demonstrates clearly that this justification is not one which carries any weight. This is evidenced by the fact that exceptions exist to the doctrine and also that the doctrine has never affected the grant of patents for processes to isolate products of nature from their environment.

Given this, is it not time to abolish any reference to the doctrine of 'products of nature'? If the concerns which it purports to embody are either ignored or dealt with in another context, what possible justification can remain for its retention? Bent *et al.*[79] recommend that the only question which should be asked is whether the inventor did anything technical at all. If so, then one should move to a consideration of questions of novelty and inventive step which will exclude applications not worthy of protection on practical and pragmatic grounds.

Whereas it could be argued that the problems which this doctrine poses are limited to a small number of claims in a small number of patents, a further problem is encountered in the context of inventions of application in medicine which is of pertinence to this work. This arises because of a further exception which operates to exclude patentability under the EPC. Article 52(4) provides that, 'methods of treatment of the human or animal body by surgery or therapy and diagnostic methods practised on the human or animal body shall not be regarded as inventions which are susceptible of industrial application'.[80] In effect this precludes inventors who have isolated a known substance from its original state which has potential for use in methods of medical treatment from reverting to the obvious means of avoiding the product of nature doctrine, namely, to apply for a use or method of use patent. White has described this as 'one of the most retrograde steps taken by legislatures in modern times, since its effect is bound to be to retard the discovery of remedies for many as yet unconquered diseases'.[81]

The NIH application

An additional problem of seeking patents for biological entities per se was highlighted recently by the activities of the National Institutes of Health (NIH) in the United States. In 1991, the NIH, as a result of its work on the Human Genome Project,[82] filed applications to patent 2412 human DNA sequences. These has been identified by the use of automatic sequencers which screen and sequence large number of DNA fragments very rapidly, even though the function of such fragments is unknown.[83] In marked contrast to the problems encountered by Genentech, NIH had produced DNA fragments never previously identified and with no known utility. Primarily because of this latter feature the US Patent and Trademark Office (PTO) rejected the applications in October 1992. The view of the PTO was that, although it is clear that such sequences could be used for a number of purposes,[84] the specification was insufficient. It stated, 'although the oligonucleotides embraced by the claims may be hybridized to a variety of different preparations of other nucleic acids, one of skill in the art has no clue as to the significance of any such hybridization because the instant application fails to provide any basis for the interpretation of any putative results'.[85] The NIH withdrew its threat to appeal in February 1994.[86] From an academic viewpoint, this is to be regretted: further analysis of the complex issues involved would be most interesting. From a practical point of view, however, it has averted a state of crisis within the biotechnology industry. As a result of the NIH's attempts, several other organisations filed applications for patents of similar DNA fragments.[87] Although most of these have been withdrawn,[88] the initial push to secure patent protection over such molecules was very revealing. In the specific context of the Human Genome Project, it casts some doubt on the extent of cooperation likely to be forthcoming from collaborators. More generally, it renders questionable the extent to which any patent system achieves its objective of encouraging research and innovation. If early protection of such products of research were allowed, this would act as a disincentive to others to engage in more complex product development based on such substances.[89] This could only be to the detriment of the community and the biotechnology industry alike.

Deposit requirements

The final requirement for a valid patent application, that of adequate disclosure of the details of the invention, has been particularly problematic for biotechnological inventions. The reason for this is explained by Bent *et al.*:

> unlike inventions of the classical model, biotechnological inventions are generally *not* assembled from simpler, well-defined elements, into similarly well-defined structures of greater complexity according to a concise set of instructions. Rather, with few exceptions biotechnological inventions entail the modification of a preexisting system of living matter already characterized by a very high degree of ordered complexity. Indeed, the raw material of biotechnology is usually so highly integrated *before* man's intervention that it defies description in terms of precisely definable, constituent elements.[90]

Such complexity makes it impossible for a patent application involving a novel microorganism to meet the requirements of disclosure by traditional means, that is, by a written description in the specification.[91] For this reason, special provisions have been instituted which require the deposit of samples of materials used in biotechnological inventions.[92] The mechanism for establishing depositories and for regulating the deposit scheme is to be found in the Treaty on the International Recognition of the Deposit of Microorganisms for the Purposes of Patent Protection – the Budapest Treaty – which was established in

1977.[93] Once a deposit is made in an internationally recognised depository, reference can be made to it in any patent application in any country which has ratified the treaty. However, the question of access to such deposits has led to considerable concern among many biotechnologists.

Controversially, the Budapest Treaty leaves the question of access to samples by third parties to the discretion of individual signatories. This has led to broad diversity of approach. In the United States, access to deposited samples will be granted, once the patent has been granted, to anyone on the payment of a standard fee.[94] This practice has given rise to heated debate about the adequacy of infringement protection for inventions.[95] In particular, recent amendment of the US patent law by Congress has led to much confusion about the scope of a patentee's rights in the field of genetic engineering.[96] Section 271(e) (1) of the patent law now provides:

> It shall not be an act of infringement to make, use or sell a patented invention (… which is primarily manufactured using recombinant DNA, recombinant RNA, hybridoma technology, or other processes involving site-specific genetic manipulation techniques) solely for uses reasonably related to the development and submission of information under a Federal law which regulates the manufacture, use, or sale of drugs.

As Hardy has noted,[97] the Supreme Court has interpreted this section as, allowing competitors, 'prior to the expiration of a patent, to engage in otherwise infringing activities necessary to obtain regulatory approval'.[98]

In Europe, access provisions are even less generous to an inventor.[99] Access to deposited materials will be granted 18 months after the patent has been filed, irrespective of whether or not a patent has been secured by this date.[100] An applicant can, however, restrict access in the period until grant[101] to nominated experts who can carry out inquiries regarding novelty and obviousness and who can continue experimentation with the subject matter on behalf of interested others. This is allowed on the proviso that release of the culture is not made to such parties. Often such an expert is working directly on behalf of an inventor's competitors. Much discontent is expressed with this system and there have been calls for Europe to adopt the US and Japanese approach of allowing access only once a patent has been granted.[102]

Two additional differences exist between US and European approaches which are worthy of note. First, in the United States a deposit is considered to be timeous provided that it is made at any time before the grant of the patent. In Europe, the deposit must be made no later than the date on which the patent application was first filed. Those dissatisfied with the 'expert access' system consider that the potential for abuse simply occurs at a much earlier stage. Second, in Europe, once a deposit has been placed it is considered to be in the public domain and as such becomes part of the state-of-the-art. This is so even if the patent application is refused or withdrawn. Clearly, this has implications for European inventors who might try to reapply for a patent at a later date. In the United States and Japan, all access to deposits is denied if no grant is awarded.[103]

The disparities which exist between the US and European systems are prejudicial to inventors in several ways. First, inventors lose complete control of their inventions. Questions of access are decided by third parties who apply criteria which are at best obscure and at worst unjust. Second, the samples at issue are generally self-replicating, thus providing a competitor with a limitless supply of materials which an original inventor has created at considerable cost in terms of both time and money. It is generally accepted that this unique feature makes the replication of the invention much easier and allows competitors an edge in an otherwise very small and fiercely competitive industry.[104] Moreover, once disclosure has occurred, access can be gained to the deposited material by anyone in a country which is a signatory to the treaty, even if no patent to protect the invention has been applied for in the country in question.[105] It is thought unlikely, however, that moves will be made to bring Europe into line with the rest of the developed world.[106] An example of this can be seen in articles 15 and 16 of the now defunct European Directive on the Protection of Biotechnological Inventions which, if passed, would have retained the 'expert access' approach.[107] Article 17 had provided, however, that in infringement proceedings involving process patents where access to a sample had been granted, the burden of proof would be reversed. That is, the onus would be on the alleged infringer to show that no infringing act had taken place.[108]

The continuation of diverse approaches to the question of access to samples can only have an adverse effect on the willingness of inventors to seek patent protection. This calls into question the accuracy of the tenet of patent law that it encourages disclosure of information and the dissemination of knowledge. In the absence of adequate protection of the initial invention, such disclosure is unlikely to be forthcoming.

The practical problems experienced by the biotechnology industry in seeking protection for its work might lead one to conclude that, in this context at least, the patent system does not fulfil its objectives. If protection is significantly more difficult to obtain, and if its scope is significantly more uncertain once it has been obtained, then this may act as a disincentive to prospective inventors to work and to invent in the biotechnology field. Furthermore, if practices such as the patenting of DNA fragments with no known utility are allowed to happen, this may lead to patents of extremely wide scope which might, in turn, raise the possibility of research by others being prevented since such work might be infringing. This would mean that the patent system would serve to inhibit, rather than encourage research – clearly not a stated or desirable aim. That said, problems such as these can be addressed from within the patent system itself and can be avoided by amendments to existing law, for example by removing the products of nature prohibition or by refusing to grant patents over unspecified DNA fragments. However, these problems of practicality represent only half the picture with biotechnology patents. They ask us to address the question, can we apply patent law to biotechnological inventions? The answer to this is yes, albeit a qualified yes. A further question however remains. Should we do this simply because we can? That is, a question not of possibility but of propriety

The Problem of Morality

In moral terms, the subject matter of the work of the biotechnological sciences has been a source of considerable consternation.[109] The manipulation of 'life' for ends which are often perceived to be purely commercial is condemned by a great many as immoral and unacceptable.[110] Objections from groups opposed to what they consider to be the misapplication of patent law have led, inevitably, to further delays for those seeking protection of their work and further arguments about the appropriateness of allowing intellectual property protection of the fruits of the labour of the biotechnology industry.[111]

Traditionally, patents were not granted over living matter per se, although patent protection was granted without question for processes involving living matter.[112] This position changed dramatically in 1980 with the seminal decision of the US Supreme Court in *Diamond* v. *Chakrabarty*.[113] In 1972, Ananada Chakrabarty filed a patent application for, inter alia, bacteria created using genetic engineering techniques. These bacteria had the unique ability, unknown in naturally occurring bacteria, to break down multiple components of crude oil. The inventor saw considerable potential for the use of his 'invention' in the treatment of oil spills. His application in this respect was denied by the patent examiner on the grounds that the microorganisms were products of nature and living things. This was rejected by the Supreme Court. In a majority decision (5 to 4) it held that such bacteria were patentable subject matter, endorsing the view that, 'the distinction [is] not between living and inanimate things, but between products of nature, whether living or not, and human-made inventions'.[114] In this way the court delivered a clear statement about its perception of the role of patents in encouraging scientific progress and securing financial return. In particular, the court refused to address the issue of the morality of patenting living entities. It adopted a strict interpretation of the statute under scrutiny and declined to apply a balancing model to the resolution of the perceived issues at stake: 'Congress intended statutory subject matter to include anything under the sun that is made by man.'[115] It was only a matter of time before this philosophy extended to higher forms of life.

In April 1988, Harvard University obtained a patent from the US Patent and Trademark Office (PTO) for a transgenic animal called Oncomouse.[116] The mouse in question was modified to possess a human cancer gene causing it to develop cancerous tumours within the first few months of life. Harvard saw considerable potential for research with such an animal and the patent was granted in the United States without question. An application for a patent in Europe did not, however, pass without objection. Indeed, after many years, proceedings before the European Patent Office (EPO) are still not finalised.[117]

The basis of the objections to the grant of a patent over Oncomouse in Europe related to the exceptions to patentability contained in Article 53(a) and 53(b) of the EPC. This provides 'European patents shall not be granted in respect of: (a) inventions the publication or exploitation of which would be contrary to 'ordre public' or morality ... (b) plants or animal varieties or essentially biological processes for the production of plants or animals'.[118] Initially, the Examining Division of the EPO rejected the Oncomouse application stating that (i) the question of morality was not one which was suitable for such a forum, and (ii) the drafters of the Convention must have intended to exclude all kinds of animal from patentability. After remittance from the Technical Board of Appeal,[119] however, the Division granted a patent for Oncomouse in October 1991.[120] The Division drew a distinction between animals per se and animal varieties in interpreting article 53(b). Only the latter are now excluded from patentability. Oncomouse was classified as the former because the claim was to a non-human 'mammal' and 'rodent' which was acceptable because it claimed a range of animals broader than a mere variety of animals.[121] The question of morality was tackled by applying a balancing test. The matters for consideration were, on the one hand, the certain suffering to the animal and the possible environmental risks,[122] and on the other, the benefit to humanity from cancer research. The Division preferred the latter and awarded the grant. Opposition proceedings are still before the EPO.[123]

By way of contrast, the EPO has rejected an application for a patent for a mouse which had been created by the insertion of an oncogene for research into hair loss in humans (Upjohn's Application).[124] The EPO refused the patent on the grounds that, applying the balancing test from Oncomouse, the benefit to humanity did not outweigh the animal's suffering through developing cancer. However, it is noteworthy that the applicants have refiled their application in such a way that will circumvent the morality exclusion.[125] All reference to the oncogene has been removed. The application is now for a genetically engineered mouse *simpliciter*. It is thought that a patent will now be granted.[126]

An account of the role of morality in patent applications cannot ignore the possibility of patents being sought over human material. Crespi has commented that, 'the patenting of human cellular material has been accepted for many years by the authorities as a natural extension of the patentability of lower life forms such as bacteria and yeasts'.[127] That is not to say, however, that this has not been the source of disputes. Unquestionably, the most famous decision on this matter to date is that of the Californian Supreme Court in *Moore v. The Regents of the University of California*.[128]

The Moore case

In 1976, John Moore sought treatment for hairy-cell leukaemia from a specialist, Dr Golde, in UCLA. The specialist removed Moore's spleen, which was grossly enlarged. Moore's condition improved. In the meantime, Golde isolated and cultivated an immortal cell line from a sample of the spleen. This proved to be very successful and was the source of a variety of products, one of which has been tested for use in the treatment of AIDS. A patent was granted in 1984 over the cell line and the products. This came to the attention of Moore, who sued on several different grounds of action[129] alleging, inter alia, conversion, lack of informed consent and breach of fiduciary duty.[130] The case was heard by the Californian Supreme Court in 1990.[131] The court rejected out-of-turn arguments based on the tort of conversion. In other words, Moore failed to establish any property rights in his cells. The court held that to allow such a tort would 'hinder research by restricting access to the necessary raw materials ... Conversion ... would threaten to destroy the economic incentive to conduct important medical research ... with every cell sample a researcher would purchase a ticket in the litigation lottery.'[132] The only ground upon which Moore won his case was in relation to the claim of breach of fiduciary duty for failure to obtain informed consent.[133,134]

Annas considers that the central issue in the decision is that of public policy regarding the nature and the future of the biotechnology industry.[135] It is axiomatic that the decision provides a degree of security for the future of the industry. What is does not do is address the multiplicity of questions of a moral nature which arise as a result. For example, the decision endorses the view that property can exist in parts of the human body; however, it precludes ownership being vested in the person from whom the parts originated. On what acceptable moral basis can such a decision be taken? Moreover, it begs the question, where do we draw the line? Can a distinction be made between the exploitation of diseased cells and of healthy organs? Or between excised and non-excised cells? Are parts of the human body suitable subjects for a patent application at all?

That such matters are a source of concern is shown by the dramatic defeat of the European Draft Directive on the Legal Protection of Biotechnological Inventions.[136],[137] Invoking for the first time powers conferred by the Maastricht Treaty, the European Parliament refused to adopt the Directive at its final reading on 1 March 1995. The Directive fell because of a dispute between the Parliament and the Council of Ministers over the question of the patentability of material taken from living organisms. Originally the Directive drew no distinction between non-human and human subject matter for patentability – even humans were not excluded – but this was amended in the light of considerable objection by a variety of bodies.[138] A Common Position document was issued by the Council of Ministers in February 1994 which was acceptable to the biotechnology industry but still met with opposition from Parliament.[139] A Conciliation Committee eventually met in January 1995 and agreed a text. The relevant passage provided that the 'human body or parts of the human body as such' would be unpatentable. It was not clear, however, whether the expression 'parts of the human body as such' included microscopic parts of the body, including genes.[140] Furthermore, many were unhappy because a literal interpretation of the passage meant that, provided material was no longer a part of a human body (as such), it could be patented. The European Parliament expressed its dissatisfaction with the text in rejecting it with a clear majority: 240 against the text, 188 in favour and 23 abstentions. Thus, for the time being, the current practices of the EPO provide the only means to address concerns about granting patents over life. Most recently, the EPO has decided that human DNA is not life. In opposition proceedings concerning the grant of a patent over human H2-relaxin,[141] the patent was held to be valid despite objections by Green MEPs that the grant was 'immoral'. It is thought that an appeal will now be lodged.[142]

Despite the favourable judgement in *Moore* for the biotechnology industry, several commentators have expressed concern about the ramifications of 'moral concerns' for the future patentability of inventions.[143] Nott, for example, is of the opinion that all reference to morality should be abolished from the EPC because such considerations are irrelevant in determining the grant of a patent and could even be counterproductive.[144] Crespi considers that the contemplation of moral matters 'involves a burden that patent officials are not trained to bear'.[145] For this reason he suggests that the morality exception should be construed very narrowly so that a patent would be refused only when faced with an overwhelming consensus that a particular invention is immoral.[146] Yet these proposals fail to take account of the depth of feeling which exists in relation to these matters. It is submitted that society cannot ignore the concerns which surround the activities of the biotechnology industry.

In examining the problem of how to address such concerns, it is important to recognise that they are of two distinct kinds. First, certain concerns do not relate to the seeking of a patent per se, but rather involve concern about the very act of creation itself. That is, the question is not should we protect, but rather should we invent? An example of this is found in the primary objection to the Oncomouse and Upjohn patents. The issue to be balanced against the potential benefit to humanity was the suffering of the animals. In other words, the concern focused on the desirability of creating animals with a very poor quality of life which were so clearly used as a means to an end. By the same token, some might argue that John Moore's cells should never have been exploited for commercial gain.[147] This follows the view that human beings, as morally autonomous agents, merit respect and should not be the subject of exploitation. While such views do not take into account utilitarian counterarguments,[148] the point to be made remains unchanged: in such circumstances the patent system is wholly ill-equipped to regulate such matters. One might argue that such creation would not occur if not encouraged by the attraction of a patent, yet this argument is flawed in that its desired result – to prevent innovation and therefore exploitation – is unlikely to happen in practice. As one commentator has said, 'it seems highly unlikely that the unavailability of patents would dampen the present escalating industrial interest in applications of genetic technology'.[149] The mechanism which exists within the patent system to refuse patents for novel inventions on moral grounds cannot control or regulate the act of invention itself.[150] At best, the 'morality' exception can draw attention to matters requiring attention and action. In reality, it demonstrates the inappropriateness and inadequacy of using such a system to regulate matters which are clearly outside its scope.

Second, even if it is generally accepted that a particular invention is morally acceptable, a moral objection might be raised against the means used to reward such innovation. This type of objection is particularly pertinent in the realm of biotechnological innovation because the benefit to mankind can be especially great. Thus, even if few would object to the use of John Moore's cells to produce useful drugs for the treatment of life-threatening conditions, an objection might nevertheless be raised to the award of exclusive control of such drugs to a small number of commercially driven companies. The objection might be based on the fact that Moore himself should receive some recognition of his role because he has a personal interest in what happens to his cells, or that one is against monopolies being granted over such important innovations in which the public has a substantial interest. Eisenberg suggests that this might be one reason why the exception relating to non-patentability of methods of medical treatment exists.[151] Such objections have, however, much more to do with the essential nature of the patent system than with the notion of patentability per se. The issues which underlie such objections are of a more fundamental nature than can be dealt with by any patent office. Arguably, it is not for the system itself to address such issues but rather for society to do so. This might entail a reassessment of the values to which we adhere and which we wish to uphold though the grant of patent. But this would require a reappraisal of the philosophy and practice of the patent system: a task once again outside the scope of any particular system. Thus, whereas one might agree that questions of morality should not be dealt with by the patent system itself, it is submitted that they are of sufficiently important and serious nature to merit considerable attention in an appropriate forum.

Conclusion

The practical problems encountered by the biotechnology industry in seeking patent protection for its work have given rise to much criticism of the patent systems of the world. While these problems have not been fatal to the majority of biotechnolgical patent applications, the experiences of Genentech and Biogen have caused much in the way of speculation about the future relationship between the industry and the world's patent offices. Moreover, the differences which exist between patent systems, and the particular idiosyncrasies internal to patent systems, continue to be a source of concern. At the present time it is unclear whether or not this is a temporary matter or something of a more permanent nature. Certainly, much can be done to ameliorate current practices. Harmonisation of laws on an international level is an obvious goal. That said, the experiences of the European Commission in trying to introduce the European Directive are not encouraging. Yet these problems have arisen because of problems of a moral, rather than a practical nature.

Objections of a moral nature relate to two issues, both of which are wider than regulation of the grant of any one patent. First, they involve concern about the actual work of the industry itself and relate only tangentially to the granting of a patent. Second, they call into question the general ethos of the patent systems of the world and in this respect transcend particular problems of particular grants. If this leads one to conclude that all reference to morality in a patent grant should be avoided, as has been suggested, then the problem arises of how to address the moral concerns which nevertheless exist. The question of adequate regulation of the activities of the biotechnology industry as a whole has never been fully addressed by the international community. Also it has been assumed for a long time that the grant of a monopoly as a means of reward for innovation is the best way, and the most desirable way, to secure the maximum number of ends and to serve the maximum number of interests. In the context of biotechnology, however, the number of interests involved increases and with this comes uncertainty about the weight which each should be given. Is this sufficient impetus to bring about a re-evaluation of the justification of our patent systems? Do patent laws continue to address and serve all interests involved? Is radical change necessary? An attempt to answer these questions is beyond the scope of this chapter. Suffice it to say that the practical and moral problems currently faced by the biotechnology industry in seeking patent protection for its work are significant. The problems faced by society in coming to terms with such work are daunting. The benefits of biotechnology could be countless. But the cost?

Notes

1 Insulin was the first therapeutic agent produced by means of genetic engineering to be made commercially available. It has been on the market since 1983: see Committee of Experts on Biotechnological Inventions and Industrial Property, Second Session, Geneva, 3–7 February 1986, reported in *Industrial Property* (June 1986), 251–74 at 257. Other valuable chemicals such as Interferon (useful in the treatment of at least one form of leukaemia) and Factor VIII (the blood-clotting agent deficient in haemophiliacs) have been successfully reproduced in laboratories.

2 The technique was carried out by a team from the National Institutes of Health in Bethesda, Maryland, on a young girl suffering from SCID (Severe Combined Immune Deficiency). In this case, the condition was caused by an inherited inability to produce an enzyme (adenosine deaminase) essential to the proper functioning of the immune system. Most persons afflicted with the condition die in early childhood, normally by succumbing to a minor infection. The technique employed by the Bethesda team was as follows. A sample of the most affected cells (white blood cells or 'T' cells) was extracted from the patient's body and subjected to genetic modification techniques which allowed the missing enzyme to be 'inserted' into the genetic make-up of each of the cells in the sample. Thereafter, the cells were allowed to divide and multiply until a sufficient quantity of the 'treated' sample was produced. This was then transfused back into the girl in the same way as an ordinary blood transfusion. Although apparently simple, this was the first time such genetically-modified material had been used in the treatment of a human being with a genetic disorder. For a fuller account of events, see T. Wilkie, *Perilous Knowledge: The Human Genome Project and its Implications*, London, Faber & Faber, 1993, pp. 16–23.

3 Ibid.

4 Tay-Sachs disease is caused by the absence of an enzyme which breaks down fatty substances in neurons. It is a fatal disorder of the nervous system which invariably results in a slow, painful death within the first five years of life.

5 This resulted in the birth of a healthy baby girl in January 1994. See J. Rennie, 'Grading the Gene Tests', *Scientific American*, **270**(6) (June, 1994), at 66–74.

6   C. Roberts, 'The Prospects of Success of the National Institute of Health's Human Genome Application', *European Intellectual Property Review*, **1**, (1994), 30–36 at 30.

7   Other areas of intellectual property law can be used in an attempt to secure protection. See, for example, I. Kayton, 'Copyright in Living Genetically Engineered Works', *The George Washington Law Review*, **50**(2), (1982), 191–218; R.S. Eisenberg, 'Proprietary Rights and the Norms of Science in Biotechnology Research', *Yale Law Journal*, **97**(2), 1987, 177–231 at 190ff discusses the merits of trade secrecy laws compared to patent protection; P. Turley and R. Siluk, 'A Trademark Primer for Biotech', *Bio/Technology*, **12**, (1994), 824–5.

8   See Committee of Experts on Biotechnological Inventions and Industrial Property, note 1, above, at 256.

9   Office of Technology Assessment, *New Developments in Biotechnology: Ownership of Human Tissues and Cells*, Washington D.C.: Harper and Row, 1988, p. 24.

10 'Bios' is the ancient Greek word for 'life', see WIPO Expert Meeting, note 8, above.

11 The cells grew from a sample taken from a woman, Henrietta Lacks, who had died eight months before from cervical cancer. The results were published in 1952; see G.O. Gey, W.D. Coffman and M.T. Kubicek, 'Tissue Culture Studies of the Proliferative Capacity of Cervical Carcinoma and Normal Epithelium', *Cancer Research*, **12**, (1952), 264.

12 The average life of a 'normal' cell is eight days; see E.F. Enayati, 'Enemies to Innovation: Protecting Biotechnological Inventions', *Computer and High Technology Law Journal*, **5**, (1989), 437–67 at 439.

13 The cells were kept alive in an environment created from chicken plasma, bovine embryo extract and serum from placental cord.

14 In honour of Henrietta, this was called the HeLa cell line. The name is a construction of the first two letters of Henrietta's forename and surname.

15 That said, problems can arise if a particular cell line is kept alive too long. Mutations can occur and cells can begin to behave in an erratic manner (for example, to shut down reproduction or to over-reproduce). To avoid such problems, scientists 'clone' and 'reclone' cell lines; that is, they establish lines from a single cell: see OTA report, note 9, above, 34–5.

16 The establishment of such cell lines is still a difficult matter. Tumour cells (by their very nature) will normally establish an immortal cell line with relative ease. Non-tumour cells have to be 'helped' to immortality through the use of chemicals and the skills of the scientist. For a good discussion of the technology involved, se OTA report, note 9, above, pp. 31–5.

17 Ibid., p. 38.

18 DNA was discovered by James Watson and Francis Crick in 1953, for which they received the Nobel Prize in 1962.

19 These chemical 'bases' are called Adenine (A), Thymine (T),. Cystosine (C) and Guanine (G).

20 An example of a section of a particular sequence might be: ACCTCAGTTC-CAAGCACATATCGAATCGACTCTGATCGAAAAGCTAGTAGAT.

21 It is estimated that between 50 000 and 100 000 human genes exist each of a length of a few thousand base pairs.

22 See Wilkie, note 2, above, pp 35–6.

23 This discovery was made in 1970 by Hamilton Smith from Johns Hopkins University in Baltimore. For discussion, see Wilkie, note 2, above, p. 58.

24 This is done through the use of 'vectors' and 'host' cells. A vector is a string of DNA from another source (for example, a bacterium or a virus) which joins onto the ends of the fragment of cut DNA to form a 'recombinant' DNA molecule. This ensures that there are no loose ends of DNA. This recombined molecule is then introduced into a host cell which has the properties of rapid reproduction. This

means that as the host cell reproduces itself it also copies the DNA of the recombinant molecule in enormous quantities. Eventually, the particular fragments of DNA that are to be studied can be isolated from the recombinant molecules using the original cutting enzyme. In this way scientists can obtain copies of the DNA fragment in a state which facilitates their examination and manipulation. For an interesting account of the development of these technologies, see H.F. Judson, 'A History of the Science and Technology Behind Gene Mapping and Sequencing', in D.J. Kevles, and L. Hood (eds), *The Code of Codes*, London, Harvard University Press, 1992, pp. 37–80.

25 See Wilkie, note 2, above, p. 59.

26 See Rennie, note 5, above: the number estimated by the author is 616. He comments that 'disease-related genes have already been located on each of the chromosomes, and new ones are constantly being discovered'. These include the genes for Cystic Fibrosis, Duchenne Muscular Dystrophy, a rare form of Alzheimer's disease and Huntington's disease. For comment on the latter, see S.K. Miller, 'To Catch A Killer Gene', *New Scientist* (April, 1993) 37–41; A.E. Harding, 'The Gene for Huntington's Disease', *British Medical Journal*, **307** (1993), 396–7. For general comment, see W. Bodmer and R. McKie *The Book of Man*, London, Little, Brown and Company, 1994, ch. 5.

27 For an example of some of the medical advances which have resulted from rDNA technology, see C.T. Caskey, 'DNA-Based Medicine: Prevention and Therapy', in D.J. Kevles and L. Hood, note 24, above, pp. 114–15. For an up-to-date account of the science of genetics and its limits, see the Third Report of the Science and Technology Committee of the House of Commons, *Human Genetics: The Science and its Consequences*, HC 41–I, 6 July 1995, HMSO.

28 Ibid.

29 Note 6, above, and text.

30 It is estimated that biotechnology companies in the United States have the potential to generate $100 billion per year by the year 2000; see C.D. Hardy, 'Patent Protection and Raw Materials: The Convention on Biological Diversity and its Implications for U.S. Policy on the Development and Commercialization of Biotechnology', *University of Pennsylvania Journal of International Business Law*, **15**(2) (1994), 299–326 at 300.

31 See A.J. Wells, 'Patenting New Life Forms: An Ecological Perspective', *European Intellectual Property Review*, **3**, (1994), 111–118 at 114.

32 For an example of some of criticism levelled at the patent system, see D. Vaver, 'Intellectual Property Today: Of Myths and Paradoxes', *Canadian Bar Review*, **69**, (1990), 98–128 at 114–24; B.S. Chimni, 'The Philosophy of Patents: Strong Regime Unjustified', *Journal of Scientific and Industrial Research*, **52**, (1993), 234–9. In particular, for comprehensive comment and criticism, see W. Kingston (ed.), *Direct Protection of Innovation*, Lancaster, Dordrecht, 1987.

33 See Eisenberg, 'Proprietary Rights and the Norms of Science in Biotechnology Research', note 7, above, 180.

34 In the United States a patent monopoly lasts for 17 years (35 USC s.154 [1988]). Under the European Patent Convention inventors can exploit their work for 20 years. In the United Kingdom this is embodied in s. 25(1) of the Patents Act 1977.

35 As stated, this is particularly true of the biotechnology industry; see Wells, note 31, above.

36. Although at present there does not exist any set of principles or universally applicable criteria for the obtaining of a patent, there is considerable similarity between the requirements for patentability in a great many countries around the world. This is especially true of the Western nations. The law for the United States is contained in 35 USC, section 101 of which states: 'Whoever invents or discovers any new and useful process, machine, manufacture, or composition of matter,

or any new and useful improvement thereof, may obtain a patent therefor subject to the conditions and requirements of this title.' Section 102 defines novelty and s.103 defines 'inventive step'/obviousness. Disclosure requirements are provided in s.112. The European Patent Convention (1973) outlines the criteria for patentability in articles 52 and 53. These are incorporated into UK law by s.1 of the Patents Act 1977.

37 See Articles 52 and 53. These exceptions are found in ss. 1(2) and 1(3) of the Patents Act 1977 for the United Kingdom. In the United States there is no mention of exceptions in the patent statute. Any objectionable applications are dealt with through the courts; see S.A. Bent, R.L. Schwaab, D.G. Conlin and D.D. Jeffery, *Intellectual Property Rights in Biotechnology Worldwide*, Basingstoke, Macmillan, 1987, p. 102.

38 It is also thought 'to encourage fresh invention'; see B.C. Reid, *A Practical Guide to Patent Law*, 2nd edn, London, Sweet & Maxwell, 1993, p. 25. An invention can be deemed to be in the public domain if it has already been described in any form of publication, or used in any sense in a 'public' forum; see R.S. Crespi, *Patents: A Basic Guide to Patenting in Biotechnology*, Cambridge, Cambridge University Press, 1988, p. 62.

39 For commentary, see K.M. Williams, 'When is a "Private" Conversation "Public" Disclosure?' *Bio/Technology*, **12**, (1994), 523–5; E.C. Rzucidlo, 'New Year's Resolutions: Ten Dos and Donts for Patenting your Research in the Coming Year', *Bio/Technology*, **12**, (1994), 79.

40 For a discussion of the concept in the context of biotechnology, see R.S. Crespi, 'Inventiveness in Biological Chemistry: An Overview of Current Trends', *Intellectual Property in Business*, 3(3), (1991), 7–16.

41 It is thought that 'the grant of a monopoly in a product or process which is … obvious is tantamount to the undesirable prohibition, or at any rate the inhibition, of competition in any field of industrial activity in which a new product or process is utilised': see J. Phillips and A. Firth, *Introduction to Intellectual Property Law*, 3rd edn, London, Butterworths, 1995, 5.13. Furthermore, the absence of 'intellectual creativity is not regarded as an appropriate subject for reward' (ibid.).

42 But see the problems experienced by the National Institutes of Health, below.

43 Above, note 32.

44 See Bent *et al.*, note 37, above, 112 and 116.

45 See Bent *et al.*, note 37, above 115–42.

46 According to Cornish, 'discovery is the unearthing of causes, properties or phenomena already existing in nature; invention is the application of such knowledge to the satisfaction of social needs', W.R. Cornish, *Intellectual Property: Patents, Copyright, Trade Marks and Allied Rights*, London, Sweet & Maxwell, 1989, para. 5–041.

47 See Eisenberg, 'Proprietary Rights and the Norms of Science in Biotechnology Research', note 7, above, 187–8. In *American Fruit Growers, Inc.* v. *Brogdex Co.*, 238 U.S. 1 the Supreme Court held invalid a patent for fresh citrus fruit the skin of which had been impregnated with small quantities of borax to prevent blue mould decay. For a discussion of the US, European and Japanese approach to this doctrine, see Bent *et al.*, note 37, above, 112–42.

48 The exact nature of the US approach has been the source of considerable confusion; see Bent *et al.*, note 37, above, 116–23.

49 Ibid., 123–7.

50 Ibid., 115–6.

51 See Genentech Inc., discussed below.

52 Guidelines for Examination in the European Patent Office, Part C(IV) 2,1.

53 The Guidelines continue, 'An example of such a case is that of a new substance which is discovered as being produced by a microorganism.'

54 Crespi, *Patents: A Basic Guide to Patenting in Biotechnology*, note 38, above, 63.

55 Such an application is valid according to European patent jurisprudence; see Crespi, ibid,. 64. Where one or more uses for a product are known it is still possible to seek a 'purpose-limited process of manufacture claim' for a 'novel' use or application: ibid., p. 65, where the author discusses a case decided by the Appeal Board of the European Patent Office which is authority for this proposition. It is important to note that the grant of such a patent is not for a patent over the original substance, material or process in question but rather it is a patent for the novel use or application only (ibid., p. 67).

56 In other words, the moral objection to patenting 'products of nature' is not the justification which is used.

57 Note, in this respect, one can also argue that the 'inventor' has done more than merely discover the substance (in the sense of stumbling upon it); rather, he has demonstrated enough 'inventiveness' to turn a discovery into an invention.

58 See Office of Technology Assessment, note 9, above, p. 50.

59 See above.

60 Mellor is of the opinion that, 'whilst research is directed at ... known proteins [tPA] the biotech industry is in a transient state. Once this technology is used to identify previously undiscovered naturally-occurring proteins ... then the industry will enter a new more stable phase': see J. Mellor, 'Patents and Genetic Engineering – Is it a New Problem?', *European Intellectual Property Review*, 6 (1988), 159–62 at 161.

61 T. Cook, C. Doyle and D. Jabbari, *Pharmaceuticals, Biotechnology and the Law*, London, Macmillan, 1991, p. 124.

62 [1989] RPC 147.

63 According to Cook *et al.*, op. cit., 125, this case 'essentially concerned a products of nature problem'.

64 He states, 'without the knowledge of those sequences human t-PA could not have been produced by recombinant DNA technology. But apart from the use of the sequences there is nothing new in the invention described in the patent' [1989] RPC 147 at 239.

65 Ibid., at 237

66 Ibid., at 240.

67 He explains, 'in so far as a patent claims as an invention the practical application of a discovery, the patent does not, in my judgement, relate only to the discovery as such, even if the practical application may be obvious once the discovery has been made, even through unachievable in the absence of the discovery' (ibid.).

68 Per Purchas L.J. at 227.

69 Ibid.

70 Ibid., at 228. Indeed, he considered that the only patentable invention specified in the application was for the method of embracing their discovery of t-PA's DNA sequence.

71 Mustill L.J. delivered a reluctant opinion on the matter of discoveries because of the lateness of the lodging of the objection. Apparently concurring with Purchas and Dillon, he commented that, 'I will ... assume ... that the identification by Genentech of a discovery of their patent is not fatal to its validity' (ibid. at 270).

72 See I. Judge, S. Cooke, M. Burdon, T. Powell, P. Gilbert and C. Hore, 'Chiron v Organon and Biogen v Medeva: A Boost for the Biotech Industry', *Patent World*, (December/January 1994), 20–26 at 20. Note that Genentech was able to secure patent protection for t-PA in the United States, Europe and Japan. However, at least in the United States, the nature of the claims was substantially different to the UK patent and, importantly, did not include any claim for the protein itself.

For comment, see C.G. Love, 'A Survey of Recent Biotechnology and Patents Litigation in the US', *Managing Intellectual Property*, **9**, (1991), 10–22 at 18–20.

73 *Chiron Corporation* v. *Organon Teknika Ltd* [1994] *Fleet Street Reports* 202.

74 *Biogen Inc.* v. *Medeva plc*, Chancery Division (Patents Court), 4 November 1993, unreported. For comment, see Judge *et al.*, note 72, above, and J. Rimmer 'The UK Patents Court Decisions in Chiron and Biogen: A Review of the Issues, *Patent World* (March 1994), 22–8.

75 Chiron had employed an 'expression screening' approach whereby plasma taken from a chimpanzee infected with HCV was analysed and the DNA isolated and synthesised using recombinant DNA technology. This was in comparison to competitors who had tried a range of 'classical' immunological and virological methods to achieve the same results. Biogen did not attempt to sequence the DNA for the hepatitis B virus at all. Rather, they were successful in expressing the DNA of the virus without having sequenced it or cloned it. This was in marked contrast to the attempt of their rivals who had adopted the traditional approach of sequencing, cloning, expressing. For a discussion of the technicalities of these matters, see Judge *et al.*, note 72, above.

76 Above, note 72.

77 *Biogen Inc.* v. *Medeva plc* [1995] *Fleet Street Reports* 4; [1995] RPC 25.

78 Ibid., at 57. Leave to appeal to the House of Lords was immediately requested after the decision of the Court of Appeal.

79 Note 37, above, 134.

80 The article continues 'this provision shall not apply to products, in particular substances or compositions, for use in any of these methods'. In this way pharmaceuticals are patentable. The justification for such an exclusion is not clear. Commentators report various justifications: for example, that it is on the grounds of lack of industrial applicability, or that ethical considerations are operative; see Eisenberg, 'Proprietary Rights and The Norms of Science in Biotechnological Research', note 7, above, 187. See also R. Moufang, 'Methods of Medical Treatment Under Patent Law', *International Review of Industrial Property and Copyright Law*, **24**, (1993), 18–49. Compare the situation in Australia where medical treatments have been accepted as patentable; see D. Kell, 'Expanding the Frontier of Patentability: Methods of Medical Treatment of the Body', *European Intellectual Property Review*, **4** (1995), 202.

81 A. W. White, 'The Patentability of Naturally Occurring Products', *European Intellectual Property Review*, **2** (1980), 37–41 at 40.

82 the Human Genome Project, which was established in 1988, seeks as its primary purpose to map and sequence the entire human genome. It is estimated that the work will be completed by the turn of the century. International coordination of the project is undertaken by the Human Genome Organisation (HUGO).

83 For comment on the technicalities of this, see S.B. Maebius, 'Novel DNA Sequences and the Utility Requirement: The Human Genome Initiative', *Journal of the Patent and Trademark Office Society* (September 1992), 651–8 at 652–4. For general comment, see Roberts, note 6, above.

84 NIH had argued that such fragments could be used as identification markers (ESTs: Expressed-sequence tags) and Sequence-tagged sites (STs) within genome research; see C. Anderson, 'US Patent Application Stirs Up Gene Hunters', *Nature*, **353**, (1991), 485–6.

85 'What the Patent Office Report Says', *Science*, **258**, 210.

86 A. Coglan, 'Applications for Gene Patents "Thrown on Bonfire"', *New Scientist* (February 1994), 4.

87 In the United Kingdom the Medical Research Council filed its own application as a direct result of NIH's acts; see Anderson, note 84, above.

88 R. Cook-Deegan and R. Eisenberg, 'Conference Examines DNA Patenting, Tech Transfer Issues', *Human Genome News*, (March 1994), 6–7; comment that EST patent applications are 'still pursued by other entities', at 7.

89 As Roberts observes, 'companies may abandon product development to take up routine genetic sequencing in order to stake a claim to as much of the genome as possible': note 6, above, 31. The United States PTO announced new guidelines for the examination of biotechnological patent applications on 22 December 1994. Central to these guidelines are clear provisions concerning utility. In essence, any credible statement of utility consistent with the scope of the claimed invention will satisfy s.101 of 35 USC. For comment, see *World Intellectual Property Report*, February 1995, 50–51.

90 Note 37, above.

91 If a microorganism is already known or used in biotechnological applications, or if such a microorganism has already been deposited by someone else, it is not necessary to make a deposit. However, adequate reference must be made to the existence of the microorganism elsewhere; see Cook *et al.* note 61, above, 130–3.

92 An overview of deposit practice around the world can be found in S.C. Jong and J.M. Birmingham, 'Disclosure Requirements for Biological Materials in Patent Law', *Advances in Applied Microbiology*, **35**, (1990), 255–93. For an historical account of the development of disclosure requirement in a variety of countries, see Bent *et al.*, note 37, above, 218–27.

93 The treaty entered into force on 19 August 1980. For a discussion of its terms, see Bent *et al.*, note 37, above, 407–21.

94 The seminal case in the United States on deposit requirements for biotechnological invention was *In re Argoudelis* 434 F.2d 1390. For a discussion, see Enayati, note 12, above, 449–52.

95 For a discussion of the US position, see Hardy, note 30, above, 309–12.

96 Ibid.

97 Ibid., at 312.

98 *Eli Lilly & Co* v. *Medtronic, Inc.* 496 US 661, 671 (1990).

99 For a good account of current European practices, see R.S. Crespi, 'The Micro-Organism Deposit System in European Patent Law – An Appraisal', *International Review of Industrial Property and Copyright Law*, **24**(1), (1993), 1–18.

100 The UK rules are embodied in the Patent Rules (SI 1990/2384), as amended by SI 92/1142 and SI 93/2423. The relevant provisions of 90/2384 are found in Rule 17, Schedule Two.

101 After the grant of the patent any third parties can apply for access.

102 See Cook *et al.*, note 61, above, 133, citing Straus and Moufang, in *Deposit and Release of Biological Material for the Purposes of Patent Procedure – Industrial and Tangible Property Issues*, Baden-Baden, Nomos Verlagsgesellschaft, 1990.

103 See Crespi, 'The Micro-Organism Deposit System in European Patent Law – An Appraisal', note 99, above, 14–18. The European Community Directive, if implemented, would have limited access in such circumstances to an independent expert for a period of 20 years from the date of filing under Article 15(4). This article was amended from an original, more generous, version which made unlimited access provisional on the grant of a patent. The redrafting was initiated after intervention by the EPO, which opined that it could not support such an approach since 'it would be incompatible with the generally accepted doctrine that whatever has become the state of the art must forever remain so': Crespi, ibid., 11.

104 Cook *et al.*, note 61, above, 131.

105 Furthermore, the existence of different systems around the world is likely to prejudice more inventors than just those in Europe. Normally, patenting is undertaken on an international scale, with several patents pending in several countries, and this is especially true in the biotechnology industry. Thus, if US

companies seek patents in Europe as well as in the United States, competitors can circumvent US protection of deposits by gaining access to the deposits in Europe. For general comment, see Crespi, *Patents: A Basic Guide to Patenting in Biotechnology*, note 38, above, 86.

106   Crespi, 'The Micro-Organism Deposit System in European Patent Law – An Appraisal', note 99, above, 14, is of the opinion that the only obstacle to Europe adopting the US and Japanese approach is the 'psuedo-legal' objection 'which insists that an early published patent application must be an enabling disclosure'. He is of the view, however, that this is not derived from the EPC, but rather stems for the 'philosophy' imposed on it by the official viewpoint. In this respect considerable resistance to change is likely.

107   European Draft Directive on the Legal Protection of Biotechnological Inventions, COM (92) 589 final – SYN 159. This directive failed at its final hurdle when the European Parliament voted to reject it on 1 March 1995.

108   Article 17 stated, 'If the subject matter of a patent is a process for obtaining a new product, any identical product produced by any person other than the patent holder shall, in the absence of proof to the contrary, be deemed to have been obtained by means of the patented process'. A new text of the biotechnology directive is being drafted and is expected to be published at the end of 1995. It is not as yet clear how much of the original articles will remain. Certainly amendments will be included concerning the patentability of genes and parts of the body. See *European Intellectual Property Review*, **10** (1995), D–304.

109   'The replication of nature … is the principle role of biotechnology … and … is the main reason why it is so difficult to obtain the protection it seeks from the patent system': see Cook *et al.*, note 61, above, 7.

110   The debate about what constitutes 'life' reaches far beyond the scope of this work and indeed that of science, and touches on the many other realms, such as metaphysics, religion and philosophy. The problem of what is or what is not life is exacerbated at the microbiological level. Cells are 'the smallest components of plants and animals that are capable of carrying on all essential life processes': see OTA report, note 9, above, 31. In this respect a cell, or even a singular-celled creature, differs from a virus which is 'incapable of performing the normal functions of life (such as reproduction) unless it is sustained by a living, "host" cell. This total dependency of viruses is called obligatory parasitism. Furthermore, unlike organisms, viruses contain no cellular structure. These unique characteristics have caused many biologists to classify viruses as somewhere between the living and the non-living': see B.C. Auerbach 'Biotechnology Patent Law Developments in Great Britain and the United States: Analysis of a Hypothetical Patent Claim for a Synthesized Virus', *Boston College International & Comparative Law Review*, 6(2), (1983), 563–90, note 19.

111   See, for example, the objections currently being voiced by 16 pressure groups in Opposition Proceedings concerning the grant of a patent for Oncomouse (discussed below) in H.R. Jaenichen and A. Schrell, 'The "Harvard Onco-mouse" in the Opposition Proceedings before the European Patent Office', *European Intellectual Property Review*, **9**, (1993), 345–7.

112   An example of this is fermentation processes using yeast.

113   447 US 303, 65 L Ed 2d 144, 100 S Ct 2204 (1980).

114   Ibid., at 152. It is estimated that in the four years subsequent to this decision the number of patent applications by universities and hospitals for inventions containing human biological materials increased threefold: see OTA report, note 9, above, 7.

115   *Diamond* v. *Chakrabarty*, above, at 150.

116 US Patent No. 4,736,866. A transgenic animal contains genes from another species which have been inserted into the genetic make-up of the former by the application of genetic engineering techniques.

117 After numerous appeals, the European Patent Office finally granted a patent for Oncomouse in October 1991. However, 16 parties lodged objections within the nine month opposition period which ensued. For an account of these, see Jaenichen and Schrell, note 111, above. It is thought that an oral hearing of these appeals will take place in November 1995.

118 European Patent Convention, art. 53(a) and (b).

119 T19/90, HARVARD/Oncomouse, OJ EPO 1990, 476.

120 [1991] European Patent Office Reports 525; Patent EP B1 0 169 672.

121 For comment, see M. Paver, 'All Animals are Patentable, But Some Are More Patentable Than Others', *Patent World* (March 1992), 9–15 at 10. It should be noted that this means that the patent granted covers all kinds of transgenic animals with inserted oncogenes and gives rise to the possibility of Onco-dog, Onco-cat and Onco-orang-utan!

122 Ibid., at 11.

123 See note 117.

124 Upjohn's Application: for a discussion, see R. Nott, 'Plants and Animals: Why They Should Be Protected By Patent and Variety Rights', *Patent World* (July/August 1993), 45–8 at 47.

125 Ibid.

126 Ibid., at 48.

127 See R.S. Crespi, 'Ethics Aspects of Patenting in Biotechnology', *Cancer Detection and Prevention*, **17**(2), (1993), 323–7 at 325.

128 793 P 2d 479, 271 Cal Rptr. 146 (1990).

129 The defendants were the university, the doctor and researcher, and the companies Genetics Institute Inc and Sandoz.

130 The list of Moore's complaints was as follows: conversion, lack of informed consent, breach of fiduciary duty, fraud and deceit, unjust enrichment, quasi-contract, breach of implied convenant of good faith and fair dealing, intentional infliction of intentional distress, negligent misrepresentation, interference with prospective advantageous economic relationship, slander of title, accounting and declaratory relief.

131 For comment, see G.J. Annas, 'Outrageous Fortune: Selling Other Peoples Cells', *Hastings Center Report*, (November/December 1990), pp. 36–9.

132 Ibid., at 37. Similarly, the court held that the plaintiff could not sue the research companies for a share of the profits from the use of his cell line. The court gave three reasons for doing so. First, no case had ever been decided that a patient had a continuing property interest in excised cells. Second, it concluded that California law drastically limits a patient's interest in excised cells. Finally, it opined that the patented cell line was 'both factually and legally distinct from the cells taken from Moore's body'.

133 The Californian Supreme Court has been the leading proponent of informed consent doctrine in the United States. It has sustained the view through much jurisprudence that a patient is entitled to an enhanced choice about treatment and thus must be provided with 'material' information with which to make that choice. This case extends this further in holding that a doctor must disclose any financial interests he or she might have in the treatment (or its consequences) because to do otherwise is a violation of trust upon which the doctor–patient relationship is based and that undermines patient autonomy. The aim is to protect patients from doctors who might have a conflict of interest in certain cases: for example, suggesting a certain procedure which could produce something with which the doctor could make money, such as another cell line. For comment, see

B. Hoffmaster, 'Between the Sacred and the Profane: Bodies, Property, and Patents in the *Moore* Case', *Intellectual Property Journal*, 7 (1992), 115–48.

134 Moore sought leave to petition the Supreme Court, but this was refused. He eventually settled the case for what has been described as a 'relatively small sum': see R. Stepney, 'Immortal, Divisible', *The Independent on Sunday*, supplement, 13 March 1994, p. 50.

135 Note 131, above at 37.

136 Note 107, above.

137 For comment on the Directive at various stages in its progression, see R. Nott, 'The Proposed EC Directive on Biotechnological Inventions', *European Intellectual Property Review*, 5, (1994), 191–4; J. Thurston, 'Recent EC Developments in Biotechnology', *European Intellectual Property Review*, 6, (1993), 187–90.

138 For comment, see D. MacKenzie, 'Europe Debates the Ownership of Life', *New Scientist* (January, 6, 1992), 9–10.

139 Common Position (EC) No. 4/94, 7 February 1994, OJEC No. C101/65. Recitals 10 and 11 suggested that both genes and proteins in their natural state and 'isolated human nucleic acids having no described application other than the expected properties attributable to any such nucleic acid, for example their ability to be used as a probe or as a primer for synthesis of further copies of nucleic acid' should be unpatentable. A new draft directive is expected by the end of 1995. See note 108, above.

140 See J. Thurston, 'Recent EC Developments in Biotechnology', note 137, above.

141 H2-relaxin is a protein produced within the ovaries which relaxes connective tissue to allow a woman's pelvic girdle to widen during pregnancy and childbirth. The proprietor of the patent (no. 112 149) is the Howard Florey Institute of Experimental Physiology and Medicine. Opposition proceedings were filed by the Fraktion der Grünen im Europäischen Parliament, and separately by their Fraktions-Präsident, Mr Paul Lannoye. The rejection of opposition arguments was given by the Chairman of the Opposition Division on 8 December 1994. For a similar decision concerning morality, see Genetics Systems/Glutamine Synthetase ... Inhibitors, Case T356/93, Technical Board of Appeal, 3.3.4, 21 February 1995, [1995] *European Patent Office Reports* (EPOR) 357, [1995] 8 *European Intellectual Property Review* (EIPR) D–240.

142 See A. Coglan, 'DNA "Not Life": Rules Patent Office', *New Scientist*, 28 January 1995, p. 15.

143 See Nott, 'Plants and Animals: Why They Should Be Protected By Patent and Variety Rights', note 124, above; Paver, note 121, above; Crespi, 'Ethical Aspects of Patenting in Biotechnology', note 127, above; N. Byrne 'Patents for Biological Inventions in the European Communities', *World Patent Information*, 15(2) (1993), 77–80. According to Byrne, 'prior to Harvard Mouse, Article 53(a) was something of a dead letter. Harvard Mouse gave it the kiss of life, so to speak. Any patent application, or granted patent, that involves a plant, an animal, a microorganism or other biological material, is liable nowadays to be attacked in patent office proceedings in Europe, on the grounds that the application or patent contravenes morality' (78).

144 For example, he argues that an overemphasis on moral issues will only result in an insupportable burden on the EPO, serious delays in the grant of patents, little if any reduction in animal suffering and possibly adverse effects for humanity, note 124, above, 47–8.

145 Crespi, note 143, above, at 326.

146 Ibid. See also S. Crespi, 'Biotechnology Patenting: The Wicked Animal Must Defend Itself', *European Intellectual Property Review*, 9 (1995), 431.

147 It is estimated that the income generated from Moore's cell line is in excess of $3 billion; see Paver, note 121, above, 15.

148 For a critique of 'utilitarian justifications' of the patent system see, Chimni, note 32, above.

149 See H.P. Green, 'Chakrabarty: Tempest in a Test Tube', *Hastings Center Report* (October 1980), 12–13 at p. 13. In *Diamond* v. *Chakrabarty*, above, it was stated, 'the grant or denial of patents on micro-organisms is not likely to put an end to genetic research or its attendant risks' (at 155).

150 See K.W. O'Connor, 'Patenting Life', *Cancer Investigation*, **10**(1), (1992), 61–70 at 68.

151 Eisenberg, 'Proprietary Rights and the Norms of Science in Biotechnology Research', note 7, above, 187, suggests that this might be one reason why the exception relating to the non-patentability of methods of medical treatment exists.

Index